Migrant Smuggling by Sea

Publications on Ocean Development
Volume 66

A Series of Studies on
the International, Legal, Institutional and Policy Aspects
of Ocean Development

General Editors: Vaughan Lowe and Robin Churchill

Migrant Smuggling by Sea

Combating a Current Threat to Maritime Security through the Creation of a Cooperative Framework

By
Patricia Mallia

MARTINUS
NIJHOFF
PUBLISHERS

LEIDEN • BOSTON
2010

This book is printed on acid-free paper.

Library of Congress Cataloging-in-Publication Data

Mallia, Patricia.
Migrant smuggling by sea : combating a current threat to maritime security through the creation of a cooperative framework / by Patricia Mallia.
p. cm. – (Publications on ocean development ; v. 66)
Includes bibliographical references and index.
ISBN 978-90-04-18209-7 (hardback : alk. paper)
1. Human smuggling. 2. Law enforcement–International cooperation. 3. Jurisdiction over ships at sea. I. Title.

K5258.M35 2010
345'.0237–dc22

2009050582

ISSN 0924-1992
ISBN 978 90 04 18209 7

Koninklijke Brill NV incorporates the imprints Brill, Hotei Publishing, IDC Publishers, Martinus Nijhoff Publishers and VSP.

PRINTED IN THE NETHERLANDS

For Mary

You are a very special little girl
who has helped me travel this long road.
I treasure and love you very much.

Contents

Part II. Tools and Constraints

Part III. State Practice

Foreword

The freedom of the high seas is probably the best known of all principles of international law, and certainly one of the oldest. The idea that ships on the high seas should be subject only to the jurisdiction of their flag State is seen as an essential corollary of that principle. In days when traders were thought benign, all governments accepted that there was open season on pirates, and naval power was in the hands of a self-selecting group of civilised Powers, this appeared (at least to those Powers) to work tolerably well. But is the principle worth retaining?

A ship encountered on the high seas may be carrying lawful commercial cargoes, illegal narcotics, lawful passengers, refugees and asylum seekers, components for weapons of mass destruction, people intent on avoiding immigration controls, or who knows what else. Should the default principle be that the ship must be left alone? Navies great and small, all around the world, are given responsibility for protecting coastal States from seaborne threats; but how can they know whether to treat a foreign ship outside their territorial seas as an innocent vessel going about its lawful business and entitled to be left alone, or as the carrier of distressed people in need of humanitarian assistance, or as a threat to the coastal State? And how should they handle whatever situation they may find on board? These are pressing problems; and they require carefully crafted legal responses, because a naval vessel visiting a foreign ship is at the centre of a web of national and international legal obligations that both limit its scope for action and require that it follow correct legal procedures if subsequent law-enforcement measures, such as criminal trials, are not to be jeopardized.

This excellent study grapples with those problems in the particular context of migrant smuggling at sea. It examines the range of legal responses to the problems and the practical steps that are being taken, both nationally and through international cooperation, to create a legal framework that goes some way towards reconciling the exigencies of twenty-first century policing with the antique legal principles that we have inherited and still (for the moment at least) appear to cherish. Dr Mallia has amassed a wealth of material on state practice, and subjected it to an incisive legal analysis. She has produced a fine monograph, and a model of the kind of critical analysis of contemporary problems that is of real value to scholars and governments alike. I watched the study grow in its original form as a doctoral thesis, and now have both the supervisor's delight in seeing a first-class thesis emerge as a first-class monograph, and the lawyer's gratitude and relief in having at my disposal a massive compilation of material assembled by someone else's untiring and intelligent labours.

Vaughan Lowe

Acknowledgements

This book is based on a Ph.D. thesis awarded by the IMO International Maritime Law Institute (IMLI) in May 2009. I would like to acknowledge the Institute's cooperation in the publication of this manuscript by waiving its own publication rights.

Thanks and much appreciation go to my supervisor, Professor Vaughan Lowe, Chichele Professor of Public International Law at the University of Oxford, for his unwavering support and help throughout the period of research. His expertise, guidance and advice were invaluable. Apart from this, his understanding of all and any mishaps along the way and his continuous enthusiasm for the project will always be deeply appreciated. I feel honoured to have been given the opportunity to work under his tutelage. I also thank him deeply for introducing me to the possibility of publishing this manuscript with Martinus Nijhoff / Brill.

I would also like to thank my mentor, Professor David Attard, Director of the IMO International Maritime Law Institute, for his constant guidance over the past 12 years and for nurturing my interest in Public International Law. I shall remain indebted to him for his interest and input generally, and more specifically in connection with this thesis.

I am also very grateful to Professor Frank Wiswall Jr., Vice-President (*Honoris Causa*) *Comité Maritime International* / Former Chairman of the Legal Committee of the IMO and Proctor and Advocate in Admiralty, for his extremely kind offer to proof read the manuscript prior to publication.

Grateful mention must also be made of the University of Malta for providing the necessary funding for me to carry out my research degree.

Lastly, I would never have been able to write this book had it not been for the unwavering belief, support and understanding of my parents. I thank them with all my heart for their encouragement and patience, always.

Patricia Mallia
Malta, September 2009

Acknowledgments

Abbreviations

ADF	Australian Defence Force
AIS	Automatic Identification System
AJHR	*Australian Journal of Human Rights*
AJIL	*American Journal of International Law*
AMIS	Australian Maritime Identification System
Aruba Agreement	Agreement concerning cooperation in Suppressing Illicit Maritime and Air Trafficking in Narcotic Drugs and Psychotropic Substances in the Caribbean Area
Aust LJ	*Australian Law Journal*
BHRC	Butterworths Human Rights Cases
BIMCO	Baltic and International Maritime Council
CATOC	United Nations Convention on Transnational Organised Crime
CETS	Council of Europe Treaty Series
CICAD	Inter-American Drug Abuse Control Commission
CIRM	*Comité International Radio-Maritime*
CMI	*Comité Maritime Internationale*
CND	Commission on Narcotic Drugs
COMSAR	Sub-Committee on Radiocommunications and Search and Rescue (IMO)
Cornell Intl L J	*Cornell International Law Journal*
Council of Europe Agreement	Agreement on Illicit Traffic by Sea, implementing Art. 17 of the United Nations Convention against Illicit Traffic in Narcotic Drugs and Psychotropic Substances which establishes a foundation for cooperation between the parties to the Agreement
CSI	Container Security Initiative
C-TPAT	Customs–Trade Partnership against Terrorism
DIAC	Department of Immigration and Citizenship
DIMIA	Department of Immigration and Multicultural Indigenous Affairs
DUSPIL	Digest of United States Practice in International Law
ECHR	European Convention for the Protection of Human Rights and Fundamental Freedoms
ECOSOC	Economic and Social Council of the United Nations
ECRE	European Council on Refugees and Exiles
EEOC	Equal Employment Opportunity Commission
EEZ	Exclusive Economic Zone
EHRR	European Human Rights Reports
EJIL	*European Journal of International Law*

EU	European Union
ExCom	Executive Committee
FAL	Facilitation Committee (IMO)
FAL Convention	International Convention for the Facilitation of Maritime Traffic
Georgetown Immigration L J	*Georgetown Immigration Law Journal*
GMDSS	Global Maritime Distress and Safety System
Hague Convention	Convention for the Suppression of the Unlawful Seizure of Aircraft
Harv LR	*Harvard Law Review*
HSC	Convention on the High Seas
IADC	International Association of Drilling Contractors
IAEA	International Atomic Energy Agency
IALA	International Association of Marine Aids to Navigation and Lighthouse Authorities
IAPH	International Association of Ports and Harbours
IARLJ	International Association of Refugee Law Judges
IAS	Immigration Advisory Service
ICCL	International Council of Cruise Lines
ICCPR	International Covenant on Civil and Political Rights
ICFTU	International Confederation of Free Trade Unions
ICJ	International Court of Justice
ICJ Rep	ICJ Reports
ICLQ	*International and Comparative Law Quarterly*
ICS	International Chamber of Shipping
IFHR	International Federation for Human Rights
IFSMA	International Federation of Shipmasters' Associations
ILC	International Law Commission
IJMLC	*International Journal of Marine and Coastal Law*
IJRL	*International Journal of Refugee Law*
ILC	International Law Commission
ILM	International Legal Materials
ILO	International Labour Organization
IMB	International Maritime Bureau
IMB-PRC	International Maritime Bureau's Piracy Reporting Centre
IMO	International Maritime Organization
IMSO	International Mobile Satellite Organization
INA	Immigration and Nationality Act
INS	Immigration and Naturalization Service (US)
INTERCARGO	International Association of Dry Cargo Shipowners
INTERTANKO	International Association of Independent Tanker Owners
IOM	International Organization for Migration
IPTA	International Parcel Tanker Association
ISF	International Shipping Federation

ISPS Code	International Ship and Port Facility Security Code
ISWG No. 1	First Meeting of the Intersessional Working Group
ISWG No. 2	Second Meeting of the Intersessional Working Group
ITLOS	International Tribunal for the Law of the Sea
IUMI	International Union of Marine Insurance
J. Int Marit Law	*Journal of International Maritime Law*
JLE	*Journal of Law and Equality*
LEG	Legal Committee (IMO)
LNTS	League of Nations Treaty Series
LOSC	United Nations Law of the Sea Convention
LRIT	Long-range Identification and Tracking System
Maritime Ports Convention	Convention on the International Regime of Maritime Ports
MARPOL	International Convention for the Prevention of Pollution from Ships
Melb JIL	*Melbourne Journal of International Law*
MPI	Migration Policy Institute
MRCC	Maritime Rescue Coordination Centre
MSC	Maritime Safety Committee (IMO)
nm	nautical miles
OAS	Organization of American States
ODCCP	Office for Drug Control and Crime Prevention (UN)
ODIL	Ocean Development and International Law
OHCHR	Office of the High Commissioner for Human Rights (UN)
OJ	Official Journal (EU)
Pac Rim L & Pol'y J	*Pacific Rim Law and Policy Journal*
PCA	Permanent Court of Arbitration
PFSP	Port Facility Security Plan
Prum Convention	Convention between the Kingdom of Belgium, the Federal Republic of Germany, the Kingdom of Spain, the French Republic, the Grand Duchy of Luxembourg, the Kingdom of the Netherlands and the Republic of Austria on the stepping up of cross-border cooperation, particularly in combating terrorism, cross-border crime and illegal migration
PSI	Proliferation Security Initiative
Pub LR	*Public Law Review*
Refugee Convention	Convention Relating to the Status of Refugees
Refugee Protocol	Protocol relating to the Status of Refugees
RHIB	Rigid Hull Inflatable Boat
Salvage Convention 1910	International Convention for the Unification of Certain Rules relating to Assistance and Salvage at Sea
Salvage Convention 1989	International Convention on Salvage
SAR Convention	International Convention on Maritime Search and

	Rescue
SAR zone	Search and Rescue zone
SIEV	Suspected Illegal Entry Vessel
SIGTTO	Society of International Gas Tanker and Terminal Operators
Smuggling Protocol	Protocol against the Smuggling of Migrants by Land, Sea and Air, Supplementing the United Nations Convention against Transnational Organized Crime
SOLAS	International Convention for the Safety of Life at Sea
SPI	Ship/Port Interface
SSAS	Ship Security Alert System
SJCRCL	*Stanford Journal of Civil Rights and Civil Liberties*
Stat	Statutes-at-Large
STW	Sub-Committee on Standards of Training and Watchkeeping (IMO)
SUA Convention	Convention for the Suppression of Unlawful Acts Against the Safety of Maritime Navigation
SUA Protocol	Protocol for the Suppression of Unlawful Acts Against the Safety of Fixed Platforms Located on the Continental Shelf
TIAS	Treaties and other International Acts Series
Tokyo Convention	Convention on Offences and Certain other Acts committed on board Aircraft
Torture Convention	Convention against Torture and Cruel, Inhuman or Degrading Treatment or Punishment
Trafficking Protocol	Protocol to Prevent, Suppress and Punish Trafficking in Persons, especially Women and Children, Supplementing the United Nations Convention against Transnational Organized Crime
TSC	Convention on the Territorial Sea and Contiguous Zone
TSO	The Stationery Office
UDHR	Universal Declaration of Human Rights
UKTS	United Kingdom Treaty Series
UNCTAD Convention	Convention on Conditions for Registration of Ships
UNDCP	United Nations International Drug Control Programme
UNGA	United Nations General Assembly
UNHCR	United Nations High Commissioner for Refugees
UNICRI	United National Interregional Crime and Justice Research Institute
UNODC	United Nations Office on Drugs and Crime
UNSC	United Nations Security Council
UNTS	United Nations Treaty Series
USC	United States Code
USCG	United States Coast Guard

USCIS	United States Citizenship and Immigration Service
US–Haiti Agreement	Agreement Relating to Establishment of a Cooperative Program of Interdiction and Selective Return of Certain Haitian Migrants and Vessels Involved in Illegal Transport of Persons coming from Haiti
UST	United States Treaties and other International Agreements
VCLT	Vienna Convention on the Law of Treaties
Vienna Drugs Convention	Convention against Illicit Traffic in Narcotic Drugs and Psychotropic Substances
Va. J. Int'l Law	*Virginia Journal of International Law*
WCO	World Customs Organization
WMD	Weapons of Mass Destruction
WNTI	World Nuclear Transport Institute

Table of Statutes

Australia

Border Protection Legislation Amendment Act 1999 (Cth) (No. 160, 1999) [p. 163, 166, 169, 173]
Border Protection (Validation and Enforcement Powers) Act 2001 (Cth) (No. 126, 2001) [p. 166, 168, 169, 172, 173, 176, 178, 189]
Crimes at Sea Act 2000 (Cth) (No. 13, 2000) [p. 166]
Customs Act 1901 (Cth) (No. 6 of 1901) [p. 166, 168, 172, 177, 184]
Migration Act 1958 (Cth) (No. 62, 1958) [p. 24, 25, 86, 87, 164–166, 168, 169, 171–174, 176, 177, 179–182, 189]
Migration Amendment (Excision from Migration Zone) Act 2001 (Cth) (No. 127, 2001) [p. 172, 179]
Migration Amendment (Excision from Migration Zone) (Consequential Provisions) Act 2001 (Cth) (No. 128, 2001) [p. 90, 172, 181, 183]
Migration Legislation Amendment Act (No. 1) 2001 (Cth) (No. 129, 2001) [p. 172]
Migration Legislation Amendment Act (No. 5) 2001 (Cth) (No. 130, 2001) [p. 172]
Migration Legislation Amendment Act (No. 6) 2001 (Cth) (No. 131, 2001) [p. 172]

Malta

Malta Maritime Authority Act, Laws of Malta, Chapter 352 [p. 68]
Merchant Shipping Act, Laws of Malta, Chapter 234 [p. 68]
Small Ships Regulations, Subsidiary Legislation 352.15 [p. 68]
Territorial Waters and Contiguous Zone Act, Laws of Malta, Chapter 226 [p. 59]

United States of America

Enhanced Border Security and Visa Entry Reform Act, Pub L No. 107–173 (14 May 2002) [p. 8, 34]
Immigration and Nationality Act, Pub L No. 82–414, c.477, 66 Stat 163, Title 8 USC 1101 (27 June 1952) [p. 85, 193, 194]
Marijuana on the High Seas Act, Pub L No. 96–350, 94 Stat 1159 (1980) [p. 71]
Refugee Act, Pub L No. 96–212, 94 Stat 107 (17 March 1980) [p. 195, 197]

Table of International Instruments

tocol adopted at San Jose 2 July 1999, entered into force 19 November 1999) Copy provided by US Coast Guard. [p. 55, 148, 150, 151]

Agreement between the Government of the United States of America and the Government of the Republic of Croatia concerning cooperation to Suppress the Proliferation of Weapons of Mass Destruction, their Delivery Systems, and Related Materials by Sea (Washington, 1 June 2005, entered into force 5 March 2007), available at www.state.gov/t/isn/trty/47086.htm [p. 154, 159]

Agreement between the Government of the United States of America and the Government of the Republic of Cyprus concerning cooperation to Suppress the Proliferation of Weapons of Mass Destruction, their Delivery Systems, and Related Materials by Sea (Washington, 25 July 2005, entered into force 12 January 2006), available at www.state.gov/t/isn/trty/50274.htm [p. 154]

Agreement between the Government of the United States of America and the Government of the Republic of Guatemala concerning cooperation to suppress illicit traffic in narcotic drugs and psychotropic substances by sea and air (Guatemala City, 19 June 2003, entered into force 10 October 2003) Copy provided by US Coast Guard. [p. 55, 150–152, 154]

Agreement between the Government of the United States of America and the Republic of Haiti concerning cooperation to suppress illicit maritime drug traffic (Port au Prince, 17 October 1997, entered into force 5 September 2002) 1997 UST LEXIS 128 [p. 55, 148, 150, 151]

Agreement between the Government of the United States of America and the Government of the Republic of Liberia concerning cooperation to Suppress the Proliferation of Weapons of Mass Destruction, their Delivery Systems, and Related Materials by Sea (Washington, 11 February 2004, provisionally applied from 11 February 2004, entered into force 9 December 2004), available at www.state.gov/t/isn/trty/32403.htm [p. 154]

Agreement between the Government of the United States of America and the Government of the Republic of the Marshall Islands concerning cooperation to Suppress the Proliferation of Weapons of Mass Destruction, their Delivery Systems, and Related Materials by Sea (Honolulu, 13 August 2004, provisionally applied from 13 August 2004, entered into force 24 November 2004), available at www.state.gov/t/isn/trty/35237.htm [p. 154]

Agreement between the Government of the United States of America and the Government of Trinidad and Tobago concerning maritime counter-drug operations (Port of Spain, 4 March 1996, entered into force 4 March 1996) TIAS 12732, 1996 UST LEXIS 59 [p. 55, 148, 150, 151]

Agreement between the Government of the United States of America and the Government of Venezuela to suppress illicit traffic in narcotic drugs and psychotropic substances by sea (Caracas, signed and entered into force 9 November 1991; amended by Protocol adopted at Caracas 23 July 1997, entered into force 23 July 1997) TIAS 11827 [p. 152]

Agreement concerning cooperation in Suppressing Illicit Maritime and Air Trafficking in Narcotic Drugs and Psychotropic Substances in the Caribbean Area (San Jose, Costa Rica, 10 April 2003, not yet in force) (Aruba Agreement), available at www.state.gov/s/l/2005/87198.htm [p. 142, 150, 206, 210, 211, 223]

Table of Selected Legal Instruments

European Union

Commission

Commission (EC) 'Towards a Common Asylum Procedure and a Uniform Status, valid throughout the Union, for Persons granted Asylum' (Communication) COM(2000) 755 final, 22 November 2000 [p. 200]

Commission (EC) 'Combating Trafficking in Human Beings and on Combating the Sexual Exploitation of Children and Child Pornography' (Communication) COM (2000)854 final/2, 22 January 2001 [p. 202]

Commission (EC) 'A Common Policy on Illegal Immigration' (Communication) COM (2001)672 final, 15 November 2001 [p. 200, 202]

Commission (EC) 'Towards Integrated Management of the External Borders of the Member States of the European Union' (Communication) COM(2002)233 final, 7 May 2002 [p. 202, 204, 205]

Commission (EC) 'Towards more Accessible, Equitable and Managed Asylum Systems' (Communication) COM(2003)315 final, 3 June 2003 [p. 200]

Commission (EC) 'On the Development of a Common Policy on Illegal Immigration, Smuggling and Trafficking of Human Beings, External Borders and the Return of Illegal Residents' (Communication) COM(2003)323 final, 3 June 2003 [p. 202, 204, 205]

Commission (EC) 'An Area of Freedom, Security and Justice: Assessment of the Tampere Programme and Future Orientations' (Communication) COM(2004)4002 final, 2 June 2004 [p. 201]

Commission (EC) 'The Hague Programme: Ten Priorities for the Next Five Years—The Partnership for European Renewal in the field of Freedom, Security and Justice' (Communication) COM(2005)184 final, 10 May 2005 [p. 201]

Commission (EC) 'Priority Actions for responding to the Challenges of Migration: First Follow-up to Hampton Court' (Communication) COM(2005)621 final, 30 November 2005 [p. 213]

Commission (EC) 'Strengthened Practical Cooperation. New Structures, New Approaches: Improving the Quality of Decision Making in the Common European Asylum System' (Communication) COM(2006)67 final, 17 February 2006 [p. 218]

Commission (EC) 'A Future Maritime Policy' (Green Paper) COM(2006)257 final, 7 June 2006 [p. 218]

Commission (EC) 'Reinforcing the Management of the European Union's Southern Maritime Borders' (Communication) COM(2006)733 final, 20 November 2006 [p. 217, 221]

Commission (EC) 'Study on the International Law Instruments in Relation to Illegal Immigration by Sea' (Staff Working Document) SEC (2007) 691, 15 May 2007 [p. 49, 54, 96, 101, 135, 221, 227]

Commission (EC) 'Future Common European Asylum System' (Green Paper) COM (2007)301 final, 6 June 2007 [p. 219]
Commission (EC) 'Report on the Evaluation and Future Development of the FRONTEX Agency' (Communication) COM(2008)67 final, 13 February 2008 [p. 204]

Council

Council Directive (EC) 2001/51 Supplementing the Provisions of Article 26 of the Convention Implementing the Schengen Agreement of 14 June 1985 [2001] OJ L187/45 [p. 7]
Council Framework Decision (JHA) 2002/946 on the strengthening of the penal framework to prevent the facilitation of unauthorised entry, transit and residence [2002] OJ L328/1 [p. 202]
Council Directive (EC) 2002/90 defining the facilitation of unauthorised entry, transit and residence [2002] OJ L328/17 [p. 202]
Council Regulation (EC) 343/2003 establishing the criteria and mechanisms for determining the Member States responsible for examining an asylum application lodged in one of the Member States by a third-country national [2003] OJ L50/1 (Dublin II) [p. 12]
Council and Parliament Regulation (EC) 725/2004 on enhancing ship and port facility security [2004] OJ L129/6 [p. 33]
Council Regulation (EC) 2007/2004 establishing a European Agency for the Management of Operational Cooperation at the External Borders of the Member States of the European Union [2004] OJ L349/1 [p. 204, 213]
Council and Parliament Regulation (EC) 863/2007 establishing a mechanism for the creation of Rapid Border Intervention Teams and amending Council Resolution (EC) No. 2007/2004 as regards that mechanism and regulating the tasks and powers of guest officers [2007] OJ L199/30 [p. 213]
Council Decision (JHA) 2008/615 on the Stepping up of Cross-border co-operation, particularly in combating terrorism and cross-border crime [2008] OJ L210/12 [p. 222]

International Maritime Organization

Resolutions

A.773(18) Enhancement of Safety of Life at Sea by the Prevention and Suppression of Unsafe Practices associated with alien smuggling by ships (4 November 1993) [p. 128]
A.867(20) Combating unsafe practices associated with the trafficking or transport of migrants by sea (27 November 1997) [p. 128, 207]
MSC.74(69) Adoption of New and Amended Performance Standards (12 May 1998) [p. 35]
A.920(22) Review of Safety Measures and Procedures for the treatment of persons rescued at sea (29 November 2001) [p. 129]
MSC.75/ISWG/INF.3 Prevention and Suppression of Acts of Terrorism against Ship-

Circulars

COMSAR

COMSAR 8/8/1 Review of the Convention Provisions regarding the treatment of persons rescued at sea: SOLAS and SAR Conventions. Report of the Correspondence Group. (12 November 2003) [p. 132]

COMSAR 8/13 Measures to enhance maritime security. Long-Range Identification and Tracking of Ships. Submitted by the United States. (10 November 2003) [p. 36, 37]

COMSAR 8/13/1 Measures to enhance maritime security. Difficulties with using VHF/MF DSC as a ship security alert system. Submitted by Finland. (27 November 2003) [p. 38]

COMSAR 8/13/2 Measures to enhance maritime security. COSPAS-SARSAT ship security alert system. Submitted by COSPAS-SARSAT. (4 December 2003) [p. 38]

COMSAR 8/13/3 Measures to enhance maritime security. Ship Security Alert System (SSAS). Submitted by Japan. (12 December 2003) [p. 38]

COMSAR 8/13/4 Measures to enhance maritime security. Long-Range Identification and Tracking of Ships. Submitted by the Rapporteur of the correspondence group on Long-range Identification and Tracking of Ships. (12 December 2003) [p. 36]

COMSAR 8/13/5 Measures to enhance maritime security. Long-Range Identification and Tracking of Ships. Submitted by the United States. (12 December 2003) [p. 36]

COMSAR 8/13/6 Measures to enhance maritime security. Requirements for the implementation of ship security alert systems (SSASs). Submitted by the United States. (12 December 2003) [p. 38]

COMSAR 8/13/7 Measures to enhance maritime security. Long-Range Identification and Tracking of Ships. Submitted by the Netherlands, Sweden and IALA. (17 December 2003) [p. 36]

COMSAR 8/INF.5 Measures to enhance maritime security. Long-Range Identification and Tracking of Ships. Submitted by the Rapporteur of the Intersessional correspondence group on Long-Range Identification and Tracking of Ships. (14 November 2003) [p. 36]

COMSAR 9/12 Measures to enhance maritime security. Outcome of MSC 78. Note by the Secretariat. (21 October 2004) [p. 35, 36, 38]

COMSAR 9/12/1 Measures to enhance maritime security. Outcome of MSC 79. Note by the Secretariat. (22 December 2004) [p. 35, 36, 38]

COMSAR 9/12/3 Measures to enhance maritime security. Long-Range Identification and Tracking of Ships. Submitted by Brazil. (3 December 2004) [p. 36]

COMSAR 9/12/4 Measures to enhance maritime security. End-to-end test and automatic acknowledgement for testing SSASs. Submitted by the Republic of Korea. (3 December 2004) [p. 38]

COMSAR 9/12/5 Measures to enhance maritime security. National Vessel Monitoring System and LRIT System. Submitted by the Republic of Korea. (3 December 2004) [p. 36]

COMSAR 9/12/6 Measures to enhance maritime security. Priority of ship security alerts. Submitted by Italy. (3 December 2004) [p. 38]

COMSAR 9/12/7 Measures to enhance maritime security. Long-Range Identification and Tracking of Ships. Submitted by Cyprus, Luxembourg, Spain, the Netherlands and Sweden. (17 December 2004) [p. 36]

COMSAR 9/12/8 Measures to enhance maritime security. Long-Range Identification and Tracking of Ships. Submitted by the United States. (29 December 2004) [p. 36]

COMSAR 9/INF.4 Measures to enhance maritime security. Satellite-based AIS Long-Range Identification and Tracking (LRIT). Submitted by Norway. (29 October 2004) [p. 35, 36]

COMSAR 9/INF.6 Measures to enhance maritime security. IALA Seminar on Long-Range Tracking: Tracking all the way. Submitted by IALA. (25 November 2004) [p. 36]

COMSAR 9/INF.8 Measures to enhance maritime security. Satellite-based AIS Long-Range Identification and Tracking (LRIT). Submitted by the United States. (3 December 2004) [p. 36]

COMSAR 9/INF.11 Measures to enhance maritime security. Experiences on ship security alerts. Submitted by Italy. (3 December 2004) [p. 38]

COMSAR 9/INF.12 Measures to enhance maritime security. Satellite-based AIS Long-Range Identification and Tracking (LRIT). Submitted by Marshall Islands. (17 December 2004) [p. 36]

COMSAR 10/10 Measures to enhance maritime security. Report of the Correspondence Group on Long-Range Identification and Tracking of Ships. Submitted by the co-ordinator of the correspondence group. (2 December 2005) [p. 36]

COMSAR 10/10/1 Measures to enhance maritime security. Long-Range Identification and Tracking (LRIT) of Ships. Submitted by CIRM. (5 December 2005) [p. 36]

COMSAR 10/10/2 Measures to enhance maritime security. Long-Range Tracking. Global Tracking. Submitted by IALA. (21 December 2005) [p. 36]

COMSAR 10/10/3 Measures to enhance maritime security. Long-Range Identification and Tracking. Submitted by ICS, BIMCO, INTERCARGO and INTERTANKO. (10 January 2006) [p. 36]

COMSAR 10/INF.7 Measures to enhance maritime security. Long-Range Identification and Tracking (LRIT) of ships. Submitted by IMSO. (12 December 2005) [p. 36]

FAL

FAL 30/9 Measures and Procedures for the treatment of persons rescued at sea: Facilitation Aspects. Note by the Secretariat. (24 October 2002) [p. 128–130]

FAL 31/9/Add.1 Measures and procedures for the treatment of persons rescued at sea: facilitation aspects. Note by the Secretariat. (12 July 2004) [p. 132]

FAL 32/22 Report of Thirty-Second session of the Facilitation Committee (25 July 2005) [p. 132]

LEG

LEG 76/11/1 Proposed Multilateral Convention to Combat Illegal Migration by Sea. Submitted by Italy. (1 Aug 1997) [p. 113, 128]

LEG 88/3/3 Review of the Convention for the suppression of unlawful acts against the safety of maritime navigation, 1988, and its Protocol of 1988 relating to the suppression of unlawful acts against the safety of fixed platforms located on the

MSC

MSC 75/17/Add.1 Prevention and suppression of acts of terrorism against shipping. IMO activities on security and the prevention and suppression of terrorism against ships. Note by the Secretariat. (17 December 2001) [p. 44]

MSC 75/17/1 Prevention and suppression of acts of terrorism against shipping. Report of the Intersessional meeting of the MSC Working Group on Maritime Security, held from 11–15 February 2002. (25 February 2002) [p. 31, 35]

MSC 75/17/3 Prevention and suppression of acts of terrorism against shipping. Proposed amendments to SOLAS regulation V/19. Note by the Russian Federation. (28 March 2002) [p. 35]

MSC 75/17/4 Prevention and suppression of acts of terrorism against shipping. Implications of a decision to advance the date of carriage requirement for AIS. Submitted by ICS. (25 March 2002) [p. 35]

MSC 75/17/5 Prevention and suppression of acts of terrorism against shipping. Application of security measures to mobile offshore drilling units. Submitted by IADC. (5 April 2002) [p. 29]

MSC 75/17/6 Prevention and suppression of acts of terrorism against shipping. Maritime security. Comments and recommendations regarding the report of the Intersessional Working Group. Submitted by the International Maritime Bureau of the ICC. (11 April 2002) [p. 31]

MSC 75/17/7 Prevention and suppression of acts of terrorism against shipping. Means of ship alerting: The use of Automatic Identification System (AIS). Submitted by IALA. (9 April 2002) [p. 35]

MSC 75/17/8 Prevention and suppression of acts of terrorism against shipping. WCO documents: Action plan to improve security at the frontier in order to combat international terrorism "SP0078" and Business partnership meeting report EC0116. Submitted by WCO. (8 April 2002) [p. 31]

MSC 75/17/12 Prevention and suppression of acts of terrorism against shipping. Consideration of proposals and information on maritime security issues. Submitted by Belgium, Finland, France, Germany, Ireland, Italy, Portugal, Spain and Sweden. (12 April 2002) [p. 29, 31, 35]

MSC 75/17/28 Prevention and suppression of acts of terrorism against shipping. Automatic identification system. Submitted by the United States. (12 April 2002) [p. 35]

MSC 75/17/44 Prevention and suppression of acts of terrorism against shipping. Information on the ownership and control of a ship. Submitted by Cyprus. (12 April 2002) [p. 29]

MSC 75/INF.30 Prevention and suppression of acts of terrorism against shipping. Observations by IUMI relating to the security of container transport. Submitted by IUMI. (12 April 2002) [p. 30]

MSC 75/INF.31 Prevention and suppression of acts of terrorism against shipping. Availability of ship data reporting systems and long-range tracking services to all Inmarsat C fitted ships. Submitted by CIRM. (12 April 2002) [p. 36]

MSC 75/ISWG/3 Prevention and suppression of acts of terrorism against shipping. Review requested in operative paragraph 1 of resolution A.924(22). Outcome of FAL 29 and the concurred session of the SPI Working Group. Report on the outcome of FAL 29 and the SPI Working Group on the prevention/suppression of acts of terrorism against shipping issue. (11 January 2002) [p. 30]

MSC 75/ISWG/5 Prevention and suppression of acts of terrorism against shipping. Proposal for an International Security code for the prevention of acts of terrorism against shipping to be annexed to the SOLAS Convention. Submitted by France. (10 January 2002) [p. 29]

MSC 75/ISWG/5/2, Annex 'Enhancing Maritime Security and Safety through Satellite Technology'. Submitted by Australia. (15 January 2002) [p. 40]

MSC 75/ISWG/5/3 Prevention and suppression of acts of terrorism against shipping. Consideration of proposals and information on maritime security issues. Public security measures in harbor terminals for passengers and vehicles accompanying passengers and the financing of the cost of their implementation. Submitted by Spain. (14 January 2002) [p. 30]

MSC 75/ISWG/5/7 Prevention and suppression of acts of terrorism against shipping. Consideration of proposals and information on maritime security issues. Measures to improve maritime security. Submitted by the United States. (15 January 2002) [p. 28, 30, 35, 38]

MSC 75/ISWG/5/9 Prevention and suppression of acts of terrorism against shipping. Consideration of proposals and information on maritime security issues. Transparency in regard to the ownership of vessels. Submitted by ICFTU. (15 January 2002) [p. 29]

MSC 75/ISWG/INF.4 Prevention and suppression of acts of terrorism against shipping. Consideration of proposals and information on maritime security issues. Tracking of vessels using Inmarsat C. Polling. Note from Australia. (14 January 2002) [p. 40]

MSC 75/ISWG/INF.6 Prevention and suppression of acts of terrorism against shipping. Consideration of proposals and information on maritime security issues. Intersessional Working Group on Maritime Security. Maritime security in the Philippines and the proposed information exchange arrangement among Indonesia, Malaysia and the Philippines. Submitted by the Philippines. (15 January 2002) [p. 1, 30, 36]

MSC 75/ISWG/INF.8 Prevention and suppression of acts of terrorism against shipping. Consideration of proposals and information on maritime security issues. Providing a chain of custody for containers from origin to destination. Submitted by Singapore. (6 February 2002) [p. 31]

MSC 75/ISWG/INF.26 Prevention and suppression of acts of terrorism against shipping. Port and maritime security IAPH policy and guidance paper. Submitted by IAPH. (9 April 2002) [p. 29]

MSC 75/ISWG/INF.33 Prevention and suppression of acts of terrorism against shipping. Reporting requirements for ships entering Canadian waters. Submitted by Canada. (12 April 2002) [p. 34]

MSC 76/4/2 Measures to enhance maritime security. Ship Security Alert. Draft recommendation on performance standards for a ship security alert system installation. Submitted by the United States. (28 October 2002) [p. 38]

MSC 76/4/21 Measures to enhance maritime security. Consideration of comments on draft Conference resolution (10). Early implementation of Long-Range Ship's Identification and Tracking. Submitted by ICS, BIMCO, IPTA, Intertanko, ICCL and SIGTTO. (1 November 2002) [p. 36]

MSC 76/22/8 Any other business: Review of safety measures and procedures for the treatment of persons rescued at sea. Note by the Secretariat. (31 July 2002) [p. 128]
MSC 76/22/10 Any other business: Review of safety measures and procedures for the treatment of persons rescued at sea. Submitted by Spain. (9 October 2002) [p. 136, 137, 139]
MSC 76/22/11 Any other business. Outcome of informal meeting on safety measures and procedures for the treatment of persons rescued at sea. Submitted by Sweden. (27 September 2002) [p. 128, 130, 131, 133–138]
MSC 76/ISWG/7/1 Consideration of proposals and information on maritime security issues. Long-range Identification and Tracking System. Submitted by Hong Kong, China. (31 July 2002) [p. 36]
MSC 76/ISWG/7/10 Consideration of proposals and information on maritime security issues. Long-range tracking. Submitted by ICS, BIMCO, IPTA and INTERTANKO. (2 August 2002) [p. 36]
MSC 76/ISWG/7/11 Consideration of proposals and information on maritime security issues. AIS—Issues arising from accelerated implementation—(proposed amendments to regulation 19 of Chapter V of Solas—safety of navigation). Submitted by ICS, BIMCO, IPTA and INTERTANKO. (2 August 2002) [p. 35]
MSC 76/ISWG/7/16 Consideration of proposals and information on maritime security issues. Intersessional Working Group on Maritime Security. Ship security alert. Submitted by the United States. (2 August 2002) [p. 38]
MSC 77/6/5 Measures to enhance maritime security. Long-range Tracking and Identification of Ships. Submitted by WNTI. (24 February 2003) [p. 36]
MSC 77/6/6 Revision of Circular MSC/Circ.967: Piracy and armed robbery against ships—Directives for MRCCs. Submitted by France. (3 March 2003) [p. 39]
MSC 77/6/11 Measures to enhance maritime security. Function requirements for long-range AIS. Submitted by the United Kingdom. (25 March 2003) [p. 36]
MSC 77/6/16 Measures to enhance maritime security. Long-range Ship's Identification and Tracking. Submitted by the United States. (8 April 2003) [p. 36, 37]
MSC 78/7/8 Measures to enhance maritime security. Long-Range Identification and Tracking of Ships. Submitted by the Netherlands and Sweden. (19 March 2004) [p. 36]
MSC 78/26/Add.1 Report of the Maritime Safety Committee on the work of its Seventy-Eighth Session (4 June 2004) [p. 14]
MSC 79/5/4 Measures to enhance maritime security. "False security alerts—Distress/security double alerts" and Long-Range Identification and Tracking. Note by the Secretariat. (20 September 2004) [p. 36]
MSC 79/5/6 Measures to enhance maritime security. Priority of ship security alerts. Submitted by Italy. (22 September 2004) [p. 38]
MSC 79/5/10 Measures to enhance maritime security. Freely available AIS generated ship data and the attendant security risks. Submitted by BIMCO, ICS, INTERCARGO, INTERTANKO and SIGTTO. (23 September 2004) [p. 35]
MSC 79/5/12 Measures to enhance maritime security. Long-range Identification and Tracking of Ships. Submitted by Australia. (24 September 2004) [p. 36]
MSC 79/22/6 Outcome of the second meeting of the UN Inter-Agency group on the

treatment of persons rescued at sea. Note by the Secretariat. (15 September 2004) [p. 80, 128, 140]

MSC 80/5/5 Measures to enhance maritime security. A practical system for implementing Long-Range Identification and Tracking of Ships (LRIT). Submitted by IMSO. (2 March 2005) [p. 36]

MSC 80/5/8 Measures to enhance maritime security. Long-Range Identification and Tracking of Ships. Submitted by the United States. (4 March 2005) [p. 36]

MSC 80/5/9 Measures to enhance maritime security. Long-range Identification and Tracking (LRIT) Project. Submitted by the Marshall Islands. (18 March 2005) [p. 36]

MSC/ISWG/LRIT 1/3 Development of the draft SOLAS amendments on Long-Range Identification and Tracking. Inclusion of LRIT regulation in SOLAS Chapter V. Proposal on application of provision for the reception of information from ships navigating within a distance from a coastal state. Submitted by the Islamic Republic of Iran. (15 September 2005) [p. 36]

MSC 81/5/11 Measures to enhance maritime security. Performance standards for the ship security alert system. Submitted by Austria, Brazil, Cyprus, Czech Republic, Denmark, Estonia, Finland, France, Germany, Greece, Hungary, Ireland, Italy, Latvia, Lithuania, Luxembourg, Malta, the Netherlands, Poland, Portugal, Slovakia, Slovenia, Spain, Sweden, the United Kingdom and the European Commission. (27 February 2006) [p. 38]

NAV

NAV 49/12 Measures to enhance maritime security. Long-Range Tracking and Identification of Ships. Submitted by WNTI. (24 February 2003) [p. 36]

NAV 49/12/1 Measures to enhance maritime security. Long-range ship's identification, position reporting and monitoring. Submitted by IALA. (24 March 2003) [p. 36]

STW

STW 34/9/4 Measures to enhance maritime security. Training in the use of shipboard AIS. Submitted by the United Kingdom. (2 January 2003) [p. 35]

STW 35/9 Measures to enhance maritime security. Shipboard AIS training. Submitted by IFSMA. (11 November 2003) [p. 35]

United Nations

UNGA Resolutions

UNGA Res 36/125 'Report of the United Nations High Commissioner for Refugees' (14 December 1981) A/RES/36/125 [p. 79, 80]

UNGA Res 48/102 'Prevention of the Smuggling of Aliens' (20 December 1993) A/RES/48/102 [p. 81, 82]

UNGA Res 51/62 'Measures for Prevention of the Smuggling of Aliens' (12 December 1996) A/RES/51/62 [p. 82]

UNGA Res 52/103 'Office of the United Nations High Commissioner for Refugees' (9 February 1998) A/RES/52/103 [p. 83]
UNGA Res 53/125 'Office of the United Nations High Commissioner for Refugees' (12 February 1999) A/RES/53/125 [p. 83]
UNGA Res 54/212 'International Migration and Development' (1 February 2000) A/RES/54/212 [p. 117]
UNGA Res 54/166 'Protection of Migrants' (24 February 2000) A/RES/54/166 [p. 81]
UNGA Res 55/92 'Protection of migrants' (26 February 2001) A/RES/55/92 [p. 81]
UNGA Res 56/170 'Protection of migrants' (28 February 2002) A/RES/56/170 [p. 81]
UNGA Res 57/218 'Protection of migrants' (4 December 2002) A/RES/57/218 [p. 81]
UNGA Res 58/190 'Protection of migrants' (22 March 2004) A/RES/58/190 [p. 81]
UNGA Res 60/169 'Protection of migrants' (7 March 2006) A/RES/60/169 [p. 81]

UNSC Resolutions

UNSC Res 1456 (20 January 2003) UN Doc S/RES/1456 [p. 141]
UNSC Res 1816 (2 June 2008) UN Doc S/RES/1816 [p. 72]
UNSC Res 1838 (7 October 2008) UN Doc S/RES/1838 [p. 72]

Table of Cases and Arbitral Awards

Chapter One

Introduction

This study is primarily concerned with the crime of migrant smuggling by sea. While not falling within the traditional definition of 'security', the admission of maritime migrant smuggling as a crime against maritime security is a reflection of the fact that 'new and evolving threats require a new vision of collective security in the twenty-first century.'[1]

The use of the term 'security' necessitates the drawing of a distinction between 'maritime safety' and 'maritime security'. 'Security' differs from 'safety' in the issue of wilfulness of the act. While safety is concerned with the avoidance of accidents, security issues are concerned with deliberate malignity. Maritime security is understood to include the preservation of territorial integrity and sovereignty, and the maintenance of peace and order, so as to ensure the safety and protection of ships together with their passengers, crews and cargoes, and the protection of property and the environment. Among the threats to maritime security are the transnational crimes of terrorism, arms smuggling, piracy, money laundering, trafficking in persons, and illicit trafficking in narcotic drugs and psychotropic substances.[2]

As far as criminal activity is concerned, all threats to maritime security share one significant common feature: the transnational link. This is a feature of all forms of organized crime, of which the crimes listed above form a part. This problem is an unintended consequence of the compression of time and distance, alongside the rapid development of information technologies. While criminal syndicates are able to operate within the global village, crossing borders with considerable ease, the majority of legislative instruments and resources for combating such crimes are limited by State boundaries. It has been recognized that '[n]ew and existing transnational threats and challenges have also highlighted the importance of international cooperation in ensuring maritime security and the need for a coordinated approach.'[3]

1 UNGA A/63/63 (10 March 2008) 15.
2 MSC 75/ISWG/INF.6 (15 January 2002), paras 3, 4.
3 UNGA A/63/63 (10 March 2008) 16.

The study is not concerned with all types of organized crime constituting a threat to maritime security. Indeed, the text only makes reference to certain other examples such as drug smuggling and maritime terrorism to give examples of cooperation in these spheres, and also, due to the fact that State vessels do not patrol the seas with the sole purpose of interdicting vessels carrying migrants, but rather, to safeguard maritime security in general. Apart from this however, the core of the book is devoted to a study of maritime migrant smuggling. There are various reasons for this. Firstly, this is a crime which admits of action, in some form or another, by different State actors, in each maritime zone. Also, the actual *locus* of the crime can be in different zones: the crime can be completed in the territorial sea, when the migrants are brought close to the shores of a State; alternatively, the offence can be partially completed on the high seas or exclusive economic zone (EEZ), such as where migrants are transferred to small, unseaworthy boats which then, in turn, take them closer to shore. The crime of migrant smuggling by sea is also extremely interesting in that it posits a number of inter-related considerations. Unlike narcotics trafficking, the subject of migrant smuggling is not a commodity but an individual, thereby importing principles of human rights, refugee and humanitarian law. This is what makes the issue uniquely complex and difficult. Furthermore, due to the extremely poor condition of the vessels which transport the migrants, the area of law requiring vessels to rescue those in distress at sea comes to the fore. The IMO has played a pivotal role here, a role which is studied in this book. Lastly, maritime migrant smuggling is of direct and immediate relevance to Malta, and a comprehensive analysis of the state of the law in this area was thus felt to be of some use in clarifying certain aspects of the problem. It is for this reason, too, that special attention is given to the Mediterranean region.

There is a difference between what actions States would like to pursue in order to carry out their aims and objectives and what States are actually empowered to do. It seems almost too basic to note that States must act within the parameters of the current legal regime, but in an area such as this, only recently regulated upon, this is of extreme importance. Furthermore, States are bound not only by the current regime of the law of the sea and the precepts of relevant customary international law, but also by the law relating to human rights and humanitarianism. Beyond the distinction between what States want to do and what States are empowered by law to do there lies another subdivision: States are not always able to do what the law permits them to do. Here, we come to technical factors which sometimes inhibit State action, thus rendering invaluable the terms of instruments which provide for the merging of State resources in this area.

Therefore, empowerment to act can be seen from two angles: firstly, States may legally act only within the constraints of international law. However, irrespective of the legal empowerment to act, States also face challenges of a practical nature. A simple example may clarify this point: while each State has an unquestionable legal power to safeguard its port facilities, it is still faced with the difficulty of ensuring the proper and effective monitoring of vessels entering its ports and the efficient but thorough inspection of containers. These 'practical' or 'technical' factors thus focus on what a State *can* do, rather than what a State is *empowered* to do. Empowerment by the law differs according to the legal classification given to a particular set of facts. This becomes relevant when one considers that the same facts may amount to different or multiple offences, thus warranting different action on the part of the State. In this way, the legal factors empowering a State to act appear to vary according to the legal nature of the offence, while the technical issues to be faced by a State remain the same irrespective of the legal nature of the offence.

The legal empowerment referred to above in fact refers to a coastal State's prescriptive and enforcement jurisdiction. These two types of jurisdiction are not necessarily always commensurate: usually, a State's prescriptive jurisdiction is wider than its enforcement jurisdiction. In other words, although a State's power to board, search and arrest a vessel in its territorial sea necessarily means that it has the prescriptive jurisdiction to create a particular offence, the existence of prescriptive jurisdiction does not automatically imply that the State has the power to enforce that particular law. This difference will be clearer once the various maritime zones are outlined: the coastal State has differing degrees of legal and enforcement power in the various maritime zones.

As far as enforcement jurisdiction is concerned, issues are complicated further when one considers that an offence may easily straddle more than one maritime zone; indeed, in the case of drug- or migrant-smuggling, the crossing of various maritime zones is often a trade mark of these offences. Another problem concerning enforcement relates to the very practical fact that it is sometimes not desirable to take enforcement action at the earlier stages of the commission of the offence but to leave it to later stages so that other offenders may be identified and arrested as well. In this way, on- and off-shore authorities may desist from taking action against a suspicious vessel approaching the land territory of the coastal State in the hope that the contacts on land may also be revealed. This, again, is extremely relevant in the case of the illegal importation of drugs and migrants, where the traffickers may also be identified, as well as the smugglers on board the vessel.

This study departs from the premise that maritime migrant smuggling presents a problem to the international community and constitutes a threat to maritime security. It is concerned with the issue of whether the existing framework governing jurisdictional powers in the law of the sea is adequate to deal with this problem. While I conclude that it is indeed possible to deal with maritime migrant smuggling within the existing framework of international law, it is not altogether easy or straightforward, precisely because of the significance of the human rights considerations mentioned above.

The approach taken in the study is first to provide a factual account of migrant smuggling by sea, presenting the crime as a threat to national security and as a facet of organized crime. I then focus on the primary tool by means of which States pursue their policy interests and aims—that of 'interception'—and on outlining various operational and technical approaches adopted by States in order to overcome practical problems inhibiting action. Part II of the book looks at the opportunities for State action and at the constraints on it. The jurisdictional powers of States under the current law of the sea regime are analysed, as is the humanitarian aspect of maritime migrant smuggling. Under this heading human rights principles are discussed, together with the duty to rescue those in distress at sea. Following the analysis of the relevant international law in this area, in a chapter on treaty modifications I will discuss instances of cooperation within the field of maritime migrant smuggling and, also, illustrations of the most advanced forms of cooperation in the fight against other crimes such as maritime drug trafficking and maritime terrorism. Following this analysis one can determine whether or not it is possible to work within the current legal regime when combating the crime of maritime migrant smuggling. The book ends with an account of State practice. This chapter aims to demonstrate the practical difficulty certain States have faced in dealing with the issue. The examples provided by Australia, the USA and the EU are the best paradigms to illustrate this fact since—and this is especially the case for Australia and the USA—these States have strayed beyond what is strictly necessary and legal in the fight against migrant smuggling. Furthermore, this chapter is significant in that, together with the previous chapter, State action in dealing with migrant smuggling can offer a way forward in the fight against this international threat—one which could signal the future orientation of international law in this area. Therefore, the chapter on State practice best demonstrates both the pitfalls and prospects of State action in this field.

Part I

Outlining the Problem

Chapter Two

Factual Background

2.1. *Preliminary Considerations*

'Migrant smuggling by sea' is a particular offence, recently defined in international treaty law, in which individuals are assisted in their attempt to enter a State's territory via the sea in a covert manner in violation of its laws, evading detection by its border control officials. Individuals seeking to enter States in this way include those who are attempting to flee conflict, persecution,[1] or natural disasters, as well as those seeking to circumvent migration and border controls, often in order to improve their economic circumstances.

Furthermore, '[t]he potential for terrorists to take advantage of human smuggling networks in attempts to circumvent border security measures cannot be ignored.'[2] In view of this, there is a trend towards more stringent migration policies and control mechanisms in a bid to combat terrorism.[3] Primarily however, the fight against migrant smuggling, whether by land, sea or air, is increasingly being perceived as a border control issue. Although the doctrine of State sovereignty generally prohibits enforcement action by one State on the territory of another, two branches of exceptions to this rule are emerging. Non-entrée policies such as visa regimes, carrier sanctions and departure control inspections[4] form the first group of exceptions. These measures

---

1 This group may comprise persons fleeing directly from the country of persecution as well as those engaged in secondary or tertiary movements from a country of first or subsequent asylum where they had or could have been provided with the necessary protection.

2 US National Strategy for Maritime Security (September 2005) 6.

3 See S. Ginsburg, 'Countering Terrorist Mobility: Shaping an Operational Strategy February' (February 2006) Migration Policy Institute Report; J.E. Lake, W.H. Robinson, L.M. Seghetti, 'The Complexity of the Challenge' (29 March 2005) CRS Report for Congress, Border and Transportation Security.

4 Carrier sanctions are found in the original Schengen Convention, Art. 26, and reinforced in Art. 4 of Council Directive 2001/51/EC of 28 June 2001 [2001] OJ L187/45; Convention on International Civil Aviation 1944, annex 9; Migrant Smuggling and Trafficking Protocols 2000, Art. 11(3). Departure site inspections are also common with the EU and UK, the

indicate a willingness on the part of States to apply their domestic immigration laws extraterritorially. The second emerging exception is of maritime enforcement increasingly being carried out outside coastal States' jurisdictional zones. International conventions increasingly provide for the exercise of jurisdiction on the high seas, as we will discuss.

2.2. *The Fastest-growing Transnational Organized Crime Recently Defined in International Law*

Migrant smuggling causes a major disruption both to national immigration policies and to the international protection framework as a whole. It is considered to be the fastest growing transnational crime today, with the number of affected countries increasing, together with the number and complexity of routes used.[5] It is also benefiting from developments in technology making possible the use of sophisticated navigational equipment and the creation of fraudulent documentation. The actual size of the problem is unknown; the statistics on the scale of the offence of migrant smuggling by land, sea and air do not necessarily reflect the true scale of the problem as they take into account only actual apprehensions of unauthorized migrants, thus only amounting to a fraction of the problem.

Any statistical data are thus bound to be unreliable, albeit staggering. Out of the estimated 191 million migrants world-wide (with Europe hosting 64.1 million, amounting to 8.8 % of the region's population)[6] there are approximately 30 to 40 million unauthorized migrants, comprising 15 to 20 % of the world's immigrant stock.[7] The Report of the Global Commission on International Migration states that an estimated 2.4 to 4 million people cross international borders without authorization annually.[8] Although no statistics are available on the total number of people who use maritime routes clandestinely,[9] the 2007 Report of the Secretary-General on Oceans and the Law of the Sea states that

Netherlands, Germany and Denmark posting immigration officers abroad. See also USA Enhanced Border Security and Visa Entry Reform Act 2002 (Pub L No. 107–173, 14 May 2002), para. 401.

5 The global profit of trafficking organizations is estimated to be between US$ 3.5 billion and US$ 10 billion per year.

6 UN, 'Trends in Total Migrant Stock: The 2005 Revision' (UN Publications, New York, 2007).

7 UN, 'Trends in Total Migrant Stock: The 2003 Revision', POP/DB/MIG/REV.2003.

8 Global Commission on International Migration, 'Migration in an Interconnected World: New Directions for Action' (October 2005), annex II. See www.gcim.org.

9 UN Doc A/61/63 (9 March 2006), para. 82.

during 2006 an unprecedented number of individuals used the maritime route to cross international borders clandestinely.[10] As far as migrant smuggling by sea is concerned, between 1 January and 31 July 2007, 79 separate incidents involving 1,253 migrants were reported to the IMO, thus bringing the total number of incidents reported to the IMO since 2001 to 1,242, involving 61,422 migrants.[11] It has also been estimated that 3,000 people died between January and July 2006 in their attempts to cross the Mediterranean.[12] The most recent statistics show that some 51,000 people arrived irregularly in Italy, Spain, Greece and Malta in 2007 and 16,767 in 2008 (up to mid-June).[13]

The link to organized crime is highlighted by the fact that the first international regulation of the offence of migrant smuggling came in the form of a Protocol to the United Nations Convention on Transnational Organized Crime (CATOC). CATOC defines an organized criminal group for the purposes of the Convention as 'a structured group of three or more persons, existing for a period of time and acting in concert with the aim of committing one or more serious crimes or offences established in accordance with this Convention, in order to obtain, directly or indirectly, a financial or other material benefit'.[14]

The term 'smuggling' will be used in this book, as opposed to 'trafficking'. These terms are defined separately in international law, although they do have certain overlapping elements. However, because trafficking requires attention to be given to post-arrival conduct (in order to prove the element of fraud or coercion, as indicated below) enforcement action may well not be taken in maritime zones, nor even at the actual border crossing onto land, but several weeks after the border crossing, in order to identify other members of the organized criminal ring.[15] A brief description of the main elements of these crimes should therefore be read with this fact in mind.

---

10 UN Doc A/62/66 (12 March 2007), para. 70.

11 MSC.3/Circ.13 Unsafe Practices associated with the Trafficking or Transport of Migrants by Sea (31 July 2007).

12 ECRE, 'Defending Refugees' Access to Protection in Europe' (December 2007).

13 A. Klug, 'The Treatment of Migrants and Refugees Rescued at Sea' presented at the Ninth Meeting of the United Nations Open Ended Informal Consultative Process on Oceans and the Law of the Sea, Panel Discussion, Segment 4: Focus on People at Sea (23–27 June 2008), 2.

14 CATOC Art. 2(a).

15 Statistics relating to human trafficking are equally staggering: 600,000 to 800,000 men, women and children are trafficked across international borders annually; approximately 80 % are women and girls and up to 50 % are minors. See US Department of State, Trafficking in Persons Report (2005) www.state.gov/g/tip/rls/tiprpt/2005/.

Undocumented migration refers to the process whereby people attempt to enter a country which is not their country of nationality or permanent residence without the proper authority.[16] When they are assisted in this process, it is referred to either as 'smuggling of migrants' or as 'trafficking in persons'. The distinction between these two terms was brought out in two of the Protocols supplementing the CATOC 2000. 'Smuggling' is defined in Art. 3(a) of the Protocol against the Smuggling of Migrants by Land, Sea and Air, Supplementing the United Nations Convention against Transnational Organized Crime (Smuggling Protocol) as:

> The procurement, in order to obtain, directly or indirectly, a financial or other material benefit, of the illegal entry of a person into a State Party of which the person is not a national or a permanent resident.

Smuggling involves the physical movement of persons across international borders on a payment-for-services basis. The focus is thus on facilitation of the illegal crossing of frontiers for profit; the subsequent treatment of the migrants is not a constitutive element of the crime. The related crime of trafficking in persons is somewhat more complex and further envisages the use of force, fraud, coercion, or exploitation directed at the individual, as noted in Art. 3(a) of the Protocol to Prevent, Suppress and Punish Trafficking in Persons, especially Women and Children, Supplementing the United Nations Convention against Transnational Organized Crime (Trafficking Protocol):

> The recruitment, transportation, transfer, harbouring or receipt of persons, by means of the threat or use of force or other forms of coercion, of abduction, of fraud, of deception, of the abuse of power or of a position of vulnerability or of the giving or receiving of payments or benefits to achieve the consent of a person having control over another person, for the purpose of exploitation. Exploitation shall include, at a minimum, the exploitation of the prostitution of others or other forms of sexual exploitation, forced labour or services, slavery or practices similar to slavery, servitude or the removal of organs.

Therefore, while the offence of smuggling requires the consent of the migrants, the crime of trafficking includes elements which are not present in smuggling, those being the improper form of recruitment, through coercion, deception or some abuse of authority, and the element of obtaining a profit as a result of an exploitative purpose for which the trafficking was undertaken, although

[16] Methods of undocumented migration other than arrival by sea include those who overstay their visa, those who work in contravention of their visas and those who travel using fraudulent travel documentation.

this aim need not necessarily be fulfilled.[17] Furthermore, while the offence of smuggling ends with the arrival of the migrants at the destination country, trafficking involves a continuing exploitative relationship in order to generate profits for the traffickers. Lastly, migrant smuggling is always transnational, whereas trafficking may also take place within the borders of a single State.

Notwithstanding their separate treatment at international law, these offences often present overlapping problems to law enforcement and prosecutorial authorities.[18] Actual cases often involve elements of both offences or may shift from one to the other, as many victims of trafficking begin their journey by consenting to be smuggled from one State to another, or smuggled migrants may later be tricked or coerced into exploitative situations and thus become victims of trafficking in human beings. A migrant may have been charged a phenomenal amount of money for the illegal transportation; this practice usually results in virtual 'debt bondage' between the migrant and his transporters once the destination is reached.[19] This in effect constitutes the crime of 'trafficking' since the migrant is exploited by the transporters so as to minimize and eventually make good his debt. Thus, there seems to be a continuum between the voluntary and non-voluntary forms of undocumented migration. Therefore, while from an enforcement point of view 'trafficking' may require greater attention to be given to post-entry behaviour than 'smuggling', resulting in a deferral of maritime seizure, efforts at curtailing migrant smuggling are primarily focussed on maritime interception (since the offence is constituted by the act of the illegal crossing of an international border).[20]

---

[17] 'Implementation of the Protocol against the Smuggling of Migrants by Land, Sea and Air, supplementing the United Nations Convention against Transnational Organized Crime, Analytical Report of the Secretariat' (2 September 2005) UN Doc CTOC/COP/2005/4, point 22. Because of this, 'trafficking' gives rise to additional human rights concerns: UNGA 'Note by the Office of the United Nations High Commissioner for Human Rights, the United Nations Children's Fund and the International Organisation for Migration on the draft protocols concerning migrant smuggling and trafficking in persons' (8 February 2000) UN Doc A/AC.254/27, 1–2.

[18] UNHCR, 'Refugee Protection and Migration Control: Perspectives from UNHCR and IOM' Global Consultations on International Protection (31 May 2001) EC/GC/01/11, para. 9.

[19] UNICRI, 'Global Programme Against Trafficking in Human Beings: Human Smuggling and Trafficking: a desk Review on the Trafficking in Women from the Philippines' (Tenth United Nations Congress on the Prevention of Crime and the Treatment of Offenders, Vienna, Austria) A/CONF.187/CRP.1 (5 April 2000) 3, 8.

[20] For general information on migrant smuggling definitions see A. Schloenhardt, *Migrant Smuggling: Human Trafficking and Organized Crime in Australia and the Asia Pacific Region* (Martinus Nijhoff, The Netherlands 2003), Chapter 1.

2.3. *Migrant Smuggling and the Southern Mediterranean: Routes and Conditions*

Southern points in Europe are attractive destinations or transit points for further journeys up into Europe. In spite of the voluminous documentation and number of measures adopted within the EU sphere, migration still remains predominantly an issue of national decision-making, supplemented by the various directives and guidelines on a supra-national level, which themselves require domestic implementation. Although the EU is prioritizing the challenge of illegal immigration, perhaps the greatest issue which militates against a true will to fight the phenomenon is the principle in the 2003 Dublin Regulation which effectively imposes a disproportionate burden on the southern EU border States, leaving the remainder of the Union unaffected by the growing influx of irregular migrants arriving at its southern shores.[21] According to the Dublin Regulation, asylum-seekers are to lodge their asylum applications in the country of first arrival. Should they fail to do so, and if it can be shown that the individual has passed through the territory of another Member State, the individual will be returned to the initial State of entry. Prior to 1997, most migrants and asylum-seekers transited Italy *en route* to the French and Austrian borders, and then further north to Germany, the Netherlands, Scandinavian countries and the UK. Due to the Dublin Regulation, what should be a European problem has been made a national problem which States such as Italy and Malta can share only with other EU States with a Mediterranean coastline.[22]

It seems obvious, therefore, that the most affected EU States in terms of arrivals by sea are Italy and Malta, followed by Spain and Greece. Italy has, for several years, received the largest number of arrivals; Malta is receiving proportionally the greatest number *per capita* of the population,[23] and in 2008, for the first time, the number of immigrant arrivals exceeded the local birth rate.[24] Since 2004 Italy has used the island of Lampedusa (where since 2003 thousands of migrants have landed)[25] as a temporary holding station,

---

[21] Council Regulation (EC) 343/2003 [2003] OJ L50/1. The Dublin Regulation seeks to avoid forum shopping where asylum-seekers would tend to choose their preferred State of asylum, and also 'asylum-seeker in orbit' situations where an individual is transferred from one State to another, with no State being willing to take responsibility for examining the claim.

[22] J. van Selm and B. Cooper, 'The New Boat People: Ensuring Safety and Determining Status' (MPI, Report) (January 2006) 59. See also ECRE, 'Report on the Application of the Dublin II Regulation in Europe' (Report) (March 2006) AD/3/2006/EXT/MH.

[23] Van Selm and Cooper (n 22) 46.

[24] Statement by Emigrants Commission (Malta), October 2008.

[25] European Commission, 'Technical Mission to Libya on Illegal Immigration, 27 November to 6 December 2004' (Report) Annex 7, Description of the Nature of Migration Flows, 7753/05, April 2005, 38.

summarily removing arrivals to Libya or Tunisia, depending upon which State areas the vessels had transited. Italy has also sought closer relations with these two North African States, particularly with Libya.[26] Italy's actions (including, collective expulsions to Libya between October 2004 and March 2005 and a bilateral agreement, with unknown contents, between the two States) have been criticized by NGOs,[27] and both the European Parliament and European Court of Human Rights have demanded that Italy provide greater transparency on the conditions on Lampedusa and its bilateral agreement with Libya.[28]

Malta has similar, and arguably more immediate, problems in this respect. Most incidents of migrant smuggling occur in the summer months via unregistered boats ranging from 15 to 30 feet long, some of which are power boats carrying anything from fewer than 50 to 250 migrants each. Situated along the natural migration route from the South (Africa, Middle East) to Europe, 290 km east of Tunisia and north of Libya and only 93 km from southern Sicily, Malta is the second most densely populated country in the world, with 400,000 inhabitants packed into 320 square metres. The incidence of such arrivals has grown radically in the past years.[29]

Most intercepted vessels will have started their journey from Libya, which operates as a transit point (as most migrants originate from Central and Northern Africa, and Asian countries), and will not have intended Malta to be a final destination. Any arrival is merely perceived as a foothold into the EU.

> There is no doubt at all that recent trends observed in landings both in Malta and in Italy indicate that organized criminals are helping illegal immigrants to leave the North African shores and then abandoning them in Malta's or Italy's search and rescue area for European coast guards to retrieve.[30]

As far as those migrants wishing to reach the borders of the EU are concerned, Malta's entry into the EU has exacerbated the problem. Furthermore, increasing surveillance of the Spanish border has shifted the migration route through

---

26 For more information see Van Selm and Cooper (n 22) 64.

27 See *ibid.*, 62–64; IFHR, 'Locking up Foreigners, Determining Refugees: Controlling Migratory Flows in Malta' (Report: International Fact-finding Mission) (September 2004) no. 403/2.

28 European Parliament, 'Resolution on Lampedusa' (14 April 2005) P6_TA(2005) 0318 [2006] OJ C33 E/598.

29 Boat arrivals in recent years are as follows: 166 people in 1998; 219 in 1999; 24 in 2000; 57 in 2001; 1,686 in 2002; 502 in 2003; 1,388 in 2004; 1,822 in 2005; 1,780 in 2006, 1,702 in 2007.

30 'Opening Address at the Libya–European Union seminar on "Saving Life at Sea and in the Desert"' Press Release (20 July 2005). Malta's search and rescue area stretches from the north of Tunisia to Crete and spans over 260,000 km. It covers the direct route taken by smugglers seeking to unload migrants in Europe.

Libya to Italy and Malta. It is further envisaged that immigration problems will escalate due to the amendments made to the 1979 International Convention on Search and Rescue (SAR Convention) which entered into force on 1 July 2006 and which will be analysed later in this study.[31]

2.4. *Unique Nature*

Migrant smuggling is a crime with unique characteristics which distinguish it from other types of organized crime such as drug smuggling by reason of the fact that the subjects of the offence are individuals as opposed to a mere commodity. Combating maritime migrant smuggling therefore poses a challenge which compels States to consider principles other than policing and interdiction since at the core of the illicit activity lie *persons* on the move, so that issues of human welfare and dignity have to be taken into consideration. States therefore have to juggle between two very different considerations: migrants are to be treated with the inherent dignity and respect to be accorded to any human being, irrespective of refugee status or otherwise. At the same time, States have security interests and are entitled to take any action in accordance with international law to protect such interests. International efforts at curbing this crime must be directed towards achieving a balance between these interests.

Furthermore, while human rights apply equally to all individuals, including drug smugglers and migrant smugglers, the smuggled migrants also enjoy further protection under the umbrella of refugee rights owing to the fact that they may be genuine asylum-seekers. The consideration of this mixed influx of arrivals must be placed at the forefront of any cooperative exercise to suppress migrant smuggling:

> Refugees are not migrants in the lay sense of the word. They move through compulsion, not on the basis of meaningful choice, and their immediate objective is to seek protection, not a migration outcome. This being said, refugees may also move—in fact increasingly do so—within a broader mixed flow which includes both forced and voluntary movements. They may even resort to migrant smugglers as one way to leave the country. At the same time, in the absence of viable, legal migration options to pursue, persons who are not refugees are nevertheless seeking to enter countries of their choice through the asylum channel, it being often the only entrance possibility effectively open to them. So the line between

[31] MSC 78/26/Add.1 Annex 5, para. 3.1.9.

> migrant and asylum-seeker progressively blurs in the public mind, just as does the distinction between migration control and refugee protection in the policies of some States.[32]

It is for this reason that a discussion of this crime will necessarily highlight a potential conflict existing between the legitimate interests of States and the mandates of international law, between jurisdictional notions and humanitarian considerations, between principles of State sovereignty and principles of protection. A cooperative framework aimed at preventing such crime must find and maintain a fine balance between these considerations in order to be effective.

Furthermore, although migrants are often portrayed as parties to the criminal transaction, the aim of international initiatives is to remove this perception.[33] They are usually transported in the basest and most hazardous and inhumane of conditions, in unseaworthy and overcrowded vessels which often cannot withstand the elements.[34] Migrants face a host of perils, including storms, leaky and overcrowded boats, lack of navigational tools, pirate attacks, starvation, dehydration and illness. It is thus the potential need for rescue which further differentiates maritime smuggling from any other crime and any other mode of arrival at a State's borders; and the duty to rescue those in distress at sea brings with it further obligations which need to be fulfilled alongside the actual interception process.

2.5. *Conclusion*

This short exposition of maritime migrant smuggling was intended to bring into relief the multi-faceted character of the crime: it is a transnational organized crime and serious threat to maritime security, but at the same time, the subject of the offence makes it radically different from other types of organized crime. The very fact that individuals are involved in maritime migrant smuggling calls into play considerations of human rights and humanitarianism. For these reasons, the search for any effective regime to repress this crime—whether existing in international law or still to be devised—is not an easy task.

---

32 UNHCR, 'Refugee Protection and Migration Control' EC/GC/01/11 (n 18), para. 2. See also UNHCR, 'Interception of Asylum-Seekers and Refugees: The International Framework and Recommendations for a Comprehensive Approach' (9 June 2000) EC/50/SC/CRP/17, para. 2.

33 Smuggling Protocol (2000), Art. 5.

34 See *Sale v Haitian Centers Council*, 113 S. Ct. 2549, 509 US 155, 125 L. (92–344) at 166–167 (1993).

Chapter Three

Pursuing State Interests: The Exercise of Maritime Enforcement Jurisdiction

3.1. *Overview*

This chapter discusses the primary tool employed by States in furthering their interest in reducing boat arrivals at their shores—that of interception. The legal regime within which this factual scenario must fit will be the subject of Part II of the book. The aim in this Part is that of identifying whether the current international legal regime is adequate to deal with this increasingly serious crime.

3.2. *State Interests*

States have an interest in upholding certain rights and policy interests. There is something of a mismatch between State interests and the rights available under the international legal system. This is brought into relief when one notes the difficulties inherent in the valid exercise of jurisdiction where the offence is situated in an area in which the State cannot legally act. It is also noted when one considers a State's sovereign right to protect its borders and, thus, protect its national security, and the equally compelling humanitarian principles of protection.

States are aware of their obligation to discharge their responsibilities as regards any refugees who may be present in the influx of migrants arriving at their shores even if they would rather not have to be in a position to deal with asylum claims. Therefore, albeit somewhat reluctantly, States realize that they must comply with obligations under the Convention Relating to the Status of Refugees 1951 (the Refugee Convention). Their primary interest in this scenario is that such obligations are discharged with minimal discomfort to themselves.

State interests in the field of irregular migration are various. States want to prevent illegal migration and they do so by repelling aliens and arresting and punishing the organizers of the offence, and even the migrants themselves to the extent that they pose a threat to the security of the State in the sense that, for example, the individual who has attempted the illegal entry has links to a terrorist organisation.[1]

An increasingly significant State policy interest in this field is the war on terror; precisely because nothing about the individual is known until that person comes into contact with national authorities, the irregular entrant may as easily be a terrorist as he is a refugee.[2] Here, migrant smuggling is framed as a threat to national security. The fight against migrant smuggling—indeed, illegal immigration generally—has been linked to the war on terror, and many restrictive State policies on entry may be a result of the over-eagerness of States to forge this link. Unilateral State action is fundamentally prompted by these concerns.

Interception of boats carrying irregular migrants is the primary tool by means of which States attempt to stem the number of arrivals at their shores and thus fulfil their main policy aim in this area.

3.3. *Interception*

3.3.1. *The Exercise of Jurisdiction*

A preliminary distinction between the terms 'jurisdiction' and 'control'[3] indicates that while both terms are often synonymous, there are instances where control can be exercised in the absence of jurisdiction; therefore, while jurisdiction includes methods of control, the opposite is not always true. Perhaps the most obvious example to cite is the right of self-defence, where control, indeed force, may be exercised by a vessel (say, an aircraft carrier) in the exercise of the inherent right of self-defence. On this reasoning, it may be argued that a State has the power to prevent a vessel from coming within half a mile of one of its aircraft carriers, and may use force in pursuit of this aim, even though there is no jurisdictional basis for such action.

The basic principle governing the exercise of enforcement jurisdiction is that it is generally limited to the territory of the State exercising jurisdiction;

---

1 Generally however, the rule is that migrants are not to be punished for their irregular entry: see Smuggling Protocol, Art. 5.

2 See R.E. Wasem, 'US Immigration Policy on Haitian Migrants' (Congressional Research Service, CRS RS21349, 31 January 2005).

3 Further explored in Chapter 5.

it cannot be exercised within the territory of another State unless the latter State consents, as otherwise that State's territorial sovereignty would be violated. On the high seas, with limited exceptions, ships are subject to the exclusive jurisdiction of the flag State. Of course, vessels may be boarded in pursuance of the right of self-defence, or when authorized by the United Nations Security Council (UNSC). However, save for a few exceptions, such as piracy and the slave trade, unauthorized broadcasting and the exercising of jurisdiction over stateless vessels, maritime interdiction or interception must be accompanied by flag State consent.[4] In these scenarios, the right of visit applies as per Art. 110 of the United Nations Law of the Sea Convention (LOSC).[5]

The right of visit has been defined as 'the right of a warship, in peacetime, to verify, in accordance with international law reflected in Art. 110 of the 1982 LOS Convention, the registry of a foreign vessel encountered on the high seas which is reasonably suspected of falling within [certain] exceptions[6] … The warship may board the foreign vessel without either the consent of the Master or the permission of the flag State.'[7] However, while consent is not needed for boarding, the powers given by the right of visit are limited. The sole purpose of this right is to verify the vessel's right to fly the flag of a State and to investigate the warship's suspicions that the vessel is engaged in one of the activities set out in Art. 110 LOSC. To this end, the right has been described as consisting in the right to approach the vessel, stop it, board it and examine the vessel's documents.[8] Once the investigation is completed, the boarding party must either depart the vessel, obtain the Master's consent to stay on board, or, if criminal or unusual activity is discovered, the enforcement officials must notify and ask their operational commander for guidance.[9]

---

4 In this regard note IMO MSC/Circ. 1133 Reminder of the Obligation to Notify Flag States when Exercising Control and Compliance Measures (14 December 2004) and MSC.1/Circ. 1191 Further Reminder of the Obligation to Notify Flag States when Exercising Control and Compliance Measures (30 May 2006).

5 This provision may be relied upon by non-parties as codifying an unwritten but universally applicable rule of customary international law. See M. Byers, 'Policing the High Seas: the Proliferation Security Initiative' (2004) 98 *AJIL* 527.

6 These are listed in Art. 110(1) LOSC.

7 Telegram from the US Department of State, 15 September 1990, reported in M. Pickering et al. (eds), *Digest of United States Practice in International Law* (Office of the Legal Advisor, United States Department of State, International Law Institute, Washington, DC, 1989–1990) See also J.C. Colombos, *International Law of the Sea* (6th edn, Longman, London, 1967) 311.

8 USCG et al., 'The Commander's Handbook on the Law of Naval Operations' (July 2007) NWP 1-14M/MCWP 5-12.1/COMDTPUB P5800.7A. The procedure is described at 7.6.1.

9 USCG, 'Model Maritime Operations Guide' (21 April 2003) 2–17.

There are various boarding scenarios and arrangements whereby flag State consent may be elicited.[10] Flag State consent is required in order for any acts of sovereignty to be conducted on board the vessel; therefore, where it is the Master alone who grants consent, such consent is usually granted only for the purposes of gathering information. It is the Master who determines the scope, conduct and duration of the boarding; however, no enforcement jurisdiction such as arrest or seizure may be exercised without the permission of the flag State, even if evidence of illegal activity is found. Thus, a consensual boarding is not an exercise of enforcement jurisdiction *per se*.[11] Where the flag State consents to boarding but the Master refuses to permit boarding by enforcement officials of another vessel, necessary force may be exercised in order to stop the vessel and allow for boarding; this is termed 'flag State-authorized non-consensual boarding'. Graduated measures are usually employed in order to stop a vessel, including attempting to hail the vessel by radio and loud-hailer, flashing signal lights, spraying water across the vessel's decks, firing warning shots across the bow, and firing small-calibre rounds at the vessel's engines in order to disable, but not sink, it.

There are also instances where formalized agreements are concluded which render *ad hoc* permission unnecessary: examples include 'Shipboarding Agreements' (bilateral in nature, which may be reciprocal, in which the flag State grants advance permission to foreign law enforcement officials to board its vessels in international waters for specified purposes, thereby removing the need for the Master's consent); 'Art. 17 Agreements' (bilateral agreements which specifically implement Art. 17 of the Convention against Illicit Traffic in Narcotic Drugs and Psychotropic Substances 1988 (Vienna Drugs Convention));[12] 'Shiprider Agreements' (also bilateral, which authorize a law enforcement official of a coastal State—'the rider'—to ride aboard a law enforcement vessel of another country to assist the coastal State in enforcing its laws against its own vessels. Such agreements may also include provisions for the law enforcement vessel to enter the coastal State's territorial sea without the shiprider if one is not readily available, to enforce the coastal State's laws against its own and third nation vessels) and 'Pursuit and Entry Agreements' (which permit foreign law enforcement vessels and aircraft to enter, on a case-by-case basis, the recognized territorial sea or sovereign airspace of a coastal State to investigate a suspect or to pursue a suspect fleeing from international waters. Such agreements may

---

[10] These are reviewed in Pickering et al. (eds) (n 7) 448–456.

[11] Commander's Handbook on the Law of Naval Operations (n 8) 3.11.2.5.2.

[12] Art. 17 sets out the procedures for verifying registry of foreign vessels suspected of engaging in illicit trafficking and the procedures required for obtaining flag State permission to board the foreign vessel and take law enforcement action.

incorporate the figure of a coastal State's enforcement authority with or without a shiprider.) These agreements provide a framework of prompt and effective law enforcement action with full respect for national sovereignty and territorial integrity, accounting for the varying capabilities of individual nations.[13]

3.3.2. *What Amounts to an Exercise of Jurisdiction*

States routinely exercise the right to approach a vessel and the right to stop it through an escalating variety of methods including signal lights, whistles, loud hailers, radio contact, warning shots or disabling fire. States also exercise the power to board, search and inspect vessels, seize and forfeit goods and arrest and prosecute those on board.[14] At what point is the line from control to jurisdiction crossed? What acts constitute acts of sovereignty and therefore require flag State consent? There is no detailed analysis in case law or treaty regarding what consitute such acts. It is therefore submitted that all methods of enforcement action listed above up to and including warning shots[15] and disabling fire constitute methods of control which do not amount to an exercise of jurisdiction. It is also arguable that boarding *per se* does not require flag State consent; it was seen above that the Master can consent to boarding by the enforcement officials of another vessel, and that this need not necessarily be accompanied by flag State consent as long as the enforcement officials limit themselves to general surveillance of the vessel. Any interrogation and search for evidence, it is submitted, crosses the line and constitutes an exercise of enforcement jurisdiction for which flag State consent is required.

3.3.3. *Defining 'Interception'*

The process of 'interception' (or interdiction), the ordinary meaning of which is to prevent something from proceeding or arriving, is not limited solely to the migrant smuggling context, but is a tool used in the suppression of other threats. The treatment of the tool in this book however will centre on its use in the fight against maritime migrant smuggling.

---

[13] USCG, 'Statement of Rear Admiral E.R. Ruitta on Maritime Bilateral Counterdrug Agreements before the Sub-Committee on Criminal Justice, Drug Policy, and Human Resources, Committee on Government Reform, US House of Representatives' (13 May 1999).

[14] As far as the power to prosecute offenders is concerned, this is more adequately classified as an exercise of a State's adjudicative powers, and will not be discussed here.

[15] Warning shots do not amount to a use of force under international law. See Commander's Handbook on the Law of Naval Operations (n 8) 3.11.5.2.

'Interception' refers to non-entrée measures used by States in order to reduce the flow of irregular migration to their territories.[16] A general definition to this end has been adopted by the UNHCR as follows:

> Interception is defined as encompassing all measures applied by a State, outside its national territory, in order to prevent, interrupt or stop the movement of persons without the required documentation crossing international borders by land, air or sea, and making their way to the country of prospective destination.[17]

These measures may be generally divided into two broad categories. The first includes passive measures such as visa regimes and carrier sanctions.[18] The second focuses on active measures taken at airports and on the sea. These active measures attracted the attention of the UNHCR which highlighted the role of interception in relation to maritime migration thus:

> ... [F]or the purposes of this conclusion, and without prejudice to international law, particularly international human rights law and refugee law, with a view to providing protection safeguards to intercepted persons, interception is one of the measures employed by States to ...
>
> (iii) assert control of vessels where there are reasonable grounds to believe the vessel is transporting persons contrary to international or national maritime law;
>
> where, in relation to the above, the person or persons do not have the required documentation or valid permission to enter; and that such measures also serve to protect the lives and security of the travelling public as well as persons being smuggled or transported in an irregular manner.[19]

In the light of the above, 'interception' involves any measure applied in order to exert control over vessels, which can amount to an exercise of enforcement jurisdiction should certain action be taken. Indeed, the scenario depicted in an interception is that where 'mandated authorities representing a State locate a boat, prevent its onward movement, and either take the passengers and crew onto their own vessel, accompany the vessel to port, or force an alteration

[16] On interception generally see A. Brouwer and J. Kumin, 'Interception and Asylum: When Migration Control and Human Rights Collide' (2003) 21 *Refuge* 4, 6–24.

[17] UNHCR, 'Interception of Asylum-Seekers and Refugees: The International Framework and Recommendations for a Comprehensive Approach' (9 June 2000) EC/50/SC/CRP.17.

[18] For more information on pre-frontier controls see T.A. Aleinikoff and V. Chetail (eds), *Migration and International Legal Norms* (TMC Asser Press, The Hague, 2003), 91–93; ECRE, 'Defending Refugees' Access to Protection in Europe' (December 2007), Chapter 3; G. Goodwin-Gill and J. McAdam, *The Refugee in International Law* (3rd edn, OUP, Oxford, 2007), 374–380; J.C. Hathaway, *The Rights of Refugees under International Law* (Cambridge University Press, Cambridge, 2005), 279 *et seq.*

[19] UNHCR ExCom Conclusion No. 97 (LIV) 'Conclusion on Protection Safeguards in Interception Measures' (2003).

in its course.'[20] Various means of control may be exerted over the vessel in order to prevent its onward movement or, indeed, to force an alteration in its course; however, taking the passengers and crew onto the enforcing vessel and accompanying the vessel to port (which in itself is akin to arresting it) constitute an exercise of enforcement jurisdiction for which flag State consent is required when on the high seas.

Interception at sea may take place either within the territorial sea or contiguous zone[21] of the country of embarkation, transit or destination, or on the high seas.[22] When exercised beyond the limits of the enforcing State's territorial jurisdiction, interception highlights the fact that a State's authority and territory are not co-extensive and a State's exercise of power is not confined to the borders of its territory: the process may involve extraterritorial exercise of jurisdiction by the interdicting State acting with consent on the high seas or in other States. Therefore, in order to secure the integrity of its borders in a pre-emptive fashion an intercepting State may be seen to take action equivalent in effect to extending the ambit of its outer borders.[23]

Interception is to be discussed mainly in the context of a unilateral State exercise. Various examples of such unilateral practice exist, such as the practice adopted by the USA in response to the number of Haitian arrivals throughout the 1990s and the Australian response to the arrival of the *MV Tampa* in the summer of 2001, which are discussed in Chapter 8. Generally, following the interdiction of vessels suspected of carrying irregular migrants or asylum-seekers, either within territorial waters or on the high seas, passengers are disembarked either on dependent territories of the intercepting country or on the territory of a third country which approves their landing. In most instances, the aim after interception is the return without delay of all irregular passengers to their country of origin. However, at this stage, State action is limited by various considerations, primarily, the potential existence of asylum-seekers on board the vessel, apart from economic and other irregular migrants—since, as was noted in Chapter 2, both groups make use of the services of people smugglers. This practice therefore risks failing to identify those groups

---

20 J. van Selm and B. Cooper, 'The New Boat People: Ensuring Safety and Determining Status' (MPI, Report) (January 2006), 5.

21 Note that the contiguous zone does not form part of the territorial sea; it constitutes part of the EEZ or of the high seas, depending on whether or not the coastal State has proclaimed an EEZ. See further Chapter 5.

22 Interception within the EEZ is equated to interception on the high seas.

23 The same result may be achieved by contracting those boundaries relative to their actual geographical territory, as was seen in Australia's attempt to excise its offshore territories. See A. Attila, 'Refugee Interdiction and the Outer Limits of Sovereignty' (2004) 3 *Journal of Law and Equality* 1, 25, 26.

deserving of protection, thus debarring them from international protection and resulting in the possible *refoulement* of asylum-seekers.[24] This possibility immediately ushers in a host of new obligations relating to refugee and human rights, as will be alluded to below.

3.4. *State Sovereignty and Humanitarian Principles of Protection*

Maritime interception is based on the classical understanding that a State has complete sovereign authority over a defined territory and, thus, has the plenary power to determine who crosses its borders. It is still generally understood that any restrictions on a State's sovereignty arise only by way of exception.[25] While this approach has been criticized as representing a state of affairs where the Executive and/or Legislature are permitted to operate without being impeded by judicial review, States have been ready to use their borders as the symbol of their power, security and protection.[26] In this light, national security appears to be used as a tool to exclude or expel persons thought to constitute a threat to the State.

In the light of this, an argument justifying broader controls may well be made. In fact, it was exactly this that the Australian government argued in the *Tampa* litigation. In *Ruddock v Valdarlis*,[27] the Government developed an argument based on sovereign prerogative; the inherent powers of any sovereign nation include a power to determine who enters that nation. This power is part of the prerogative of the Crown, exercisable by the Executive, and it may be exercised regardless of the provisions of domestic legislation; in this case the Migration Act 1958. In effect therefore, it was argued that this power can oust that of Parliament. The Government won the appeal.

After the events of 11 September 2001, the sovereignty argument becomes all the more convincing—especially since the language of sovereignty has come to include assumptions about security and public safety. However, can the 'sovereignty' premise incorporate the absolute right to exclude people from entering the territory of a State? The *Tampa* litigation seems to accept this as a

---

[24] See UNHCR, 'Interception of Asylum-Seekers and Refugees' EC/50/SC/CRP.17 (n 17), para. 6; UNHCR, 'Note on International Protection' (3 July 1998) A/AC.96/898, para. 16. The doctrine of *non-refoulement* is discussed in Chapter 6.

[25] Aleinikoff et al. (n 18), Chapters 3, 7 and 16.

[26] J.C. Morris, 'The Spaces in Between: American and Australian Interdiction Policies and their Implications for the Refugee Protection Regime' (2003) 21 *Refuge* 4, 56; J. Dench and F. Crepeau, 'Interdiction at the Expense of Human Rights: A Long-term Containment Strategy' (2003) 21 *Refuge* 4, 2–5.

[27] (2001) 110 FCR 491 (Fed. Ct.).

general principle, and thus a State's right to exercise migration control appears to be generally unassailable. In considering the Commonwealth's power to exclude, North J referred to *Chu Kheng Lim v The Minister for Immigration, Local Government and Ethnic Affairs*[28] where the High Court of Australia considered the nature of the power to deport aliens as an incident of executive power. In determining that the Migration Act 1958 was intended to regulate the whole area of removal of aliens he cited the following passage from the above case:

> The power to exclude or expel even a friendly alien is recognised by international law as an incident of sovereignty over territory. As Lord Atkinson, speaking for a strong Judicial Committee of the Privy Council, said in *Attorney-General (Canada) v Cain and Gilhula*:[29]
>
> One of the rights possessed by the supreme power in every State is the right to refuse to permit an alien to enter that State, to annex what conditions it pleases to the permission to enter it, and to expel or deport from the State, at pleasure, even a friendly alien, especially if it considers his presence in the State opposed to its peace, order, and good government, or to its social or material interests: Vattel, Law of Nations, book 1, s.231; book 2, section 125.[30]

This citation was also used by Beaumont J in the Full Federal Court decision in *Ruddock v Vadarlis*[31] where reference was also made to the long-standing position of the English courts regarding the general proposition of international law whereby 'the supreme power of every state has a right to make laws for the exclusion or expulsion of a foreigner.'[32]

However, it is submitted that the admission of aliens should not be regarded as an unlimited discretionary power within the exclusive domestic jurisdiction of States. Therefore, even if the sovereign power to exclude exists, this power is not absolute. There is a convincing basis for a *qualified* duty of States to admit aliens, according to a principle that an alien may be excluded only if he poses a serious danger to the public safety, security, general welfare or essential institutions of the State. However, even this formulation would need to be refined since it still leaves considerable discretion to States.[33] Furthermore,

28 (1992) 176 CLR 1.

29 [1906] AC 542, 546.

30 However, with reference to the quotation from Vattel see J.A. Nafziger, 'The General Admission of Aliens under International Law' (1983) 77 *AJIL* 4, 811–812 where he states that Vattel is often selectively used and that parts of his treatise actually reflect a different conclusion.

31 (2001) 110 FCR 491 (Fed. Ct.), para. 114.

32 *Ibid.*, French J in para. 186, quoting *inter alia Re Adam* [1837] 1 Moo PC; 12 ER 889 and *Musgrove v Toy* [1891] AC 272. French J adopted a stance similar to that of Beaumont J: see para. 196. The same principle was enunciated in *Nishimura Ekiu v United States*, 142 U.S. 651 at 659 (1892).

33 Nafziger (n 30) 846.

this formulation does not take due account of humanitarian principles which also must operate in such sphere. Issues and priorities have indeed changed over the years: the issue of State security has only recently come to the fore in effecting a change to domestic policies on migration, and the threat of terrorist infiltration was not necessarily considered an immediate threat until a few years ago. However, basic human needs still need to be respected.[34] Therefore, the correct formulation of the argument seems to be that there is indeed a right to exclude aliens, subject to the overriding obligation to respect human rights and humanitarian principles.[35] This seems to be the current interpretation given in judicial pronouncements.[36]

3.5. *Conclusion*

It has been noted that maritime interception is classically based on the approach that a State has complete sovereign authority over its territory, which in turn is premised on the fact that any restrictions on a State's sovereignty arise only by way of exception. Viewed in this light, there seems to be an inherent understanding that State sovereignty and humanitarian principles of protection are diametrically opposed in their aims and purposes. This understanding necessarily frames State policies in dealing with alien arrivals.

Rather than the two issues being juxtaposed however, perhaps what is needed is a mental shift in approach whereby humanitarian principles of protection are considered a facet of sovereignty—not something which hampers a State in the exercise of its sovereign powers, but which helps it in upholding its international obligations. In this way, protection principles will not be considered as exceptions to State sovereignty, to be interpreted as restrictively as possible; rather, perceived as an aspect of a State's sovereign powers, humanitarian principles of protection contribute to our understanding of a State. This shift in approach could be effective in beginning to alter the course of State policies in this area.

---

[34] In this regard see *Saadi v Italy* (2008) Application No. 37201/06, Grand Chamber (28 February 2008).

[35] See UDHR (1949), Art. 14; ICCPR (1966), Art. 9.

[36] *Minister for Immigration and Multicultural Affairs v Khawar* [2002] HCA 14 (per McHugh and Gummow JJ); *R v Immigration Officer at Prague Airport et al, ex parte European Roma Rights Centre et al.* [2004] UKHL 55, para. 19.

Chapter Four

Security: Operational and Technical Approaches

4.1. *The Emerging Security Regime*

This chapter considers tools which States have employed in order to be in a better position to combat new threats to maritime security, and thus provides a few of the more important examples of control and monitoring regimes devised as a result of the changing security environment.

In the post-September 2001 environment of an increased awareness of the threat of terrorism, the IMO spearheaded developments in this area when its Assembly called for a revision of IMO measures to combat acts of violence at sea.[1] A conference was convened in December 2002 and numerous amendments were made to the 1974 International Convention for the Safety of Life at Sea (SOLAS)[2] with the aim of detecting and taking preventive measures against security incidents affecting ships or port facilities used in international trade.[3] The main feature of the ensuing regime is the International Ship and Port Facility Security Code (ISPS Code), implemented through Chapter XI-2 of SOLAS, entitled 'Special Measures to Enhance Maritime Security', which came into force on 1 July 2004. The purpose of the Code is to provide a standardized, consistent framework for evaluating the risk management involved in the operation of ships and port facilities, and also to determine what security response measures are appropriate, through the assessment of each individual case.

The Code is designed to reduce the occurrence of breaches of maritime security by means of the assessment of risk and response strategies. It requires the mandatory implementation of certain rules and then goes on to introduce

---

1 Assembly Resolution A.924(22) (22 January 2002), para. 1.

2 For a succinct overview of the recent amendments see H.G. Hesse, 'Maritime Security in a Multilateral Context: IMO Activities to Enhance Maritime Security' (2003) 18 *IJMLC* 327–339.

3 Furthermore, a number of resolutions were adopted which set the direction of future work on maritime security.

guidelines; in line with this approach, the structure of the Code is in fact made up of two parts—a mandatory Part A, and Part B which contains the non-mandatory guidelines.

The most noteworthy feature of these amendments is that the measures introduced thereby—indeed the very rationale of the ISPS Code—are *preventive* in nature and are aimed at safeguarding the security of ships and ports world-wide by averting threats before they arise. These initiatives therefore saw the introduction of a new approach, directly related to the changing security environment; they are novel in the sense that international law is generally based on acting after the event in punishing the perpetrators rather than allowing States to prevent such acts from occurring.

4.2. *Focus on Ports*

The main aim of this overhaul in port security regulation has thus been to reduce the vulnerability of port systems. The seeds of this overhaul were sown in the form of an assessment of maritime security, conducted by the US after the events of 11 September 2001, which incorporated elements of awareness, prevention, response and consequence management. The first two of these elements were considered to provide the best return on investment. The assessment indicated that there were a number of initiatives that ought to be taken to improve maritime domain awareness[4] and security within the US and that these measures ought to be taken world-wide. The initiatives were taken to the IMO and they focus on four main components: the ship, its cargo, the port facility and those on board ships and ashore.[5]

The reason for focussing on ports became all too clear in the aftermath of the 2001 attacks on the Twin Towers and the Pentagon. The economic importance of most ports for the national economy of States and the fact that they represent a large contribution to States' gross national product makes ports extremely valuable. Apart from the obvious fact that ports are the place where ships land people and cargoes, both local and foreign, thus increasing the ramifications of an attack on port systems, international ports have 'international zones', operating outside the customs sphere, which offer unique possibilities for smuggling. At the same time, the existence of open frontiers leading to less control from regulatory authorities makes them excessively vulnerable as it

4 'Maritime Domain Awareness' refers to the collection, fusion and dissemination of enormous quantities of data with the purpose of generating actionable intelligence. See www.globalsecurity.org/intell/systems/mda.htm.

5 MSC 75/ISWG/5/7 (15 January 2002), para. 2.

creates ample opportunity for criminal organizations to infiltrate the system. The submission of the International Association of Ports and Harbours (IAPH) to the 75th session of the Maritime Safety Committee (MSC) stressed the significance of port systems and the fact that they are attractive to criminals. It emphasized the need for a port security plan which addressed all elements of criminal activity, from simple fraud to potential terrorist activities.[6]

As far as ships at port facilities are concerned, it is also necessary to consider that not only may attacks be directed *against* a ship, but a ship may also be a *means* of perpetrating a terrorist attack against a city or industrial facility.[7] A ship may either be used in the transportation of persons or equipment for the purpose of committing an unlawful act, or alternatively, it can itself be used as a weapon in an unlawful act; or else, it can be employed in a lawful trade for the purpose of generating funds to finance unlawful acts.[8] While this last-mentioned point is not of immediate concern when considering the security of port facilities, the transport of persons is a very real and direct concern insofar as landed illegal immigrants may also hide a terrorist in their midst, for example.

4.3. *New Challenges and New Approaches*

That a port State has the right to control access to and close its ports and exercise jurisdiction over events, people and things within its port is undisputed. The current challenge is to prevent threats from materializing and, thus, the key issue relates to the efficiency or otherwise of the current legal regime in enabling a port State to detect such threats, thus allowing it to take the required and permitted action before it occurs. 'Security' is a hazard management activity and, as with all hazard management efforts, the most appropriate course of action is first to remove the hazard. Therefore, to deny a vessel entry into port, while somewhat of a deterrent and deflection, does not remove the hazard; removal of the hazard consists in removing those who would commit acts of terrorism and organized crimes such as migrant smuggling or otherwise threaten the security of ships, ports, and offshore facilities.[9] In order to be

6 MSC 75/ISWG/INF.26 (9 April 2002), para. 1. See also MSC 75/17/12 (12 April 2002), para. 5.1.

7 MSC 75/ISWG/5 (10 January 2002), para. 4.2. The point was also made that the fact that seagoing vessels have access to certain rivers means that such a risk is not solely restricted to coastal areas or port cities. See also MSC 75/ISWG/5/9 (15 January 2002), para. 3.

8 MSC 75/17/44 (12 April 2002), para. 3.

9 MSC 75/17/5 (5 April 2002), para. 4.

effective, any new regulatory regime purporting to safeguard a State's security would have to empower and oblige the State to act in furtherance of this aim.

In the post-2001 environment, it is widely acknowledged that coastal State port security measures must constitute an effective and credible means of detecting and intercepting any illegal or dangerous persons who could arrive at the shores of the coastal State as smuggled migrants. The new direction taken by maritime security measures addresses this point, primarily through amendments to the SOLAS Convention and the new ISPS Code. These instruments aim to set in place an intricate, technical mechanism for port security while at the same time stopping short of disrupting the seamless flow of international trade.[10]

4.4. *The Container Threat*

Possibly the most obvious threat to the security and safety of any port comes in the form of containerized cargo: more than 200 million cargo containers travel between major seaports annually and 90 per cent of world cargo moves by container. As far as container security risks from terrorism are concerned, containers could be used to transport people, in which case the threats of piracy, hijacking and illegal migration come to the fore. Furthermore, the movement of cargo such as weapons, ammunition and explosives is likely to assist terrorism. Here, potential threats could relate to the smuggling of valuable cargoes for monetary benefit or the use of the container or cargo as terrorist weapons.[11]

Early on in the deliberations within the MSC, it was recognized that securing a chain of custody for containers could not be assured with currently available technology and that the lack of knowledge of the contents of freight containers had serious security implications.[12] Furthermore, any security measures adopted needed to respect the essential balance between the facilitation of maritime traffic and maritime security.[13]

Physical improvements with few cost implications and relative ease of implementation relate to design changes, such as altering door hinges and security bars. However, innovations with substantial cost and maintenance implications

[10] MSC 75/ISWG/5/3 (14 January 2003), paras 3, 3.1, 3.2.

[11] MSC 75/INF.30 (12 April 2002), para. 2.

[12] MSC 75/ISWG/3 (11 January 2002), paras 26, 27. Similar subjects were considered during ISWG No. 1 in February 2002. Among them: US submission MSC 75/ISWG/5/7 (15 January 2002), paras 18, 19, and Philippine submission MSC 75/ISWG/INF.6 (15 January 2002), paras 23, 24, are worthy of note.

[13] See E.E. Mitropoulos, Secretary-General of the IMO, 'Vessel Tracking and Identification 2006, Freedom and Security of the Seas' (Speech) (London, 24 April 2006).

are also necessary. These measures mainly relate to the fitting of electronic seals and alarms,[14] an open information exchange supported by world-wide detection infrastructure at key ports and terminal locations, and a global-tracking platform.[15] Furthermore, cooperation between all the parties involved in the transport chain was encouraged by the first meeting of the Intersessional Working Group (ISWG No. 1), and to this end the Working Group agreed that direct, immediate and closer cooperation with the World Customs Organization (WCO) was necessary in order to implement the partnership concept between the industry, workers' unions and administrations.[16] This cooperation was formalized by a Memorandum of Understanding to strengthen the cooperation between the IMO and WCO in July 2002. Furthermore, Resolution 9, adopted at the December 2002 IMO conference, provides for the enhancement of security in cooperation with the WCO in relation to closed cargo transport units.[17]

The initiatives taken by the US in the field of container security provide a clear illustration of measures aimed at reducing the risk of container cargoes being exploited by terrorists. On 19 August 2002, the Sea Cargo Targeting Initiative was launched and provided an automated system which better identifies high-risk cargo destined for US ports and establishes new ways of dealing with such cargo.[18] Apart from this Automated Commercial Environment, US Customs is also endeavouring to gain the support of the trade community in protecting global trade from terrorism; hence, such programmes as the Customs–Trade Partnership Against Terrorism (C-TPAT).[19] However, possibly the most internationally known initiative is the Container Security Initiative (CSI), launched on 17 January 2002.[20] This initiative replaced previous

---

14 An IMB–ICC submission reviews the ramifications of conventional and electronic container seals in MSC 75/17/6 (11 April 2002), paras 4.1–4.8.

15 MSC 75/ISWG/INF.8 (6 February 2002), paras 1–4.

16 MSC 75/17/1 (25 February 2002), paras 5.44–5.49. This cooperation was welcomed by the Member States' delegations. See, e.g., MSC 75/17/12 (12 April 2002), para. 11.2(b). For information on the WCO's work in the field of container security see MSC 75/17/8 (8 April 2002).

17 Resolution (No. 9) on the Enhancement of Security Cooperation with the World Customs Organisation (Closed Cargo Transport Units).

18 See 'US Customs Implements Enhanced Anti-Terror Sea Cargo Targeting at All US Seaports' (9 March 2002) News Release.

19 See US Customs and Border Protection, 'Customs-Trade Partnership against Terrorism: A Year in Review' (31 January 2008) News Release.

20 For general information on CSI and C-TPAT see United States Department of Homeland Security: 'Statement of R.M. Jacksta' (Hearing Before the Senate Committee on Commerce, Science and Transportation) (17 May 2005), 2–3; 'Statement of Rear Admiral C. Bone, and

customs practice whereby the US Customs and Border Protection Service[21] made informed, risk-based decisions as to which trucks, railcars and sea containers were to be targeted and examined. After 11 September 2001, the US determined that in order to deal effectively with potential threats such as the smuggling of weapons of mass destruction, it was necessary to work together with foreign counterparts to screen containers earlier on in the importation process as opposed to conducting examinations solely at the port of entry.[22]

By way of the CSI, high-risk cargo containers are identified and examined for weapons of mass destruction at foreign ports prior to their being shipped to the US. The programme is a reciprocal one, in that it allows participant countries the opportunity to send their customs officers to major US ports in order to target ocean-going containerized cargo destined for their countries. It is the host country officials who carry out any examinations; US Customs and Border Protection officials merely observe these operations (and vice versa when the containers are inspected at a US port of export). The US has also published a regulation on advanced cargo manifest information which obliges carriers to provide electronic manifest data to US customs authorities 24 hours before loading sea containers bound for the US.[23] The latest step in the CSI is for major container ports to install networks of sensors to detect nuclear and other radioactive materials at major container ports throughout the world, much like airport screening.

The US initiative was not at first kindly received by the EU, and in January 2003 the EU launched infringement proceedings against four Member States (Germany, France, the Netherlands and Belgium) which had signed the CSI. The Commission's concern was that these measures would have a negative effect on trade flows and that they would lead to competition between EU ports. Furthermore, any differences in treatment would run counter to EU trade and transport policies. These proceedings were later dropped after an agree-

M. Hatfield on the National Strategy for Maritime Security' (Statement before the Committee on Transportation and Infrastructure Subcommittee on Coast Guard and Maritime Transportation) (US House of Representatives, 24 January 2006), 6–7.

21 Note that US Customs became Customs and Border Protection under the new Department of Homeland Security on 1 March 2003.

22 Note however that a recent report by the US Government Accountability Office found the CSI programme to be defective notwithstanding the fact that it was operational in 58 seaports through which around 86 % of all US-bound containers passed. See Report to Congressional Requesters, 'Supply Chain Security: Examinations of High-Risk Cargo have Increased, but Improved Data Collection and Performance Measures are Needed' (January 2008) GAO-08–107.

23 The EU also plans to introduce a similar rule. However it is not expected that the July 2009 deadline for implementation will be met. See 'EU "24 hour" rule running late', *Fairplay Daily News* (4 April 2008).

ment was reached between the EU and the US in 2004, which was intended to improve security on a reciprocal basis for both the EU and the US.[24] Furthermore, in November 2004, the EU and the US adopted, via the EU–US Joint Customs Co-operation Committee, Recommendations on Strengthening the Security of Maritime Transport of Containers under the Agreement.[25]

The EU has also taken security initiatives on its own initiative. Apart from the regulation on enhancing ship and port facility security,[26] which *inter alia* transposes the provisions of Chapter XI-2 of SOLAS and the ISPS Code, the EU has also been active in the field of container security and traders are required to provide customs authorities with information on goods prior to import into or export from the EU.[27] On a more global level, the WCO adopted a resolution in June 2002[28] which enables ports in all 161 of its Member States to begin the development of programmes using CSI principles. In June 2005 it adopted the Framework of Standards to Secure and Facilitate Global Trade, which draws heavily upon US-led initiatives such as the CSI and the C–TPAT.[29] The most recent step was a 2006 resolution dealing primarily with the implementation of these standards.[30]

4.5. *Control: Surveillance and Monitoring*

The measures outlined below have increased maritime domain awareness, and thus made it possible for States to exercise jurisdiction over vessels in instances where it might not otherwise have been possible, thus highlighting the aim of detecting events prior to their occurrence and preventing them from arising altogether.

4.5.1. *Pushing Borders Further Outwards*

Examples exist which demonstrate the readiness of States to push their borders further outwards and thus enable the investigation and interception of vessels

---

24 [2004] OJ L304/34.

25 For more information see http://europa.eu/scadplus/leg/en/lvb/l06026.htm.

26 Regulation (EC) No. 725/2004 [2004] OJ L129/6.

27 For information on EU security initiatives see the EU Customs Union website: http://europa.eu.int/comm/taxation_customs/customs/information_notes/containers_en.htm.

28 Resolution of the Customs Cooperation Council on Security and Facilitation of the International Trade Supply Chain (June 2002). A second resolution was adopted in June 2004.

29 See United States, Customs and Border Protection, 'Historic Adoption of the Framework of Standards to Secure and Facilitate Global Trade' (24 June 2005) Press Release.

30 Resolution of the Customs Co-operation Council on the Framework of Standards to Secure and Facilitate Global Trade (June 2006).

several miles out to sea. In a rule which may be categorized as a law under the power given to coastal States under Art. 25(2) of LOSC, according to the US 96-hour Advance Notice-of-Arrival rule (as opposed to 24 hours' prior notice before 11 September 2001),[31] vessels over 300 gross tons proceeding to a US port must give an Advance Notice of Arrival 96 hours prior to entering the US port.[32] This must contain certain detailed information relating to the place of destination, the vessel, its owner, operator, classification society, cargo, passenger and crew lists and details of a 24-hour point of contact for each US port included in the Notice, and the location or position of the vessel when the Notice is submitted. If any of this information raises the suspicions of the Coast Guard, officers will board the vessel 12 to 20 miles offshore.[33] Exemptions to this requirement exist *inter alia* for vessels arriving at US ports under *force majeure*.[34] A similar approach was taken by Australia in its establishment of the Australian Maritime Identification System (AMIS).[35]

4.5.2. *Other Means of Control*

In recognition of the fact that ships out at sea need to be detected because they may constitute a threat to coastal States, technology has been developed for that purpose in a bid to give the coastal State time to take preventive action. During the discussions on amendments to SOLAS, much debate centred around three methods of ship detection: Automatic Identification Systems (AIS), Long-range Identification and Tracking Systems (LRIT) and Ship Security Alert Systems (SSAS). These various systems have one aim: to remove the anonymity of ships during passage so as to monitor movements of potentially dangerous vessels—whether on the high seas or closer to the coastal State's borders.

---

[31] A similar requirement was imposed by the US Immigration and Naturalization Service (INS)—now known as the US Citizenship and Immigration Service (USCIS)—where s.402 of the Enhanced Border Security and Visa Entry Reform Act 2002 (Pub. L. 107–173) requires the submission of arrival and departure manifests electronically in advance of an aircraft's or vessel's arrival in or departure from the US (68 Fed. Reg. 292, 3 January 2003). Such notification requirements have also been adopted by other States such as Canada and Colombia: MSC 75/ISWG/INF.33 (12 April 2002); SOLAS/CONF.5/15 (6 December 2002).

[32] For vessels on voyages of less than 96 hours the required information must be submitted 24 hours prior to arrival.

[33] The final rule was promulgated by the US Coast Guard on 23 February 2003, effective from 1 April 2003 (68 Fed. Reg. 9537–9547). It replaces a temporary rule in place since 4 October 2002.

[34] See Chapter 5.

[35] See Chapter 8.

4.5.2.1. *Automatic Identification System*

The AIS, operating in the VHF maritime band, was developed to deliver digital information conveying a vessel's position, identity, and other related information automatically from ship to ship and from ship to shore.[36] This system allows ships and coastal authorities to detect the position of other ships, even in situations where physical obstructions would prevent radar detections.[37] During the deliberations in the MSC the system's implementation deadline was brought forward, following a proposal by the USA, notwithstanding concerns voiced by certain delegations.[38] SOLAS Chapter V/19 mandates that AIS equipment be fitted aboard all ships of 300 gross tonnage and upwards engaged on international voyages, all cargo ships of 500 gross tonnage and upwards not engaged on international voyages, and all passenger ships[39] regardless of size not later than 1 July 2004.

One of the concerns raised regarding the use of AIS is worthy of comment as it relates to the security of information transmitted via AIS. The International Chamber of Shipping (ICS) commented that discussions on AIS matters had centred upon the use of the data in support of defensive security measures, with little being said about the implications arising out of the misuse of the data, compromising both commercial confidentiality and maritime security. AIS has the potential to place in the public domain a vast amount of data about ships, cargoes, destinations, positions, and estimated times of arrival. These data are available to any person or organization with the right equipment, positioned within 20 or 30 miles of the ship. The ship will be unaware that the data are being gathered and by whom. There is consequently little to prevent

36 See SOLAS Chapter V/19. For IMO documentation on AIS issues see Resolution MSC.74(69) (12 May 1998); SN/Circ.227 (6 January 2003); Resolution A.917(22) (25 January 2002); MSC 75/17/4 (25 March 2002); MSC 75/17/7 (9 April 2002); MSC 75/17/28 (12 April 2002); MSC 76/ISWG/7/11 (2 August 2002); MSC 79/5/10 (23 September 2004); COMSAR 7/16/1 (7 November 2002); COMSAR 9/12 (21 October 2004); COMSAR 9/12/1 (22 December 2004); COMSAR 9/INF.4 (29 October 2004); STW 34/9/4 (2 January 2003); STW 35/9 (11 November 2003).

37 See MSC 75/17/1 (25 February 2002).

38 For relevant documents regarding the accelerated implementation deadline see MSC 75/ISWG/5/7 (15 January 2002), para. 3; MSC 75/17/3 (28 March 2002); MSC 75/17/4 (25 March 2002); MSC 75/17/12 (12 April 2002); MSC 75/17/28 (12 April 2002); MSC 76/ISWG/7/11 (2 August 2002); SOLAS/CONF.5/9 (1 November 2002). See also A.917(22) Guidelines for the onboard operational use of shipborne automatic identification systems (25 January 2002); SN/Circ.227 Guidelines for the installation of a shipborne Automatic Identification System (6 January 2003).

39 A 'passenger ship' is defined in SOLAS Chapter 1 Reg. 2, as a 'ship which carries more than twelve passengers.'

their potential use by terrorists, pirates, or belligerent nations to identify a particular ship or type of ship.[40]

4.5.2.2. *Long-range Identification and Tracking System*

Another system providing for the tracking of ships is the LRIT operated via satellite and designed to enhance the security of the coastal State by providing information about vessel traffic in a timely manner so as to enable States to take appropriate action.[41] The system should enable the identification and tracking of ships at sea; provide the competent authority of the Contracting State with the identity and position of the ship; and ensure that the information is provided to the competent authority in a secure and confidential manner, with due regard to commercial sensitivity. Moreover, it should not provide information to other ships and must be capable of working with different densities of shipping.[42] In fact, one of the significant distinctions between AIS and LRIT, apart from the one of range, is that whereas AIS is a broadcast system, data derived through LRIT will be available only to the recipients

---

40 This concern did not seem to be directly addressed by the conference insofar as the ICS's recommendation was that the Master retain his discretion to switch off the AIS when, in his judgment, the security of his ship was threatened. The provision found in the final SOLAS text states that 'ships fitted with AIS shall maintain AIS in operation at all times except where international agreements, rules or standards provide for the protection of navigational information.'

41 For IMO documentation on LRIT see COMSAR 8/13 (10 November 2003); COMSAR 8/13/4 (12 December 2003); COMSAR 8/13/5 (12 December 2003); COMSAR 8/13/7 (17 December 2003); COMSAR 8/INF.5 (14 November 2003); COMSAR 9/12 (21 October 2004); COMSAR 9/12/1 (22 December 2004); COMSAR 9/12/5 (3 December 2004); COMSAR 9/12/3 (3 December 2004); COMSAR 9/12/7 (17 December 2004); COMSAR 9/12/8 (29 December 2004); COMSAR 9/INF.4 (29 October 2004); COMSAR 9/INF.6 (25 November 2004); COMSAR 9/INF.8 (3 December 2004); COMSAR 9/INF.12 (17 December 2004); COMSAR 10/10 (2 December 2005); COMSAR 10/10/1 (5 December 2005); COMSAR 10/10/2 (21 December 2005); COMSAR 10/10/3 (10 January 2006); COMSAR 10/INF.7 (12 December 2005); MSC/ISWG/LRIT 1/3 (15 September 2005); MSC 75/ISWG/INF.6 (15 January 2002); MSC 75/INF.31 (12 April 2002); MSC 76/4/21 (1 November 2002); MSC 76/ISWG/7/1 (31 July 2002); MSC 76/ISWG/7/10 (2 August 2002); MSC 77/6/5 (24 February 2003); MSC 77/6/11 (25 March 2003); MSC 77/6/16 (8 April 2003); MSC 78/7/8 (19 March 2004); MSC 79/5/4 (20 September 2004); MSC 79/5/12 (24 September 2004); MSC 80/5/5 (2 March 2005); MSC 80/5/8 (4 March 2005); MSC 80/5/9 (18 March 2005); MSC Res 210(81) (19 May 2006); MSC Res 211(81) (19 May 2006); NAV 49/12 (24 February 2003); NAV 49/12/1 (24 March 2003); MSC.1/Circ.1256 (5 June 2008); MSC.1/Circ.1257 (5 June 2008); MSC.1/Circ.1258 (5 June 2008). See also M. Tsamenyi et al., 'Legal Considerations in the Implementation of Long-range Identification and Tracking Systems for Vessels' (2007) 13 *J. Int Marit Law* 42–55.

42 MSC 77/6/16 (8 April 2002). Note that concerns similar to those voiced with respect to the AIS were expressed by ICS et al. in this regard: MSC 76/ISWG/7/10 (2 August 2002); MSC 76/4/21 (1 November 2002).

who are entitled to receive such information and safeguards concerning the confidentiality of data have been built into the regulatory provisions. SOLAS Contracting States will be entitled to receive information about ships navigating within not more than 1,000 nm off their coasts.[43]

LRIT is therefore intended to enhance security for Contracting Governments, without unduly impacting on the security of ships. Apart from it being an integral part of any maritime security regime, an active and accurate LRIT system also has potential safety benefits, mostly for maritime search and rescue. Accurate information on the location of the ship in distress as well as ships in the vicinity which could lend assistance will save valuable response time to effect a timely rescue.[44]

At the SOLAS conference, Resolution No. 10 called for 'Early Implementation of Long-Range Ship's Identification and Tracking'. SOLAS Regulation V/19-1 introduces the LRIT as a mandatory requirement on the following ships engaged on international voyages: passenger ships, including high-speed craft; cargo ships of 300 gross tonnage and upwards, and mobile offshore drilling units. This regulation entered into force on 1 January 2008 and applies to all ships constructed on or after 31 December 2008, with a phased-in implementation for vessels constructed before that date.[45] Ship-based LRIT equipment must be capable of being configured to transmit information on the identity of the ship, its position and the date and time of that position every six hours.

4.5.2.3. *Ship Security Alert System*

Another security measure, different however in purpose from the AIS and LRIT, is the SSAS. This was conceived of because a vessel in the process of being hijacked had no simple and unobservable means of activating an alarm to notify authorities and other ships. The USA submitted that Global Maritime Distress and Safety System (GMDSS) equipment had a 'piracy/armed robbery attack' type of distress capability, but selecting this alert took time and could

---

43 During the SOLAS deliberations, the US recommended that the State should be entitled to track a vessel when it was within 2,000 nm from its coast since the US believed that these distances were necessary to provide enough time for a Contracting Government to detect, identify, and classify the security risk posed by a ship, and respond, if needed, in order to intercept and interdict the ship away from the State's waters and preserve its security. See MSC 77/6/16 (8 April 2003); COMSAR 8/13 (10 November 2003).

44 COMSAR 8/13 (10 November 2003), para. 3. See also Circular Letter No. 2507 (10 November 2003).

45 See COMSAR 8/13 (10 November 2003), paras 6, 7, 11. For a general overview of the concept of LRIT see Mitropoulos (n 13).

not be done surreptitiously since activation would sound an alarm. Apart from text messaging, AIS equipment does not provide this function either, although the AIS 'type of ship' report does include reserved characters which could conceivably be used for this purpose.[46]

Through the SSAS it is possible to send a covert signal or message from a ship which will not be obvious to anyone on the ship who is not aware of the alert mechanism.[47] It is of use therefore in circumstances where a ship wishes to inform a person ashore of a problem with a minimum number of those onboard becoming aware of the action.[48]

Apart from MSC Circular 1072 which provides guidance on the design of SSAS, SOLAS Chapter XI-2/6 lays down the SSAS requirements facilitating fast and efficient reactive measures in the case of a security threat or breach. On activation and until it is reactivated or reset, the SSAS is to initiate and transmit a ship-to-shore alert to a competent authority designated by the administration, which identifies the ship and its location and indicates that the ship's security is under threat or has been compromised.[49] The covert nature of the alert is emphasized by means of references in the regulation that no form of alert is to be sent to any other ships, nor is there to be any indication on board the ship that the alert has been activated.[50]

In June 2003, the MSC approved a revised Circular 967[51] with regard to the reception of a ship security alert. This includes provisions for the handling by Maritime Rescue Coordination Centres (MRCCs) of alerts received from ships in response to acts of violence, including terrorist acts and other security

[46] MSC 75/ISWG/5/7 (15 January 2002), para. 22.

[47] See SOLAS Chapter XI-2/6. For IMO documentation on the SSAS see IMO Documents: MSC.1/Circ.1190 (30 May 2006); MSC/Circ. 1072 (26 June 2003); MSC/Circ.1109 (7 June 2004); MSC/Circ.1109/Rev.1 (14 December 2004); MSC/Circ.1155 (23 May 2005); COMSAR 8/13/1 (27 November 2003); COMSAR 8/13/2 (4 December 2003); COMSAR 8/13/3 (12 December 2003); COMSAR 8/13/6 (12 December 2003); COMSAR 9/12 (21 October 2004); COMSAR 9/12/1 (22 December 2004); COMSAR 9/12/4 (3 December 2004); COMSAR 9/12/6 (3 December 2004); COMSAR 9/INF.11 (3 December 2004); MSC 76/4/2 (28 October 2002); MSC 76/ISWG/7/16 (2 August 2002); MSC 79/5/6 (22 September 2004); MSC 81/5/11 (27 February 2006); MSC Res 136(76) (11 December 2002); MSC Res 147(77) (29 May 2003).

[48] MSC/Circ.1072 Guidance on Provision of Ship Security Alert Systems (26 June 2003).

[49] Chapter XI-2/6.2. Very significantly, there is to be no attempt by an MRCC to communicate with the vessel, contrary to the case in a distress alert, where the MRCC immediately attempts to make contact with the ship. See MSC/Circ.1073 Directives for MRCCs on Acts of Violence against Ships (10 June 2003).

[50] Note however certain concerns with regard to the effectiveness of this device. See 'Are Security Alert Systems any use?', *Fairplay Daily News* (28 March 2008).

[51] MSC/Circ.1073 (10 June 2003).

incidents. It follows a proposal from the French delegation to the effect that MSC/Circ.967[52] should now be capable of integration within maritime security measures generally.[53]

The requirements provide that all vessels are to carry an onboard SSAS which should be able to be operated from two positions.[54] The system is also to be designed so as to protect against inadvertent operation.[55] Although it was primarily designed with ship security in mind, the protection of the coastal State is thereby safeguarded. SOLAS Chapter XI-2/6.6 provides that when an administration receives notification of a ship security alert, it is immediately to notify the State(s) in the vicinity of which the ship is operating. Furthermore, the next sub-section states that when a Contracting Government receives notification of a ship security alert from a ship which is not entitled to fly its flag, that Contracting Government shall immediately notify the relevant administration and, if appropriate, the State(s) in the vicinity of which the ship is currently operating. It is understood that arrangements for assistance and enforcement jurisdiction will therefore be made.

4.5.3. *Conclusion*

These technological measures increase awareness of the maritime domain. In the context of the SSAS, it is supposed that assistance is given in circumstances where coastal authorities would not otherwise have been aware of an attack on a particular vessel. The AIS and LRIT equipment has the benefit of eliminating the anonymity of ships whilst *en route* by identifying their location, monitoring their movements, and picking up any suspicious occurrences such as 'power down' or 'antennae disconnect' situations.[56]

Unlike the AIS, both the LRIT and SSAS are operated via satellite. Satellite communications technology has the capability to enhance both ship and port security and reduce the potential for shipping to become a target for international terrorism as the identification of non-compliant or suspicious vessels is made more readily recognizable, allowing early action to avert threats to coastal

[52] MSC/Circ.967 Piracy and Armed Robbery Against Ships. Directives for MRCCs (6 June 2000).

[53] MSC 77/6/6 (3 March 2003).

[54] Chapter XI-2/6.3. MSC 77 adopted a revised MSC Res 147(77) on Performance Standards for a Ship Security Alert System (29 May 2003), to update Res MSC.136(76) on Performance Standards for a Ship Security Alert System (11 December 2002).

[55] Chapter XI-2/6.4.

[56] At a more basic level, requirements to have some form of radio equipment (depending on the type of vessel) on board vessels makes possible the exercise of hot pursuit via radio contact.

State security.[57] It has an advantage over AIS devices in that the latter form of communication is freely available via VHF, which is not the case for satellite communications.

Furthermore, this technology may be equally useful in other areas, such as the monitoring of fishing vessels and maritime traffic control. As far as LRIT is concerned, the MSC has recently adopted a resolution on the Use of the Long-Range Identification and Tracking Information for Maritime Safety and Marine Environmental Protection Purposes,[58] where it was agreed that Contracting States may request, receive and use LRIT information for these purposes. The fact that there are a number of uses for these types of systems increases the reasonableness of the IMO mandates that all ships must carry the equipment.

The indication of a readiness on the part of States to pre-empt and prevent threats to ships and ports signals a welcome development in the evolution of international law—a development which is also apparent in treaty regimes such as the 1988 Convention for the Suppression of Unlawful Acts against the Safety of Maritime Navigation (SUA Convention), recently amended to permit preventive action in a bid effectively to fight threats to maritime security.[59] This approach is especially relevant in the case of maritime migrant smuggling: repressive action must be taken further out at sea before the vessel approaches a State's shores, as at this point, at the very latest, the coastal State becomes bound by a number of obligations of protection towards any potential asylum-seekers on board the migrant-smuggling vessel.

[57] See also MSC 75/ISWG/5/2, Annex (15 January 2002); MSC 75/ISWG/INF.4 (14 January 2002).

[58] Res MSC.242(83) (12 October 2007).

[59] See further Chapter 7.

Part II

Tools and Constraints

Chapter Five

Zonal Jurisdiction

There are various maritime zones which a vessel carrying irregular migrants will cross on its way to its destination. State action against such practice is dependent upon the location of the vessel at any particular time. This chapter presents analyses of the existing regime relating to the powers of States under the international law of the sea. It is the first branch of two chapters which attempt to outline the existing rights and obligations of States under international law. The law of the sea regime may be presented as providing the 'opportunities' open to States in the fight against maritime migrant smuggling, as opposed to the regime discussed in the following chapter, dealing with humanitarian principles of protection, which are portrayed as 'constraints' or limitations on State action.

5.1. *Internal Waters*

Internal waters are assimilated to land territory and reflect the full sovereignty which the coastal State enjoys therein.[1] The internal waters therefore, constitute the maritime zone in which the coastal State is best placed to exercise both prescriptive and enforcement jurisdiction, based on the territoriality principle, especially in view of the fact that this zone is the place where activity detrimental to the State actually touches the land. Although waters such as bays and estuaries constitute internal waters,[2] the focus of a discussion related to security understandably falls upon ports and harbours. These centres of economic activity witness the importation and transit of vast amounts of goods and numbers of people. Any form of security breach within these hubs of commerce would have devastating repercussions on both the immediate port environment and the general flow of international trade.

1 This was codified in Art. 1 TSC and Art. 2(1) LOSC and was also stated to be a reflection of customary international law in *Military and Paramilitary Activities in and against Nicaragua (Nicaragua v USA)* [1986] ICJ Rep 14.

2 LOSC Art. 8 and TSC Art. 5.

The LOSC contains only a few provisions on internal waters,[3] with other regulatory provisions left to be provided for in conventions such as the 1923 Convention on the Regime of Maritime Ports and, more recently, in IMO instruments such as the International Convention for the Prevention of Pollution from Ships (MARPOL), the International Convention for the Facilitation of Maritime Traffic (FAL) and the SOLAS Convention. The briefest of mentions in the LOSC could be due to the fact that, being considered as part of the land territory, internal waters need not necessarily form part of a Constitution regulating the ocean space. This was the approach adopted by the IMO until recently: prior to 2001, few instruments directly addressed the issue of security measures on ships and in ports.[4] The post-September 2001 environment however led the IMO Assembly to call for a revision of IMO measures to combat acts of violence at sea, as was noted in the previous chapter.

There is a general presumption in favour of entry by merchant vessels to ports used for international trade. This, however, is a mere presumption which is not based on a legal obligation (absent a right of access due to treaty obligation)[5] but is founded on a practice based upon convenience and interest in the smooth flow of international trade. It is also subject to the State's decision to close its ports for any reason—as long as that stance is taken on a non-discriminatory basis.[6] On this reasoning, any threat to the security of a port could lead to a legitimate closure of all the ports of the relevant State; even when ports are open to international trade or where such right of access is granted by treaty, a State retains its right to deny entry where its vital interests are threatened.[7]

The only exception to this, where a clear right of entry exists in customary international law, is in the case of distress, where a ship needs to enter internal

3 LOSC Art. 2(1) and 8–12; TSC Art. 1(1), 5 and 7–9.

4 These are Res A.584(14) Measures to Prevent Unlawful Acts which Threaten the Safety of Ships and the Security of their Passengers and Crews (20 November 1985); MSC/Circ.443 Measures to Prevent Unlawful Acts Against Passengers and Crew on Board Ships (26 September 1986); the 1988 SUA Convention and Protocol; MSC/Circ.754 Passenger Ferry Security (5 July 1996). For a useful summary of these documents see MSC 75/17/Add.1 (17 December 2001).

5 The 1923 Maritime Ports Convention establishes a reciprocal right of access to, and equality of treatment in, ports (Art. 2) however, this Convention has few ratifications and cannot be taken as evidence of a wider right under customary international law. See R. Barnes, 'Refugee Law at Sea' (2004) 53 *ICLQ* 57.

6 For more see A.V. Lowe, 'The Right of Entry into Maritime Ports in International Law' (1977) 14 *San Diego Law Review* 621; L. De La Fayette, 'Access to Ports in International Law' (1996) 11 *IJMLC* 1–22; G. Kasoulides, *Port State Convention and Jurisdiction—Evolution of the Port State Control Regime* (Martinus Nijhoff, Dordrecht, 1993), Chapter 1.

7 See, e.g., Art. 16 of the Maritime Ports Convention and Art. 5(2) of the FAL Convention.

waters to shelter in order to preserve human life.[8] In this regard, the discussion of the International Law Commission (ILC) on State responsibility and the decision of the tribunal in the *Rainbow Warrior* arbitration throw some light on the meaning of 'distress'.[9] The ILC maintains that a situation of distress 'may at most include a situation of serious danger, but not necessarily one that jeopardizes the very existence of the person concerned.'[10] Relying on the statements of the ILC, the tribunal in the *Rainbow Warrior* arbitration held that distress involved 'the existence of very exceptional circumstances of extreme urgency involving medical or other considerations of an elementary nature.'[11]

The foundations for the exercise of jurisdiction, should the State deem it necessary to act, are clear and easily discernible from the general LOSC framework. However, in deference to the vessel's temporary presence in the port, and even more so, owing to the concurrent jurisdiction of the flag State, the port State will not usually take any action, according to the doctrine of the 'internal economy of the vessel.'[12] Therefore, other than in response to a request to do so, local jurisdiction will not be exercised unless the tranquillity of the port is disturbed or the peace and dignity of the coastal State are involved, in either a literal or a constructive sense. According to the former approach, jurisdiction will be exercised only when the offence relates to and has some effect upon the port itself, such as in the case of a customs offence or harm done to the environment. Taking a constructive—and, therefore, wider—approach, jurisdiction will also be exercised even if there is no direct effect on the port itself, as in the case of a homicide on board a ship in harbour which, by a constructive analogy, is taken to affect the peace and good order of the port.

8 See *The Creole* (1853) Moore, International Arbitration 824 and *The Rebecca* (the Kate E. Hoff case) (1929) VI RIAA 444. It is unclear whether this right of access exists in order to save a ship's cargo when human life is not in danger. See however *The New York* (1818) 16 US 59, 3 Wheat. 59; 4 L. Ed. 333 as a case dealing with the case of loss of cargo, where the vessel entered a port due to stress of weather.

9 Barnes (n 5) 60.

10 [1973] *ILC Yearbook*, Vol II, 135, para. 10.

11 *Rainbow Warrior (New Zealand v France)*, Arbitration (1990) 82 ILR 499.

12 Two schools of thought exist in this regard, both leading to the same result: the Anglo-American approach (summarized in the British statement to the preparatory committee for the 1930 Hague Codification Conference, cited in R. Jennings and A. Watts (eds), *Oppenheim's International Law* vol. I, *Peace* (9th edn, Harlow, Longman, 1996), 623 and in US cases such as *Cunard Steamship Co Ltd v Mellon* 262 U.S. 100 (1923)), bases itself on the premise that coastal State jurisdiction over foreign vessels is complete. However, the State may waive the exercise of its jurisdiction out of considerations of public policy. The French approach, on the other hand, follows the system of '*partial desinteressement*' according to which no jurisdiction can be exercised over purely internal affairs on board foreign ships in port. The French approach derives from the *Avis* of the *Conseil d'Etat* in *The Newton and the Sally* in 1806 (1806 *Bulletin des Lois* No. 126, 602) on which subsequent French practice was based.

Other instances where coastal States will exercise jurisdiction include cases where their intervention is requested by the Captain or Master of the ship, or the consul of the flag State. Pollution, pilotage and navigation laws are other examples of laws enforced against vessels in port; and ships may be arrested in the course of civil proceedings in the coastal State.[13]

The spectre of irregular immigrants constitutes a problematic reality for many southern European States. Quite apart from any threat of terrorist infiltration, regular influxes of irregular immigrants constitute a threat to the security and stability of the coastal State. At the same time however, there is also the danger of human rights violations occasioned by measures which may be employed by States to protect their interests and security by limiting boat arrivals. This concern was voiced by the United Nations High Commissioner for Refugees (UNHCR) in 'Ten Refugee Concerns in the Aftermath of September 11'.[14] This document highlights both the increasing public perception of refugees and asylum-seekers as criminals and the tendency to create unwarranted links between refugees and terrorism. While it reports that the implementation of additional, security-based procedural safeguards is reasonable, it must, however, be ensured that any such safeguards strike a proper balance with any refugee protection principles which may be at stake. The main concerns of the UNHCR are that *bona fide* asylum-seekers may be victimized as a result of public prejudice and unduly restrictive legislation or administrative measures and that carefully constructed refugee protection standards may be eroded.

The balance is a difficult one to strike: how is a coastal State to distinguish the *bona fide* asylum-seeker from the potential terrorist? Apart from this, there are also substantial obligations which the coastal State must respect once the immigrants reach land. Foremost among these is the principle of *non-refoulement*. Insofar as the prevention of migrant smuggling is concerned, there is little, if anything, that a port State can do, due to humanitarian obligations incumbent upon it. This will be discussed later. Control must therefore be exercised further away from the State's shores to the extent that the coastal State has jurisdiction to act.

It is hoped that a short look at the current port facility security regime would have made the point that ports are not to be seen in isolation: they are part of a complex network in the international transport system. In this

13 However, a similar course of reasoning does not apply in cases where ships are driven into internal waters by *force majeure* or distress. See *The Enterprise*, (1853) II Moore's *Digest*, 350–351.

14 23 October 2001, annexed to document MSC 75/ISWG/INF.3 (15 January 2002).

way, control should be exercisable by the coastal State throughout the passage and not just at the coastal State's frontiers.[15] While unilateral initiatives are understandable, it is important that they fall within the parameters of what is being created on the global scale as, otherwise, the competitive edge of such ports would be minimized and the security risk would merely be transferred to other ports.

5.2. *Territorial Sea*

5.2.1. *The Traditional Framework established in the LOSC*

The territorial sea, as an extension of the coastal State's territory, is subject to the sovereignty of the coastal State, which is thus entitled to exercise territorial jurisdiction over this belt of sea adjacent to its coasts.[16] Notwithstanding this, the quality of sovereignty differs from that examined with respect to the internal waters. A predominant difference between the two regimes is the doctrine of innocent passage: a long-standing doctrine which developed alongside the doctrine of coastal State sovereignty over the territorial sea.[17]

The issue to be determined at this point is how far innocent passage can be considered to impede the capacity of the coastal State in the protection of its security interests, notably, insofar as maritime migrant smuggling is concerned. The LOSC states that innocent passage is a right of an exceptional nature and one based on navigational expediency.[18] As far as the requirement of innocence is concerned, Art. 19(1) LOSC (Art. 14(4) TSC) stipulates that 'passage is innocent so long as it is not prejudicial to the peace, good order or security of the coastal State.' The provision then goes on, in Art. 19(2), to provide a list of activities purporting to define instances of a breach of the coastal State's peace, good order or security. The inclusion of a list of activities indicates that the LOSC permits a wider definition of 'security' than is ordinarily inferred: apart from military security, the LOSC includes examples of threats which might

[15] See S.E. Flynn, 'Bolstering the Maritime Weak Link', Hearing on 'Weak Links: Assessing the Vulnerability of U.S. Ports and Whether the Government is adequately structured to safeguard them' presented before the US Senate Committee on Governmental Affairs US Senate (6 December 2001).

[16] This sovereignty over the belt of sea to a limit of 12 nm measured from the coastal State's baselines also extends to the air space over the territorial sea: LOSC Art. 2(1)(2), 3.

[17] LOSC Art. 17; TSC Art. 14(1).

[18] LOSC Art. 18; TSC Art. 14.

be deemed harmful to the security of the sovereignty of the coastal State.[19] Furthermore, it is arguable that this list is not exhaustive.[20]

In a case of non-innocent passage, the conventional regime on the law of the sea provides for an amount of coastal State protection: the State is empowered to 'take the necessary steps to prevent passage which is not innocent' (Art. 25(1) LOSC) and may also temporarily suspend innocent passage in certain areas of its territorial sea if such suspension is essential for the protection of its security (Art. 25(3) LOSC).[21] However, it is doubtful whether merely preventing non-innocent passage, for instance in the case of a vessel carrying migrants (to the extent that this is permitted), would be an effective tool in the wider scheme of coastal State security protection.

A coastal State would have more interest in actually enforcing its laws against that vessel rather than merely having the capacity to prevent the passage of a non-innocent vessel in a wide variety of instances. The two are not synonymous: a breach of innocent passage need not signify a violation of the coastal State's laws, nor need a breach of the coastal State's laws amount to a violation of Art. 19 relating to innocent passage. Maritime migrant smuggling, however, falls under both heads: it is a breach of the innocence requirement and also a breach of coastal State law, and thus allows for jurisdiction to be exercised against the perpetrators.

With regard to prescriptive jurisdiction, Art. 21 LOSC seems to have preserved the wide basis for exercising jurisdiction that existed under Art. 17 TSC, and the list of laws and regulations in Art. 21(1) relating to innocent passage may be read as being merely examples of the laws which the coastal State is entitled to enact. Passing on to how a coastal State can respond to breaches of its laws, a measured effective response is through the invocation of Art. 25(2) LOSC (Art. 16(2) TSC), which provides that should the vessel be proceeding to the coastal State's port then the coastal State has the right to take the necessary steps to prevent its entry on the basis that it is entitled to 'prevent any breach of the conditions to which admission of those ships to internal waters ... may be subject.' This indicates the possibility of exercising enforcement jurisdiction over the vessel; a right which is provided for in Art. 27 LOSC.

---

19 S. Kaye, 'Freedom of Security in a Post 9/11 World: Security and Creeping Jurisdiction' in D. Freestone, R. Barnes and D. Ong (eds), *The Law of the Sea: Progress and Prospects* (OUP, Oxford, 2006), 349.

20 See Art. 19(2)(l). In contrast, note however the 1989 Uniform Interpretation of Norms of International Law Governing Innocent Passage annexed to the US–Soviet 1989 Joint Statement.

21 While the LOSC does not expressly state that vessels may be excluded from the territorial sea, this right should be understood to exist in customary law. See R.R. Churchill and A.V. Lowe, *The Law of the Sea* (3rd edn, Manchester University Press, Manchester, 1999), 87.

In the case of enforcement jurisdiction, Art. 27(1) deals with criminal jurisdiction and provides that the coastal State should not exercise its jurisdiction on board a foreign vessel passing through its territorial sea to arrest any person or conduct an investigation in connection with a crime committed during its passage except in four circumstances: if the consequences of the crime extend to the coastal State; if the crime is of a kind to disturb the peace of the country or the good order of the territorial sea; if the assistance of the local authorities has been requested by the Master of the ship or by a diplomatic agent or consular officer of the flag State; or if such measures are necessary for the suppression of illicit traffic in narcotic drugs or psychotropic substances. This limitation upon the exercise of jurisdiction is, however, not mandatory: States are *expected* but not obliged to desist from enforcing their laws in respect of crimes committed on passing ships in cases other than the exceptions just outlined.[22]

At any rate, even if this limitation was mandatory, the coastal State would nevertheless be empowered to exercise criminal jurisdiction prior to the vessel entering internal waters in the case of migrant smuggling, since the consequences of the crime extend to the coastal State and the crime itself is of a kind to disturb the peace of the country. Furthermore, should such vessel be merely crossing through the territorial sea of a coastal State, in an EU context it may be considered an *obligation* for that coastal State to intervene if a vessel making use of the right of innocent passage in its territorial waters has the intention to disembark migrants in another Member State.[23]

Art. 27(2) LOSC then continues by stating that the limitation in Art. 27(1) is not operative when the foreign ship is passing through the territorial sea after having left the coastal State's internal waters. Therefore, in the event that jurisdiction was not exercised while the vessel was proceeding into internal waters, coastal State authorities may arrest the vessel after it has left internal waters and is sailing through the territorial sea. Enforcement jurisdiction in respect of the unloading of illegal immigrants may lawfully be exercised in the territorial sea. Furthermore, should the vessel, after having unloaded migrants and left a State's internal waters, attempt to flee to the contiguous zone, the coastal State may pursue and arrest it within that zone in virtue of its powers to punish offences in its territory or territorial sea.[24] Even an attempt to evade jurisdiction by sailing out to the EEZ or high seas would allow apprehension in furtherance of Art. 111 and the doctrine of hot pursuit.

---

22 In this way, what was mandatory under the Hague regime became a matter of comity under the 1958 and 1982 Conventions.

23 See Commission (EC), 'Study on the International Law Instruments in Relation to Illegal Immigration by Sea' (Staff Working Document) SEC (2007) 691, 15 May 2007, 691, para. 2.1.3, discussed below.

24 LOSC Art. 33.

It should however be noted that the current discussion relates only to a State's powers under the LOSC. The broader picture shows that a coastal State has concurrent obligations incumbent upon it, notably the obligation of *non refoulement* which applies, at the latest, once the vessel has reached the territory of the coastal State. Since the territorial sea is considered part of a State's territory,[25] this obligation can be understood to arise irrespective of whether or not the coastal State intercepts the vessel. Therefore, while criminal jurisdiction may be exercised against the perpetrators of the offence, humanitarian obligations equally apply. Thus, 'people flows' invoke the ever-struggling dichotomy between human rights protection and the protection of national security.[26]

Only one express limitation on the exercise of enforcement jurisdiction is provided for: the coastal State may not take any steps on board a foreign ship passing through the territorial sea without entering the internal waters in connection with a crime which was committed before the ship entered the territorial sea.[27] This provision constitutes an unwelcome limitation in the context of maritime security. It is also unclear and apparently contradictory. It is unclear due to the fact that no time limit is placed on this prohibition. It is contradictory owing to the fact that the LOSC apparently appears to prohibit the coastal State from taking any action against a vessel which has sailed into its territorial sea after having unloaded a boatful of individuals in the State's contiguous zone.[28] It therefore seems to be in direct conflict with the very purpose of the contiguous zone, which permits a coastal State to take action to prevent and punish immigration offences in its territorial areas. Although it is highly improbable that the vessel will proceed into the territorial sea after committing such offence, it does not make sense that a coastal State is prohibited from taking action when it is arguable that a vessel carrying migrants in the contiguous zone can be intercepted under Art. 33 when it is reasonable to suspect that it intends to proceed to the territorial sea in breach of the coastal State's immigration law. It is also possible, it seems, to apprehend a vessel which has unloaded migrants onto a smaller vessel in the contiguous zone and which then proceeds outwards away from the State's territorial sea, on the basis that this was part of the wider offence of illegally entering a State's territory. There seems to be no reason why jurisdiction can be exercised when the vessel

---

25 See LOSC Art. 2.

26 A reconciliation of these opposing positions is attempted in the Smuggling Protocol. See Chapter 7.

27 Art. 27(5) LOSC and Art. 19(5) TSC.

28 Likewise, it is powerless to act against a vessel the crew of which has earlier blown up an offshore facility in the EEZ of the coastal State, and this on the mere ground that the vessel is not approaching the ports of the coastal State.

proceeds outwards away from the contiguous zone but cannot be exercised when it subsequently enters the territorial sea. This provision does not sit well with the current security climate: today, attacks against a State's security can occur many miles out at sea and it is essential that action can be taken against such attacks if prevention has not proved possible.

5.2.2. *Focus on Maritime Migrant Smuggling*

It has been seen that Art. 25(1) LOSC gives the State the right to take necessary steps in its territorial sea to prevent non-innocent passage. Since a foreign ship the passage of which is not innocent may be excluded from the territorial sea by the coastal State, a vessel carrying inadmissible passengers seeking to effect unauthorized entry may thus be expelled from the territorial sea. Under Art. 27(1)(a)(b) LOSC, illegal immigration is also a matter over which the coastal State is allowed to exercise criminal jurisdiction in respect of occurrences on board a ship. Furthermore, under Art. 21 LOSC, a State is permitted to adopt laws and regulations relating to innocent passage in its territorial sea in order to prevent *inter alia* violations of its immigration laws; and, in the case of ships proceeding to internal waters, the coastal State also has the right to take the necessary steps to prevent any breach of the conditions to which admission of those ships to internal waters is subject.[29] In this way, as far as entry into port is concerned, the potential infringement of immigration laws upon landing at the coastal State's territory can justify any action taken by the State in repelling such boat arrival.

Therefore, it appears from a reading of these provisions alone that boat people do not have a right to enter the territorial sea of a State and, if they do so, they may be expelled therefrom; neither do they have the right of entry into port. However, there are two added considerations which arise from the fact that there may be asylum-seekers on board the vessel or that the vessel is in distress. As regards the presence of asylum-seekers on board, Goodwin-Gill argues that the fact that a vessel carries asylum-seekers who intend to request the protection of the coastal State removes that vessel from the category of innocent passage. Even if the refugee nature of those on board was considered compatible with innocent passage, this alone would not entail a right of entry into any port although other rules of international law may affect or control the decision as to what is to be done with respect to any particular vessel.[30]

---

29 LOSC Art. 25(2).

30 G. Goodwin-Gill and J. McAdam, *The Refugee in International Law* (3rd edn, Oxford, OUP, 2007), 274–275.

In particular, it is quite certain that non-admission to internal waters would amount to rejection at the frontier should any migrant on board request refugee status, that is, if any asylum-seeker is on board the vessel. On the same reasoning, the same result ensues in the case of non-admission to the territorial sea, on the basis that the territory of a State is usually defined as including *inter alia* such sea.

Rescue at sea may be discussed by taking the *Tampa* as an example.[31] The vessel was in innocent passage before it was requested to rescue persons in peril at sea. However, when it arrived off Christmas Island it was arguably a vessel in distress and was not claiming innocent passage. Thus, those rescued had a right to temporary assistance to alleviate the danger and distress to which they had been subjected at sea. This would entail an undisputed right to enter port; but was the vessel actually in distress?

At this stage, it should be highlighted that the general understanding is that unseaworthiness alone does not mean the same thing, nor bring with it the same rights, as distress, and that it is only where such unseaworthiness gives rise to a threat to human life that the vessel may claim a right of refuge.[32] The condition of distress seems therefore to necessitate an immediate threat and not a more remote or conditional threat, such as persecution if the individual on board is returned to a particular country. In the case of the *Tampa* it was claimed by both the Government of Norway (the flag State of the rescuing vessel) and the owner of the *Tampa* that the vessel had rendered itself unseaworthy by discharging its duty to rescue and taking on the asylum-seekers, as she thereby became subject to the additional obligations of Chapter III of SOLAS and did not have adequate safety equipment to deal with them.[33] Furthermore, a strong argument can be made that it was a case of distress due to the fact that the sanitary conditions on board were deteriorating rapidly. According to this view, Australia had a duty to allow the vessel into port, regardless of whether or not asylum-seekers were on board. It should however be pointed out that the issue is still not settled. It has been noted that where there are a number of options available to those in distress it does not follow that they may demand entry into port and they may be required to take other action. Further, if the reason for seeking entry into port was to disembark asylum-seekers in accordance with their demands (a number of passengers were ill and some were acting in a hostile manner, threatening to jump ship should the vessel be returned to Indonesia), this seems more like duress and a coastal State can reasonably

31 Further discussed in Chapter 8.

32 Barnes (n 5) 60.

33 Circular Letter No. 2337, The MV Tampa Incident, Communication by the Government of Norway (31 August 2001).

refuse entry. Furthermore, any decision to admit vessels in distress is made by the coastal State, and in cases like the *Tampa* it has been argued that coastal States have clear policy reasons for refusing entry.[34]

The right of entry into port owing to a state of distress stems from a humanitarian obligation and is relevant in considering the State's powers to act in the face of incoming vessels laden with irregular migrants. It should also be noted that no qualification has been given to the term 'distress', making it arguable that self-induced distress also obliges the coastal State to permit entry into port. The IMO Guidelines on the Treatment of Persons Rescued at Sea explain that although the LOSC does not specifically address the issue of whether there is a right to enter ports in the case of distress:

> [U]nder customary international law, there may be a universal, albeit not absolute, right for a ship in distress to enter a port or harbour when there exists a clear threat to safety of persons aboard the ship … Nevertheless, the right of the ship in distress to enter a port involves a balancing of the nature and immediacy of the threat to the ship's safety against the risks to the port that such entry may pose. Thus, a coastal State might refuse access to its ports where the ship poses a serious and unacceptable safety, environmental, health or security threat to that coastal State after the safety of persons onboard is assured.[35]

In this case the State may be obliged to permit the ship to shelter in its territorial sea if not in its ports. Still, it should be noted that these Guidelines are not binding; they are intended, rather, to provide general guidance to Contracting Governments and to shipmasters with regard to humanitarian obligations and obligations under the relevant international law relating to the treatment of those rescued at sea.[36]

Owing to the fact that a vessel carrying irregular migrants may also be carrying a terrorist who intends to enter a State under that guise it is also useful to consider the case in which a vessel is traversing the territorial sea and known to be carrying a terrorist. It could be argued that the manner of this vessel's passage breaches the innocence requirement whether the vessel is merely traversing the territorial sea or proceeding to internal waters. In the event that a vessel is known to be on a terrorist mission or involved in terrorist activities against the coastal State, 'there is no doubt that the coastal State has the right to board, search, seize and arrest the ship, crew and passengers' as her passage would breach the innocence requirement as clearly prejudicial to the

---

34 Barnes (n 5) 60–61.

35 MSC.167(78) Guidelines on the Treatment of Persons Rescued at Sea (in MSC 78/26/Add.2) (20 May 2004) Some Comments on Relevant International Law—Appendix, para. 6.

36 *Ibid.*, para. 1.1. See further Chapters 6 and 7.

security of the coastal State.[37] The only doubt arises where it is unclear whether the vessel is actually engaged in these activities; in such an eventuality, it has been recommended that reasonableness and proportionality be exercised in verifying whether this suspicion is well-founded. Therefore, stop-and-search exercises may be justified in the case of reasonable grounds for suspicion that a vessel may be on a terrorist mission against the coastal State.[38] If after such exercises no evidence emerges to substantiate this suspicion, the coastal State authorities may not exercise any enforcement action against the vessel; in such case, they should warn other States in the vicinity of the vessel's circumstances.

5.2.3. *The European Dimension*

The EU Commission's 2007 Staff Working Document, 'Study on the International Law Instruments in Relation to Illegal Immigration by Sea' sets out to provide a valuable exposition of State powers within each maritime zone.[39] There follow the findings on the basic framework existing in the territorial sea of Member States:

> A ship which has the intention to disembark passengers in contravention of the coastal state's immigration laws cannot benefit from [the right of innocent passage]. The coastal state has the right to escort such a ship to the high seas or proceed with arrests.
>
> In the same situation and in a Community context it could be regarded as an obligation for Member State X to intervene if a ship making use of the right of innocent passage in its territorial waters has the intention to disembark illegal immigrants in Member State Y. Such an obligation, while not explicitly established, should be considered as flowing from the Community's policies on the crossing of external borders and the establishment of an area without internal frontiers.
>
> Patrols can only intervene in a third country's territorial sea in the context of search and rescue. However, with the permission of the coastal state, other country's patrols may carry out surveillance and interception in the territorial sea of the former, including, in specific cases, with regard to ships flying a third country's flag.[40]

The EU therefore seems to acknowledge further powers of the Member States in the Community context. Interestingly, it is also admitted that, on the lines of

---

37 J.L. Jesus, 'Protection of Foreign Ships against Piracy and Terrorism at Sea: Legal Aspects' (2003) 18 *ILMLC* 363 *et seq*, 397.

38 *Ibid.*, 398.

39 In effect, it is the analysis relating to State powers within the territorial sea which is particularly interesting; the section on 'waters beyond the territorial sea' merely reproduces existing law.

40 Commission Staff Working Document (n 23), paras 2.1.2–2.1.4.

cooperation in fighting a common threat, power to use enforcement jurisdiction within the territorial seas may be delegated to another Member State. The obligation on coastal States to take action against a vessel passing through its territorial sea and intending to disembark migrants in another Member State is a welcome stipulation in the effort to conceive of migrant smuggling as a Community problem. On the other hand, the Working Document's specification that patrols can intervene in another Member State's territorial sea only in the context of search and rescue, although commendable, does not necessarily seem to be correct as a matter of law. It would seem that some agreement between the patrolling State and the coastal State is necessary in order to permit this, as search and rescue operations do not fall under the innocent passage regime.[41]

5.2.4. *Conclusion*

The current legal regime acknowledges the fact that the coastal State is susceptible to various attacks on its security via its territorial sea. The LOSC acknowledges the territorial sea as an extension of the coastal State's territory, and therefore sovereignty. However, it does not adequately cater for the threats which currently plague coastal States:

> In the 20 years since the adoption of the Convention on the Law of the Sea, crimes at sea have become more prevalent and are increasing. The framers of the Convention never envisaged many of the crimes that exist today, and as a result either included only a general provision or none at all regarding their suppression.[42]

Recent international efforts have attempted to rectify this position so as better to cater for a preventative approach to safeguarding coastal State security.

---

41 This is also the case for counter-drug patrols: the US Shiprider Agreements, to be discussed in Chapter 7, indicate that some authorization to this end is necessary. This is what makes the US Shiprider Agreements especially interesting and innovative: they allow for shipriders (as representatives of the State Party) on board US vessels to authorize anti-drug patrols by US vessels within the territorial waters of the other State Party. See, e.g., Agreement with Antigua and Barbuda, Art. 5(c) and 8(a); Agreement with Belize, Art. 5(c) and 8(a); Agreement with Dominica, Art. 5(c) and 8(a); Agreement with the Dominican Republic, Art. 5(c) and 8(a); Agreement with Grenada, Art. 5(c) and 8(a); Agreement with St. Kitts and Nevis, Art. 5(c) and 8(a); Agreement with St. Lucia, Art. 5(c) and 8(a); Agreement with St. Vincent and the Grenadines, Art. 5(c) and 8(a); Agreement with Trinidad and Tobago, Art. 5(c) and 8(a); Agreement with Costa Rica, Art. 2(c) and 6(a); Agreement with Haiti, Art. 5(c) and 9(a); Agreement with Suriname, Art. 4(3)(c) and 6(2)(a); Agreement with Honduras, Art. IV(2)(c) and V(1)(a); and Agreement with Guatemala, Art. 5(4)(d) and 6(2)(a).

42 Oceans: The Source of Life, United Nations Convention on the Law of the Sea, 20th Anniversary (1982–2002), 8.

Various international instruments have sought to provide for control measures to be employed by the States Parties, even permitting interdiction in certain circumstances, as shall be discussed. All these efforts represent a universally felt need to push the areas of control outwards at least to the borders of the territorial sea and to utilize coastal State powers to the full at such point. While international maritime law does not appear to disallow such measures, how far they will be interpreted as impinging upon other cardinal principles of international law is still a matter of debate.

5.3. *Contiguous Zone*

The contiguous zone, regulated in Art. 33 LOSC (Art. 24 TSC), is not part of the territorial sea; it constitutes part of the EEZ or of the high seas (depending on whether or not the coastal State has proclaimed an EEZ) and freedom of navigation exists therein. This has an effect on the quality and extent of the coastal State's powers within this zone. The LOSC conceives of the contiguous zone as a zone adjacent to the territorial sea (of not more than 24 nm from the baselines)[43] where a specific power is given, in that the coastal State may exercise the control necessary with respect to two functions: to prevent and to punish the infringement of customs, fiscal, immigration and sanitary regulations within its territory or territorial sea.[44] The coastal State's rights in this zone were understood to be of a 'functional' and 'protective' nature, as shall be determined below.[45]

5.3.1. *The Meaning of 'Control'*

As far as the quality of control which can be exercised in this zone is concerned, Fitzmaurice put forward the argument that there is no legislative jurisdiction with regard to the commission of acts within the zone, and therefore no offence can be committed within the contiguous zone.[46] He therefore advanced the

---

[43] This is the breadth recognized under the LOSC. Other States, non-parties to the Convention, have claimed maritime zones of greater breadth than that allowed under the LOSC. For example, Syria has claimed a 35 nm territorial sea and a 41 nm contiguous zone. This has been met with protests from other States. See Legislative Decree No. 304 of 28 December 1963 and Law 37 of 16 August 1981.

[44] LOSC Art. 33; TSC Art. 24.

[45] 2 UNCLOS III OR 121–123, 233–235, 31st meeting, 7 August 1974.

[46] G. Fitzmaurice, 'Some Results of the Geneva Convention on the Law of the Sea' (1959) 8 *ICLQ* 73, 113. It should be noted that this view was opposed *inter alia* in the First Committee of the Geneva Conference on the Law of the Sea: see the intervention of the Italian delegation (UN Conference on the Law of the Sea, Vol III p. 113) and the Polish delegation

argument that a distinction existed regarding the application of the two paragraphs of Art. 33: the power to 'punish' infringements in the territorial areas could be applied only to outgoing ships, after an offence had been committed in the territorial areas. There could be no punishment inflicted upon incoming ships since, as such ships had not yet entered the territorial sea, no offence could yet have been committed.[47] Therefore, arrest and forcible taking into port are thus excluded from this interpretation of 'control' (in paragraph (a)) and are thereby prohibited, since this exercise of enforcement jurisdiction would presuppose a measure of legislative jurisdiction for conduct occurring within the contiguous zone. This understanding presupposes a distinction between jurisdiction and control, where control is taken to refer to administrative action as opposed to actual enforcement jurisdiction.

Fitzmaurice's view does not however accord with practice prior to the 1958 Convention nor with the interpretations of leading scholars.[48] It is indeed possible to advance another argument: that legislative jurisdiction may exist within the contiguous zone, and this even on the basis of a textual interpretation of Art. 33. In this regard, O'Connell[49] writes that the statement that the coastal State may not enact laws at all to apply in the contiguous zone would limit the notion which gave rise to the zone in the first place, since early unilateral claims asserted the right both to prescribe and to enforce regulations in the extended zones.[50] However, these laws must be limited in scope to prevent the violation of other laws, such as laws respecting customs duties, passports or health control, which are laws administered at the frontier. In other words, it would seem that the coastal State could adopt laws prohibiting activity in the contiguous zone, which activity would involve an infringement of the laws within the territory or territorial sea of the coastal State. The one essential requirement is that there must be some relevant link to the territorial areas of

---

(A/CONF.13/C.1/L.28) who maintained that coastal State action should be permitted in respect of offences committed within the contiguous zone. In point of fact, the provision adopted by the First Committee did not leave any room for Fitzmaurice's view. The Plenary Meeting however went back to the original draft which could be interpreted in accordance with Fitzmaurice's interpretation (UN Conference on the Law of the Sea, Vol II, p. 40).

47 This however may not be entirely precise. Taking the case where the offence in the territorial sea which is to be prevented is an offence to be committed by a ship coming from shore to rendezvous with the foreign ship, in such a scenario preventive measures may need to be taken against the *outgoing* vessel leaving the territorial waters on its way to committing an offence against the territorial areas of the coastal State outside the territorial sea.

48 See S. Oda, 'The Concept of the Contiguous Zone' (1962) 11 *ICLQ* 131, 133 *et seq*.

49 D.P. O'Connell, *The International Law of the Sea* (ed. T.A. Shearer, Clarendon Press, Oxford, 1984) vol. II, 1058–1059.

50 O'Connell is referring to the British Hovering Acts and similar legislation elsewhere in both Common Law and Civil Law systems: *ibid*., 1034–1043.

the coastal State since 'the power of the coastal State to punish infringements of the stated laws committed outside the territorial areas or in the contiguous zone, is not generally permissible in relation to vessels merely located within the contiguous zone and not proven to have some relevant connection with territorial areas.'[51] According to this reading, the coastal State is empowered, for certain limited purposes, to exercise the same quality of power as that exercised over the territorial sea, thus operating as an extension of coastal State jurisdiction.[52] Therefore, while there is a difference in the number of rights exercised in the contiguous zone, there is no difference in the quality of rights exercised.[53]

Furthermore, the right of hot pursuit from the contiguous zone exists with regard to offences against the four types of regulations committed in the coastal State's territory or territorial sea. In other words, should the vessel, having breached any other type of regulation when in the territorial sea, be in the contiguous zone, hot pursuit may not be commenced.[54] On the other hand, hot pursuit of a vessel which has committed a relevant offence within the territorial sea may commence even though the vessel was first sighted not within the territorial sea, but within the contiguous zone. Furthermore, the right of hot pursuit extends also to mother ships which have stayed outside the limits of a State's jurisdiction and deployed smaller boats to ferry people into the territorial sea or contiguous zone. Perhaps the flight of a ship from the contiguous zone after a failed attempt to unload illegal passengers, or where it was clear that illegal entry had been intended, is an example of where hot pursuit may be exercised, particularly if a State's domestic laws prohibit attempts or conspiracy to enter unlawfully, or the organization of unlawful entry.[55]

Therefore, for example, prescribing laws to prohibit and punish the passage of a boat laden with illegal immigrants[56] through the Maltese contiguous zone when the vessel is not destined for Malta but headed for Italy would seem to be beyond the parameters of the control which is allowed to be exercised. It is possible that policing measures could be carried out by the Maltese authorities

---

[51] *M/V 'Saiga' (No. 2) (St. Vincent and the Grenadines v Guinea) Judgment* [1999] ITLOS Reports 10 (1 July 1999) Judge Laing, Separate Opinion, paras 14–15.

[52] This was the view of the majority of the ILC during the 1956 Session, according to François's report, A/CN.4/97 (*ILC Yearbook*, 1956, Vol II, 6, paras 32–34).

[53] [1956] *ILC Yearbook*, Vol I, 76.

[54] LOSC Art. 111(1).

[55] See P. Mathew, 'Legal Issues concerning Interception' IARLJ Conference 2002, 91. (The article originally appeared at (2003) 17 *Georgetown Immigration Law Journal* 221–249). However, note O'Connell (n 49) 1088–1089 who notes that it is controversial whether there can be hot pursuit for attempted offences.

[56] The ILC had removed reference to 'immigration' in its final session. See [1956] *ILC Yearbook*, Vol I, 75.

so as to verify that the vessel is not actually headed for Malta. Should the vessel laden with migrants clearly be proceeding towards the territorial sea, action could indeed be taken against her on the basis of infringement of immigration regulations within the Maltese territorial areas.[57] Still, it should be recalled that maritime entries offer a unique scenario in which human rights and humanitarian issues apply concurrently with immigration laws and a State's powers under international maritime law, as has been alluded to above.

As regards whether the rights of the coastal State within the contiguous zone include the interception and redirection of vessels believed to be carrying asylum-seekers, it is arguable that the existing powers in the contiguous zone may be inferred by reference to the purpose for which the zone exists. In other words, the exercise of jurisdiction in this zone should be consonant with the purpose for which the zone exists: if one is to draw the conclusion that prevention and punishment of certain core laws and regulations is the main aim, and that such powers must be greater than those which exist on the high seas (where stopping and boarding vessels is permitted in certain cases, even without flag State consent), then there is a strong argument for permitting interception and possibly redirection out of that zone, irrespective of flag State consent.

5.3.2. *State Practice and Protective Jurisdiction*

As far as the type of control that Art. 33 authorizes is concerned, terms such as 'sovereign rights' and 'jurisdiction' are evident in State legislation incorporating the provision into domestic law. The laws of Antigua and Barbuda and Dominica[58] refer to 'sovereign rights' being exercised within the contiguous zone, while the laws of Argentina, Chile, Haiti, Jamaica, the Maldives and Malta all provide for the exercise of 'jurisdiction'.[59] An approach adopted in other domestic laws focuses on allowing the State to exercise 'all necessary powers

57 Note also Australian legislation which empowers interdiction of vessels by authorized officials in the contiguous zone. See Chapter 8.

58 Antigua and Barbuda: Maritime Areas Act, 1982, Act No. 18 of 17 August 1982, Art. 5(3); Dominica: Territorial Sea, Contiguous Zone, Exclusive Economic and Fishery Zones Act, 1981, Act No. 26 of 25 August 1981, Art. 2.

59 Argentina: Act No. 23 of 14 August 1991, Art. 4; Chile: Law No. 18.565 amending the Civil Code with regard to Maritime Space, 13 October 1986, Art. 1 amending Art. 593 of the Civil Code; Haiti: Decree No. 38 of 8 April 1977, Art. 4; Iran: Act of the Marine Areas of the Islamic Republic of Iran in the Persian Gulf and Oman Sea, 1993, Art. 13; Jamaica: Maritime Areas Act of 1996, Art. 20; the Maldives: Maritime Zones of Maldives Act No. 6/96, Art. 10; Malta: Territorial Waters and Contiguous Zone Act of 10 December 1971, Chapter 226, Art. 4(1).

and measures'.[60] Many of these laws purport to allow the coastal State to exercise jurisdiction in accordance with the relevant international law, thus indicating that 'control' under the LOSC regime entails the exercise of jurisdiction. Viewed in this light, it may be that the problem with the notion of control, considered above, is only apparent. It seems to be accepted in State practice that the effective exercise of control denotes an amount of legislative and enforcement jurisdiction: if enforcement jurisdiction is included in the second limb of Art. 33(1) providing for punitive measures, there is no reason why it should not be admitted in the first limb as well.

As far as concerns the permitted interests in regard to which action may be taken, some States have created other interests apart from the four abovementioned where action may be taken within the contiguous zone. Some domestic legislation provides for powers of prevention and control with regard to infringements of 'any law or right,'[61] while others prefer the wider term 'financial' instead of 'fiscal'.[62] Some laws provide for maritime interests;[63] and quite a number provide for the control necessary to prevent environmental damage, although this could arguably be included in the meaning of 'sanitary'.[64]

At this point it should be noted that a distinction exists between laws embodying a contiguous zone claim and those purporting to permit a wider claim of protective jurisdiction.[65] This latter approach appears to be in keeping with the general concept of the contiguous zone as being one where the control exercised by the coastal State is based on the principle of protective jurisdiction[66] whereby a State is entitled to prosecute crimes occurring outside

60 Madagascar: Ordinance No. 85–013 determining the limits of the Maritime Zones of the Democratic Republic of Madagascar, 16 September 1985, as amended and ratified by Law No. 85–013 of 11 December 1985, Art. 3; Pakistan: Territorial Waters and Maritime Zones Act of 22 December 1976, Art. 4(2); Samoa: Maritime Zones Act No. 18, 25 August 1999, Art. 18(2); South Africa: Maritime Zones Act, No. 15 of 1994, Art. 5(2); Vanuatu: Maritime Zones Act No. 23 of 1981, Art. 7(2).

61 The Gambia: Territorial Sea and Contiguous Zone Act, 1968, as amended by the Territorial Sea and Contiguous Zone (Amendment) Act, 1969, Art. 3.

62 Bulgaria: Maritime Space, Inland Waterways and Ports Act of the Republic of Bulgaria, 28 January 2000, Art. 38; Egypt: Decree Concerning the Territorial Waters of the Arab Republic of Egypt, 15 January 1951, as amended by Presidential Decree of 17 February 1958, Art. 9.

63 Iran: Act of the Marine Areas of the Islamic Republic of Iran in the Persian Gulf and Oman Sea, 1993, Art. 13; Saudi Arabia: Royal Decree No. 33 of 16 February 1958, Art. 8.

64 Iran (n 63); Samoa: Maritime Zones Act No. 18, 25 August 1999, Art. 18(2); Sierra Leone: the Maritime Zones (Establishment) Decree, 1996, Art. 7(2)(a).

65 While all contiguous zone claims fall under the notion of protective jurisdiction, the converse is not necessarily true.

66 M.H. Nordquist (ed.-in-chief), *United Nations Convention on the Law of the Sea 1982: A Commentary* (Martinus Nijhoff, The Netherlands, 1985), Vol II, para. 33.8(d) at 274.

its territory which threaten the State, its security or vital economic interests.[67] It may seem strange that, while the contiguous zone is perceived as a protective zone, any mention of 'security' is lacking in Art. 33. Inclusion of security interests had been suggested in the First Committee of the 1958 Conference. Ultimately, however:

> The Commission did not recognize special security rights in the contiguous zone. It considered that the extreme vagueness of the term 'security' would open the way for abuses and that the granting of such rights was not necessary.[68]

Nevertheless, the most prominent claims in this regard are security claims.[69] These claims to security zones have however been met with protests from other States, possibly owing to the fact that this could curtail the freedom of navigation in the contiguous zone. In fact, some are of the opinion that the extension of such rights would go far in equating coastal State powers in the contiguous zone with all the powers existing in the territorial sea. This however, does not seem to be completely justified: conceiving of the contiguous zone as a security zone could not automatically extend the jurisdictional powers of the coastal State to those present in the territorial sea, where it has been seen that these powers are nearly complete. The EEZ/high seas nature of the contiguous zone would always impact upon the purview of the coastal State's powers therein.

---

67 Accepted in various decisions such as: *Joyce v DPP* [1946] AC 347; *Attorney-General of the Government of Israel v Eichmann* (1961) 36 ILR 5.

68 [1956] *ILC Yearbook*, Vol II, 295. The term 'security' was included in the initial intervention by François, the special *rapporteur* on the topic of the high seas, in 1950 A/CN.4/17, para. 86 ([1950] *ILC Yearbook*, Vol II, 47) and deleted in the second session in 1951 A/CN.4/42, para. 123 ([1951] *ILC Yearbook*, Vol II, 94).

69 Bangladesh: Territorial Waters and Maritime Zones Act 1974, Act No. XXVI, Art. 4(2)(a); People's Republic of China: Law on the Territorial Sea and the Contiguous Zone, 25 February 1992, Art. 13; Egypt: Decree Concerning the Territorial Waters of the Arab Republic of Egypt, 15 January 1951, as amended by Presidential Decree of 17 February 1958, Art. 9; Haiti: Decree No. 38 of 8 April 1977, Art. 4; India: Territorial Waters, Continental Shelf, Exclusive Economic Zone and other Maritime Zones Act, 1976, Act No. 80 of 28 May 1976, Art. 5(4)(a); Iran: Act of the Marine Areas of the Islamic Republic of Iran in the Persian Gulf and Oman Sea, 1993, Art. 13; Democratic People's Republic of Korea: Army Command Announcement of 1 August 1977 established a 50nm military zone; Myanmar: Territorial Sea and Maritime Zones Law, 197, Pyithu Hluttaw Law No. 3, 9 April 1977, Art. 11(a); Pakistan: Territorial Waters and Maritime Zones Act of 22 December 1976, Art. 4(2)(a); Saudi Arabia: Royal Decree No. 33 of 16 February 1958, Art. 8; Sri Lanka: Maritime Zones Law No. 22 of 1 September 1976, Art. 4(2)(a); Sudan: Territorial Waters and Continental Shelf Act, 1970, Art. 9(a); United Arab Emirates: Federal Law No. 19 of 17 October 1993 in respect of the delimitation of the Maritime Zones on the United Arab Emirates, Art. 10(1); Yemen: Act concerning the Territorial Sea, Exclusive Economic Zone, Continental Shelf and other Marine Areas, No. 45 of 17 December 1977, Art. 12(a).

A justification for claims to a security zone within the contiguous zone could be founded on the argument that States enjoy wider contiguous zone rights in customary law than they do under the LOSC.[70] If this maritime space is increasingly perceived as protective, then this could lead to wider claims being exercised therein. After all, the increase in international terrorism and drug smuggling in recent years has led to a greater acceptance of the protective principle of jurisdiction.[71] As far as drug trafficking is concerned, the US has resorted to the exercise of protective jurisdiction in order to combat threats of this nature in areas further out than the contiguous zone itself.[72] Other States have acquiesced in this practice—no doubt because of the serious nature of the threat posed by narcotics trafficking; however, they have fallen short of carrying out such arrests themselves, preferring to enter into treaty arrangements regulating enforcement in matters relating to the suppression of narcotics dealing.[73]

5.4. *High Seas*[74]

The freedoms of the seas apply to the high seas and are outlined in a non-exhaustive list in Art. 87 LOSC. The freedom of navigation is of most direct significance for immediate purposes. This freedom, while not expressly made subject to any other provisions of the LOSC, is however to be exercised subject to the flag State's duty to act in accordance with its international obligations[75]

---

70 See, e.g., *US v F/V Taiyo Maru*, 395 F. Supp. 413 (1975).

71 See, e.g., *Liangsiriprasert (Somchai) v US Government* [1991] 1 AC 225.

72 Discussed below at 5.4.1.2.

73 See, e.g., *Regina v Charrington and others*, where a Maltese-registered vessel, the *Simon de Danser*, laden with narcotics, was boarded by UK officials on 5 May 1997, when the vessel was in international waters about 100 miles off the coast of Portugal. The judgment is unreported, but see C. Warbrick and D. McGoldrick (eds), 'Current Developments: Drug Trafficking at Sea: The Case of R v Charrington and Others' (2000) 49 *ICLQ* 447–489.

74 A State has a right to declare an EEZ; this is an area which extends beyond the territorial sea to a distance of not more than 200 nm from the baselines from which the territorial sea is measured (Art. 57 LOSC). This zone is perhaps of least relevance for the purposes of this study as the rights granted to the coastal State are in the nature of sovereign rights to explore, exploit, conserve and manage natural resources in the waters, seabed and subsoil (Art. 56(1)(a)). Jurisdiction also extends to the establishment and use of artificial islands, installations and structures, marine scientific research and the protection and preservation of the marine environment (Art. 56(1)(b)). The EEZ is therefore only of relevance insofar as the provisions of the high seas regime (Art. 88–115 LOSC) are applicable to the regime of the EEZ by virtue of Art. 58(2) LOSC. In this way, the EEZ is given the status of the high seas with all the freedoms found therein.

75 See, e.g., Art. 94 (3)(4), 192.

and to the due regard obligation, an obligation of good faith requiring that rights are to be exercised reasonably.[76] Through Art. 90 LOSC, the freedom of navigation is expressed as the right given to every State (whether coastal or land-locked) to sail ships flying its flag on the high seas.[77]

Art. 92(1) LOSC provides that 'ships shall sail under the flag of one State only and, save in exceptional cases expressly provided for in international treaties or in this Convention, shall be subject to its exclusive jurisdiction on the high seas.' This rule was inserted as an adjunct to the principle of freedom of the seas due to the recognition that 'the absence of any authority over ships sailing the high seas would lead to chaos.'[78] Any action by non-flag States must be accompanied by flag State consent.[79] Even if a vessel's Master consents to her being boarded this is generally understood as consent given in order for the enforcing authorities to gather information; no enforcement jurisdiction, such as arrest or seizure, may be exercised during a consensual boarding without the permission of the flag State.[80] The aim at this point is, therefore, to establish exceptions to this general principle and to examine the extent of control by non-flag States over vessels carrying migrants on the high seas notwithstanding lack of consent by the flag State.

5.4.1. *Exceptions to Flag State Exclusivity of Jurisdiction*

5.4.1.1. *Exceptions in the LOSC*

Absent any agreement between the flag State and the State wishing to take enforcement action, the LOSC permits non-flag State action in only a limited number of instances: the suppression of the slave trade (Art. 99),[81] piracy (Art. 100 *et seq.*), illicit traffic in narcotic drugs and psychotropic substances (Art. 108), and unauthorized broadcasting (Art. 109). However, these provisions are relatively weak and of questionable effectiveness in view of the current maritime security scenario. Moreover, the right of visit is limited to verifying the right of the ship to fly the flag of the visiting party and such right cannot be exercised in the case of narcotics trafficking.

---

76 D. Anderson, 'Freedoms of the High Seas in the Modern Law of the Sea', in Freestone et al. (n 19) 330–332.

77 This text is also found in the UNCTAD Convention (1986).

78 See the Report of the ILC covering the work of its Eighth Session (A/3159), Art. 29 [1956] *ILC Yearbook* Vol II, 279, para. 3.

79 This is also the position taken under the Smuggling Protocol where, in Art. 8, authorization must be requested from the flag State prior to any action being taken with regard to a vessel reasonably suspected to be engaged in the smuggling of migrants by sea.

80 It does not seem that the Master is empowered to give wider permission; consent for enforcement action must emanate from the flag State.

81 To be dealt with separately below at 5.4.1.1.b.

Also, in cases where it is considered that the conditions on board a vessel are such that a rescue at sea operation is required, Art. 98 LOSC imposes a duty on Masters to render assistance to those in distress at sea, and therefore any boarding by non-flag State vessels is permitted insofar as it is incidental to the required rescue operation. However, while the obligation of every State to require the Master of a ship flying its flag to render assistance to those in distress while on the high seas provides an instance of intervention by non-flag State actors,[82] this provision does not sanction subsequent seizure and arrest of the vessel and/or those on board.

5.4.1.1.a. *Hot Pursuit and Constructive Presence*

The doctrine of hot pursuit pre-dates the law of the sea conventions,[83] being recognized as a principle of international law by the Supreme Court of Canada in *The North*,[84] and later, in the *I'm Alone* case.[85] The right was also recognized as already established by the ILC in its 1956 Report to the General Assembly.[86] Hot pursuit is designed to facilitate the effective enforcement of laws by ensuring that offenders do not simply escape jurisdiction by fleeing the territorial seas or contiguous zone of the coastal State.

This right allows the coastal State to pursue a vessel and arrest her on the high seas when it has good reason to believe[87] that she has violated its laws within one of its jurisdictional zones. Hot pursuit may thus be used as a tool to further the jurisdictional reach of non-flag State actors to vessels over the high seas, thus limiting the freedoms of the seas in the cause of coastal State protection. Hot pursuit enables a coastal State effectively to enforce its laws far beyond its territorial sea by maintaining an uninterrupted and continuous chase of a vessel which has violated its laws and has managed to escape. The justification for such extension of jurisdiction outside the traditional zones of control is that hot pursuit is, in essence, a continuation of a validly-commenced act of jurisdiction, commenced in the zone where the vessel violated the coastal State's applicable law. For this reason, hot pursuit must begin in the zone where

---

82 LOSC Art. 98(1). See also Salvage Convention, Art. 10; SOLAS, Arts V/7, V/33.

83 Note the discussion of the doctrine in older texts such as P.C. Jessup, *The Law of the Territorial Waters and Maritime Jurisdiction* (G.A. Jennings Co Inc, New York, 1927) and W.E. Masterson, *Jurisdiction in Marginal Seas* (The Macmillan Co, New York, 1929).

84 (1905) 11 Ex. Rep. 141; British Columbia Law Reports 473. See also Jessup (n 83) 106 *et seq.*

85 *Canada et al v US (I'm Alone)* (1935) III RIAA 1609. See W.C. Dennis, 'The Sinking of the *I'm Alone*' (1929) 23 *AJIL* 351–362. See also *The Vinces* 20 Fed. (2d) 164, discussed in Masterson (n 83), 238–240.

86 [1956] *ILC Yearbook*, Vol II, 285.

87 Some tangible evidence or reason to suspect a violation is therefore required; a mere suspicion does not suffice: see *M/V 'Saiga' (No. 2) (St. Vincent and the Grenadines v Guinea) Judgment* [1999] ITLOS Reports 10 (1 July 1999) para. 147.

the vessel violated the applicable law[88] and ceases in two instances: if the pursuit is interrupted, thus losing its continuous and uninterrupted character, as explained in Art. 111(1). Alternatively, should the pursued vessel enter the territorial sea of the flag State or another State, as envisaged in Art. 111(3), the hot pursuit must end in deference to the sovereignty of that State.

Notwithstanding the detailed provision in the LOSC, the right of hot pursuit is capable of being given a more extensive interpretation in practice, thus allowing intervention in a wider range of circumstances than perhaps originally intended. For instance, the LOSC provides that pursuit must not begin until a signal to stop—visual or auditory—has been given at a distance at which it can be seen or heard by the foreign ship. However, a readiness to admit that the order to stop may be given via radio is apparent in various judgments.[89]

Further extension of the coastal State's right of arrest and prosecution lies in the doctrine of constructive presence. Under customary international law, there is a right to arrest foreign ships which use their boats to commit offences within the territorial sea while they themselves remain on the high seas. In such a case, the mother ship may be pursued and arrested on the high seas without it ever having left those seas. The ship, in such cases, is deemed to be constructively present in the territorial sea within which the other boats are operating. Gilmore, citing Lord McNair, writes that 'when a foreign ship outside territorial waters sends boats into territorial waters which commit offences there, the mother ship renders herself liable to seizure by reason of these vicarious operations.' The exercise of this right is therefore likened to the exercise of objective territorial jurisdiction.[90]

Constructive presence is implicitly recognized in the 1958 and 1982 Conventions (extended to apply also to the contiguous zone, the EEZ and the continental shelf), through the use of phrases such as 'the foreign ship or one of its boats' and 'the ship pursued or one of its boats or other craft working as a team and using the ship pursued as a mother ship.'[91] Both conventions admit of the doctrine of simple constructive presence (i.e. where a ship actually uses its own boats and sends them to shore) and that of extensive constructive presence (i.e. where other boats are used which put out of the coastal State by prearrangement). Yet again, however, the interpretation given by domestic courts

88 Note what was stated above in relation to the contiguous zone.

89 It has sometimes been held that the signal requirement may even be done away with in certain circumstances: see *The Newton Bay*, 36 F. 2d, 729 (2d Circuit 1929); *R v Mills and Others*, Unreported, 1995, Croydon Crown Court, Judge Devonshire; *R v Sunila and Soleyman* (1986) 28 DLR (4th) 450.

90 W.C. Gilmore, 'Hot Pursuit and Constructive Presence in Canadian Law Enforcement: A Case Note' (1988) 12 *Marine Policy* 1, 109.

91 See HSC, Art. 23(1) and (3) and LOSC, Art. 111(1) and (4).

may evidence a wider application of the doctrine than was originally intended. For example, the court in *R v Mills*[92] gave an interpretation of 'extensive constructive presence' which seems to say that any vessel which colludes with a ship on the high seas which latter ship commits an illegal act within the jurisdiction of a State may be subject to arrest by that State on the high seas. In this regard, when commenting on the extensive interpretation given in *R v Mills*, Bantekas and Nash suggest that 'although this case does not conform to the spirit of Art. 111 of UNCLOS, its evolution will undoubtedly depend on relevant State protests and consensus emanating from recent international criminal co-operation initiatives in the spheres of organized crime, drug-trafficking and terrorism.'[93] This position therefore serves as an example of international cooperation to broaden coastal States' rights outside the treaty-making process.

At this point it should be emphasized that pursuit and arrest in furtherance of these doctrines is permissible only if the relevant powers have been given to the coastal State under its domestic law; otherwise, unless the LOSC, as an international convention, is automatically applicable within the domestic legal system (as in the case of monist systems), no enforcement jurisdiction can be exercised by the coastal State, save in the case of self-defence—one example where the control exercised need not have any domestic jurisdictional basis. While this has been recognized as one of the exceptions to the principle of flag State exclusivity[94] however, for a coastal State to be entitled to act in self-defence upon the high seas the ship must present 'an unquestionable, imminent and exceptionally serious danger to the security and the existence of the State in question.'[95] On this understanding, it is difficult to formulate an argument in support of the exercise of self-defence by one State's vessel against a vessel carrying irregular migrants, as the threat, if it exists at all at that stage, is too far removed from any particular State to warrant action.

5.4.1.1.b. *Slavery*

Art. 99 LOSC directs every State to take 'effective measures to prevent and punish the transport of slaves in ships authorized to fly its flag and to prevent the unlawful use of its flag for that purpose. Any slave taking refuge on board

---

92 Unreported, 1995, Croydon Crown Court, Judge Devonshire.

93 I. Bantekas and S. Nash, *International Criminal Law* (2nd edn, Cavendish Publishing, London, 2003), 108. For other cases on constructive presence see also *The Araunah* (1888) Moore, *International Arbitration* 824; *The Tenyu Maru* (1910) 4 Alaska 129 (1910); and *The Grace and Ruby* (1922) 283 Fed 475.

94 Dupuy and Vignes state that this understanding is generally adopted by English authors and refer to Colombos and Higgins: R.J. Dupuy and D. Vignes, *A Handbook on the New Law of the Sea* (Martinus Nijhoff, Dordrecht, 1991), Vol. 1, 412.

95 *Ibid.*

any ship, whatever its flag, shall *ipso facto* be free.' In support of this general prohibition, Art. 110(1)(b) allows for the right of visit by any warship, if carried out according to the conditions specified therein,[96] and the right of hot pursuit is also provided for under Art. 111. However, no power is given to non-flag States to seize or arrest those on board, thus weakening the ability adequately to address threats of such a nature.[97] Today of more topical significance are migrant smuggling and trafficking in human beings where criminal syndicates use sub-standard and overcrowded vessels to transport migrants to other States' shores. Neither of these crimes is mentioned in the LOSC; however, due to the nature and conditions of the operation, these crimes may arguably be included within the general term of 'slavery'. There is a growing awareness of the need to control such practices which are harmful to the migrants themselves and a threat to the vital interests and security of the coastal State. The rationale for taking action on the high seas is therefore two-fold: firstly, the link to organized crime necessitates concerted international action in its repression; secondly, suppression of migrant smuggling on the high seas reduces the problems faced by coastal States once migrant vessels approach their shores. However, Art. 99 is not effective in combating migrant smuggling due to the absence of any enforcement mechanism.

5.4.1.1.c. *Stateless vessels*[98]

'Stateless' simply means 'without nationality'. However, the relevant question at this point is whether an unregistered vessel necessarily becomes stateless. Registration—the administrative act which evidences the nationality of the vessel—has been described as needing to have 'substance'; it must reflect the actual control that the flag State is able to enforce over its ships.[99] However, the question of the consequences of lack of registration remains, as does the precise nature of the relationship between registration and the nationality of a vessel. Could lack of registration render the vessel devoid of nationality? A tentative answer may be reached by reference to the case of vessels too small to register.

---

96 Art. 110 indicates that the right of visit consists in boarding (para. 1) and inspection (para. 2) of the ship. See Chapter 3.

97 This is different from the situations in piracy (Art. 105) and unauthorized broadcasting (Art. 109(4)) where powers of seizure and arrest are given to non-flag States. Of course, if the apprehension of a slave vessel takes place on the high seas following an uninterrupted pursuit from the territorial sea of a coastal State, the vessel may be detained and arrested.

98 'Stateless vessels' are discussed at this point because this exception to flag State exclusivity of jurisdiction is found in the LOSC. However, it is also to be linked to the consideration of a 'lack of an effective or genuine link' below, at 5.4.1.3.

99 *'Grand Prince' (Belize v France) Prompt Release, Judgment* [2001] ITLOS Reports (20 April 2001). Declaration by Judge Wolfrum, ITLOS Reports 2001, para. 3.

The laws of most States have registration requirements for ships over a certain size. In the Maltese legal system, while vessels of a certain size are required to register under the Maltese flag, vessels falling below this threshold need not or cannot do so. In other words, this second category is divided into two: vessels falling below the threshold have a choice whether or not to register under the Maltese flag, and even smaller vessels are barred from registering under the Maltese flag but must register under the Small Ships Register instead. The position under the Maltese legal system therefore is that vessels over 24 metres in length must be registered under the Maltese flag, irrespective of whether or not they intend to leave Maltese territorial waters.[100] Vessels under six metres in length must be registered under the Small Ships Register and, consequently, do not fly the Maltese flag and cannot leave Maltese territorial waters.[101] Vessels between six and 24 metres have a choice; however if they opt for the latter form of registration, they cannot leave Maltese territorial waters and are not given a flag.[102]

Although it seems that it is registration under the Maltese flag that gives the vessel the capacity to travel out of territorial waters, the Merchant Shipping Act gives the enjoyment of 'the rights and privileges of a Maltese ship or [recognition] as a Maltese ship' to vessels registered under the Maltese flag but also to ships not exceeding 24 metres in length if not registered elsewhere.[103] Therefore, vessels registered under the Small Ships Register are still considered to be Maltese ships even though they do not fly the Maltese flag. The position in Maltese law therefore reflects the view that while the flying of a State's flag is determinant of its nationality, the nationality of a vessel does not necessarily depend on that vessel flying a State's flag. In the Maltese scenario, it is *registration*—under either register—which gives the vessel its nationality, irrespective of whether or not that vessel flies the Maltese flag.[104] This strengthens the link—

[100] Merchant Shipping Act, Laws of Malta, Chapter 234, Art. 3(1) and (7).

[101] *Ibid.*, Art. 3(7); Malta Maritime Authority Act, Laws of Malta, Chapter 352, Art. 29(1); Small Ships Regulations, Subsidiary Legislation 352.15, Art. 3(1).

[102] *Ibid.*, Art. 3(2).

[103] See Merchant Shipping Act, Art. 3(1): 'no ship, other than a ship exempted from registry, or a ship referred to in subarticle (7), shall enjoy the rights and privileges of a Maltese ship or be recognized as a Maltese ship unless such ship is registered under this Act; Art. 3(2): ships registered under the Malta Maritime Authority Act, 1991 not exceeding twenty-four metres in length shall be exempted from registry, and such ships, if not registered elsewhere ... shall also be deemed to be Maltese ships: Provided that ships of length of six metres or over not employed solely in navigation on the coasts of Malta, shall also be deemed to be Maltese ships; Art. 3(7) Notwithstanding any other provision of this Act, ships under six metres in length shall not be registrable under this Act.'

[104] It should be noted however that registration alone does not always grant nationality to vessels.

made amply clear in the LOSC—between nationality and registration, showing registration—and the right to fly the flag of the State—to be the formal evidence of nationality.

A State wishing to intervene on the high seas may attempt to show that boats carrying asylum-seekers are effectively ships without nationality and are thus subject to boarding and inspection under the right of visit.[105] This is especially relevant in the case of migrant smuggling, as many boats used by migrant smugglers are stateless vessels.[106]

Art. 110 LOSC confers a right to board and inspect ships without nationality on the high seas. Clearly, there can be no possibility of flag State consent for further enforcement action to be taken; however, it would seem that even in the case of stateless vessels some form of jurisdictional link must exist between the vessel and the State exercising jurisdiction in order for any enforcement jurisdiction to be exercised. Therefore, it has been suggested that jurisdiction could be asserted over stateless ships by the national State of their owners if they are outside the territorial areas of any State.[107] Further, the national State of those on board would arguably be entitled to exercise diplomatic protection.[108] Therefore, it seems that a State must be able to rely on some basis of jurisdiction in order to exercise enforcement action over vessels and that this could potentially be the law of the national State of their owners. In the words of O'Connell:

> When a ship loses its formal nationality, whatever that may be, its status is then a question of the municipal law of the owners, and it is likely that this would then claim to regulate the ship, and, in that sense, to become a law of the ship's nationality.[109]

However, it has also been argued that ships without nationality are effectively ships without protection, and therefore any State can exercise jurisdiction over such vessels as if they were their own (on the basis of personal jurisdiction).[110] *Naim Molvan v Attorney-General for Palestine*[111] determined that such ships enjoy the protection of no State, the implication being that if jurisdiction was indeed asserted, no State could legitimately object to its exercise.

---

105 LOSC, Art. 110(d).

106 See UNGA A/53/456 (5 October 1998), para. 135L; Commission Staff Working Document (n 23), para. 5.

107 See Churchill and Lowe (n 21), 214, and O'Connell (n 49), 756.

108 Churchill and Lowe (n 21) 214.

109 O'Connell (n 49), 756, citing various US cases, among them *The Chiquita* 19 F. 2d. 417 (CCA 5th 1927) and *The Alta* 136 Fed. 513 (CCA 9th 1905).

110 O'Connell (n 49), 755–756.

111 The *Asya* [1948] AC 351.

The Smuggling Protocol in its Art. 8(1) provides that 'a State Party that has reasonable grounds to suspect that a vessel that is flying its flag or claiming its registry, that is without nationality or that, though flying a foreign flag or refusing to show a flag, is in reality of the nationality of the State Party concerned is engaged in the smuggling of migrants by sea may request the assistance of other States Parties in suppressing the use of the vessel for that purpose. The States Parties so requested shall render such assistance to the extent possible within their means'. In the context of drug smuggling, a similar provision—Art. 17(2) of the 1988 Vienna Drugs Convention—has been interpreted as placing a ship without nationality in the same category as a ship in respect of which a State exercises jurisdiction by virtue of the fact that it sails under its flag, thereby implying that a State can take the same enforcement measures with respect to ships without nationality as it can with respect to ships flying its flag.[112]

5.4.1.2. *Protective Jurisdiction*

The principle of protective jurisdiction may also provide an argument for action on the high seas as it allows a State to prosecute crimes occurring outside its territory which threaten it, its security or vital economic interests.[113] In this way, a State may punish acts prejudicial to its security, even when such acts are committed by foreigners abroad, since the focus of this principle is the 'nature of the interest injured rather than the place of the act or the nationality of the offender.'[114] The protective principle has been accepted in a number of judgments,[115] and while it is usually discussed in terms of legislative jurisdiction, the aspect of enforcement jurisdiction may be usefully illustrated by reference to a few cases evidencing US practice in the fight against maritime drug trafficking; this principle has been cited as a valid ground upon which foreign drug smugglers apprehended on non-US flag vessels on the high seas

[112] R. Lee and M. Hayashi (eds), 'Piracy, Drug Trafficking, and Other Crimes at Sea' in *New Directions in the Law of the Sea: Global Developments* (Oceania Publications, Dobs Ferry, NY, 1996).

[113] Art. 7 of the Harvard Research Draft Convention on Criminal Jurisdiction provides that '[a] State has jurisdiction with respect to any crime committed outside its territory by an alien against the security, territorial integrity or political independence of that State, provided that the act or omission which constitutes the crime was not committed in exercise of a liberty guaranteed the alien by the law of the place where it was committed': Harvard Research in International Law, 'Draft Convention on Jurisdiction with Respect to Crime' (1935) 29 *AJIL* Supplement.

[114] 'Article 7. Protection—Security of the State' (1935) 29 *AJIL* Supplement 543–561, at 543.

[115] For example: *Joyce v DPP* [1946] AC 347; *AG of the Government of Israel v Eichmann* (1961) 36 ILR 5.

have been successfully prosecuted.[116] In a decision of the US Court of Appeals for the Eleventh Circuit in *US v Gonzalez*,[117] six foreign crewmen on board a Honduran-flagged vessel on the high seas, classified as 'customs waters' of the US, were charged with possessing marijuana with intent to distribute it, in violation of the Marijuana on the High Seas Act.[118] This judgment was also considered in *US v Tinoco*[119] where it was recalled that:

> Congress, under the "protective principle" of international law, may assert extraterritorial jurisdiction over vessels in the high seas that are engaged in conduct that "has a potentially adverse effect and is generally recognized as a crime by nations that have reasonably developed legal systems".[120]

The US District Court for the Northern District of California, in *US v Biermann*,[121] referred to trafficking in controlled substances as a specific threat to the security and well-being of the US and, again, asserted jurisdiction on the basis of the protective principle of jurisdiction.

Furthermore, the US law relating to the prevention of manufacture, distribution or possession with intent to manufacture or distribute controlled substances on board vessels defines a ship without nationality as being subject to the jurisdiction of the US, thus invoking the protective principle of jurisdiction.[122] To this end, in *US v Marino-Garcia*[123] it was held that the federal Government has criminal jurisdiction over all stateless vessels on the high seas engaged in the distribution of controlled substances. Again, although the defendants in *US v Pinto-Mejia*[124] argued that there was insufficient nexus between the vessel *Ricardo* and the US, this was not upheld by the court, which held that Congress was not bound by international law and thus could legislate in excess of the limits imposed thereby. At any rate, it was held that Congress's understanding was that international law does not require such nexus anyway. Therefore, it was held that:

---

116 USCG et al., 'The Commander's Handbook on the Law of Naval Operations' (July 2007), NWP 1-14M/MCWP 5-12.1/COMDTPUB P5800.7A, 3.11.1.5.

117 776 F. 2d 931 (1985).

118 Pub. L. No. 96-350, 94 Stat. 1159 (1980). This Act relates to the customs waters of the US, defined in 19 USC s. 1401(j). In this case, the consent of the Honduran Government, relayed by telephone after the boarding and searching of the vessel situated 125 miles off the Florida coast, was found to constitute an 'arrangement' necessary for the exercise of enforcement jurisdiction.

119 304 F.3d 1088 (11th Cir 2002).

120 776 F. 2d 931 (1985), at 939.

121 678 F. Supp. 1437 (1988).

122 Title 46 USC app. Section 1903(c)(1)(A).

123 679 F. 2d 1373 (1982).

124 720 F.2d 248 (2d Cir. 1983), modified, 728 F.2d 142 (2d Cir. 1984).

> Stateless vessels on the high seas are, by virtue of their statelessness, subject to the jurisdiction of the United States ... even absent proof that the vessel's operators intended to distribute their cargo in the United States.[125]

The policy argument here is that the US does not assert a right to exercise enforcement jurisdiction, but maintains that there is no duty *not* to take action in cases outside the jurisdiction of any State in circumstances where no State is able or prepared to take action. A somewhat parallel approach can be seen to be emerging in the repression of piracy off the coast of Somalia. A resolution on Piracy and Armed Robbery against Ships in Waters off the Coast of Somalia, adopted on 29 November 2007 at the 25th IMO Assembly (revoking a previous resolution, A.979(24), adopted in 2005 at the 24th IMO Assembly) requests the Transitional Federal Government of Somalia *inter alia* to inform the Security Council that it 'consents to warships ... operating in the Indian Ocean, entering its territorial sea when engaging in operations against pirates or suspected pirates and armed robbers endangering the safety of life at sea'.[126] The UN Security Council, having previously issued a Presidential Statement[127] in response to the IMO Assembly's 2005 Resolution, consequently unanimously adopted Resolution 1816 (2008) on 2 June 2008 which, for a period of six months, permits States cooperating with the Transitional Federal Government of Somalia in the fight against piracy and armed robbery at sea off the coast of Somalia, for which advance notification has been provided by the Transitional Federal Government to the Secretary-General, to enter the country's territorial waters and to use all necessary means to repress acts of piracy and armed robbery at sea in a manner consistent with the international law of the sea.[128] The underlying reasoning is that the continuing political instability and unrest do not allow for adequate policing and supervision. Therefore, the understanding is that other States can and should step in where the State which would rightfully be able to take action is unable to do so.

5.4.1.3. *Lack of an Effective or Genuine Link*

The above policy argument is only a small step away from the assertion of jurisdiction by non-flag States due to non-recognition of vessels on the basis

[125] This was also held in *US v. Howard-Arias* 679 F.2d 363 (4th Cir. 1982), cert. denied, 459 U.S. 874, 103 S.Ct. 165, 74 L.Ed.2d 136 (1982).

[126] Para. 6.3. Note also in this regard MSC.1/Circ.1233 Piracy and Armed Robbery Against Ships in Waters off the Coast of Somalia (15 June 2007).

[127] UNSC, Presidential Statement 11 (15 March 2006) S/PRST/2006/11.

[128] Para. 7. A recent Resolution, adopted on 7 October 2008 (UN Doc S/RES/1838), further calls upon Member States, in para. 2, actively to participate in the fight against piracy on the high seas off the coast of Somalia by deploying naval vessels and aircraft. Para. 4 of the Resolution reiterates the call made in Res 1816.

of an ineffective link between the flag State and its vessels. In other words, it is arguable that where the flag State is unwilling or unable to exercise jurisdiction over its vessels, then other States can step in on the premise that there is no duty *not* to take action in the case where the State which can rightfully take action under international law fails to do so.

5.4.1.3.a. *Absence of a definition*

Art. 91(1) LOSC states that there 'must' exist a genuine link between the State and the vessel. The introduction of this concept into the international law of the sea brought with it a number of concerns due to its 'vague and imprecise nature'.[129] In view of the lack of elaboration in the LOSC, the criterion of the genuine link has often been interpreted in the context of the International Court of Justice's judgment in the *Nottebohm case*,[130] concerning the 'genuine link' between people and their State of nationality. The Court in this case established the notion of the genuine link to illustrate the need for some form of connection between the State granting nationality and the individual in the context of diplomatic protection.

Transposing the context of this judgment to vessels has resulted in equating the genuine link requirement with concepts relating to nationality. However, this judgment does not shed any light on indicators of nationality or the actual substance of the genuine link. At any rate, reliance on the *Nottebohm* holding would seem to be dangerous: the Court was dealing with nationality in the context of a claim for diplomatic protection, and furthermore it did not establish that a genuine link is necessary in all circumstances. Above all, it has also been pointed out that the criteria laid down for giving content to the genuine link requirement may not easily be applied to inanimate objects such as ships.[131] In this regard, 'there is no analogy between the nationality of ships and the concept of nationality as applied to individuals or corporations.'[132]

In the absence of a definition of the concept, considerations of ownership and nationality have featured prominently in describing the genuine link requirement. In a bid to give substance to the notion of the genuine link, the United Nations Convention on Conditions for Registration of Ships 1986 (UNCTAD Convention) attempted to introduce a regulatory framework which would supplement the provisions in the law of the sea conventions of 1958 and 1982. The objectives of the Convention are set out in Art. 1 wherein each State Party is

[129] [1956] 1 YBILC at 72.
[130] [1955] ICJ Rep. 4.
[131] See M.S. McDougal, W.T. Burke and I.A. Vlasic, 'The Maintenance of Public Order at Sea and the Nationality of Ships' (1960) 54 *AJIL* 25–116, for more on this issue.
[132] Nordquist (n 66), 106.

exhorted to apply the Convention's provisions with the aim of 'strengthening the genuine link between a State and ships flying its flag and ... to exercise effectively its jurisdiction and control over such ships with regard to identification and accountability of ship owners and operators as well as with regard to administrative, technical, economic and social matters.' In furtherance of these aims, flag States are to have effective national maritime administrations and must implement international measures and ensure that ships flying their flag carry documents necessary for the identification and accountability of ships.[133] Provision is also made with respect to the ownership and manning of vessels (Art. 8 and 9) and to the corporate ownership of vessels (Art. 10). However, the Convention has not yet come into force and it is unlikely to do so.[134] Even if it does, it is unlikely that the provisions on corporate ownership of vessels will be effective in addressing the complex methods which are used today to hide the beneficial ownership of vessels.[135] To this end, 'many of the complex financial structures developed to allow individuals to hold assets anonymously for perfectly legitimate reasons are also capable of being used to hide the involvement of a terrorist organisation in the ownership or control of a vessel.'[136]

Ultimately, there does not appear to be one single criterion which gives substance to the genuine link, and establishing these requirements seems to be for the discretion of the flag State. The ILC in its Commentary had discussed the possibility of incorporating more definite limits regarding the link between the State of registration and its vessels. It however concluded that existing State practice was too divergent to be governed by a few criteria.[137]

5.4.1.3.b. *Consequences of a Lack of a Genuine Link*

It is recognized that 'the ability of a flag State to effectively exercise its responsibilities appeared to be contingent upon a sufficiently strong link between the flag State and the ships flying its flag.'[138] In other words, without a genuine link the effective exercise of jurisdiction by the flag State over vessels flying its flag is, at best, dubious. In the absence of a genuine link, a State may feel justified

[133] Art. 5.

[134] See Art. 19(1). To date, there are 14 signatories and 11 parties to the Convention.

[135] See LEG 84/13/3, Annex, 'Maritime Security—The Prevention of Terrorism and Lifting of the Corporate Veil', submitted by the UK; OECD, 'Behind the Corporate Veil. Using Corporate Entities for Illicit Purposes' (Paris, OECD, 2001); OECD, Maritime Transport Committee, 'Ownership and Control of Ships' (March 2003).

[136] LEG 84/13/3, Annex, para. 13. See also MSC 75/17/26 (12 April 2002).

[137] Report of the ILC covering the work of its Eighth Session (A/3159), Art. 29 *Commentary*, para. (3), [1956] II YB ILC 279 *et seq.*

[138] UNGA 'Note by the Secretary-General' (17 July 2006) UN Doc A/61/160, Report of the Ad Hoc Consultative Meeting on senior representatives of international organizations on the "genuine link", paras 10–11.

in disregarding the status of the flag State and exercising jurisdiction itself. The possibility of non-recognition owing to a lack of a genuine link was suggested by Advocate General Mischo in *ex p Factortame*[139]and was central to Guinea's defence in the *M/V Saiga* case.[140] This is, however, not the accepted position today. In this respect, the IMO Council, in commenting on the Report of the Ad Hoc Consultative Meeting of senior representatives of international organizations on the genuine link during its 96th Session (19–23 June 2006) noted that 'sanctions consisting of suspension of registration and the use of the flag, which was one possibility mooted by the Meeting,[141] could be counterproductive and lead to the unwanted consequences of re-registration with countries not properly fulfilling the "genuine link" requirements regulated by the United Nations Convention on the Law of the Sea.'[142]

An early draft of the provision calling for a genuine link stated that 'for purposes of recognition of the national character of the ship by other States, there must exist a genuine link between the State and the ship'.[143] The removal of this phrase could arguably be interpreted as disallowing the possibility of denying recognition to vessels without a genuine link to their flag State. However, if no consequences followed a lack of a genuine link, such requirement would be redundant. In this regard, it has been indicated that through the basic maxim of treaty interpretation provisions are to be interpreted so as to be effective and have meaning and purpose, some consequences must necessarily follow from the lack of a genuine link.[144]

The International Labour Organization (ILO) put forward a related opinion in its Examination and Clarification of the role of the "genuine link" in relation to the duty of flag States to exercise effective control over ships flying their flags, including fishing vessels.[145] Its argument was based on Art. 228 LOSC wherein the flag State, within the context of marine pollution by its vessels outside the

---

139 Case C-221/89, *R v. Secretary of State for Transport ex p. Factortame* [1991] ECR I-3905.

140 *M/V 'Saiga' (No. 2) (St. Vincent and the Grenadines v Guinea) Judgment* [1999] ITLOS Reports 10 (1 July 1999).

141 See Report of the Ad Hoc Consultative Meeting, UN Doc A/61/160 (17 July 1006), para. 45. This recommended that '[a]side from penalties of a financial nature, sanctions should include suspension from registration and the use of flag, and in cases of persistent violations, deletion from the flag State's registry.'

142 UNGA 'Note by the Secretary-General' (17 July 2006) UN Doc A/61/160, Annex: Letter dated 23 June 2006 from the Secretary-General of the International Maritime Organization addressed to the Secretary-General, 2–54.

143 ILC Report to the General Assembly covering the work of its Eighth Session, UN Doc A/3159, 1956 in [1956] II ILC Yearbook, final draft Art. 29 at 260–261.

144 *Ibid.*, referring to I. Sinclair, *The Vienna Convention on the Law of Treaties* (2nd edn, Manchester University Press, Manchester, 1984), 121.

145 UNGA A/61/160 (17 July 2006) Appendix 1.

territorial sea of another State, may lose its claim to jurisdictional primacy over its vessels in cases where it has 'repeatedly disregarded its obligations to enforce effectively the international rules and standards in respect of violations committed by its vessels.' The ILO argued that the legal system could potentially be developed in such a way as to lead to the flag State losing 'its right to be considered the "flag State" with respect to the right of primary control over the ship, in matters other than marine pollution'. This falls short of the 'extreme response of non-recognition of its flag by other States.'[146]

5.5. *SAR Zones*

Although not mentioned in the LOSC, no analysis of zonal jurisdiction would be complete without mention of the so-called 'SAR zone' and the responsibilities of States within such zone. Following the adoption of the SAR Convention, the IMO divided the world's oceans into 13 areas in each of which the countries concerned have delimited search and rescue regions.[147]

A SAR region is defined in the Annex to the Convention as an 'area of defined dimensions associated with a rescue co-ordination centre within which search and rescue services are provided.'[148] This area defines which State has primary responsibility for coordinating rescue operations in response to a distress situation. Each region has an associated Rescue Coordination Centre (RCC) which is defined as 'a unit responsible for promoting efficient organisation of search and rescue services and for co-ordinating the conduct of search and rescue operations within a search and rescue region.'[149] The SAR Convention provides, in paragraph 3.1.6.4 of its Annex, that it is the States' responsibility to cooperate with other RCCs to identify the most appropriate place(s) for disembarkation of persons found in distress at sea.

A fundamental duty of States Parties to the Convention is that of cooperation in the conduct of search and rescue operations. Chapter 3 of the Annex states that '[p]arties shall co-ordinate their search and rescue organizations and should, whenever necessary, co-ordinate search and rescue operations with those of neighbouring States.'[150] They are also required, unless otherwise agreed, to authorize 'immediate entry into or over its territorial sea or territory

[146] *Ibid.*, paras 28–29.

[147] Map available at www.oceansatlas.com/unatlas/issues/emergencies/gmdss_sar/SARMAP.PDF.

[148] Chapter 1, para. 1.3.4.

[149] Chapter 1, para. 1.3.5.

[150] Para. 3.1.1.

of rescue units of other Parties solely for the purpose of searching for the position of maritime casualties and rescuing survivors of such casualties.'[151] This last-mentioned obligation is of significance also in that it implies that there is no automatic right to enter the territorial sea of another State in the context of a search and rescue operation. While the coastal State must authorize such entry, as stated above, a request must be made beforehand.[152] Very significantly, a new amendment to the SAR Convention provides for the duty of cooperation and coordination among States in releasing the Master of a rescuing vessel from his obligations to assist survivors from assisting ships and to deliver them to a place of safety.[153]

In addition, other international conventions define the obligations of States Parties to ensure coordination in rescue operations. Art. 98(2) LOSC, under Part VII of the Convention which deals with the high seas, obliges every coastal State Party to:

> [P]romote the establishment, operation and maintenance of an adequate and effective search and rescue service regarding safety on and over the sea, and, where circumstances so require, by way of mutual regional arrangements co-operate with neighbouring States for this purpose.

Furthermore, SOLAS Chapter V, Regulation 7.1 requires that States Parties:

> [E]nsure that necessary arrangements are made for distress communication and co-ordination in their area of responsibility and for the rescue of persons in distress at sea around its coasts. These arrangements shall include the establishment, operation and maintenance of such search and rescue facilities as are deemed practicable and necessary ... and shall, so far as possible, provide adequate means of locating and rescuing such persons.

There is also an obligation, imposed by Chapter 2.1.1 of the Annex to the SAR Convention that, on receiving information that a person is in distress at sea in an area within which a Party provides for the overall coordination of search and rescue operations, the responsible authorities of that Party are to take urgent steps to provide the most appropriate assistance available. The Guidelines on the Treatment of Persons Rescued at Sea[154] note that the intent of the recently amended paragraph 1.1 of SOLAS Chapter V, Regulation 33

---

[151] Para. 3.1.2.

[152] One can surmise, however, that should no coastal State response be forthcoming and the circumstances be of an urgent nature, then the vessels conducting the search and rescue mission could enter the territorial seas nonetheless, on the understanding that consent *ex post facto* will be attained.

[153] Para. 3.1.9. Newly amended SOLAS Chapter V/33.1.1 imposes the same obligation on Contracting Governments, further discussed in Chapter 7.

[154] Res MSC 167(78), adopted in May 2004 by the MSC, together with the SAR and SOLAS amendments.

and paragraph 3.1.9 of the Annex to the SAR Convention[155] is that in every case a place of safety is to be provided within a reasonable time. To this end, paragraph 2.5 of the Guidelines states that 'the responsibility to provide a place of safety, or to ensure that a place of safety is provided, falls on the Government responsible for the SAR region in which the survivors were recovered.'

Malta has a vast SAR area, spanning more than 250,000 square kilometres, an area linked to its flight information region. This has a direct impact on its international obligations regarding search and rescue, as will be discussed in the following chapters.

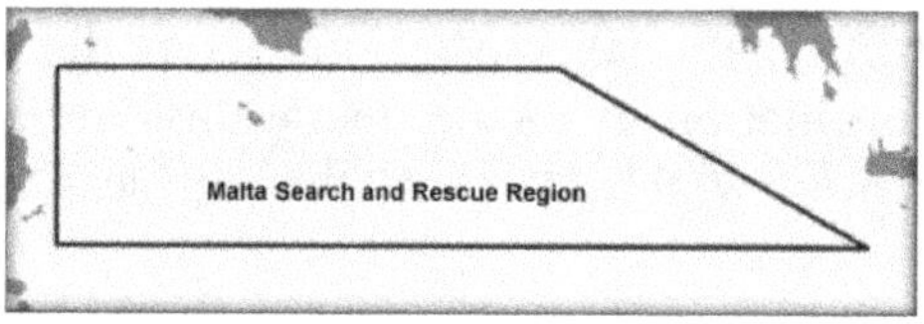

Taken from 'Search and Rescue Malta'.
www.sarmalta.gov.mt/sar_in_Malta.htm

[155] Discussed in Chapter 6.

Chapter Six

Humanitarian Obligations

6.1. *Preliminary Clarifications and Parameters of Discussion*

This section will attempt to analyse the acts of interception, search, rescue and disembarkation in relation to migrant smuggling in the context of humanitarian obligations incumbent upon States. The section on humanitarian considerations is especially significant because it is this aspect which makes migrant smuggling crucially different from an international law point of view from other maritime security threats.

An initial distinction must be made between the *act of rescue* and the *subsequent processing of any asylum claims*.[1] Both involve the granting of humanitarian assistance, but the latter falls outside the parameters of the present discussion.[2] The act of rescuing a vessel in distress is an international duty, and involves the granting of humanitarian assistance. The act of processing and hearing claims for asylum and the granting of refugee status in the case of a successful claim is a separate act of humanitarian assistance which follows interception or rescue, but which is quite distinct from this.[3] I make this point due

1 This distinction was also highlighted in the IMO forum. See, e.g., MSC 75/11/2 (11 March 2002), para. 7.

2 It is to be noted, however, that the rescuing ship's flag State can be subjected to certain obligations should asylum-seekers be among those rescued. In this regard, the UNHCR maintains that State responsibility under the Refugee Convention is activated once it is clear that there are asylum-seekers among those rescued. In such case, the State is to ensure admission, at least on a temporary basis, in order to process and verify these claims: see 'Background Note on the Protection of Asylum Seekers and Refugees Rescued at Sea' (18 March 2002), para. 18 (final version as discussed at the expert roundtable *Rescue-at-Sea: Specific Aspects Relating to the Protection of Asylum-Seekers and Refugees*, held in Lisbon, Portugal on 25–26 March 2002).

3 Note: that the definition of asylum-seeker is historically closely related to UNHCR ExCom Conclusion No. 22 (XXXII)—1981, endorsed by UNGA Res 36/125. The term can refer either to an individual whose refugee status has not yet been determined by the authorities but whose claim to asylum entitles him or her to a certain protective status on the basis that he or she could be a refugee, or to large-scale influxes of mixed groups in a situation where individual determination of refugee status is impractical.

to the mistaken tendency to link the mode of arrival to the granting of refugee protection. These two humanitarian aspects cannot be merged. The right to protection cannot be connected to the mode of arrival, but must be based on the reasons for flight. What is being considered here is the mode of arrival by sea coordinated by migrant smugglers: an act which is both a crime and a threat to maritime security. The only area in which attention will be given to potential refugee status is in considering the doctrine of *non-refoulement* and how it impacts upon actions taken by States under the current international legal framework.

International law has had to cater for diverse, often conflicting, interests when framing responses to the threat of migrant smuggling. Once again, the thorny issues of State sovereignty and human rights come to the fore. The key issue in this tension is that of disembarkation: while international law indicates that asylum claims should normally be heard on land, thereby indicating the necessity of disembarkation,[4] State sovereignty interests call for restraint in opening a State's doors to aliens. This leads to complex problems such as 'refugees in orbit' where the rescuing vessel may sail for days, looking for a State port which will allow it entry.[5] Apart from the *Tampa* incident, one can also refer to the case of the *Cap Anamur* which on 20 June 2004 rescued 37 migrants in international waters between the Libyan coast and Lampedusa. It then sailed for weeks without finding a State which would allow disembarkation.[6] Finally, after the Captain reported that the passengers were threatening to throw themselves overboard, permission was given to land in Italy. The ship consequently docked in Agrigento, Sicily, on 12 July 2004. The rescuees were disembarked, issued with expulsion orders and detained in Agrigento's detention centre. Their claims were processed, the crew was ordered to leave the vessel and the three Europeans in charge of the vessel were arrested immediately on disembarkation on the charge of promoting illegal immigration. Their release was ordered on 16 July 2006 and trial began on 27 November 2006 in Agrigento.[7] Similarly, on 16 July 2006, a Spanish trawler, *Francesco y Catalina*, rescued a boatful of migrants, mostly Eritreans, which

4 See, e.g., 'Global Consultations on International Protection, Rescue-at-Sea: Specific Aspects Relating to the Protection of Asylum-Seekers and Refugees', Expert Roundtable, Lisbon 25–26 March 2002, Summary of Discussions, pt. 14: determination of character or status should normally be effected on dry land.

5 See UNGA A/RES/36/125 (14 December 1981) which *inter alia* draws attention to the problem of refugees rescued at sea and the difficulties encountered in their disembarkation, involving threats of *refoulement*.

6 See MSC 79/22/6 (15 September 2004), para. 14.

7 At the time of writing, the trial was proceeding at a very slow pace.

had set sail from Libyan shores. The boat was rescued in Libya's SAR area, 100 miles south of Malta; after the rescue, the vessel proceeded to a point 18 miles from Maltese shores. Malta refused permission to enter port as the vessel was not in imminent danger and had been rescued a long way outside Malta's SAR area.[8] It was only six days after the rescue that Spain, as the flag State, agreed to allow entry. The 2007 *Report of the Secretary-General on Oceans and the Law of the Sea* also reports the February 2007 case of the *Marine I*, located off the West African coast and carrying about 400 people, the individuals on which were not permitted to disembark for several days.[9] This difficulty in finding a place for disembarkation leads to a general reticence among ship Masters to aid vessels in distress, a fact of grave concern to international bodies.[10]

The international legal regime recognizes and accepts the need for States to control their borders and, indeed, calls for cooperative efforts to combat migrant smuggling by sea.[11] At the same time, it provides ample illustration of the dilemma brought on by the issues of sovereignty and human rights. A number of resolutions and conference conclusions reaffirm respect for the sovereignty and territorial integrity of all States, including their right to control their borders, while at the same time calling upon States to cooperate in the interest of the safety of life at sea, to increase their efforts to prevent the smuggling of aliens on ships[12] and to ensure, in accordance with their national

---

8 Malta's understanding is that a border State unduly burdened by a sudden influx of immigrants rescued by EU vessels in areas falling under the responsibility of non-Member States of the EU should be able to share this burden with other Member States. See T. Borg, Deputy Prime Minister of Malta, 'Address by the Deputy Prime Minister Tonio Borg at the JHA Council in Luxembourg' (Press Release) (12 June 2007).

9 UNGA A/62/66/Add.1 (31 August 2007), para. 90, also referring to UNHCR, 'UNHCR urges disembarkation for people on boat in West Africa' (Press Release) (8 February 2007).

10 See UNHCR, 'Report on the Meeting of the Working Group of Government Representatives on the Question of Rescue of Asylum-Seekers at Sea', Geneva (5–7 July 1982) EC/SCP/21. See also UNHCR ExCom Conclusions: No. 26 (XXXIII)—1982; No. 31 (XXXIV)—1983; No. 34 (XXXV)—1984; No. 38 (XXXVI)—1985.

11 It is interesting that specific references to 'migrant smuggling' are relatively recent, as early references were only to 'trafficking'. The first time the smuggling of aliens was referred to by the UNGA was in Resolution 48/102 of 20 December 1993.

12 Various resolutions of the UN General Assembly emphasize the need to protect the rights of migrants, while encouraging States to 'enact domestic criminal legislation to combat international trafficking of migrants, which should take into account, in particular, trafficking that endangers the lives of migrants or includes different forms of servitude or exploitation, such as any form of debt bondage, sexual or labour exploitation, and to strengthen international cooperation to combat such trafficking': see UNGA A/RES/54/166 (24 February 2000), para. 7. This is reiterated in subsequent resolutions such as: UNGA A/RES/55/92 (26 February 2001), para. 9; UNGA A/RES/56/170 (28 February 2002), para. 10; UNGA A/RES/57/218 (4 December 2002), para. 12; UNGA A/RES/58/190 (22 March 2004), para. 13; UNGA A/RES/60/169 (7 March 2006), para. 22.

legislation, that prompt and effective action is taken against maritime migrant smuggling.[13] Issues recognized by the IMO as being at stake are:

> [T]he need of States to respect and ensure respect for the rights and dignity of the persons rescued at sea regardless of their status; their legitimate interest to maintain effective border and immigration controls and to prevent and combat transnational organized crimes such as the smuggling of migrants and trafficking in human beings; the need to meet the immediate humanitarian requirements of rescued persons and stowaways and to ensure that those who seek asylum are protected from immediate danger and are granted prompt access to fair and efficient status determination procedures in full compliance with respect to the principle of *non refoulement*; and the need to maintain security and stability in international shipping.[14]

International cooperation is fundamental. This is made all the clearer when one considers the transboundary nature of the crime.[15] International cooperation thus depends upon certain general responsibilities being accepted by all actors concerned, primarily, coastal States and flag States.[16] As far as flag States are concerned, a major cause for concern in the international arena is the lack of control exercised by flag States in this—and other—fields:

> At the root of far too many of these problems is the unwillingness or lack of capacity of certain States, especially flag States, to fulfil their international legal obligations. It is essential to reinforce the control of flag States over their vessels.[17]

6.2. *The Impact of the* Non-refoulement *Obligation*

The Refugee Convention provides protection for any person having the status of a refugee or seeking to attain that status; in other words, refugees and asylum-seekers. The instrument is clearly humanitarian in character, the core principle of which is *non-refoulement*, set out in Art. 33(1) and relating to the prohibition of expulsion or return ('*refouler*') of a refugee (or asylum-

---

13 UNGA A/RES/51/62 (12 December 1996).

14 Contribution of the IMO to the Secretary-General's Report on Oceans and the Law of the Sea (A/RES/57/141); Report—Record of Decisions on the United Nations Inter-Agency Meeting on the Treatment of Persons Rescued at Sea (Geneva 2 and 3 July 2002). See also UNHCR, 'Regional Workshops in Ottawa, Ontario (Canada) and in Macau—Incorporating Refugee Protection Safeguards into Interception Measures' Ottawa, Ontario, Canada (14–15 May 2001) EC/GC/01/13, paras 2 and 3.

15 UNGA A/RES/48/102 (20 December 1993).

16 Global Consultations (n 4), point 13.

17 UNGA A/58/65 (3 March 2003), para. 249; also mentioned in Human Rights Watch, 'Statement to the United Nations Open-Ended Informal Consultative Process on Oceans and the Law of the Sea' (2 June 2003).

seeker)[18] 'in any manner whatsoever to the frontiers of territories where his life or freedom would be threatened on account of his race, religion, nationality, membership of a particular social group or political opinion'. This duty may be stated to be an obligation imposed on *any* State—irrespective of ratification of the Refugee Convention—by reason of its customary international law status.[19] The UNHCR Executive Committee (ExCom) has even gone as far as to state that the principle is progressively acquiring the status of a peremptory norm of international law.[20]

The Refugee Convention was however devised in the post-World War Two period and focuses mainly on the effects of Nazi war-time persecutions. It presupposes a refugee problem based solely on the grounds stipulated in Art. 1; that is, applying to an individual who 'owing to well-founded fear of being persecuted for reasons of race, religion, nationality, membership of a particular social group or political opinion, is outside the country of his nationality and is unable, or owing to such fear, is unwilling to avail himself of the protection of that country; or who, not having a nationality and being outside the country of his former habitual residence as a result of such events, is unable or, owing to such fear, is unwilling to return to it.'[21] Since the 1980s, movements of persons have been more likely to be the result of natural disasters and famine, and other dire social conditions. Although the plight of such people is obvious, it

[18] This guarantee of protection does not refer solely to 'declared' refugees. Art. 1A (2) of the Refugee Convention as amended by Art. I(2) of the 1967 Protocol defines a refugee, significantly omitting any reference to formal recognition of refugees. In this way, *non-refoulement* obligations fall upon a State once an asylum claim is made, irrespective of whether or not the person seeking asylum has been declared a refugee. See in this regard UNHCR, *Handbook on Procedures and Criteria for Determining Refugee Status under the 1951 Convention and 1967 Protocol relating to the Status of Refugees* HCR/IP/4/Eng/REV.1 (UNHCR 1979; re-edited, Geneva, January 1992), para. 28; ExCom Conclusions: No. 6 (XXVIII)—1977, para. (c); No. 79 (XLVII)—1996, para. (j); No. 81 (XLVIII)—1997, para. (j); UNGA Resolutions: UNGA, A/RES/52/103 (9 February 1998), para. 5; UNGA A/RES/53/125 (12 February 1999), para. 5; UNGA A/RES/55/74 (12 February 2001), paras 6, 10; G. Gilbert, 'Is Europe living up to its Obligations to Refugees?' (2004) 15 *EJIL*, 966.

[19] The customary international law status of the *non-refoulement* principle is however denied by a minority of commentators. In this regard see J. Bedlington, 'The Hows and the Whys of Interception—A State Perspective', presented at the 5th IARLJ Conference 'Stemming the Tide of Keeping the Balance—the Role of the Judiciary' (Wellington, New Zealand, 2002); G. Goodwin-Gill and J. McAdam, *The Refugee in International Law* (3rd edn, OUP, Oxford, 2007), 345–354; J.C. Hathaway, *The Rights of Refugees under International Law* (Cambridge University Press, Cambridge, 2005), 363–365.

[20] Conclusion No. 25 (XXXIII)—1982, para. (b).

[21] Due to further refugee situations arising since the conclusion of the Convention, the 1967 Protocol provided that protection was to be given to all refugees without any time (the Convention imposed an original date restriction of 1 January 1951) or geographical limitation. See 1967 Protocol, Art. 1(2)(3).

is doubtful whether they can demonstrate the well-founded fear of persecution required for the application of the Convention. Furthermore, the Convention does not provide an answer for problems arising from situations of mass influx (such as boat arrivals), focussing as it does on individually-targeted persecutions by an oppressive regime. The effect of this is that the tools available to protect individuals have been overtaken by events: new classes of individuals requiring protection (e.g. stateless individuals, internally displaced persons, persons fleeing from natural disasters) have been added to the traditional definition of 'refugee'.[22] This is not to mention the economic and other irregular migrants who abuse the current system of protection by entering a State on the pretext of seeking asylum. States are bound by principles and procedures established by an instrument which was created in a completely different international environment:

> States face considerable challenges as they try and reconcile their obligations under the Convention with problems raised by the mixed nature of migratory movements, misuse of the asylum system, increasing costs, the growth in smuggling and trafficking of people, and the struggle to manifest international solidarity to resolve the refugee situation.[23]

It is useful to look at the ramifications of the *non-refoulement* obligation when considering that a number of interception measures do actually result in individuals being turned back, away from their intended destination and, potentially, towards the State of departure or a third State which could send them back to the original frontiers of persecution. Therefore, measures to repress migrant smuggling are to be implemented with due regard to the international legal framework and a State's international obligations.[24] There is concern that '[i]mmigration control measures do not necessarily distinguish between asylum-seekers and refugees and other intercepted persons. In the absence of adequate safeguards, this may result in persons in need of international protection being turned back, sometimes to situations of danger.'[25]

---

22 See generally UNHCR, 'Note on International Protection' (7 September 1994) A/AC.96/830.

23 UNHCR, 'Note on International Protection' (3 July 1998) A/AC.96/898, para. 1.

24 UNHCR ExCom Conclusion No. 97 (LIV)—2003, para. 19; UNHCR ExCom Conclusion No. 89 (LI)—2000, Preambular para. (A/AC.96/944 para. 23); UNHCR, 'Refugee Protection and Migration Control: Perspectives from UNHCR and IOM' Global Consultations on International Protection (31 May 2001) EC/GC/01/11, para. 14; UNHCR, 'Interception of Asylum-Seekers and Refugees: The International Framework and Recommendations for a Comprehensive Approach' (9 June 2000) EC/50/SC/CRP.17, para. 17.

25 UNHCR, Regional Workshops in Ottawa and Macau (n 14), para. 3. See also UNHCR, 'Interception of Asylum-Seekers and Refugees' EC/50/SC/CRP.17 (n 24), para. 17.

6.2.1. *Geographic Operation of the Principle*

Most State actions have turned upon an interpretation of the scope of operation of the *non-refoulement* principle.[26] This obligation clearly comes into play when the asylum-seeker is in a State's territory, as it does at the State's borders. Having said this, the issue of non-rejection at the frontiers was not always generally accepted. Unanimity did not exist in 1951 as to whether the principle applied in cases where the refugee presented himself for entry at a State's borders as opposed to cases where the refugee had already entered the State's territory.[27] However, since then, State practice has contributed to the further development of the law, and today various Conclusions of the UNHCR ExCom also express the view that the principle applies 'both at the border and within the territory of a State'.[28] This is also held to be the case in situations of mass influx,[29] with stowaways[30] and, of most direct relevance, in the case of boat arrivals.[31] There is no doubt, therefore, that a State is bound by the obligation not to *refoule* an asylum-seeker once on the territory of that State or at its borders.[32] This would also seem to be true as far as the territorial sea is concerned since the general understanding is that a State's territory extends beyond the land mass to encompass the territorial sea. However, the point has been made that the physical territory of a State need not necessarily correlate with the definition of 'territory' for immigration law purposes. For example, the US Immigration and Nationality Act 1952 (INA) draws a distinction between 'entry' and 'admission' in order to restrict access to unauthorized migrants, so that 'entry into the territory—the material act of crossing of the geographical border and physically being present within the jurisdiction of the United States,

26 A. Brouwer and J. Kumin, 'Interception and Asylum: When Migration Control and Human Rights Collide' (2003) 21 *Refuge*, 13.

27 In fact, several European nations, including Switzerland, Belgium and the Netherlands, advocated a restrictive approach at the 1951 Conference. See Goodwin-Gill et al. (n 19), 206–208; A. Grahl-Madsen, *Commentary on the Refugee Convention 1951, Articles 2–11, 13–37* (reprinted by UNHCR, Geneva, 1997). See also 'Summary Record of the Sixteenth Meeting' Conference of Plenipotentiaries on the Status of Refugees and Stateless Persons (11 July 1951) UN Doc A/CONF.2/SR.16, at 6.

28 UNHCR ExCom Conclusion No. 6 (XXVIII)—1977, para. (c); UNHCR, 'Interception of Asylum-Seekers and Refugees' EC/50/SC/CRP.17 (n 24), para. 21.

29 UNHCR ExCom Conclusion No. 22 (XXXII)—1981.

30 UNHCR ExCom Conclusion No. 53 (XXXIX)—1988.

31 UNHCR ExCom Conclusion No. 15 (XXX)—1979.

32 In this regard Goodwin-Gill et al. (n 19), 208 cite *R (European Roma Rights Centre and others) v Immigration Officer at Prague Airport (UNHCR Intervening)* [2005] 2 AC 1, [2004] UKHL 55, para. 26 (Lord Bingham).

does *not* equate with gaining immigration-related procedural protections that would apply to those who have been admitted'.[33]

There are apparent *lacunae* in both the law of the sea and refugee law, as far as a State's powers and obligations within the territorial sea are concerned. Indeed, Goodwin-Gill states that 'neither branch of law resolves the question of whether entering a State's territorial waters constitutes entry to State territory'.[34] However, it is submitted, that while this observation is true as far as entry for the purposes of immigration law is concerned, there cannot be any argument to defend the failure to process any asylum claims made by people on the vessel while it is in the territorial waters of a State. In other words, while under the law of the sea regime a State may turn back vessels at the borders of its territorial sea and also order a vessel to leave the territorial sea in furtherance of its powers under Art. 25 LOSC, once a claim for asylum is made within the territorial sea, the coastal State is obliged to arrange for the processing of such claim in order to ensure that it does not violate the *non-refoulement* obligation.

Notwithstanding this, various States have employed measures whereby, through a legal fiction, this maritime belt is not considered to be State territory for asylum-seeking purposes.[35] As far as a denial to consider asylum claims made in the territorial sea is concerned, Australia has proved to be the archetypical example. It is arguable that the Australian definition of the 'Migration Zone',[36] together with excision of some of its offshore territories from that zone, constitutes a breach of the right to seek asylum. There is however an argument that such actions are licit under the 1951 Convention: the text of the Convention does not determine what constitutes entry into a Contracting State for the purpose of claiming its benefits, and Art. 33 (encapsulating the *non-refoulement* obligation) is clearly premised upon entry into the territory of a State Party, apart from the return to a threatening frontier.[37]

It is submitted that such legal fictions employed by States in a bid to avoid formal acknowledgement of the arrival of asylum-seekers constitute a breach of Art. 33. There is thus no international legal difference between opting not to consider the refugee status of people present in excised territories and refusing to consider the refugee status of persons clearly acknowledged to be on

---

33 A. Shachar, 'The Shifting Border of Immigration Regulation' (2007) 3 *Stanford Journal of Civil Rights and Civil Liberties* 165, 171.

34 *Ibid.*, at 279. See also Goodwin-Gill et al. (n 19), at 273–274.

35 See Chapter 8 regarding Australian legislation in relation to the *Tampa* case.

36 The 'migration zone' is the area in which valid applications for an Australian visa may be made. It is defined in s. 5 of the Migration Act 1958 and refers to the physical territory and proclaimed ports.

37 R. Piotrowicz and S. Blay, 'The Case of the MV *Tampa*: State and Refugee Rights Collide at Sea' (2002) 76 *Aust LJ*, 15.

the State's territory.[38] Furthermore, the prohibition of the return 'in any manner whatsoever' of persons to places where they may face persecution means that the obligation applies to State action '*wherever* it takes place, whether internally, at the border, or through its agents outside territorial jurisdiction.'[39]

In defence of its excision policy, the Australian Government has stated that the Refugee Convention still applies in excised areas. The only difference is that non-citizens applying for recognition as refugees in these areas will not be able to apply for Australian visas, necessary in order legally to enter and remain in Australia; however, they are still guaranteed access to asylum determination processes to ensure that any protection needs are identified and addressed as they can make visa applications of a specified class.[40] Furthermore, Australian legislation permits asylum-seekers intercepted at sea to be taken to declared countries:[41] section 245F(9) of the *Migration Act* provides that where a ship has been detained under that section, those on board the ship may be taken to a place 'outside Australia'. Still, while processing will take place here, there is no guarantee under Australian domestic legislation that such 'declared countries' must be States Parties to the Refugee Convention and, thus, *refoulement* is a real possibility.[42]

The most logical conclusion regarding the application of the principle, it is submitted, is that entry into the territorial sea in any situation will have brought

---

38 See Hathaway (n 19), at 321 *et seq*, also citing *Amuur v France* [1996] ECHR 25 (ECHR, 25 June 1996), at para. 52, regarding the designation by France of part of its territory as an 'international zone' in which it exercised authority but assumed no protection responsibility.

39 G. Goodwin-Gill et al. (n 19), at 248; P. Mathew, 'Legal Issues concerning Interception', IARLJ Conference 2002, 95; see http://www.upf.pf/IMG/pdf/06_Mathew.pdf.

40 For information on the Australian visa system see J. Vrachnas et al., *Migration and Refugee Law—Principles and Practices in Australia* (Cambridge University Press, Cambridge, 2005), Chapter 4, and DIAC Factsheets: 64, 'Temporary Protection Visa' (27 June 2007); 64a, 'New Measures for Temporary Protection and Temporary Humanitarian Visa Holders' (30 January 2007); 64b, 'Reintegration Package for Temporary Protection, Temporary Humanitarian and Return Pending Visa Holders' (30 January 2007); 64c, 'Return Pending Visa' (30 January 2007); 64d, 'New Onshore Visa Options for Temporary Protection and Temporary Humanitarian Visa Holders' (10 September 2007); 65, 'New Humanitarian Visa System' (30 January 2007); 70, 'Border Control' (30 January 2007).

41 A 'declared country' is one specified in writing by the Minister and provides people seeking asylum with access to effective procedures for assessing their claims. See s.198A Migration Act 1958.

42 Regarding the prohibition of 'chain *refoulement*' (i.e. causing a person to return to another place from which *refoulement* occurs) see Mathew (n 39), at 95. See also E. Lauterpacht and D. Bethlehem, 'The Scope and Content of the Principle of *Non refoulement*' in E. Feller et al. (eds) *Refugee Protection in International Law: UNHCR's Global Consultations on International Protection* (Cambridge University Press, Cambridge, 2003), para. 83.

the vessel within the territorial jurisdiction of the coastal State and, thus, the *non-refoulement* principle is activated if any asylum claims are made once the vessel is within the territorial sea, even if the coastal State has not exercised any form of jurisdiction or control over that vessel.

6.2.1.1. *Extraterritorial Application?*

The Refugee Convention's *travaux préparatoires* are not specific about the geographical operation of the principle. There is an argument for the conclusion that Art. 33(1) was not intended by the original drafters to apply extraterritorially and that Art. 33 'may only be invoked in respect of persons who are already present—lawfully or unlawfully—in the territory of the Contracting State'.[43] However, the UNHCR suggests[44] that the physical act of interception by a State engages that State's protection obligations in respect of those intercepted, irrespective of the location of that interception.[45] Therefore, the exercise of State action is the determining factor in whether or not the *non-refoulement* obligation is triggered in extraterritorial areas.

In the context of *non-refoulement*, Art. 33(1) therefore applies 'whenever a State acts', a term which includes territorial and extraterritorial waters.[46] Indeed, the obligation applies to the conduct of State officials or those acting on behalf of the State wherever such conduct occurs.[47] As mentioned above, the obligation applies within the areas of a State's territorial jurisdiction, even without any exercise of jurisdiction on the part of the coastal State. When jurisdiction is exercised in extraterritorial areas, the *non-refoulement* obligation applies nonetheless, extending therefore to interceptions taking place prior to arrival at port:

> The principle of *non refoulement* does not imply any geographical limitation. In UNHCR's understanding, the resulting obligations extend to all government agents acting in an official capacity, within or outside their national territory.

43 A. Grahl-Madsen, *The Status of Refugees in International Law* (A.W. Sijthoff, Leiden, 1972), vol. 2, 94.

44 While the UNHCR has a supervisory role under Art. 35 of the Refugee Convention, its pronouncements are not binding. Having said this, the Conclusions on the International Protection of Refugees adopted by the Executive Committee of the High Commissioner's Program 'have strong political authority as consensus resolutions of a formal body of government representatives'. See Hathaway (n 19), at 113, see further at 112–118.

45 UNHCR, 'Interception of Asylum-Seekers and Refugees' EC/50/SC/CRP.17 (n 24), para. 4.

46 UNHCR, Brief of the Office of the United Nations High Commissioner for Refugee as *Amicus Curiae* in Support of Respondents in *McNary v Haitian Centres Council*, 509 US 155 (1993), (Case no. 92–344) 18 reprinted in (1994) 6 *IJRL* 85. See also Art. 3(1) of the Declaration on Territorial Asylum (1967).

47 Lauterpacht and Bethlehem (n 42), para. 67.

> Given the practice of States to intercept persons at great distance from their own territory, the international refugee protection regime would be rendered ineffective if States' agents abroad were free to act at variance with obligations under international refugee law and human rights law.[48]

6.2.2. *Actions which do not amount to* refoulement

It has been stated that the simple denial of entry of ships to territorial waters cannot be equated with a breach of the *non-refoulement* principle as this requires that State action result in the return of refugees to territories where they face persecution. In this way, Goodwin-Gill says, mere denial of entry to internal or territorial waters is to be distinguished from programmes of interdiction of boats which are accompanied by the actual physical return of passengers to their country of origin where such passengers face persecution.[49] To support this, he cites the observations of the *Ad Hoc Committee* on the draft Refugee Convention:

> [T]he obligation not to return a refugee to a country where he was persecuted did not imply an obligation to admit him to the country where he seeks refuge. The return of a refugee-ship, for example, to the high seas could not be construed as a violation of this obligation.[50]

It is also arguable that as long as the interdicting State ensures that *non-refoulement* is respected, sending asylum-seekers interdicted at sea to another country (even without the consent of the asylum-seekers) is permissible under refugee law.

The *non-refoulement* principle is not without its critics. In the light of the climate in which the Refugee Convention was drafted, the principle makes sense. However, it overlooks the fact that anyone may make an asylum claim, and only after due processing can its veracity or otherwise be proven. No account is taken of the fact that the world's migrant population has significantly increased since the Convention was drafted and no provision is made for burden-sharing among States Parties.[51] Furthermore, the Convention seems to give priority to

---

48 UNHCR, 'Interception of Asylum-Seekers and Refugees' EC/50/SC/CRP.17 (n 24), para. 23; see also UNHCR, 'Note on International Protection' (13 September 2001) A/AC.96/951 para. 16.

49 Goodwin-Gill et al. (n 19), at 277; G. Goodwin-Gill, '*Non refoulement* and the new asylum-seekers' (1986) 26 *Va. J. Int'l Law* 897, 902.

50 UN Doc E/AC.32/L.32/Add.1 (10 February 1950).

51 A. Millbank, 'The Problem with the 1951 Refugee Convention' (Research Paper No. 5 2000–2001) (5 September 2000), Department of the Parliamentary Library, Australia, 12; See also Vrachnas et al. (n 40), Chapter 18.

asylum-seekers on the move—that is, to those who can afford, in some way or another, to employ the services of people smugglers, while those with perhaps the greatest need remain in refugee camps.[52]

6.2.3. *Evaluation*

In light of the above, the Refugee Convention is not tied to the exercise of State jurisdiction; rather, the obligation of *non-refoulement* is triggered wherever a State *acts*. The key, at this point, is to note that we are concerned with *effective* action. It can therefore be convincingly argued that any action which would have the effect of returning a refugee to a place of persecution would violate the *non-refoulement* obligation.

According to this understanding, should a Coast Guard vessel or any other official State vessel come upon a vessel carrying irregular migrants, merely using a loud hailer to attempt to turn it back would not qualify as action by a State capable of activating the *non-refoulement* obligation. On the other hand, forcibly turning back a ship would amount to effective action sufficient to trigger responsibility. However, although the obligation is triggered, this would not amount to *refoulement* as the action would not have the effect of returning the boat to the borders of persecution; turning a vessel back onto the high seas does not amount to *refoulement*.[53] It is quite a different story should shots be fired at the vessel when it is leaving the waters of the State where those on board face persecution; in this case, the obligations under the *non-refoulement* principle would apply and this action would indeed amount to *refoulement*, as the vessel would be forced back to those borders.

An interesting point to determine is what happens when asylum claims are made while the State is exercising effective action when attempting to turn the vessel back. The Refugee Convention does not grant the right to asylum, nor does it oblige a State to hear and process asylum applications. However, it is often necessary for a status determination procedure to be carried out in order to ascertain that no asylum-seeker will be returned to a place where he risks persecution. In this regard, it has been stated that 'where States are not prepared to grant asylum to persons who have a well-founded fear of persecution, they must adopt a course that does not lead to *refoulement*'.[54] In both interception

[52] See in this regard The Hon. Philip Ruddock, MP, 'Migration Amendment (Excision from Migration zone) (Consequential Provisions) Bill 2001' (Second Reading Speech, House of Representatives, Debates, 18 September 2001).

[53] UN Doc E/AC.32/L.32/Add.1 (10 February 1950).

[54] Lauterpacht and Bethlehem (n 42), para. 76.

measures and rescue at sea scenarios it is only a determination of status which will draw the distinction between a genuine asylum-seeker and an illegal immigrant. A State would therefore be held to be in breach of the principle of *non-refoulement* were it to intercept and turn back a vessel to the borders of persecution without reviewing any asylum claims made on board.

It is generally recommended that the status of rescued people is best determined by the appropriate authorities on land:

> In UNHCR's view, the identification and subsequent processing of asylum-seekers is an activity most appropriately carried out on dry land … Onboard processing may be appropriate in some limited instances depending on the number and conditions of the persons involved, the facilities on the vessel and its physical location. It would, however, be impractical for situations involving large numbers of people or where their physical and mental state is not conducive to immediate processing. Onboard processing is inappropriate where the rescued persons are aboard a commercial vessel. The first priority in most instances remains prompt and safe disembarkation followed by access to fair and efficient asylum procedures. An effective response to the challenge of properly identifying asylum-seekers should therefore acknowledge that the status of the rescued persons is best determined by the appropriate authorities after disembarkation.[55]

Disembarkation is therefore necessary, at least on a temporary basis, to allow access to asylum procedures. This consequently raises the question of determining the State responsible for admitting asylum-seekers, at least on a temporary basis.[56] The UNHCR Background Note, rather simplistically, states that this is usually the coastal State in the immediate vicinity of the rescue, and then goes on to consider the responsibility of the flag State in this regard, as shall be discussed below.[57]

---

55 UNHCR, 'Background Note' (n 2), paras 23–24; See further T.A. Aleinikoff and V. Chetail (eds), *Migration and International Legal Norms* (The Hague, TMC Asser Press, 2003), 143–144.

56 International refugee and maritime law suggest that this is usually the responsibility of the State in which disembarkation occurs. It is clear that the State within whose sovereign territory, or territorial waters, interception takes place has the primary responsibility for addressing any protection needs of intercepted persons (UNHCR ExCom Conclusion No. 97 (LIV)—2003). However, problems arise when States intercept vessels far from their territorial waters and close to the waters of another State as that State is then charged with the processing of such claims.

57 UNHCR, 'Background Note' (n 2), paras 25 *et seq.* It is in this light that burden-sharing arrangements appear to be an essential tool for the effective implementation of the separate but inter-linked aspect of humanitarianism mentioned at the outset of the chapter.

6.3. *Human Rights Considerations*

All persons at sea have basic human rights under general international law and also under regional instruments such as the European Convention on the Protection of Human Rights and Fundamental Freedoms (ECHR) if they are in the jurisdiction of a State Party to that instrument.[58] The humane treatment of all those rescued at sea is of utmost importance and noted in international instruments, for example, in the recently amended SOLAS Convention, where Masters of ships who have embarked people in distress at sea are to treat them with humanity.[59]

The discussion has hitherto focussed upon the *non-refoulement* obligation under the Refugee Convention. Other international instruments however also deserve mention at this point as they are directed towards the protection of fundamental rights of individuals generally. Foremost amongst these is the ECHR. Art. 1 provides that '[t]he High Contracting Parties shall secure to everyone within their jurisdiction the rights and freedoms defined in Section 1 of this Convention,' *inter alia*, the right to life, enshrined in Art. 2, and protection against torture or inhuman or degrading treatment or punishment, guaranteed in Art. 3.[60] While the level of torture or degrading or inhuman treatment in Art. 3 depends upon the circumstances of the case and must reach a 'minimum level of severity'[61] in order to qualify as such. Art. 3 contains no qualifications, exceptions or restrictions to the right guaranteed. The fundamental nature of this article is demonstrated by the recent judgment of the

58 For more on the applicable human rights standards see UNHCR, 'Reception of Asylum Seekers, Including Standards of Treatment, in the context of Individuals Asylum Systems' (4 September 2001) EC/GC/01/17.

59 Chapter 5/33.6. This is also noted in Art. 10(a) of the Operational Procedures for Boarding and Inspecting Vessels Suspected of Illicit Traffic in Narcotic Drugs and Psychotropic Substances and of Smuggling Migrants by Sea, concluded between the Bureau of the Merchant Navy and Coastal Affairs of Ecuador and the United States Coast Guard (copy provided by US Coast Guard). Here, the 'safety and humane treatment of the persons on board' is to be assured.

60 There are a number of international instruments which provide for protection against torture or inhuman or degrading treatment or punishment, or actually reflect the substance of the terms of Art. 33 of the Refugee Convention. See Principles Concerning Treatment of Refugees (1966), Art. III(3); Declaration on Territorial Asylum (1967), Art. 3; Organisation of African Unity Convention concerning the Specific Aspects of Refugee Problems in Africa (1969), Art. II(3); American Convention on Human Rights (also known as the Pact of San Jose) (1969), Art. 22(8); Cartagena Declaration on Refugees (1984) Section III, para. 5; Torture Convention (1984), Art. 3; ICCPR (1966), Art. 7; European Convention on Extradition (1957), Art. 3(2); Inter-American Convention on Extradition (1981), Art. 4(5).

61 *Ireland v United Kingdom* (1997) 23 EHRR 413 (18 January 1978).

Grand Chamber of the European Court of Human Rights in *Saadi v Italy*, where the absolute prohibition on *refoulement* in terrorism extradition cases was reasserted, as was the absolute nature of Art. 3.[62]

Failure to assist people in distress at sea can be interpreted as a violation of both Art. 2 and 3. Furthermore, the *refoulement* of migrants to the frontiers of persecution may amount to a violation of Art. 3 due to its extraterritorial effect, as determined in the *Soering case*[63] where the Court held that Art. 3 could be violated if the actions of the Contracting State could expose the individual to torture or inhuman or degrading treatment outside the jurisdiction of the Contracting State.[64]

As far as the application of Art. 3 is concerned, this is premised upon the precondition that the individual is 'within the jurisdiction' of the Contracting State Party. While predominantly signifying a territorial interpretation, a look at some of the decisions of the European Court of Human Rights regarding the application of the ECHR serves to illustrate the point that this phrase too has been given an extraterritorial meaning. An overview of this jurisprudence would be useful in light of the fact that in the event of the Refugee Convention not being held applicable[65] (in the exceptional case where no asylum claims are made) the ECHR may apply nonetheless. The term 'jurisdiction' in Art. 1 of the ECHR has been held to apply beyond a State's territory when 'acts of their authorities, whether performed within or outside national boundaries ... produce ... effects outside their own territory'.[66] However, in *Bankovic v Belgium*[67] the Court stressed the exceptional nature of this principle, that is, that the term 'jurisdiction' in Art. 1 of the Convention is premised upon a territorial interpretation of the notion of jurisdiction.[68] The Court concluded:

> [T]he case law of the court demonstrates that its recognition of the exercise of extra-territorial jurisdiction by a contracting state is exceptional; it has done so when the respondent state, through its effective control of the relevant territory and its inhabitants abroad as a consequence of military occupation or through the consent, invitation or acquiescence of the government of that territory, exercises all or some of the public powers normally to be exercised by the Government ...

---

62 *Saadi v Italy* App. No. 37201/06, Grand Chamber (28 February 2008), para. 127.

63 *Soering v United Kingdom*, (1989) 11 EHRR 439, para. 85 (7 July 1989).

64 *Ibid.*, para. 91. Examples of other relevant judgments are: *Chahal v United Kingdom* (1997) 23 EHRR 41 (15 November 1996) and *D v United Kingdom* (1997) 24 EHRR 423 (2 May 1997).

65 There is no need for such analysis when considering the application of the Refugee Convention because this instrument is not conditional upon 'jurisdiction' for its application.

66 *Loizidou v Turkey* (1995) 20 EHRR 90, para. 62.

67 (2001) 11 BHRC 435. See also A. Ruth and M. Trilsch, 'Bankovic v Belgium (Admissibility) App. No. 52207/99' (2003) 97 *AJIL* 168–172.

68 *Bankovic v Belgium* (2001) 11 BHRC 435, paras 61 and 67.

> Additionally, the court notes that other recognised instances of the extra-territorial exercise of jurisdiction by a state include cases involving the activities of its diplomatic or consular agents abroad and on board craft and vessels registered in, or flying the flag of the state. In these specific situations, customary international law and treaty provisions have recognised the extra-territorial exercise of jurisdiction by the relevant state.[69]

However, this interpretation has not formed part of the Court's later judgments. As Goodwin-Gill reports, 'post-*Bankovic* decisions … [have] extended the concept of "jurisdiction" to other types of conduct occurring *outside* the territorial boundaries of Contracting States'.[70]

The key terms in determining whether jurisdiction can apply extraterritorially are 'authority and/or effective control', as was maintained in *Issa and others v Turkey*:[71]

> [A] State's responsibility may be engaged where, as a consequence of military action—whether lawful or unlawful—that State in practice exercises effective control of an area situated outside its national territory …
>
> … a State may also be held accountable for violation of the Convention rights and freedoms of persons who are in the territory of another State but who are found to be under the former State's authority and control through its agents operating—whether lawfully or unlawfully—in the latter State.[72]

For our purposes, the scenario to be considered is when a Coast Guard vessel or any other official State vessel comes upon a vessel carrying irregular migrants either in the course of an interception exercise or in a rescue at sea scenario. It must be ascertained whether the State is thus exercising its authority and/or its effective control over the vessel in question. Taking the less stringent interpretation outlined above, the Court in *Issa* seems to have indicated that there must be effective control by the State over an area situated outside its national territory. This seems very much linked to a territorial area of control and thus may not be applicable to the maritime scenario, even though it may be argued that through

69 *Ibid.*, paras 71 and 73.

70 Goodwin-Gill et al. (n 19), at 246. In support of this contention Goodwin-Gill et al. cite *inter alia: Ocalan v Turkey* (2000) 30 EHRR CD 231 (Admissibility); *Ocalan v Turkey* (2003) 37 EHRR 10 (Merits); *Ocalan v Turkey* (Grand Chamber) (12 May 2005); *Issa v Turkey*, App. No. 31821/96 (Admissibility) (30 May 2000); *Issa v Turkey*, App. No. 31821/96 (Merits) (16 November 2004).

71 *Issa v Turkey*, App. No. 31821/96 (Merits) (16 November 2004) 41 EHRR 567, para. 72.

72 *Ibid.*, paras 69 and 71. Note however, that the House of Lords in *Al Skeini and others v Secretary of State for Defence* [2007] UKHL 26, on appeal from [2005] EWCA Civ 1609 relied heavily on the *Bankovic* decision at the expense of that in *Issa v Turkey*. For an overview of *Bankovic* and later cases and their application to the case see Lord Rodger of Earlsferry, at paras 68–91; Lord Brown of Eaton-Under-Heywood, at paras 108–132.

its agents the flag State is exercising effective control over an area outside its territory when it intercepts and boards the vessel, which is sometimes described as an extension of the State's territory. Another instance of jurisdiction being exercised extraterritorially may however more convincingly be applied to the case at hand. A State may also be held accountable for violating the rights and freedoms laid down in the ECHR in the case of people who are in the territory of another State but who are found to be under the former State's authority and control by reason of the fact that its agents are operating in the latter State. Once again, transposing this to the maritime scenario, through interception and boarding a State's agents are exercising authority and control over those on a vessel, which represents an area or an entity outside the flag State as such. Moreover, the Court in *Issa* explained that '[a]ccountability in such situations stems from the fact that Art. 1 of the Convention cannot be interpreted so as to allow a State Party to perpetrate violations of the Convention on the territory of another State, which it could not perpetrate in its own territory'.[73] In the maritime scenario, this can be interpreted as meaning that the consequences of a State's exercise of jurisdiction and control over a vessel in an interception or rescue scenario should be the same wherever such jurisdiction and control are exercised. A State cannot ignore obligations on a humanitarian level merely on account of the fact that it exercises its jurisdiction outside its territorial areas.[74]

The point thus seems to be whether the relevant conduct amounts to an exercise of jurisdiction—whether authority and/or effective control is evident, and not whether the conduct takes place within the territory of that State or outside it. As the judgments outlined above indicate, as a general proposition States are responsible for conduct in relation to those subject to or within their jurisdiction, and this is not conditional upon their presence within the territory of the State purporting to exercise jurisdiction, but rather whether they were under the effective control of such State or its agents.[75] It is submitted that from the initial interception the officials of the intercepting State are exercising effective control and authority over the intercepted vessel and, therefore, are subject to whatever obligations arise in the exercise of jurisdiction.

---

73 *Issa v Turkey*, App. No. 31821/96 (Merits) (16 November 2004) 41 EHRR 567, para. 71.

74 Similar reasoning is evident in *Legal Consequences of the Construction of a Wall in the Occupied Palestinian Territory*, Advisory Opinion [2004] ICJ Rep 136, paras 109–111.

75 See further, e.g., ICCPR (1966), Art. 2(1); Optional Protocol to ICCPR (1966), Art. 1; UNGA Res 2200A (XXI); American Convention on Human Rights (1969), Art. 1(1); *Lopez Burgos v Uruguay*, Human Rights Committee, Communication No. 52/1979, Views of the HRC of 29 July 1981, paras 10.1–10.3.

6.4. *Rescue at Sea*

The duty of States to rescue vessels in distress and the subsequent responsibility that falls upon the flag State of the rescuing vessel (especially if the rescue operation was carried out in the course of an interception operation[76]) or State of disembarkation all bring into play the obligation of *non-refoulement*.[77] It is made clear in relevant international instruments that 'all rules have to be applied without prejudice to the obligations deriving from international humanitarian law and international human rights law, including in particular the prohibition of *non refoulement*'.[78]

The duty to rescue those in distress at sea is enshrined in Art. 98 LOSC and may be regarded as part of customary international law.[79] The terms of Art. 98 impose obligations on both the flag and coastal States in this regard, obligations which also impact on ships' Masters. The provision dictates that every State is to require the Master of a ship flying its flag, insofar as he can do so without serious danger to the ship, crew or passengers, to render assistance to any person found at sea in danger of being lost and to proceed with all possible speed to the rescue of persons in distress once informed of their need for assistance and insofar as such action can be reasonably expected from him.[80] Furthermore, every coastal State is to promote the establishment, operation and maintenance of an adequate and effective search and rescue service, and to cooperate with neighbouring States to this end.[81]

Although the duty to rescue has been repeatedly emphasized in international documentation, 'what the lawmakers systematically had in mind were classic shipwrecks and sailors surrounding whom no attendant legal problem was suspected. Nationals of any given State, they could expect to be repatriated from the rescue ships' first port of call. In the case of asylum-seekers, however, repatriation must be ruled out. Whose responsibility they should become

[76] *Ibid.*, paras 9, 26: when vessels engage in rescue operations in territorial waters, the responsibility for those rescued devolves upon that State. Arguably, this is also the case where such scenarios occur on the high seas.

[77] See MSC.167(78) Guidelines on the Treatment of Persons Rescued at Sea (20 May 2004).

[78] Commission (EC), 'Study on the International Law Instruments in Relation to Illegal Immigration by Sea' (Staff Working Document) SEC (2007) 691, 15 May 2007, 691. This is also affirmed in Art. 19(1) of the Migrant Smuggling Protocol.

[79] This duty is also provided for in other international instruments such as: Salvage Convention 1910; SOLAS 1925; HSC 1958; SOLAS 1960; SOLAS 1974; SAR 1979, Annex; Salvage Convention 1989. Note also the ILC's view that this duty is also part of general international law: UN Doc A/3179 (1956) regarding the proposed draft of Art. 12 of the 1958 HSC. See also R. Barnes, 'Refugee Law at Sea' (2004) 53 *ICLQ* 49.

[80] LOSC Art. 98(1).

[81] LOSC Art. 98(2).

is something on which international law is practically silent.'[82] Once again therefore, international legal norms are faced with developments unforeseen at the time of their drafting; nevertheless, these same international norms are the only ones which apply in these new scenarios.

While the duty to rescue is clearly stated, until recently nothing in the international legal regime had indicated what was to occur once the rescue had been effected. The obligation to rescue therefore presented the problem of what happened after the actual rescue operation, which only terminated once those rescued were delivered to a place of safety.[83] Although not explicitly mentioned, disembarkation is necessary for such delivery. Various States are potential locations for disembarkation: the flag State of the rescuing ship; the closest land to where the rescue takes place; the next port of call on the rescuing ship's established route;[84] the nation from which the rescued persons originally set out to sea; and SAR States.[85] The traditional assumption that the ship's Master would consult with owners and relevant authorities on the most appropriate place to take survivors, depending on the individual circumstances surrounding each case, and that survivors would be processed by border control authorities of the relevant port State is no longer tenable. This tradition was based on the assumption that there were a relatively small number of boats and survivors, not the increasing trend in unauthorized arrivals in overcrowded and unseaworthy vessels, sometimes using force or threats to coerce the Masters and crews of rescuing ships to transport them to a particular chosen destination. States are understandably reluctant to permit the disembarkation of asylum-seekers without resettlement guarantees, with the result that ships' Masters are equally concerned about the time and consequent expense which could be spent in a rescue operation following which there is no given State which is actually obliged to permit disembarkation.[86] This is a preoccupying trend.

---

82 2 Refugees 21 (February 1984) cited in L.B. Sohn and J.E. Noyes, *Cases and Materials on the Law of the Sea* (Transnational Publishers, New York, 2004), 98.

83 Generally, the rescuing ship cannot be considered to be a 'place of safety'.

84 The UNHCR ExCom Conclusions state that those rescued at sea 'should normally be disembarked at the next port of call', but has also made recommendations for determining 'the most appropriate port for disembarkation purposes', thereby suggesting that the next port of call may not always be the most appropriate port for disembarkation, particularly if it is the country of origin of people claiming to be refugees. See UNHCR ExCom Conclusion No. 23 (XXXII)—1981, para. 3; UNHCR, 'Background Note' (n 2) sec. II (31).

85 Recent IMO amendments to the SOLAS and SAR Conventions require that governments which are party to SOLAS and have search and rescue regions are to be responsible for coordinating disembarkation in cases of rescue. See further Chapter 7.

86 Note the case of the *Clementine Maersk*, a Danish ship which rescued 27 migrants in the Mediterranean in June 2005 and disembarked the migrants at the next scheduled port of

Another problem is that 'distress' is not qualified, and thus arguably includes 'self-induced' distress as a type of distress in need of rescue.[87] The 2004 amendments to the SAR Convention have now amplified the original definition of 'persons in distress', as shall be seen. However this point was not considered.[88]

Furthermore, any asylum claims must also be assessed. If a boat reaches a port of call, the State of that port is expected to take on responsibility for the people rescued and assess their status and situation (although that State need not be the place in which long-term protection needs are met). However, sometimes States seek to avoid being put in that position. The ship's Master, according to the IMO Guidelines on the Treatment of Persons Rescued at Sea must take protection needs into account and weigh this factor in determining where to disembark.[89] In reality, this does not negate the possibility that the Master may determine that the country of origin may be the most favourable place for disembarkation. This option however is often met with much resistance from those on board, refusal to disembark and violent behaviour on the part of those rescued.

Moreover, while the rescue obligation exists almost unconditionally (the only reservation being that such action must not seriously endanger the rescuing ship and its crew or passengers), enforcement of such duty is difficult, especially considering that it is mainly the flag State which can enforce the obligation[90] and that nearly one-third of all ocean-going vessels are registered under flags of convenience.[91] The rather incomplete exposition of the obligation, which makes no reference to obligations incumbent upon States after the immediate alleviation of distress, is another drawback. The challenge therefore is to find elements which will build an effective cooperative framework with the aim of defining responsibilities and providing for burden-sharing between the relevant actors.

---

call, in the UK. The craft had floated for 8 days, being passed by cargo ships, some of which informed it that they would request coast guard assistance, though none came.

87 Note, however, that this is not unanimously accepted. See M. Pugh, 'Europe's Boat People: Maritime Cooperation in the Mediterranean' (July 2000) *Chaillot Paper* 41, Institute for Security Studies Western European Union, 57. Pugh argues that a group of determined people who have set out on a risky voyage in a substandard vessel may not be easily recognized as being in a condition of distress.

88 See SAR Convention, Annex, Chapter 2, para. 2.1.1.

89 See n 77 above. Note also IMO / UNHCR, 'Rescue At Sea: A Guide to Principles and Practice as applied to Migrants and Refugees' (2006).

90 The remedy provided in Art. 94(6) LOSC is ineffective.

91 For concern at ignoring distress signals and problems caused by flags of convenience see 79 Department of State Bullettin No. 2031 at 2, 3 (October 1979), cited in Sohn and Noyes (n 82), 99.

Rescue at sea is different from the act of maritime enforcement amounting to interception, differing in both intention and purpose. However, the two sometimes overlap, and disembarkation is common to both processes.[92] Interception is reserved to State authorities and is an exercise of a programme of maritime enforcement. However, interception may pre-empt the need for a rescue.[93] Often, Masters of non-State—that is, private—vessels find themselves rescuing a vessel in distress. Having said this, rescue operations are sometimes carried out by State authorities conducting surveillance activities due to the unseaworthiness of the vessels used to carry irregular migrants, and in this case a situation akin to that of interception may ensue: State authorities coming across the vessels are required to assist the passengers, probably by transferring them to their own Coast Guard vessels. If the migrants are later to be disembarked, this will usually be either in the State whose Coast Guard has conducted the rescue or at a location with which that State has an established agreement for such disembarkations. The point to be made at this stage is that sometimes an operation which is characterized as a rescue operation may actually be designed to avoid having to seek flag State authorization prior to intercepting and boarding vessels on the high seas, or even in the contiguous zone of other States.[94] The result of this may be that in such cases, where a rescue operation is more akin to an interception exercise, the State whose authorities carried out the exercise is to take responsibility for disembarkation and processing of any asylum claims.

6.4.1. *Relevant Responsibilities*

6.4.1.1. *Masters of Ships*

The obligation of the ship's Master to provide assistance is repeatedly provided for in international maritime law. The nature of the obligation is not in doubt; it is its application which gives rise to problems. A rescue operation is not terminated until those rescued are delivered to a place of safety.[95] The Master has a wide discretion as to how he conveys them to such a place, and in so doing he has the right to require support both from the coastal State and from those States whose nationals he has rescued from danger.[96]

---

[92] Brouwer and Kumin (n 26), 11.

[93] UNHCR, 'Background Note' (n 2), para. 26 states in this regard that 'the responsibility [for admitting asylum-seekers] accruing to the flag State would be stronger still, where the rescue operation occurs in the context of interception measures.'

[94] See Brouwer and Kumin (n 26), 11, 14.

[95] SAR Convention, Annex, Chapter 1, para. 1.3.2.

[96] M. White, 'MV Tampa and Christmas Island Incident' (August 2001—copy available was to be published in BIMCO Review (2002) 116–123) 4–5.

SOLAS provides for the responsibility of the Master in this respect. Chapter V Regulation 33.1 provides *inter alia* that the:

> [M]aster of a ship at sea which is in a position to be able to provide assistance, on receiving a signal from any source that persons are in distress at sea, is bound to proceed with all speed to their assistance, if possible informing them or the search and rescue service that the ship is doing so.

The 2004 amendments to SAR 1979 have added a new paragraph which makes it clear that disembarkation is indeed part of the rescue operation. The recent amendments have introduced paragraph 3.1.6.4 into Chapter 3 of the Annex, dealing with cooperation between States, which now provides for assistance to be given to the Master in delivering those rescued at sea to a place of safety. The text reads that States are to 'make the necessary arrangements in cooperation with other RCCs to identify the most appropriate place(s) for disembarking persons found in distress at sea.'

Furthermore, in answer to the concern voiced by the UNHCR that the reluctance of States to permit disembarkation was leading to a reluctance on the part of ships' Masters to answer distress calls,[97] the amendments to the SAR Convention have sought to minimize the burden on the ship's Master. Paragraph 3.1.9 of the Annex, introduced by Resolution MSC. 155(78), states:

> Parties shall co-ordinate and co-operate to ensure that masters of ships providing assistance by embarking persons in distress at sea are released from their obligations with minimum further deviation from the ships' intended voyage, provided that releasing the master of the ship from these obligations does not further endanger the safety of life at sea. The Party responsible for the search and rescue region in which such assistance is rendered shall exercise primary responsibility for ensuring such co-ordination and co-operation occurs, so that survivors assisted are disembarked from the assisting ship and delivered to a place of safety, taking into account the particular circumstances of the case and guidelines developed by the Organization. In these cases, the relevant Parties shall arrange for such disembarkation to be effected as soon as reasonably practicable.

It will be noted that the general obligation upon States is one of coordination and cooperation. The obligation of the State in whose SAR area the assistance was given is to exercise primary responsibility for ensuring that such coordination and cooperation occur so that disembarkation takes place and a place of safety is provided. However, this begs the question of what happens in default of agreement. The new provision may not therefore be clear enough in its terms,

[97] UNCHR, 'Problems related to the Rescue of Asylum-Seekers in Distress at Sea' (26 August 1981) EC/SCP/18, paras 3–11.

as it still fails to stipulate a State of disembarkation.[98] Also, the new amendment does not take into account the fact that certain countries have not defined their SAR zones.[99] This could lead to a situation where no State is legally bound to coordinate such cooperative exercises. The issue of what such cooperation could involve has been addressed by the Commission's Study on the International Law Instruments in Relation to Illegal Immigration by Sea as including agreements covering entry by States' vessels into territorial waters for search missions.[100]

As far as ships' Masters are concerned, the MSC Guidelines on the Treatment of Persons Rescued at Sea[101] emphasize the obligations incumbent upon Masters to provide for the safety of life at sea and also the integrity of global search and rescue services.[102] Furthermore, the IMO/UNHCR Guide to Principles and Practice as Applied to Migrants and Refugees (2006) guides the Master as to his actions in the event that asylum claims are made. In this case, he is to alert the closest RCC, inform the UNHCR and ensure that he does not request disembarkation in the country of origin or the country which the asylum-seekers had fled. Lastly, he is not to share personal information regarding the asylum-seekers with the authorities of that country or with others who may convey this information to those authorities.[103]

6.4.1.2. *Coastal States*

As far as the coastal State is concerned, its powers to prevent non-innocent passage have already been discussed. These powers are, however, subject to the concomitant duty to rescue vessels in distress at sea. The responsibility of States in this regard is set out in the LOSC as the obligation to develop adequate search and rescue services according to Art. 98 LOSC. This duty clearly applies to the high seas and, from a reading of Art. 58(2) and 86 LOSC, to the EEZ as well. Despite the fact that no such obligation is articulated for the purposes of the territorial sea, this has been argued to be a mere technical oversight and

---

98 This point was also noted by the European Commission, which pointed out that not only is there 'no rule designating by default a State responsible for receiving the rescued passengers', but also that 'the issue of the repartition of responsibilities between the different countries with regard to the protection of refugees is still open': see Commission Staff Working Document (n 78), paras 2.3.2 and 2.3.4.

99 *Ibid.*, para. 2.3.3.

100 *Ibid.*, para. 2.1.3.

101 See n 77 above.

102 Guidelines (n 77), para. 5.1. Ships are also urged, in para. 6.2, to participate in ship reporting systems established for the purpose of facilitating SAR operations.

103 Note also MSC.1/Circ.1182 Guide to Recovery Techniques (31 May 2006) aimed at providing specific guidance to seafarers on recovery techniques.

a duty which may be implicit in the provisions on innocent passage.[104] The responsibility of the coastal State in waters around its coasts is also provided for under SOLAS, obliging States Parties to 'ensure that necessary arrangements are made … for the rescue of persons in distress at sea around its coasts'.[105]

Specific arrangements for the provision of search and rescue services are found in the SAR Convention which, in paragraph 2.1.1 of the Annex, imposes an obligation on States Parties to ensure that necessary arrangements are made for the provision of adequate search and rescue services for persons in distress at sea round their coasts. A definition of 'persons in distress at sea' was introduced at the end of this paragraph by Resolution MSC. 155(78) of May 2004, which amendment entered into force on 1 July 2006. Persons in distress are now stated to include 'persons in need of assistance who have found refuge on a coast in a remote location within an ocean area inaccessible to any rescue facility other than as provided for in the annex.'[106]

On receipt of information that a person is in distress at sea in an area within which a Party provides for the overall coordination of search and rescue operations, the responsible authorities of that Party are to take urgent steps to ensure the provision of the necessary assistance.[107] The obligation requires States Parties to assist those in distress at sea 'regardless of nationality or status of such a person or the circumstances in which that person is found.'[108]

The SAR Convention also provides a definition of a rescue operation as 'an operation to retrieve persons in distress, provide for their medical or other needs, and deliver them to a place of safety'.[109] Prior to the 2004 amendments, with no express mention of a duty of disembarkation anywhere in the SAR Convention, this definition of rescue was used in order to indicate that disembarkation was obligatory as a result of the reference to 'delivery to a place of safety,' which necessitated disembarkation.

Another provision used to indicate that disembarkation was mandatory was paragraph 3.1.2, which calls for the coastal State to permit immediate entry *inter alia* into its territorial sea for the purpose of searching for the position of maritime casualties and rescuing the survivors of such casualties:

> Unless otherwise agreed between the States concerned, a Party should authorize, subject to applicable national laws, rules and regulations, immediate entry into or over its territorial sea or territory of rescue units of other Parties solely for the purpose of searching for the position of maritime casualties and rescuing the

[104] Barnes (n 79), 52.
[105] SOLAS Chapter V/7.
[106] This definition originated from a French proposal: see MSC 75/11/1 (4 March 2002).
[107] SAR Convention, Annex, Chapter 2, para. 2.1.1.
[108] *Ibid.*, para. 2.1.10.
[109] *Ibid.*, Chapter 1, para. 1.3.2.

> survivors of such casualties. In such cases, search and rescue operations shall, as far as practicable, be co-ordinated by the appropriate search and rescue co-ordination centre of the Party which has authorized entry, or such other authority as has been designated by that Party.

However, this provision, apart from the fact that disembarkation is not mentioned, is also subjected to applicable national laws, rules and regulations and has not been considered to be a satisfactory statement of the obligation, if indeed such obligation existed.[110]

The question of disembarkation is no longer an issue post-SAR and SOLAS amendments, to be discussed in Chapter 7. Clear indications of the necessity of disembarkation are now found throughout the SAR Convention, such as in paragraph 3.1.9, discussed above, specifically mentioning disembarkation. Similarly, paragraph 3.1.6.4 proceeds on this premise by requiring States 'to make the necessary arrangements in cooperation with other RCCs to identify the most appropriate place(s) for disembarking persons found in distress at sea.'

6.4.1.3. *Rescue Co-ordination Centres (RCCs)*

According to paragraph 4.8.5 in Chapter 4 of the Annex to the SAR Convention, relating to operating procedures, RCCs are to initiate the process of identifying the most appropriate places for disembarking those found in distress at sea:

> The rescue co-ordination centre or rescue sub-centre concerned shall initiate the process of identifying the most appropriate place(s) for disembarking persons found in distress at sea. It shall inform the ship or ships and other relevant parties concerned thereof.

As has been mentioned, both the LOSC and SAR Convention impose upon States the obligation to develop and maintain adequate search and rescue services. RCCs are the embodiment of such obligation, being charged with receiving distress calls and responsible for coordinating rescue operations in response to such calls. The MSC Guidelines provide that normally any SAR coordination which takes place between a rescuing ship and any coastal State(s) should be handled by the responsible RCC which should be prepared to act quickly on its own, or have processes in place as necessary to involve other authorities in order that timely decisions can be reached with regard to the handling of survivors.[111] The motivating concern of the Guidelines and the 2004 amendments are recognized in paragraph 6.3 of the Guidelines which

---

[110] See Barnes (n 79), 53, citing E. Rosaeg, 'Refugees as Rescuees—the Tampa Problem', section 3.4, who maintains that there is no duty on coastal States to allow disembarkation of rescuees.

[111] Guidelines (n 77), para. 6.4.

states that '[a] ship should not be subject to undue delay, financial burden or other related difficulties after assisting persons at sea; therefore coastal States should relieve the ship as soon as practicable.'

On their part, Governments are to ensure that the RCCs and other national authorities concerned have sufficient guidance and authority to be able to fulfil their duties under the relevant treaties and MSC Guidelines; they must also ensure that their RCCs and rescue units are operating in accordance with the standards and procedures found in the IAMSAR Manual.[112] Each RCC is charged with having effective plans of operation and arrangements in place in order to respond to all types of SAR situations. These plans and arrangements should cover incidents which occur within the associated SAR region, and they should also cover incidents outside their SAR region if necessary, until the RCC responsible for the region in which assistance is being given or another RCC better situated to handle the case accepts responsibility.[113] In this regard, it is stated that, where appropriate, the first RCC contacted should immediately begin efforts to transfer the case to the RCC responsible for the region in which assistance is being given. When the latter RCC is notified of the situation, it should immediately accept responsibility for coordinating the rescue efforts, since related responsibilities, including arrangement for a place of safety for survivors, fall primarily on the Government responsible for that region. As indicated above, the first RCC is however responsible for coordinating the case until the responsible RCC or other competent authority assumes responsibility for such coordination.[114]

Furthermore, paragraph 6.6 of the Guidelines states that plans of operation, liaison activities and communications arrangements providing for proper coordination in advance of and during a rescue operation should be made with shipping companies and national or international authorities which may need to be involved in response or disembarkation efforts. RCCs are also to attempt to obtain certain information from the Master of the assisting vessel.[115] In some cases it may be advisable for the RCC to arrange for SAR or other personnel to visit the assisting ship in order better to assess the situation on board, to help in meeting the needs on board, or to facilitate the safe and secure disembarkation of the survivors.[116]

Finally, the Guidelines emphasize that '[g]overnments and the responsible RCC should make every effort to minimize the time survivors remain aboard

[112] *Ibid.*, paras 6.1 and 6.2.
[113] *Ibid.*, para. 6.5.
[114] *Ibid.*, para. 6.7.
[115] Details of the information required are laid out in *ibid.*, para. 6.10.
[116] *Ibid.*, para. 6.11.

the assisting ship' and that '[r]esponsible State authorities should make every effort to expedite arrangements to disembark survivors from the ship; however, the Master should understand that in some cases necessary coordination may result in unavoidable delays.'[117]

6.4.1.4. *Flag States*

As far as the flag State is concerned, the UNHCR Background Note reports that the responsibility of flag States has sometimes been invoked partly on the basis of the vessel being considered as a 'floating extension' of the State in question, notwithstanding the fact that this position may not have a firm legal basis and that it leads to problems with respect to flags of convenience which do not adequately carry out the duties of a flag State. Nevertheless, this understanding apparently contributed to the practice of 'attributing certain responsibilities to flag States and/or commercial vessels operating under their authority.'[118] Briefly, the situation regarding flag State responsibility may be summed up thus:

> While ... there is a clear duty for ship's masters, their owners and their Governments to rescue asylum-seekers at sea, there is no obligation under international law for the flag State of a rescuing vessel to grant durable asylum to rescued refugees. It is, of course, correct that by boarding a vessel, the refugee comes under the jurisdiction of the flag State which is considered to exercise jurisdiction over the ship on the high seas. There is, however, no valid legal basis for considering that by boarding a vessel a refugee has entered the territory of the State exercising jurisdiction over the ship. Moreover, even if physical presence on the ship were regarded as tantamount to presence in the territory, this would not in the present status of international law constitute an obligation for the flag State to grant durable asylum.[119]

A clear instance of flag State responsibility for those on board exists where a State's vessels (such as naval vessels, coast guard vessels and national lifeboats specifically tasked with search and rescue operations) are concerned. Where such vessels carry out a rescue operation in territorial waters, responsibility for those rescued would devolve upon the flag State of the State's vessel. This is also arguably the case where such scenarios take place on the high seas, particularly, in the view of the UNHCR, if such rescue occurs in the context of interception measures.[120]

---

[117] *Ibid.*, paras 6.8–6.9.

[118] UNHCR, 'Background Note' (n 2), para. 8.

[119] UNHCR, EC/SCP/18 (n 97), para. 23. Note, however, that this exercise of jurisdiction would give rise to the duty of *non-refoulement*.

[120] UNHCR, 'Background Note' (n 2), paras 9 and 26.

6.4.2. *The* lacuna

The point was made above that, although the duty to rescue those in distress at sea is firmly established, none of the various conventions addressed the issue of what was to happen after assistance had been given; more specifically, no mention was made of disembarkation. Of them all, only the SAR Convention implied subsequent disembarkation in its terms, by indicating the necessity to deliver those rescued to a place of safety. It could have been argued that bringing those rescued on board the rescue vessel or transferring them to another vessel amounted to delivery to a place of safety; however, this was not perceived by the UNHCR as a satisfactory resolution of the matter.[121] It maintained that the fulfilment of SAR obligations necessitated disembarkation; 'delivery to a place of safety' could not mean keeping the rescuees on board the rescuing vessel indefinitely, although it was admitted that the rescuing ship could be a temporary place of safety.[122]

Faced with this lack of clarity, the UNHCR consistently advocated the 'next port of call' as the appropriate place for disembarkation and as a solution for the legal lacuna existing in post-rescue operations.[123] It indicated that disembarkation and processing at the next port of call were considered so obvious that express inclusion in international instruments was considered superfluous.[124] However, the UNHCR's pronouncements do not amount to rules of international law, and this 'solution' was therefore dependent on the discretion of the coastal State.[125] Moreover, this gave rise to certain difficulties: while commercial and flag State interests would no doubt be comfortable with such arrangement, it is not difficult to understand why coastal States would be reluctant to agree to the 'next port of call' rule. At best, they would do so only if the rule were linked to a system of resettlement guarantees.[126] Technical

---

121 See Barnes (n 79), 52; UNHCR, 'Background Note' (n 2), para. 12.

122 Guidelines (n 77), para. 6.13.

123 UNHCR, EC/SCP/18 (n 97), para. 25(c). See also UNHCR, 'Background Note' (n 2), para. 12; ExCom Conclusions: No. 14 (XXX)—1979, para. (c); No. 15 (XXX)—1979, para. (c); No. 23 (XXXII)—1981, para. 3.

124 UNHCR, EC/SCP/18 (n 97), paras 19–20. However, note that the costs to the State of disembarkation, together with the rejection of the Stowaways Convention 1957, which in Art. 2(2) states that stowaways are to be disembarked to the appropriate authority, seem to indicate the contrary.

125 UNHCR ExCom Conclusions are not binding; at best, they constitute soft law. See n 44 above; and also J. Sztucki, 'The Conclusions on the International Protection of Refugees adopted by the Executive Committee' (1989) 1 *IJRL* 285; Annex 14, 'Background Note Concerning the Competence of the United Nations High Commissioner for Refugees (UNHCR) in Relation to Rescue at Sea Matters', prepared for COMSAR 6 (in COMSAR 6/22), para. 7.

126 By means of resettlement guarantees, flag States would agree to take responsibility for settling the asylum-seekers if the coastal State permitted them to disembark there. See, e.g., the

difficulties would also arise when considering the suitability of the next port of call for disembarkation purposes.

Furthermore, the actual meaning of the 'next port of call' was not clear. Alternative references had indeed been formulated by the UNHCR, including: the nearest port in terms of geographical proximity (especially where the incident involved large numbers of rescuees); the port of embarkation (due to the responsibility of this State to prevent unseaworthy vessels from leaving its territory);[127] the next scheduled port of call (in cases where the number of rescuees was small and the safety of the vessel and those on board was not endangered nor likely to necessitate a deviation from its intended course); the port best-equipped for the purposes of receiving traumatized and injured victims and subsequently processing any asylum applications; and, in instances involving States' vessels intercepting illegal migrants, the nearest port of that State could be regarded as the most appropriate one for disembarkation.[128]

The identification of the next port of call was informed by a number of considerations; foremost amongst these were the legal obligations of States under both international maritime law and international refugee law. Other considerations included the safety and humanitarian concerns of both the rescuees and the rescuing vessel and its crew; the number of persons rescued and the consequent need to ensure prompt disembarkation; the technical suitability of the port in question to allow for disembarkation; the need to avoid disembarkation in the country of origin for those alleging a well-founded fear of persecution; and the financial implications and liability of the shipping companies involved in undertaking rescue operations.[129]

Considering that the effectiveness of the international search and rescue system depends upon certainty and the predictable action of all concerned, this limbo constituted a severe handicap in the workings of the system. The IMO sought to rectify this situation and the 2004 amendments to the SAR and SOLAS Conventions together with the associated Guidelines on the Treatment of Persons Rescued at Sea[130] have the aim of helping to 'ensure that persons

---

Disembarkation Resettlement Offers Scheme (DISERO) and the Rescue-at-Sea Resettlement Offers Scheme (RASRO) in UNHCR, 'International Protection Problems related to the rescue of Asylum-Seekers in Distress at Sea' (1 September 1983) EC/SCP/30; UNHCR, 'International Protection, Problems related to the rescue of Asylum-Seekers in Distress at Sea' (8 July 1985) EC/SCP/42.

[127] The reference to the port of embarkation seems erroneous as *per se* it can hardly be conceived of as the next port of call, although it may be the closest port geographically or the actual port of destination should the vessel be returning to the original port of embarkation.

[128] UNHCR, 'Background Note' (n 2), para. 30.

[129] Aleinikoff et al. (n 55), 146.

[130] See n 77 above.

in distress are assisted, while minimizing the inconvenience to assisting ships and ensuring the continued integrity of SAR services,'[131] as shall be discussed below.[132]

Ultimately, the problem arose from an inherent paradox: while there was a sacrosanct duty to rescue those in distress at sea, there was no corresponding duty to receive the rescued. This need for reform was expressed *inter alia* by the UNHCR ExCom at its 53rd Session (October 2002) where it referred to the need to reach common understandings on responsibilities in the context of rescue at sea and the disembarkation of those rescued.

An attempt to address these issues took place in 2004 when the IMO carried out amendments to the SOLAS[133] and SAR[134] Conventions,[135] to the effect that Contracting Governments are now obliged to coordinate and cooperate to release Masters who have assisted persons in distress at sea from their obligations with minimum further deviation from the ship's voyage. The Contracting Government responsible for the SAR area in which the assistance is rendered is charged with exercising primary responsibility for ensuring that such coordination and cooperation occur in order to disembark survivors and take them to a place of safety.[136]

In this way the amendments 'aim at maintaining the integrity of the SAR services, by ensuring that people in distress at sea are assisted while minimizing the inconvenience to the assisting ship. They require the Contracting States/Parties to:

- co-ordinate and co-operate to ensure that masters of ships providing assistance by embarking persons in distress at sea are released from their obligations with minimum further deviation from the ship's intended voyage; and
- arrange disembarkation as soon as reasonably practicable'.[137]

---

131 Guidelines (n 77), para. 2.3.

132 Illustrations of States endeavouring to solve the problem are also apparent. One such example is the Australian Guidelines for Commercial Shipping Rescuing Persons at Sea In or Adjacent to the Australian Search and Rescue Region (Department of Transport and Regional Services, June 2005) which are to be interpreted in the light of the mentioned IMO Guidelines.

133 Chapter V/33.1.1.

134 Para. 3.1.9.

135 These amendments came into force on 1 July 2006. Associated Guidelines were also adopted in order to provide guidance to governments and to shipmasters in the implementation of the amendments. See further Chapter 7.

136 These amendments are discussed in detail in the next chapter.

137 They also oblige Masters 'who have embarked persons in distress at sea, to treat them with humanity, within the capabilities of the ship'. See IMO/UNHCR, 'Rescue at Sea' (n 89), 6.

6.5. *Concluding Observations*

This chapter has attempted to analyse two branches of international law which are intricately linked to the fight against maritime migrant smuggling. The principle of *non-refoulement*, applicable extraterritorially wherever a State exercises effective control over a vessel, together with the duty to rescue all those in distress at sea, renders the fight against maritime migrant smuggling vitally different from that against any other threat to maritime security. These considerations must therefore be at the forefront of any effective cooperative measure to repress this threat, as is seen in the instruments to be considered in the next chapter.

Chapter Seven

Treaty Modifications Demonstrating International Co-Operation

7.1. *Overview*

There is an acknowledged need for cooperation among States, not least because maritime enforcement efforts are needed over vast ocean areas and incidents occur at all and any hours of the day or night, often on the high seas where the flag State has no presence at the time of the occurrence. One finds mention of the duty of cooperation in a large number of international law instruments to the extent that '[i]t may be said that a cooperative international law based on a community of interests has developed in the field of crime prevention and punishment.'[1] The obligation to cooperate has a specific legal content and imposes action which goes beyond the expectation of good faith among the Parties to a treaty regime.[2] It is a distinct and independent obligation. In this area therefore, the obligation implies a positive duty of action on the part of States called on to cooperate with others in combating a specific threat to maritime security.

The aim of this chapter is to examine treaty modifications to the existing legal framework as implementations of the duty to cooperate, a duty which has again found recent expression in the IMO amendments to the SOLAS and SAR Conventions imposing an obligation of coordination and cooperation among States Parties. The first part of the chapter will examine the two major treaty modifications to the general regime in the field of migrant smuggling and rescue at sea. The chapter will begin with an analysis of the terms of the Migrant Smuggling Protocol as the most recent—and indeed first—expression of the duty of cooperation in this field. The next major treaty amendment process,

---

1 L. Reydams, *Universal Jurisdiction: International and Municipal Legal Perspectives* (OUP, Oxford, 2003), 17.

2 For detailed analysis see *Lac Lanoux* Arbitration (*France v Spain*) (English Translation) (1957) 24 ILR 119; *MOX Plant Case (Ireland v United Kingdom) Provisional Measures, Order of 3 December 2001* [2001] ITLOS Reports 95.

spearheaded by the IMO in relation to the SOLAS and SAR Conventions will then fall to be considered. Here, it is not only the amended text which will be the focus of attention, but also the considerations made in the course of amending those treaties due to their significant contributions to the understanding of certain core precepts in this field.

The second part of the chapter will discuss the most advanced areas of international cooperation, notably in combating illicit drug trafficking. During the analysis a pattern will be noted, primarily in instances of permitted entry into the territorial waters of States Parties and the boarding procedures seawards of the territorial sea, especially in the area of authorization to board vessels suspected of engaging in the illicit activity proscribed by the treaties under consideration.

The aim of this exercise is to discover whether the requisite tools exist to fight maritime migrant smuggling using the existing legal framework and to examine what can be done in the field if States have the necessary will and intention effectively to fight this threat to maritime security. In other words, the chapter will elicit whether it is possible to work within the existing legal framework or whether more crucial inroads to the prevailing regime are necessary.

7.2. *Treaty Modifications*

7.2.1. *The Smuggling Protocol*

The Smuggling Protocol (supplementing the CATOC)[3] aims to fight the crime of migrant smuggling by creating a framework for legal and judicial cooperation while ensuring the protection of victims and respect for their inherent rights. The seeds of such initiative were sown in 1997 by two proposals prepared by Austria and Italy which were merged in 1998, following Italy's unsuccessful initiative at the IMO,[4] and presented to the Ad Hoc Committee on the Elabora-

---

3 Regarding the relationship of the Protocols to the main text see UNGA A/AC.254/5/Add.3 (9 February 1999) Addendum, 2, 10; UN Doc A/55/383/Add.1 (3 November 2000) Report of the Ad Hoc Committee on the Elaboration of a Convention against Transnational Organized Crime on the work of its First to Eleventh Sessions, Addendum: Interpretative Notes for the official records (*travaux préparatoires*) of the negotiation of the United Nations Convention against Transnational Organized Crime and the Protocols thereto (Interpretative Notes); United Nations Legislative Guide for the Implementation of the UN Convention against Transnational Organized Crime and the Protocols thereto (UN Publications, New York. 2004) (Legislative Guide), 329–332. See also CATOC Art. 37 and Smuggling Protocol Art. 1.

4 The Italian proposal enjoyed the support of most delegations; however, questions arose over the competence of the IMO since the draft mainly focussed on the creation of an international

tion of a Convention against Transnational Organized Crime at its fourth session.[5] The final text was approved by the UNGA on 15 November 2000, during its 11th session of the Ad Hoc Committee.[6]

The Protocol is especially interesting, not only because it recognizes that migrant smuggling requires universal criminalization and a consequent cooperative framework for its prevention, but also because it contains a section on migrant smuggling by sea. The origins of this Part lie in the 1997 Italian proposal, now Arts. 7–9 of the Protocol, which contained provisions concerning cooperation in apprehending, boarding and seizing vessels and preventing entry and diverting vessels from ports.[7]

7.2.1.1. *The 1997 Italian Proposal*[8]

The preamble to Italy's 1997 draft proposal for a Multilateral Convention to Combat Illegal Migration by Sea[9] noted the 'rapid development of illegal trafficking and transport of migrants, especially by sea' and the fact that only a global approach to the phenomenon could lead to effective suppression of the crime.[10] The proposal sought to establish a range of measures to combat migrant smuggling, calling for international cooperation and the extradition of offenders. It introduced consideration of elements such as the offence sanctioned by stating that:

> Any person who intentionally procures, for his or her profit, repeatedly and in an organized manner, the illegal entry of a person into another State of which

criminal offence. It was also stated that the Italian proposal might cause overlaps with initiatives taken up by other international organisations. In November 1997, the IMO Legal Committee, followed in December by the MSC, supported the purpose of the proposal but agreed that it was necessary to wait for the outcome of work done by other international organisations. The IMO Assembly later declared itself not competent, thus rejecting the Italian proposal.

5 UNGA A/AC.254/4/Add.1 (15 December 1998).

6 UN Doc A/55/383 (2 November 2000).

7 Austria's proposal focused on a definition of the offence under international law and measures to facilitate investigation, prosecution and extradition.

8 For background information on the origins of the Protocol see A. Schloenhardt, *Migrant Smuggling: Human Trafficking and Organized Crime in Australia and the Asia Pacific Region* (Martinus Nijhoff, Leiden, 2003), 346 *et seq.*

9 LEG 76/11/1 (1 August 1997).

10 UNGA A/AC.254/4/Add.1 (15 December 1998). It should be noted that at this point the crimes of trafficking and smuggling were being considered together and subject to the same regulatory framework. For eventual separate consideration of the two crimes following government contributions regarding the distinction between the two offences see UNGA A/AC.254/5/Add.3 (9 February 1999) 5; UNGA A/AC.254/4/Add.3/Rev.1 (22 February 1999).

> the latter person is not a national or not a permanent resident commits the offence of 'illegal trafficking and transport of migrants' within the meaning of this Protocol.[11]

Art. F safeguards the continued operation of rules of international law by stating that nothing in the Chapter is to affect States' powers in relation to vessels not flying their flag as far as investigative and administrative functions are concerned. It also provides for rights of action of any State (according to the terms set out in Arts. H and I) in relation to stateless vessels flying no flag or flying the flag of more than one country, using them at their convenience in international waters. However, such rights of action are granted only in one of two situations, indicating that a link with the acting State must exist. Rights of action are granted only if the vessel is 'undoubtedly' bound for the State's coasts or if the vessel is 'armed or governed or manned by its nationals'. These requirements are not in the final text. Their omission is interesting. It could arguably indicate a shift in the general understanding that a State must be able to rely on some basis of jurisdiction in order to exercise enforcement jurisdiction over the vessel in the case of migrant smuggling. In other words, migrant smuggling may be increasingly being recognized as a crime which affects the security of States generally.

Art. F concludes by providing that 'if a measure is taken in implementation of this article, the States Parties concerned shall take into due account the need not to impair the security of human life at sea and the safety of the vessel and its cargo, as well as the commercial and legal interests of any other State concerned and those of the State of which the migrants and crew are nationals.'

The rights of action provided for when the conditions outlined in Art. F subsist are laid out in Arts. G and H.[12] Art. G states that when a State Party has 'reasonable grounds to believe that a vessel flying its flag—or flying no flag, or a vessel which, even if flying a foreign flag or refusing to fly its flag, has actually the same nationality as the vessel exercising the right under Art. F, paragraph 1(b)—is involved in the trafficking of migrants, [it] may request the assistance of other States Parties to combat such trafficking. The requested Parties shall offer any reasonable assistance necessary in order to achieve this goal.' Art. H continues by providing that:

> Each State Party that has reasonable grounds to believe that a vessel flying the flag of or registered with another State Party, navigating freely in accordance with international law, is involved in the trafficking of migrants may notify the State whose flag it flies, request a verification of the registration and, after receiving

---

[11] Art. A. Criminalization of the attempt or complicity in the offence is provided in Art. B.

[12] Arts. G and H correspond to the final Art. 8(1) and (2).

confirmation, may request authorization to adopt the necessary measures to guarantee the control and containment of the flow of individuals bound for its territory, which may include verifying the vessel's right to fly its flag, stopping the vessel, boarding it and diverting it.

It should be noted that the general principle of prior flag State consent has not been dispensed with here. What is especially interesting is the reference to the possibility of requesting authorization 'to adopt the necessary measures to guarantee the control and containment of the flow of individuals bound for its territory'. As for the types of action which may be considered 'necessary', it is submitted that these may not differ greatly from the inclusive examples which follow, that is, 'verifying the vessel's right to fly its flag, stopping the vessel, boarding it and diverting it', as defined in draft Art. I, discussed hereunder. Of course, the principles of human rights and *non-refoulement* must be guaranteed in such actions. The corresponding text in the final draft of the Protocol (Art. 8(2)) retains the same possibility of requesting authorization from the flag State but, however, removes the somewhat liberal wording of the original draft. Instead, it states that the State Party may 'request authorization from the flag State to take appropriate measures with regard to that vessel. The flag State may authorize the requesting State, *inter alia*:

a. To board the vessel;
b. To search the vessel; and
c. If evidence is found that the vessel is engaged in the smuggling of migrants by sea, to take appropriate measures with respect to the vessel and persons and cargo on board, as authorized by the flag State.'[13]

When considering permissible State action, Art. I provides a useful guide defining certain basic steps in enforcement jurisdiction, such as what stopping, visiting and diversion amount to:

a. Verifying the vessel's right to fly its flag: the vessel may be requested to give information on its nationality and the nationality of its crew, its port of departure and its destination;
b. Stopping the vessel: the vessel may be ordered to stop or to change course and reduce speed appropriately, following the procedures mentioned in subparagraph (a) above, so that a team of inspectors may board the vessel to ascertain the truth of the information communicated and whether any migrants are on board;
c. On-board visit: when the vessel is stopped or has changed course as ordered and at the speed ordered, the aforementioned inspection team shall board the vessel to carry out the necessary verification of documents and inspections, in order to ascertain whether the vessel is involved in the trafficking of migrants;

---

[13] See further the discussion on Art. 8(2) below.

d. Diversion: if the vessel refuses to permit an on-board visit or if the on-board inspection reveals that irregularities are being committed, the vessel shall be ordered to go back to the port of departure or to divert to the nearest port of a Contracting Party, designated according to Art. L,[14] and the State of which the migrants are nationals shall be informed of the outcome of the on-board visit. If the vessel fails to comply with such order, it shall be escorted to the prescribed destination.

Art. I finds no equivalent in the final text. The absence of such definition section is unfortunate; clear descriptions of what is permitted and what each method of control consists of would be of very great use in providing certainty, especially when one considers the dearth of information in this area.

Like Art. F, discussed above, where the necessity for a jurisdictional link was omitted in the final text, another article in the initial proposal which was removed from the final text was Art. M, which provided for the necessity of a territorial link. According to this provision, the above Arts. F–K were to apply in only two cases, where:

a. the vessel on which the trafficking or transport of migrants is under way is entering into the territorial waters of a Contracting Party;
b. there are reasonable grounds to suspect that such vessel is bound for entering into the territorial waters or otherwise procuring the illegal entry of migrants into the territory of a Contracting Party.[15]

Apart from the omission of these references, the substance of the joint proposal remained unchanged, as we will see when discussing Part II of the Protocol: the smuggling of migrants by sea.

7.2.1.2. *Main Features of the Smuggling Protocol*

The approach adopted in the Smuggling Protocol is not innovative and falls within the existing jurisdictional framework insofar as it requires States Parties to criminalize certain acts in their domestic law, to make them punishable by appropriate sanctions and to subject them to various measures such as extradition and mutual legal assistance.[16] Early treaties condemning white slave traffic[17] and the 1950 Convention for the Suppression of Traffic in Persons and of

[14] Art. L provided *inter alia* for the designation of ports to which vessels caught *in flagrante delicto* transporting migrants could be diverted. This article finds no equivalent in the final text, possibly owing to its requirement to take control of the vessel in its ports, which could lead to required disembarkation of any asylum-seekers.

[15] The applicable article with respect to jurisdiction is the present Art. 15 CATOC.

[16] Smuggling Protocol, Art. 6; CATOC, Art. 16. A similar pattern is found in other conventions such as the Vienna Drugs Convention 1988.

[17] Protocol amending the International Agreement for the Suppression of the White Slave Traffic 1904; International Agreement for the Suppression of White Slave Traffic 1905; International

the Exploitation of the Prostitution of Others also contained these features.[18] What is noteworthy however is the recognition of the link between organized crime and migrant smuggling—a relationship which has emerged only in the past decade.[19] From a policy point of view it is also valuable in that it takes due account of the many characteristics that distinguish migrant smuggling from other forms of organized criminal activity, consequently providing for the safeguarding of migrant rights as well as providing a comprehensive framework for action at the domestic and international levels, including, in Art. 18, the return of smuggled migrants. Another innovation is the attention given to maritime migrant smuggling requiring 'States to cooperate to the fullest extent possible to prevent and suppress the smuggling of migrants by sea, in accordance with the international law of the sea.'[20]

These innovations are recognized in the Preamble to the Protocol, which notes the significant increase in the activities of organized criminal groups in the smuggling of migrants, that this crime endangers the lives and security of migrants and that there is as yet no universal instrument which addresses all aspects of migrant smuggling, a crime which requires a 'comprehensive international approach.' The need to treat migrants humanely and with full protection of their rights is also stressed. The final text refers to the UNGA Resolution of 22 December 1999,[21] in which the Member States and the UN system were urged to strengthen international cooperation in the area of international migration and development so as to address the root causes of migration, especially those related to poverty, and to maximize the benefits of international migration to those concerned.

The fundamental points of attention in the Protocol emerge as the prosecution of migrant smuggling as a transnational offence which involves organized criminal groups and the protection of the rights of victims of such offences.[22] This is reflected in Art. 2 of the Protocol which states that '[t]he purpose of this

Convention for the Suppression of the White Slave Traffic 1910; International Agreement for the Suppression of the White Slave Traffic, signed at Paris on 18 May 1904, amended by the Protocol signed at Lake Success, New York 1949; International Convention for the Suppression of the White Slave Traffic, signed at Paris on 4 May 1910, amended by the Protocol signed at Lake Success 1949.

18 Regional efforts also exist to combat migrant smuggling, but they will not be discussed here. See further Schloenhardt (n 8), Chapter 18.

19 See UNGA A/AC.254/5/Add.21, Addendum, Proposal of Italy and Austria (11 February 2000); amendments previously issued in document A/AC.254/L.71 (27 September 1999).

20 UNGA UN Doc A/59/62 (4 March 2004).

21 UNGA A/RES/54/212.

22 For definitions of 'transnational' and 'organized criminal group' see CATOC Art. 3(2) and 2(a), respectively.

Protocol is to prevent and combat the smuggling of migrants, as well as to promote cooperation among States Parties to that end, while protecting the rights of smuggled migrants.'

The smuggling of migrants has a specific definition in the Protocol, found in Art. 3(a) and stated to be: 'the procurement, in order to obtain, directly or indirectly, a financial or other material benefit, of the illegal entry[23] of a person into a State Party of which the person is not a national or a permanent resident.'[24] Art. 6 requires that the smuggling of migrants and connected offences be rendered crimes in the domestic law of each State Party to the Protocol. The Interpretative Notes explain that such offences are to be seen as being part of the activities of organized criminal groups and, in this regard, the Protocol follows the precedent set in the CATOC Art. 34(2).[25] However, throughout the Protocol one notes a firm intention to protect the rights of smuggled migrants. Furthermore, Art. 5 expressly states that smuggled migrants are not to be liable to criminal prosecution solely by reason of being smuggled. During negotiations it was however equally clear that States retained the right to apply their domestic laws if a migrant had engaged in conduct which constituted an offence under its laws.[26] To this end, it has been pointed out that this article does not give smuggled migrants immunity from prosecution should, for example, they commit acts of criminal damage during their journey. To this end, Art. 6(4) of the Protocol states that '[n]othing in this Protocol shall prevent a State Party from taking measures against a person whose conduct constitutes an offence under its domestic law.'[27]

Various measures, found in Part III of the Protocol, are intended to support the main aim of the instrument. Training and technical assistance, together with increasing public awareness and the promotion of development programmes and cooperation at the national, regional and international levels are

23 Until the draft considered during the 11th session (UN Doc A/AC.254/4/Add/1/Rev.6, 19 July 2000) reference was made to 'illegal residence'. During the fourth session and at informal consultations held during the fifth session, several delegations expressed concern that the Protocol should focus on illegal entry and not illegal residence, and preferred the text proposed by Mexico.

24 The text for this provision was adopted at the eighth session of the Ad Hoc Committee and is based on the proposal of Austria and Italy (A/AC.254/L.179, 28 February 2000).

25 Interpretative Notes (n 3), 17, para. 92.

26 See UN Doc A/AC.254/5/Add.21, Addendum, Proposal of Canada (11 February 2000); amendments previously issued in document A/AC.254/L.59 (6 July 1999): 'migrants who engage in criminal activity ought not to be above the law in the State in which they find themselves, nor should a person who actively participates in a migrant smuggling ring (e.g. as an instigator or a provider of fraudulent documents) be immune from prosecution just because he or she can also claim to be a migrant.'

27 D. McClean, *Transnational Organized Crime: A Commentary on the UN Convention and its Protocols* (OUP, Oxford, 2007), 389.

seen as necessary in this regard.[28] The same goes for border control, which States Parties are required to strengthen to the greatest extent possible as well as considering strengthening cooperation between border control agencies.[29] Carrier sanctions are also provided for, according to the terms of Art. 11(2)–(4); however, the obligation is on States Parties to impose a duty on commercial carriers to ascertain that passengers have the necessary documents; they are not called upon to make any judgment on their validity or authenticity. It seems therefore that the obligation could arguably have been made more onerous in this respect. Nevertheless, the measures established under the instrument do not unduly limit the discretion of States not to hold carriers liable for the transportation of undocumented refugees.[30]

Throughout, one finds references to the preservation of relevant rules of international law. This is noted, for example, in Art. 16 providing for protection and assistance measures and for the protection of the rights of smuggled migrants. Primarily however, it is Art. 19[31] which expressly stipulates that:

> [n]othing in this Protocol shall affect the other rights, obligations and responsibilities of States and individuals under international law, including international humanitarian law and international human rights law and, in particular, where applicable, the 1951 Convention and the 1967 Protocol relating to the Status of Refugees and the principle of non-refoulement as contained therein.[32]

It should be noted that this provision is not intended to create new obligations beyond those established in the Protocol and those already existing in international law (whether treaty law or customary international law) in respect of any given State. This was made clear in response to a concern voiced at the eighth session of the Ad Hoc Committee, regarding the implications of this provision for States which were not Parties to the other international instruments referred to in the Protocol. In particular, the delegations of Saudi Arabia and the United Arab Emirates were concerned that, as a result of this wording, their

---

28 Arts. 14 and 15.

29 Legislative Guide (n 3) 385, para. 93(b), commenting on Art. 11(1)(6).

30 *Ibid.*, 373, para. 85; Interpretative Notes (n 3) 19, para. 103.

31 This text originally appeared in Art. 5(2) in UN Doc A/AC.254.4/Add.1/Rev.4 (27 December 1999) and earlier drafts. At the eighth session it was decided to replace the original text of Art. 5(2) with a new text based on the proposal of Belgium and Norway (A/AC.254.L.189, 1 March 2000) and Art. 13 of the revised draft Trafficking Protocol (A/AC.254/4/Add.3/Rev.5, 1 January 2000) as agreed at the seventh session. This formed the substance of the present Art. 19(1), initially appearing as Art. 15*bis*; see UN Doc A/AC.254/4/Add.1/Rev.5 (20 March 2000).

32 UN Doc A/AC.254/4/Add.1/Rev.5 (20 March 2000).

governments might be subject to obligations under those instruments to which they were not Parties, should they choose to become Parties to the CATOC Convention and Protocol. It was however pointed out that while the opening words protected the integrity of existing obligations, it could not be interpreted as creating new ones. Therefore, any State which becomes a Party to this Protocol but is not a Party to another international instrument referred to in the Protocol will not become subject to any right, obligation or responsibility under that other instrument.[33] It is however submitted that this is a moot issue: the principles embodied in the instruments mentioned in the Protocol all constitute customary international law and are therefore binding upon those States irrespective of the fact that they are not Parties to those instruments. A more pertinent point is the inclusion of the principle of *non-refoulement*, which may seem rather superfluous since the instruments mentioned in Art. 19 themselves contain references to the principle. Furthermore, reference to a specific principle of international law could lead to the mistaken impression that the other established principles might not apply. The principle was clearly included owing to its fundamental significance in this field; however, the drafting method for its inclusion is not ideal.

7.2.1.3. *Smuggling of Migrants by Sea*

The provisions relating to migrant smuggling by sea are primarily based upon Art. 17 of the 1988 Vienna Drugs Convention and are drafted in conformity with LOSC 1982. The Interpretative Notes explain that the *travaux préparatoires* should indicate that it is generally understood that the measures set out cannot be taken in the territorial sea of another State except with the permission or authorization of the coastal State concerned.[34] It is stated that this principle is well established in the law of the sea and consequently need not be restated in the Protocol.[35] Similarly, the understanding is that no action can be taken on the high seas without the authorization of the flag State. However, the wording of Art. 9(3), entitled 'Safeguard Clauses,' may lead to some inconsistent interpretation. It is stated that '[a]ny measure taken, adopted or implemented in accordance with this chapter shall *take due account* [emphasis added] of the need not to interfere with or to affect:

---

33 Interpretative Notes (n 3) 21, para. 118.

34 See also United Nations Office on Drugs and Crime, *Travaux Préparatoires of the negotiations for the elaboration of the United Nations Convention against Transnational Organised Crime and the Protocols thereto* (United Nations, New York, 2006), 494, 510, 512.

35 Interpretative Notes (n 3) 18, para. 98. See also Informal consultations of the ninth session Doc A/AC.254/L.195 (9 June 2000).

a. the rights and obligations and the exercise of jurisdiction of coastal States in accordance with the international law of the sea; or
b. the authority of the flag State to exercise jurisdiction and control in administrative, technical and social matters involving the vessel.'[36]

The whole provision imposes only an obligation to 'take due account' of the need not to interfere with or to affect the protected rights. In view of this, the Protocol may be seen as failing to use sufficiently strong wording for its terms to be interpreted as a prohibition not to interfere with or affect the rights protected under the international law of the sea.[37]

The general obligation in Part II stems from the overriding duty to 'cooperate to the fullest extent possible to prevent and suppress the smuggling of migrants by sea, in accordance with the international law of the sea.'[38] Action is predicated upon two main factors: that a State Party establishes jurisdiction over vessels sailing on the high seas and that the vessel is indeed a migrant smuggling vessel. The Legislative Guide for the Implementation of the CATOC and its Protocols notes that establishment of jurisdiction over smuggling at sea is a prerequisite for the effective implementation of Part II. Art. 15(1)(b) CATOC requires States Parties to establish jurisdiction when offences have been committed on board a vessel flying their flag. In addition, although it is not a requirement under the Convention or Protocol, it would also be useful for States Parties to establish their jurisdiction over vessels on the high seas flying the flag of another State Party as well as over those without nationality, as this will ensure the proper functioning of the measures provided for under Part II of the Protocol.[39] Furthermore, the enactment of implementing legislation providing for enforcement powers in respect of foreign flag vessels is also necessary. Issues to

36 This text of Art. 9(3) was proposed by the USA at the informal consultations of the ninth session (A/AC.254/ L.195, 9 June 2000) based on a proposal of Singapore made at the sixth session, and Art. 17(11) of the 1988 Vienna Drugs Convention. The language is derived from Art. 17(11) of the 1988 Convention and para. 6 of the IMO Interim Measures (MSC/Circ.896, Annex).

37 Art. 9 as found in Draft 6 contained sub-art. 5 which provided that 'no measures taken pursuant to this chapter shall be taken in the territorial sea, except with the permission of or as otherwise authorized by the coastal States.' This was a proposal by the US at the informal consultations of the ninth session (A/AC.254/L.195). Mexico stated that it agreed with the principle expressed, but it voiced concerns about redundancy with the international law of the sea. It suggested that an interpretation note be prepared and incorporated into the *travaux préparatoires*.

38 Art. 7. The language of this article is derived from Art. 17(a) of the Vienna Drugs Convention and from para. 8 of the IMO Interim Measures (MSC/Circ.896, Annex). Note that 'general law of the sea' includes the LOSC and other relevant international instruments. See Interpretative Notes (n 3) 18, para. 98.

39 Legislative Guide (n 3), 386, para. 95.

be addressed in such legislation include the provision of powers to search and obtain information, powers of arrest and seizure, the use of reasonable force, the production of authoritative evidence and the provision of appropriate legal protection for the officers involved.

Insofar as the object of the action taken is concerned, reference should be made to the definition of a migrant smuggling vessel. As far as the term 'engaged' (used in paragraphs 1, 2 and 7 of Art. 8) is concerned, during informal consultations held during the ninth session of the Ad Hoc Committee, it was proposed that the word 'engaged' be replaced with 'involved', which some delegations felt would include vessels less directly involved in smuggling. The words 'taking part in' and 'participating in' were also considered, but there was no consensus to change the text. 'Engaged' is intended to be understood broadly, as referring to both direct and indirect engagement. This includes cases where a mother ship has already transferred migrants to smaller vessels for landing, or has picked up migrants while at sea for the purposes of smuggling them. It does not include a vessel which had simply rescued migrants who were being smuggled by another vessel.[40]

The general rubric of permissible action at sea is laid out in Art. 8,[41] which opens by stating that where a State Party has reasonable grounds to suspect that a vessel flying its flag or a stateless vessel is involved in migrant smuggling, the State Party may request the assistance of other States Parties in suppressing such use of the vessel.[42] This assistance must be provided to the extent possible and within the means of the requested States Parties (Art. 8(1)).[43]

The Protocol falls short of detailing the type of assistance that may be requested, as does the Vienna Drugs Convention. However, a look at the Commentary on the Drugs Convention shows that a wide interpretation is given to the equivalent provision:[44]

40 Interpretative Notes (n 3), 18, para. 100; Legislative Guide (n 3), 386, para. 97.

41 The origins of the text of this article can be found in Art. 17 of the 1988 Convention and para. 11 of the IMO Interim Measures (MSC/Circ.896, Annex).

42 Note that any measure taken pursuant to Part II is to be carried out only by warships or military aircraft, or by other ships or aircraft clearly marked and identifiable as being on government service or authorized to that effect. See Art. 9(4), the text of which derives from Art. 17(10) of the 1988 Convention and para. 6 of the IMO Interim Measures (MSC/Circ.896, Annex).

43 The language in this provision is taken from Art. 17(2) of the 1988 Convention and para. 11 of the IMO Interim Measures (MSC/Circ.896, Annex). During the sixth session, it was decided to replace the words 'as is reasonable under the circumstances' with 'within the means available to them', to bring the wording closer to the 1988 Convention.

44 United Nations, *Commentary on the UN Convention against Illicit Traffic in Narcotic Drugs and Psychotropic Substances 1998*, E/CN.7/590 (United Nations, New York, 1998), para. 17.44.

> [A]ssistance can also be sought for a wide range of other purposes. These might include searching for the suspect vessel, preventing it from unloading or trans-shipping its cargo, facilitating the presence of the law enforcement officials of the flag State on board the pursuing vessel, and like matters.

Art. 8(2) specifies that in cases where a State Party has reasonable grounds to suspect that a vessel exercising the freedom of navigation in accordance with international law and registered or flagged to another State Party is engaged in migrant smuggling, that State Party may so notify the flag State, request confirmation of registry and, if confirmed, request authorization from the flag State to take appropriate measures with regard to that vessel. The article goes on to specify the actions which may be authorized by the flag State as including boarding and searching the vessel and, if evidence of smuggling is found, taking other appropriate measures as authorized by the flag State. The Agreement on Illicit Traffic by Sea, implementing Art. 17 of the United Nations Convention against Illicit Traffic in Narcotic Drugs and Psychotropic Substances (Council of Europe Agreement) provides more detail in this regard, stating, in Art. 9, that:

> Having received the authorisation of the flag State, and subject to the conditions or limitations, if any, made under Art. 8, paragraph 1, the intervening State may take the following actions:

i.

- a. stop and board the vessel;
- b. establish effective control of the vessel and over any person thereon;
- c. take any action provided for in sub-paragraph ii of this article which is considered necessary to establish whether a relevant offence has been committed and to secure any evidence thereof;
- d. require the vessel and any persons thereon to be taken into the territory of the intervening State and detain the vessel there for the purpose of carrying out further investigations;

ii. and, having established effective control of the vessel:

- a. search the vessel, anyone on it and anything in it, including its cargo;
- b. open or require the opening of any containers, and test or take samples of anything on the vessel;
- c. require any person on the vessel to give information concerning himself or anything on the vessel;
- d. require the production of documents, books or records relating to the vessel or any persons or objects on it, and make photographs or copies of anything the production of which the competent authorities have the power to require;
- e. seize, secure and protect any evidence or material discovered on the vessel.

However, the lack of detail in the Smuggling Protocol is not to be seen as a shortcoming, as the use of the words '*inter alia*' in Art. 8(2) indicates that the list is not exhaustive and any of the above measures may be authorized by the flag State; after all, it is within the discretion of the flag State to authorize any measures necessary, subject to its obligation under Art. 7 to 'cooperate to the fullest extent possible to prevent and suppress the smuggling of migrants by sea, in accordance with the international law of the sea.' The implication is that, while in theory the flag State may decline to give its authorization for any or some actions, the obligation in Art. 7 prevents it from doing so if the flag State's refusal would amount to a lack of cooperation in the suppression of maritime migrant smuggling. The same interpretation may be given to Art. 8(5) which, itself subject to the terms of Art. 7, states that flag State authorization may be subject to certain conditions (such as conditions relating to responsibility and the extent of effective measures to be taken) to be agreed between the flag State and the requesting State.[45] It is implied that these conditions must be reasonable and not unfounded.

Art. 8(2) mentions boarding and searching. As far as the meanings of 'board' and 'search' are concerned, during the sixth session of the Ad Hoc Committee, several delegations expressed concern about the exact meaning of the word 'board' and its translation into other languages. At issue was the extent to which the term would authorize the boarding of a vessel against the will of the person in charge of it. The word 'board' appears in both the 1988 Vienna Drugs Convention and the 2001 IMO Interim Measures.[46] A similar issue arose with regard to the use of the term 'search' during the informal consultations of the ninth session. There was discussion regarding whether the word 'inspect' or 'search' was more appropriate here. Some delegations preferred an inspection power, as being broader and less intrusive; others preferred the power to search, being more suitable for the examination of a vessel believed to be engaged in criminal smuggling activities. Several delegations preferred the use of the words matching Art. 17(4) of the Vienna Drugs Convention; however, it was noted that while the English text of the Convention used the word 'search', the French and Spanish texts used words more closely corresponding to 'inspection'.[47] It is for this reason that the lack of definitions of the type in the original Italian proposal is a grave shortcoming, as they would no doubt have facilitated and clarified such operational aspects.

---

[45] Earlier drafts included the words 'including the use of force' after 'the extent of effective measures to be taken.' At the informal consultations held during the ninth session, it was agreed to recommend the deletion of these words.

[46] MSC/Circ.896.Rev.1 Advisory Circular outlining Interim Measures for combating unsafe practices associated with the trafficking or transport of migrants by sea, para. 12.

[47] The first five drafts used the word 'inspect.'

Furthermore, Art. 8(2) states that if evidence is found that the vessel is engaged in the smuggling of migrants, the State Party may take appropriate measures with respect to the vessel and people and cargo on board, as authorized by the flag State (Art. 8(2)).[48] 'Appropriate measures' are not specified and there are two possible interpretations. The appropriate measures could be specified by the requesting State to the flag State and flag State authorization be given for each action, or, alternatively, the authorization of the flag State is for the requesting State to take all appropriate measures deemed necessary by the requesting State. The latter alternative seems to be preferable: it permits more efficient action and, consequently, more effective suppression of migrant smuggling on the part of the requesting State. Furthermore, the vessel is safeguarded by Art. 9(2), which states that where 'the grounds for measures taken pursuant to Art. 8 ... prove to be unfounded, the vessel shall be compensated for any loss or damage that may have been sustained, provided that the vessel has not committed any act justifying the measures taken.' Any actions taken which are not deemed 'appropriate' could be seen to be actions taken on unfounded grounds.

No other measures can be taken without express flag State authorization, unless necessary to relieve imminent danger to life or any measures provided for in relevant bilateral or multilateral agreements (Art. 8(5)).[49] At the sixth session many delegations expressed the view that the words 'imminent danger' were too broad and required clarification. Some delegations sought clarification that the danger referred to was 'to life.' Others expressed a preference for limiting this provision to cases where there was danger to the lives of migrants. Others pointed out that cases could arise where the lives of crew members or boarding parties exercising their powers under paragraph 2(a) might be endangered, and that the wording should provide for this. At the informal consultations of the ninth session, it was agreed to recommend the removal of 'safety' from the phrase 'to the lives or safety of persons.'[50]

The results of any measure taken in furtherance of such authorization must be promptly relayed to the flag State (Art. 8(3)). Furthermore, any requests must be considered and responded to 'expeditiously' (Art. 8(4)) and, in order

48 During the informal consultations, the Danish delegation raised a reservation to this provision and indicated that, as a matter of Danish constitutional law, it could not expressly authorize another State to search a ship of Danish registry. It indicated that it could however undertake not to pursue any claims under Danish or international law against another State which took such action of its own accord, provided that such action was consistent with the Protocol.

49 The Protocol does not specify whether such bilateral agreements are limited to those with the flag State or can also include agreements with the national State of those on board. Arguably, any such bilateral agreements would fall under this sub-article.

50 This limited the scope of permissible action without flag State authorization. Some delegations expressed concern that the exceptions did not cover all the operational scenarios which might arise.

to expedite the process of receiving authorization, each State Party is required to designate an authority or authorities to receive and respond to requests for assistance in maritime cases (Art. 8(6)).

Should a State Party have reasonable grounds[51] to suspect that a vessel is engaged in the smuggling of migrants by sea and is without nationality or may be assimilated to a vessel without nationality, it may board and search it (Art. 8(7)). If there is evidence confirming this suspicion, that State Party is obliged to take appropriate measures in accordance with relevant domestic[52] and international law. At the sixth session, in response to concerns about the meaning of 'to board' in various languages, the wording was changed to 'to board and inspect'. The informal consultations held during the ninth session recommended revising the sentence by replacing the words 'shall board' with 'may board' and replacing the word 'inspect' with the word 'search'.

7.2.1.4. *The Particular Nature of Migrant Smuggling*

While the law enforcement and cooperation regime defined in Part II has been inspired in large part by the set of measures included in Art. 17 of the Vienna Drugs Convention, because of the fundamental difference between trafficking in drugs and smuggling of persons, the Smuggling Protocol considers specific factors in judging the appropriateness of intervening at sea against migrant smuggling and in ensuring that adequate safeguards are taken regarding the safety and humane treatment of people on board. In this regard, the Legislative Guide draws attention to the fact that the focus, in Arts. 7 and 8, on the suppression of a criminal activity should not lead law enforcement officers to overlook the duty established under maritime law and custom to rescue those in peril at sea. Vessels used for smuggling may be confiscated if apprehended and smugglers often use dilapidated vessels as a result. In some cases, vessels are encountered at sea overloaded with migrants and in imminent danger of sinking. Legislation should therefore be drafted and implemented so as to ensure that officials are aware that the duty to effect a rescue takes priority (presumably over the suppression of criminal activity) in such circumstances, and that where there is evidence of peril at sea vessels should be boarded, whether or not smuggling is suspected.[53]

51 The informal consultations held during the ninth session recommended replacing the words '[w]hen there are reasonable grounds', present in the earlier drafts, with '[a] State Party that has reasonable grounds'. One delegation expressed concern that this might make assessment of 'reasonable grounds' a subjective matter for the State involved. Other delegations pointed out that since the provision dealt only with the boarding of stateless vessels, only one State would be in a position to make this determination in any event.

52 The reference is presumably to the enforcing State's domestic law.

53 Legislative Guide (n 3), 386, para. 97.

Furthermore, the IMO and UNHCR had expressed concern that unnecessary search or detention of vessels could deter Masters from meeting fundamental humanitarian requirements, including that of effecting rescue operations. In establishing and implementing powers to stop and search vessels and to detain them or crew members who may be witnesses (but not criminal suspects), legislators should bear in mind that procedures of stopping and boarding should be carefully considered and used with as much restraint as possible. Art. 9 is in part a response to such concerns.[54] Entitled 'Safeguard Clauses,' Art. 9 instructs States Parties taking action against vessels under Art. 8 to ensure the safety and humane treatment of those on board; to ensure, within available means, that any measures taken are environmentally sound; to take due account of the need not to endanger the security of the vessel and its cargo and not to prejudice the commercial and legal interests of the flag State or any other interested State (Art. 9(1)). As mentioned earlier, if the grounds for measures taken prove to be unfounded, the vessel is to be compensated for any loss or damage which may have been sustained, provided that she has not committed any act justifying the measures taken (Art. 9(2)).[55]

Apart from this framework, the Protocol amplifies the duty to cooperate in the repression of migrant smuggling to the fullest extent by expressly providing for further agreements of a bilateral or regional nature to be established in order to create the most appropriate and effective measures to prevent and combat the crime of migrant smuggling and further to increase the effectiveness of the Protocol among the Parties themselves.[56]

The Smuggling Protocol is valuable in a number of respects. Most obviously, it indicates a readiness to recognize migrant smuggling as a type of organized crime which needs effective action to combat it. Secondly, despite not being provided for in the LOSC, the regulation of enforcement activity in its repression does not proceed along new lines; rather, the measures build on previous experience in the fight against maritime drug trafficking and proceed to create enforcement procedures which leave untouched the general principles of the law of the sea. In this way, the *lacunae* in the general rubric of the international law of the sea are filled in a way which strengthens—rather than challenges—it.

---

54 *Ibid.*, 367, para. 78; 386, para. 100.

55 This proposal was made by China at the sixth session UN Doc A/AC.254/5/Add.21 (11 February 2000); amendments were previously issued in document A/AC.254/L.51 (2 July 1999). The text is based on Art. 110(3) LOSC.

56 Smuggling Protocol, Art. 17 (originally, Art. 7*quater* in the first five drafts).

7.2.2. The 2004 Amendments

The IMO played a pivotal role in the creation of the recent amendments. Initially, the concern of the IMO was more particularly focussed on the unsafe practices of migrant smuggling by sea which often placed passengers' lives at risk. This is evidenced both by the 1993 Resolution on the Enhancement of Safety of Life at Sea by Prevention and Suppression of Unlawful Practices associated with alien smuggling by ships[57] and the 1997 Resolution on Combating Unsafe Practices Associated with the Trafficking or Transport of Migrants by Sea.[58]

Italy's proposal to the IMO for a Multilateral Convention to Combat Illegal Migration by Sea[59] acted as a catalyst in the process of creating a framework for combating maritime migrant smuggling. Despite the fact that the IMO ultimately declared itself incompetent to consider such proposal,[60] work within the Organization quickly led to the establishment of interim measures which built upon the 1997 Resolution and on the proposals contained in the Italian draft. The resulting Interim Measures for Combating Unsafe Practices associated with the Trafficking or Transport of Migrants by Sea of 16 December 1998 were the primary guide in relation to maritime migrant smuggling until the coming into force of the CATOC and its Protocols.[61]

During the deliberations within the various IMO sub-committees, a number of important principles were stated and significant points discussed which elaborate on the interplay between rescue at sea and maritime interception. The amendments to the SOLAS and SAR Conventions are therefore discussed in the light of the various proposals made by States (primarily, France, Germany and Norway), the ideas developed by the Inter-Agency Group during its meeting in Geneva in July 2002[62] and the Informal Meeting held in Sweden in September 2002.[63]

---

57 A.773(18) (4 November 1993).

58 A.867(20) (27 November 1997).

59 LEG 76/11/1 (1 August 1997).

60 See Schloenhardt (n 8), 292.

61 MSC/Circ. 896, revised and updated in June 2001, MSC/Circ.896.Rev.1. See also MSC 74/23/8 (9 April 2002). The measures seek to establish mechanisms for inter-State cooperation *inter alia* to ensure maritime safety standards, to apprehend and inspect suspect vessels and to ensure the humane treatment of those on board.

62 Participating organizations were: the United Nations Division for Ocean Affairs and the Law of the Sea, the Office of the UNHCR, the ODCCP, the OHCHR, IOM and the IMO Secretariat. For conclusions see FAL 30/9 (24 October 2002), Note by the Secretariat (also reported in MSC 76/22/8, 31 July 2002). Another inter-agency group meeting was held in July 2004 at the IMO Headquarters, after the amendments had been adopted: see MSC 79/22/6 (15 September 2004).

63 Conclusions contained in MSC 76/22/11 (27 September 2002).

The logical starting point in this analysis would be the proposal, at the opening of the twenty-second Assembly in 2001, by former Secretary-General of the IMO, Mr W. O'Neill, to review existing legislation in order to identify any *lacunae*, inconsistencies or ambiguities therein. Consequently, Resolution A.920(22) on the Review of Safety Measures and Procedures for the Treatment of Persons Rescued at Sea called for a review of existing treaties and IMO instruments and for appropriate action to be undertaken within the context of an inter-agency group. The intended result of such review was *inter alia* that survivors of distress incidents would be given assistance, regardless of nationality or status or circumstances in which they are found; that rescuing ships would be able to deliver the survivors to a place of safety; and that survivors, regardless of nationality or status (including undocumented migrants, asylum-seekers, refugees and stowaways), would be treated, while on board the vessel, in the manner prescribed in the relevant IMO instruments and in accordance with relevant international agreements and long-standing humanitarian maritime traditions.

7.2.2.1. *Priorities when Amending the Existing Legal Framework*

There was a general recognition that *lacunae* existed in both the SOLAS and SAR Conventions in relation to the disembarkation of those rescued at sea and the requirement of bringing them to a place of safety.[64] In this regard, an important distinction drawn early on in the deliberations was that there were two issues which, although related, had to be kept distinct. These were the purely SAR aspect of rescuing those in distress at sea regardless of their nationality, status or circumstances and the concomitant necessity of delivering them to a place of safety under the SOLAS and SAR Conventions, and the related but distinct considerations of the status of such persons after the rescue when other related international instruments would subsequently have to be taken into consideration.[65] This point was outside the IMO's remit and was to be handled by the inter-agency group, mentioned above.[66]

Priorities and considerations were diverse and compelling. The resultant framework would need to cater for the need of States to respect and ensure respect of the rights and dignity of people rescued at sea regardless of their status, as well as for their need to maintain effective border and immigration controls and to prevent and fight the smuggling of migrants and trafficking in human beings. Of paramount importance was the need to preserve the integrity

64 FAL 30/9 (24 October 2002), para. 9.

65 COMSAR 6/22 (8 March 2002). See also MSC 75/11/2 (11 March 2002), para. 7.

66 For discussion of issues outside the IMO's remit see MSC 75/11/2 (11 March 2002), para. 10; FAL 30/9 (24 October 2002) Annex.

and effectiveness of the international system for search and rescue and the role of commercial shipping in providing assistance to those in distress at sea.[67] In order for such framework to exist and operate effectively, coastal States needed to accept their obligation to facilitate rescue operations by ensuring that the necessary enabling arrangements are in place. Furthermore, flag States had the obligation of ensuring that Masters of ships flying their flag proceeded to the assistance of people in distress at sea. Ultimately, the entire international community had to cooperate in such a way as to uphold the integrity of the search and rescue system.[68]

A principal concern related to the risk of compromising the duty to rescue and the search and rescue system put in place by the IMO. It was also seen to be important that the Master was not to be left alone with his responsibilities (in other words, that he had a right to expect cooperation from governments) and that there was to be a closer balance between the obligations of States and ships' Masters. Clarification of the meaning of a 'place of safety' was thus seen to be essential to the exercise, as it was a central element in the obligation of the Master to deliver those rescued at sea to such a place of safety and of Contracting Governments to accept those so delivered.

The Norwegian delegation was especially interested in this point since, following its experience with the *Tampa*, delivery to a place of safety without undue delay would minimize any burdens on the rescuing ship, thus implying less risk of distress calls remaining unheeded, and the threat to the international search and rescue regime would thus be averted.[69] The inter-agency meeting also noted the importance of such *lacuna*. Concerns involved whether 'safety' referred only to protection from physical elements or included other dangers as well, and whether the obligation placed on mariners to take rescued persons to a place of safety should be accompanied by a reciprocal duty on the part of States to allow entry and disembarkation in such place of safety.[70]

At an informal meeting held in Sweden in September 2002 on Safety Measures and Procedures for the Treatment of Persons Rescued at Sea (IFM), it was made clear that a place of safety would normally be located ashore; however it could also be a properly equipped and staffed ship. It was recognized that one of the most important issues was to get the distressed persons off the assisting ship as quickly as possible since that ship would not usually have the appropriate facilities and equipment to sustain the additional persons on board without

[67] FAL 30/9 (24 October 2002). The essence of these considerations was echoed at the Swedish IFM of September 2002. See MSC 76/22/11 (27 September 2002), para. 2.2.

[68] FAL 30/9 (24 October 2002) Annex, para. 13.

[69] MSC 75/2/2/Add.2 (12 March 2002) para. 7.

[70] FAL 30/9 (24 October 2002), para. 7.

endangering its own safety and to permit proper care of those rescued.[71] However, no definition of 'place of safety' was found to be needed at that stage, and the phrase remains undefined to date.[72] The Guidelines on the Treatment of Persons Rescued at Sea[73] however stipulate that a place of safety is a location where rescue operations are considered to end and that it is also a place where the survivors' safety of life is no longer threatened and where their basic human needs (such as food, shelter and medical needs) can be met. It is a place from which transportation arrangements can be made to the survivors' next or final destination.[74] An assisting ship should not be considered a place of safety solely on the basis of the fact that the survivors' life is no longer in immediate danger once they are on board the vessel. That vessel may not have appropriate facilities for dealing with the survivors without endangering itself. Even if the ship is capable of safely accommodating the survivors it should still be relieved of this responsibility as soon as alternative arrangements can be made.[75] The selection of a place of safety will need to account for a variety of factors such as the situation on board the assisting ship, on-scene conditions, medical needs, the availability of transportation or other rescue units.[76] Governments are urged to cooperate with each other with regard to the provision of suitable places of safety for survivors after considering relevant factors and risks.[77] A place of safety may be on land, or aboard a rescue unit or other suitable vessel or facility at sea which can serve as a place of safety until the survivors are disembarked to their next destination.[78] It is also stated that often the assisting ship or another ship may be able to transport those rescued to a place of safety; however, if performing the function would be a hardship for the vessel, then RCCs should attempt to arrange for the use of other reasonable alternatives for this purpose.[79]

7.2.2.2. *The Amendments*[80]

On 20 May 2004, during its seventy-eighth session, the MSC adopted amendments to the SOLAS and SAR Conventions concerning the treatment of those

---

71 For considerations of consequent unseaworthiness see Germany's proposal: MSC 75/11/2 (11 March 2002), para. 11.

72 MSC 76/22/11 (27 September 2002), paras 3.4 and 3.5.

73 MSC.167(78) adopted on 20 May 2004.

74 *Ibid.*, para. 6.12.

75 *Ibid.*, para. 6.13.

76 *Ibid.*, para. 6.15.

77 *Ibid.*, para. 6.16.

78 *Ibid.*, para. 6.14.

79 *Ibid.*, para. 6.18. Note that the obligation of *non-refoulement* is also alluded to in para. 6.17.

80 The need for updating the international law instruments relating to illegal migration by sea has also been examined by the EU. See Conclusions of 2 December 2004 evaluating the progress made with regard to the implementation of the Programme of measures to combat

rescued at sea, and/or asylum-seekers, refugees and stowaways,[81] together with Guidelines on the Treatment of Persons Rescued at Sea.[82] The SOLAS Convention obliges ships and thus flag States to render assistance to those in distress at sea, and the SAR Convention obliges coastal States to assist persons in distress at sea.[83] The Guidelines sum up in a nutshell the main effect of the amendments to the SAR and SOLAS Conventions:

> Specifically, paragraph 1–1 of SOLAS regulation V/33 and paragraph 3.1.9 of the Annex to the SAR Convention, as amended, impose upon Governments an obligation to co-ordinate and co-operate to ensure that masters of ships providing assistance by embarking persons in distress at sea are released from their obligations with minimum further deviation from the ship's intended voyage.
>
> As realized by the MSC in adopting the amendments, the intent of new paragraph 1–1 of SOLAS Regulation V/33 and paragraph 3.1.9 of the Annex of the International Convention on Maritime Search and Rescue, 1979, as amended, is to ensure that in every case a place of safety is provided within a reasonable time. The responsibility to provide a place of safety, or to ensure that a place of safety is provided, falls on the Government responsible for the SAR region in which the survivors were recovered.[84]

The Guidelines provide general guidance to ships' Masters, governments and RCCs. Their purpose is stated to be to provide 'guidance to Governments and to shipmasters with regard to humanitarian obligations and obligations under the relevant international law relating to treatment of persons rescued at sea':[85]

> The obligation of the master to render assistance should complement the corresponding obligation of IMO Member Governments to co-ordinate and co-operate in relieving the master of the responsibility to provide follow up care of survivors and to deliver the persons retrieved at sea to a place of safety.

illegal migration across the maritime borders of the Member States of the European Union, 15087/04 FRONT 201 COMIX 709, 22 November 2004. Here, special attention was to be given to rescue on the high seas and whether a specific arrangement could be developed for the Mediterranean Sea. See also Global Approach to Migration: Policy Actions focusing on Africa and the Mediterranean, in Presidency Conclusions, Brussels European Council, 15–16 December 2005, 15914/1/05 REV 1, CONCL 3.

81 Draft guidance to Governments and to Shipmasters was initially developed and approved by COMSAR at its eighth session: COMSAR 8/8/1 (12 November 2003).

82 See n 73.

83 FAL 32/22 (25 July 2005). An amendment to the FAL Convention relating to those rescued at sea was also adopted to be included in Section 2—Arrival, Stay and Departure of the ship. This amendment requires public authorities to facilitate the arrival and departure of ships engaged in the rescue of those in distress at sea in order to provide a place of safety for such people. (See FAL 31/9/Add.1 (25 March 2004) for text of amendments).

84 Guidelines (n 73), paras 2.4–2.5.

85 *Ibid.*, para. 1.1.

> These Guidelines are intended to help Governments and masters better understand their obligations under international law and provide helpful guidance with regard to carrying out these obligations.[86]

It is stressed that when ships assist persons at sea, coordination is needed among all concerned to ensure that priorities are met in a manner which takes due account of border control, sovereignty and security concerns consistent with international law.[87] The priorities mentioned are that all those in distress at sea should be assisted without delay; that prompt assistance provided by ships at sea is an essential element of global search and rescue services; and, lastly, that both flag and coastal States should have effective arrangements in place for prompt assistance to shipmasters in relieving them of those recovered by ships at sea.[88]

Insofar as the SOLAS Convention is concerned, the relevant aspects are provided in Chapter V, Regulation 7 entitled 'Search and Rescue Services' and Regulation 33 on 'Distress messages: Obligations and Procedures'. The main changes to the SOLAS Convention concern definitional aspects and the level of cooperation which must exist between the Parties concerned.

Chapter V, Regulation 2.5 now includes a definition of 'search and rescue service,' developed by the IFM, as consisting of:

> The performance of distress monitoring, communication, co-ordination and search and rescue functions, including provision of medical advice, initial medical assistance, or medical evacuation, through the use of public and private resources including co-operating aircraft, ships, vessels and other craft and installations.

The Norwegian delegation had stated that the obligations imposed by SOLAS on Contracting Governments to provide assistance to those in distress at sea were not precise and, moreover, certain key terms (such as: 'rescue'; 'around its coasts'; 'as are deemed practicable and necessary'; 'so far as possible') remained undefined, thus leading to the risk of different interpretations being given to the same terms.[89] This was affirmed by the Swedish IFM which proceeded to develop a definition of 'search and rescue service'.[90] Another definitional point concerned the clarification of 'persons in distress at sea', found in Regulation V/33. Regulation 33.1 now stipulates that any person in distress at sea

86 *Ibid.*, para. 1.2.

87 Parties concerned include the Master of the rescuing vessel, the flag State of the rescuing vessel and the State in whose SAR area the assistance has been rendered. The flag State of the rescued vessel and the States of nationality of those on board in distress at sea could also be relevant.

88 *Ibid.*, para. 3.1.

89 There was an initial hesitation regarding the definition of 'search and rescue service' since this is covered by the SAR Convention. See MSC 75/2/2/Add.2 (12 March 2002), paras 16–17.

90 MSC 76/22/11 (27 September 2002).

is to be given assistance 'regardless of the nationality or status of such persons[91] or the circumstances in which they are found,' emulating paragraph 2.1.10 of the SAR Convention.[92]

The most significant amendment relates to the notion of assistance and the duty of cooperation in this regard. The Swedish IFM noted the need to balance the obligations of the Master to render assistance with a corresponding obligation on Contracting States to coordinate and cooperate in relieving the Master of his burden and to deliver the rescued to a place of safety. It was proposed that the Contracting State responsible for the SAR region in which the operation took place should have the responsibility for coordination and cooperation between the Parties concerned.[93]

Norway had voiced concern that the current provisions in SOLAS did not specify what a ship was to do after having retrieved the persons in distress. It maintained that the intent of the provisions was to establish both a duty and a right to deliver them to a suitable place of safety without undue delay. Unless this principle was clearly established in an IMO Convention, Norway feared that this could cause vessels to violate their duty to provide assistance to those in distress at sea. It consequently advocated that a ship having retrieved persons in distress at sea should be given certain reasonable rights to decide which port or territorial waters the people rescued could be delivered to.[94] France had proposed a similar option as paragraph 7 of Regulation V/33 in that 'Masters of ships that have retrieved rescued persons should be able to put them ashore at the nearest appropriate [place] [port] taking into account the number of persons rescued, the size of the ship and her route.'[95] The Swedish IFM however agreed that the draft text it developed would cover this latter proposal which could thus be deleted.[96] To be able to comply with such proposal, the Norwegian delegation maintained that a corresponding obligation had to be created requiring Contracting Governments to allow such ships access to their territorial waters and ports, a right which, Norway maintained, was part of customary international law.[97]

---

[91] Determination of status was not to be relevant in rescue operations since any determination of status was part of the post-SAR operations and outside the remit of the IMO. These issues however did need to be considered by the UNHCR and other relevant organizations, in order to develop burden-sharing agreements and procedures and to discourage people from trafficking and smuggling. See MSC 76/22/11 (27 September 2002), paras 3.7–3.8.

[92] For relevant contributions see MSC 75/2/2/Add.2 (12 March 2002), para. 20; MSC 75/11/1 (4 March 2002).

[93] MSC 76/22/11 (27 September 2002), para. 3.6.

[94] MSC 75/2/2/Add.1 (12 February 2002), paras 21 and 22.

[95] MSC 75/11/1 (4 March 2002).

[96] MSC 76/22/11 (27 September 2002), para. 3.1.

[97] MSC 75/2/2/Add.2 (12 March 2002), para. 23. For the text of proposal see paras 21–23.

Norway's proposal was not, however, fully endorsed by the IFM. The draft alternative text developed during this meeting was considered to go a long way in reassuring a Master that he would be able to disembark persons rescued from distress at sea at the earliest opportunity.[98] While Norway expressed support for the text produced in Sweden it also voiced serious concerns that the 'system' described must be expected to fail in certain circumstances. Such failures could indeed result in Masters having rescued persons in distress at sea not being permitted by any coastal State to disembark the survivors to a place of safety within a reasonable period of time. These concerns could well prevent some Masters from fulfilling their obligation to rescue those in distress at sea. Norway was therefore of the opinion that additional provisions needed to be developed and added to the text produced at the Swedish IFM both in SOLAS and SAR so as to eliminate these concerns. While a number of delegations such as that of Denmark supported this view, a significant number supported the report of the SAR Working Group and the compromise text of the proposed draft amendments to the SOLAS and SAR Conventions.[99]

It is submitted that Norway was correct in its observation that the devised system could not be successful in 'all extraordinary, isolated cases.'[100] After all, what has been imposed upon States is an obligation to cooperate rather than one to ensure that a place of safety is provided. In this way, a rather hefty burden is placed upon the State in whose SAR area the assistance is rendered, as it is that State which is held responsible for coordinating such cooperative efforts. It seems, therefore, that in default of agreement it is this State which must bear responsibility for those rescued at sea within its search and rescue area. This was also observed in the EU Commission's Study on the International Law Instruments in Relation to Illegal Immigration by Sea, which states:

> Besides the principle according to which the State responsible for the SAR zone should provide such a [safe] place or to make sure that such a place is found, there is no rule designating by default a State responsible for receiving the rescued passengers such as, for example, the State of nationality or of residence of the persons, the flag State or the State of departure of the ship.[101]

The resulting provision, developed by the IFM, is Regulation V/33.1.1, which states as follows:

---

98 It was recognized that the regulation would not be able to ensure that this could be assured for all extraordinary, isolated acts. For that particular purpose, further guidance was needed in the IAMSAR manual. See MSC 76/22/11 (27 September 2002), para. 3.10.

99 COMSAR 7/23 (20 February 2003), paras 8.17 *et seq.*

100 MSC 76/22/11 (27 September 2002), para. 3.10.

101 Commission (EC) 'Study on the International Law Instruments in Relation to Illegal Immigration by Sea' (Staff Working Document) SEC(2007)691, 15 May 2007, 691.

> Contracting Governments shall co-ordinate and co-operate to ensure that masters of ships providing assistance by embarking persons in distress at sea are released from their obligations with minimum further deviation from the ships' intended voyage, provided that releasing the master of the ship from the obligations under the current regulation does not further endanger the safety of life at sea. The Contracting Government responsible for the search and rescue region in which such assistance is rendered shall exercise primary responsibility for ensuring such co-ordination and co-operation occurs, so that survivors assisted are disembarked from the assisting ship and delivered to a place of safety, taking into account the particular circumstances of the case and guidelines developed by the Organization. In these cases the relevant Contracting Governments shall arrange for such disembarkation to be effected as soon as reasonably practicable.

Coupled with this amendment is the introduction of another provision (Regulation V/34.1) also developed by the IFM, relating to the Master's discretion. According to this provision '[t]he owner, the charterer, the company operating the ship ... or any other persons shall not prevent or restrict the master of the ship from taking or executing any decision which, in the master's professional judgment, is necessary for safety of life at sea and protection of the marine environment.'[102] Furthermore, there is a new obligation imposed on the Master of the rescuing vessel who has embarked persons in distress at sea to treat such persons 'with humanity, within the capabilities and limitations of the ship'.[103]

Clearly, the issue of delivery to a place of safety was the most thorny issue in the IMO deliberations, where varying interests surfaced, reflecting the particular situations of various States. States such as Spain were adamant in maintaining that proposals made should not hinder national and international efforts to eradicate all forms of illegal immigration by sea.[104] Consequently, it did not agree with the Norwegian proposal which attempted to include an obligation on any particular State to admit rescuees.[105] It maintained that the discretion of the Master to decide upon a suitable port or territorial waters, and the corresponding obligation placed upon coastal States to accept and act upon this decision raised 'real concern as to the use of such rights and obligations by illegal migrant trafficking networks by sea which, with total disregard for the safety of the lives of the immigrants they transport by sea, seek to exploit those rights and obligations to promote this kind of activity, and consequently endanger the safety of life at sea ... [Spain feared] that such broad amendments could under-

---

102 This provision was the result of a French proposal, subsequently developed by the Swedish IFM. See MSC 76/22/11 (27 September 2002), para. 3.11.

103 SOLAS Chapter V/33.6.

104 MSC 76/22/10 (9 October 2002).

105 MSC 76/22/11 Annex 1 (22 September 2002); and MSC 75/2/2/Add.2 (12 March 2002), paras 21 and 22.

mine national and international efforts to eradicate all forms of illegal immigration by sea.' Consequently, it was of the opinion that this must be limited to cases 'justified by objective reasons of safety of the ship, serious humanitarian grounds or saving life at sea.'[106]

Similarly, the delegation of Australia, supported by the US, opposed any proposals for amendments of the SOLAS and SAR Conventions which would have the effect of extending convention obligations to encompass the disembarkation of rescued persons at a particular port or any implied or direct provision that the Master should have the ultimate right to decide this. It was of the view that this was the responsibility of the relevant authorities of the coastal States in conjunction with those of the flag State.[107]

Perhaps the best description of the new provision came from the US delegation, which expressed the view, supported by a number of other delegations, that two competing interests exist in the rescue-at-sea scenario: that of the Master to deliver those rescued at sea to a place of safety within a reasonable period of time and the interest of the State in protecting its borders and other sovereignty concerns. Both interests could conflict at times, but the latter was not within the remit of the IMO. The US felt that the compromise text developed at the IFM in Sweden was well-balanced and that the new draft SOLAS Regulation V/33.1 *bis* should provide a sufficient basis for reminding Contracting States of their treaty obligations in case of need. Any attempt to try to regulate any further into the delivery process would run the risk of exceeding the remit of the IMO. The new provision thus represented the best possible compromise for the time being.[108]

Moving on to the SAR Convention, this instrument obliges Contracting Governments to provide assistance at sea. The aim of this Convention is to impose obligations on Contracting Governments regarding facilities, procedures and cooperation with other States for the purpose of rescuing those in distress at sea.

To begin with the definitional aspects, the notion of a person in distress at sea has been supplemented, and paragraph 2.1.1 now includes 'persons in need of assistance who have found refuge on a coast in a remote location within an ocean area inaccessible to any rescue facility other than as provided for in the annex.'[109] Perhaps more significant, however, are the obligations of cooperation which have been introduced in Chapter 3 of the Annex. Arising out of a French

[106] MSC 76/22/10 (9 October 2002), paras 10–14.

[107] COMSAR 6/22 (8 March 2002).

[108] COMSAR 7/23 (20 February 2003), paras 8.29 and 8.30.

[109] Note: MSC 76/22/11 (27 September 2002), para. 6.1. France's proposed amendments to paras 2.1.1 and 2.1.10 of the Annex to the SAR Convention were considered not to be appropriate since the first addressed 'whole land areas' ashore and would therefore not fit in the SAR

proposal, subsequently developed at the Swedish IFM, paragraph 3.1.6.4 now obliges Contracting Parties 'to make the necessary arrangements in cooperation with other RCCs to identify the most appropriate place(s) for disembarking persons found in distress at sea.'[110] The IFM had agreed that the RCCs should be the focal point for handling the delivery of those rescued at sea to a place of safety and that after the RCCs had handed the case over to another authority the SAR operation was completed. It was also held that Contracting Parties should have plans and arrangements in place for the delivery of survivors to a place of safety, the determination of which is currently agreed between the RCC and the SAR facility.[111]

In furtherance of the aim of striking a balance between the obligations of the Master to come to the assistance of persons in distress at sea and the obligations of Contracting States to permit and assist the Master in disembarking such persons to a place of safety within a reasonable time, following a proposal by France[112] and developed at the IFM, paragraph 3.1.9 was introduced. It states:

> Parties shall co-ordinate and co-operate to ensure that masters of ships providing assistance by embarking persons in distress at sea are released from their obligations with minimum further deviation from the ships' intended voyage, provided that releasing the master of the ship from these obligations does not further endanger the safety of life at sea. The Party responsible for the search and rescue region in which such assistance is rendered shall exercise primary responsibility for ensuring such co-ordination and co-operation occurs, so that survivors assisted are disembarked from the assisting ship and delivered to a place of safety, taking into account the particular circumstances of the case and guidelines developed by the Organization. In these cases, the relevant Parties shall arrange for such disembarkation to be effected as soon as reasonable practicable.[113]

Linked to paragraph 3.1.9 is paragraph 4.8.5 relating to operating procedures, again proposed by the French delegation and later developed at the IFM, which

Convention addressing rescue from ships in peril, and the second would require an explicit amendment procedure and did not improve the provisions sufficiently to justify such a major amendment. For France's proposals see MSC 75/11/1 (4 March 2002).

110 For the text of French proposal see MSC 75/11/1 (4 March 2002).

111 It was noted that guidance to this effect was given in the IAMSAR manual. Since the obligation of Contracting Parties/Governments to receive the persons rescued at sea could be a burden, guidance has to be developed on how burden-sharing should work in the future. See MSC 76/22/11 (27 September 2002), para. 6.3.

112 For the text see MSC 75/11/1 (4 March 2002).

113 COMSAR 7/23 (20 February 2003). While a number of delegations thought that although the balance was well struck by the text produced in Sweden additional guidance was needed to assist the Master on the one hand and the Contracting States on the other clearly to understand what the provisions of this new draft regulation actually meant. Consequently, references to 'guidelines developed by the Organization' were included in both SOLAS Regulation V/33.1*bis* and para. 3.1.9 of the Annex to the SAR Convention.

sought further to ensure that an appropriate place for disembarking those rescued at sea would indeed be found. This is done by placing the primary responsibility in this regard on rescue coordination centres. In the words of the French proposal:

> The rescue coordination centre or rescue sub-centre concerned shall seek to locate, for a vessel or vessels rescuing persons, the most appropriate [place] [port] for disembarking such persons taking into account, *inter alia*, the wishes of the master, the number of persons rescued, their needs, the facilities of the rescue vessel, [its original destination] [its originally intended first port of call]. It shall inform the vessel or vessel concerned thereof.[114]

Currently, the State in the search and rescue area of which the rescue takes place bears the main responsibility for the rescue and disembarkation of rescuees.[115] This is not, however, a solution which has met with the approval of all Contracting Parties. The Maltese delegation, supported by only a few other delegations, did not agree with placing the final responsibility for accepting people rescued at sea on the Contracting Government responsible for the search and rescue area in which the rescue took place. It feared that this arrangement would encourage trafficking in illegal migrants, since the vessels carrying them would simply have to enter the closest neighbouring SAR area and call for assistance. The Contracting Government of that SAR area would then have to come to their assistance and effectively provide them with a place of safety. There is scope for a solution to this problem to be found at the European level, especially in terms of financial aid and the deployment of resources, as stated in the Joint Letter of 25 September 2006 addressed to the EU Presidency from the Heads of States of Cyprus, France, Greece, Italy, Malta, Portugal, Spain and Slovenia.[116] Besides this, an EU arrangement focussed on the notion of burden-sharing would no doubt serve to assist States most affected by the influxes of irregular migrants. In this regard, Malta's success in ensuring the insertion of an intra-EU voluntary burden-sharing mechanism into the European Pact on Immigration and Asylum is to be lauded as a sure step in the right direction.[117]

---

[114] MSC 75/11/1 (4 March 2002). Note that Germany supported France's proposals regarding the introduction of paras 3.1.6.4; 3.1.9; and 4.8.5. See docs MSC 75/11/2 (11 March 2002) and MSC 76/22/10 (9 October 2002). The text of para. 4.8.5 runs as follows: '[t]he rescue co-ordination centre or rescue sub-centre concerned shall initiate the process of identifying the most appropriate place(s) for disembarking such persons found in distress at sea. It shall inform the ship or ships and other relevant parties concerned thereof.'

[115] MSC 78/26 (28 May 2004), paras 16.48–16.54.

[116] Also referred to in UNGA UN Doc A/62/66 (12 March 2007), para. 74.

[117] This Pact was adopted by the European Council at its meeting of 15–16 October 2008. See Presidency Conclusions, Brussels European Council, 15–16 October 2008 (16 October 2008) 14368/08 CONCL 4.

A second meeting of the inter-agency group, held in 2004, concluded that the IMO Member States had 'arrived at a very carefully crafted compromise' which seemed to balance all of the often conflicting interests of the parties concerned. It noted that by these amendments the provisions, for the first time, placed obligations on Contracting Governments to coordinate and cooperate so that survivors assisted are disembarked from the assisting ship and delivered to a place of safety within a reasonable time. Significantly, it also noted the views of the majority of the delegations of Member States that, while the Contracting Governments responsible for the SAR region in which such assistance is rendered are to exercise primary responsibility for providing a place of safety or ensuring that a place of safety is provided, this does not oblige those Governments to disembark those rescued in its territory.[118]

Relevant legal principles and practical procedures are now helpfully laid out in a document produced jointly by the IMO and UNHCR in a bid further to amplify the relevant obligations of the Master and the relevant coastal States so as to ensure prompt disembarkation following a rescue operation.[119] These, together with the 2004 amendments and associated Guidelines, present a hope for the future resolution of disembarkation situations; a solution based on the prerequisite of cooperation and coordination of all parties concerned, both States and non-State actors. However, by failing to specify a particular State which is obliged to permit disembarkation and process any asylum claims made, it may be said that the refugee protection perspective and sharing of responsibilities in this regard have not been adequately catered for:

> In spite of the recent revision of the SAR regime undertaken by the IMO and the drafting of accompanying guidelines relating to the determination of the place of disembarkation, the issue of repartition of responsibilities between the different countries with regard to the protection of refugees is still open.[120]

It is true of course that such protection perspective is outside the remit of the IMO as such. Therefore, it seems that agreements to this end would have to be concluded possibly within a regional ambit, such as that of the European Union.

---

[118] MSC 79/22/6 (15 September 2004), paras 17–18.

[119] IMO and UNHCR, 'Rescue at Sea: A Guide to Principles and Practice as applied to Migrants and Refugees' (2006). This document has no legal force; it is merely intended as a useful reference guide in which all provisions of the various relevant international instruments are laid out, thus providing a central source of reference for obligations and definitions in international maritime and refugee law in the context of rescue at sea.

[120] Commission Staff Working Document (n 101).

7.3. *Detailing Cooperation*

7.3.1. *Drug Smuggling by Sea*[121]

Maritime drug smuggling is a concern both in itself and by reason of its link to international terrorism. UN Security Council Resolution 1456 of 2003[122] reaffirms the need to prevent terrorists from making use of other criminal activities such as transnational organized crime and, *inter alia*, illicit drugs and drug trafficking.[123] A core theme in the fight against drug smuggling is the need for cooperation.[124] According to the Working Group on Maritime Cooperation of the UN Commission on Narcotic Drugs (CND), the barriers to international cooperation include the inability of some States to exercise effective jurisdiction over vessels flying their flag outside the territorial sea, and, accordingly, their inability to reply to requests by other States to board such vessels, as well as the inability of States to exercise criminal jurisdiction over offenders other than their nationals on board vessels beyond the territorial sea. Furthermore, maritime law enforcement capability is often weak, and domestic legal restrictions in some States regarding the use of naval vessels in drug law enforcement operations further limit the interception capabilities of several coastal States.[125]

Prominent in the multilateral framework is the 1988 Vienna Drugs Convention, Art. 17 of which provides for combating the illicit traffic in drugs at sea. The Convention builds upon the general requirement in Art. 108 LOSC that States cooperate in the suppression of the illicit traffic in drugs at sea. The stated aim in Art. 2(1) is to 'promote co-operation among the Parties so that they may address more effectively the various aspects of illicit traffic ... having an international dimension.' The Convention recognizes that although drug-trafficking

[121] The following analysis of instruments will focus on the relevant provisions for immediate purposes, notably those from which a common pattern may be noted.

[122] UN Doc S/RES/1456.

[123] The IMO has also been active in this area: see MSC.228(82), Revised Guidelines for the prevention and suppression of the smuggling of drugs, psychotropic substances and precursor chemicals on ships engaged in international maritime traffic (7 December 2006) in MSC 82/24/Add.2, Annex 14.

[124] See ECOSOC, 'Enhancing multilateral cooperation in combating illicit traffic by sea' (15 March 2000) CND Res 43/5; ECOSOC, 'Enhancing multilateral cooperation in combating illicit traffic by sea' (28 March 2001) CND Res 44/6; ECOSOC, 'Report of the Executive Director on the Progress made in the development of technical assistance and training to promote maritime cooperation' (7 February 2003) E/CN.7/2003/8.

[125] See UNGA A/53/456 (5 October 1998); ECOSOC, E/CN.7/1995/13 (6 March 2005) Chapter II, paras 13, 20 and 22.

is an international criminal activity, States Parties are to develop procedures in domestic law to identify, arrest, prosecute and convict those who traffic drugs across national borders.[126]

The general framework of the Convention follows a familiar pattern: establishing the relevant offences as serious offences in domestic law; providing for extradition in respect of those offences; and providing for mutual legal assistance and cooperation in the investigation and prosecution of those offences. What is of direct interest at this point, however, is Art. 17, which dictates that States Parties 'cooperate to the fullest extent possible to suppress illicit traffic by sea, in conformity with the international law of the sea' (Art. 17(1)) and, in so doing, 'the Parties shall consider entering into bilateral or regional agreements or arrangements to carry out, or to enhance the effectiveness of, the provisions of this article' (Art. 17(9)).[127] This provision has formed the basis of both regional and bilateral arrangements in combating the illicit flow of drugs.

7.3.1.1. *Regional Initiatives*

Looking at regional initiatives following on from the 1988 Vienna Convention, Council of Europe action in relation to the suppression of illicit drug trafficking on the high seas has come in the form of the Council of Europe Agreement which establishes a foundation for cooperation between the Parties to it. However, by far the most interesting regional maritime counterdrug agreement is the Agreement concerning cooperation in suppressing illicit maritime and air trafficking in narcotics and psychotropic substances in the Caribbean Area (Aruba Agreement), opened for signature at Costa Rica on 10 April 2003.[128] Focussing on maritime cooperation in the fight against drug trafficking it represents further evidence of a willingness on the part of States to increase action on the high seas and in coastal waters in the cause of safeguarding maritime security. Applicable in the Caribbean area,[129] it covers a wide range of maritime cooperation issues, *inter alia*, the coordination of law enforcement operations, the identification of suspect vessels, boarding and searching, the use of force and jurisdiction over offences, vessels and persons.

[126] To this end, Art. 3 obliges States Parties to criminalize such offences within their domestic legal framework. Art. 4 provides for cases in which it is mandatory for the State Party to take the measures necessary to establish its jurisdiction over offences and other cases where it is discretionary upon the State to do so. However, it is to be noted that the 1988 Convention stops short of requiring the establishment of jurisdiction over stateless vessels and those assimilated to stateless vessels.

[127] See also L.B. Sohn and J.E. Noyes, *Cases and Materials on the Law of the Sea* (Transnational Publishers, New York, 2004), 193 *et seq.*

[128] Aruba Agreement noted in CND Res 43/5 and E/CN.7/2003/8. This Agreement has still to be ratified by the requisite minimum 5 States to enter into force.

[129] Art. 1(j) and 39.

By virtue of Art. 7, each Contracting Party undertakes to establish the capability at any time *inter alia* to respond to requests for verification of nationality;[130] authorize the boarding and searching of suspect vessels; and authorize the entry into its waters (and air space) of law enforcement vessels in support of law enforcement operations of the other Parties. Furthermore, Art. 9 gives each Party the power in its discretion to permit designated law enforcement officials of another Party to embark on its law enforcement vessels (this may be subject to conditions). The powers given to such law enforcement officials are listed in the Agreement as being the power to:[131]

a. embark on law enforcement vessels of any of the Parties;
b. enforce the laws of the designating Party[132] to suppress illicit traffic in the waters of the designating Party, or seaward of its territorial sea in the exercise of the right of hot pursuit or otherwise in accordance with international law;
c. authorise the entry of the law enforcement vessels on which they are embarked into and navigation within the waters of the designating Party;
d. authorise law enforcement vessels on which they are embarked to conduct counter-drug patrols in the waters of the designating Party;
e. authorise law enforcement officials of the vessel on which the law enforcement officials of the designating Party are embarked to assist in the enforcement of the laws of the designating Party to suppress illicit traffic; and
f. advise and assist law enforcement officials of other Parties in the conduct of boardings of vessels to enforce the laws of those Parties to suppress illicit traffic.[133]

As far as action in the territorial waters of a Party is concerned, this is always to be subject to the authority and authorization of that Party (Art. 11), and such requests for authorization are to be responded to 'expeditiously' (Art. 11(2)). Furthermore, in accordance with Art. 11(3), law enforcement operations are to be carried out by, or under the direction of, the law enforcement authorities of the coastal State, thus preserving the priority accorded to the coastal State in the territorial sea. Art. 12(1) permits a law enforcement vessel of a Party to follow a suspect vessel 'into the waters of another Party and take actions to prevent the escape of the vessel, board the vessel and secure the vessel and persons on board awaiting an expeditious response from the other Party if either:

130 Note Art. 6(4) stating that requests for verification of nationality are to be responded to as soon as possible and in any event no later than 4 hours after the request is made.

131 These powers mirror those given to the shiprider in the bilateral agreements to be considered below.

132 See Art. 9(1): the designating Party is the State which designates qualified law enforcement officials to act as embarked law enforcement officials on vessels of another Party.

133 Art. 9(3). Note that these powers are subject to 'the domestic laws and regulations of the designating Party.'

a. the Party has received authorisation from the authority or authorities of the other Party . . . ; or
b. on notice to the other Party, when no embarked law enforcement official or law enforcement vessel of the other Party is immediately available to investigate. Such notice shall be provided prior to entry into the waters of the other Party, if operationally feasible, or failing this as soon as possible.'

Parties are to elect either of the above two procedures and notify the Depositary of their choice; until such election, Parties are deemed to have accepted the first option (Art. 12(2)).[134]

In the case of operations seaward of the territorial sea, when law enforcement officials of one Party encounter a suspect vessel claiming the nationality of another Party, located seaward of any State's territorial sea, Art. 16(1) states that the Agreement itself constitutes 'the authorization by the claimed flag State Party to board and search the suspect vessel, its cargo and question the persons found on board by such officials in order to determine if the vessel is engaged in illicit traffic.'[135] However, according to Art. 16(2)(3), it is possible for a Party to notify the Depositary that boarding is to occur only upon express consent. It is also possible for a Party to notify the Depositary that Parties shall be deemed to be granted authorization to board vessels located seaward of the territorial sea of any State which flies its flag or claims its nationality and to search the suspect vessel or cargo or question persons on board if there is no response to the request or the requested Party can neither confirm nor deny nationality within four hours following receipt of an oral request for verification of nationality of a vessel. When evidence of illicit traffic is found as a consequence of the boarding of the vessel, the law enforcement officials of the boarding Party may then detain the vessel, cargo and persons on board pending expeditious disposition instructions from the flag State Party (paragraph 5).[136]

---

[134] Note that Art. 15 provides for the possibility of extending the application of the Agreement to some or all of a State's internal waters upon notification to the Depositary. This provision should be read together with the definition of the 'Caribbean Area' in Art. 1(j) and with Art. 39 on territorial application. See W.C. Gilmore, *Agreement Concerning Co-operation in Suppressing Illicit Maritime and Air Trafficking in Narcotic Drugs and Psychotropic Substances in the Caribbean Area, 2003* (TSO, London, 2005), 28.

[135] Art. 17 safeguards all other boardings according to international law in that this Agreement is stated not to apply to or limit such boardings based *inter alia* on the right of visit, rendering assistance to persons, vessels or property in distress or peril, or an authorization from the flag State to take law enforcement action.

[136] Notwithstanding the above, law enforcement officials of one Party may board a suspect vessel located seaward of the territorial sea of any State, claiming the nationality of another Party for the purpose of locating and examining the documents of that vessel when it is not flying the flag of that other Party; it is not displaying any marks of its registration; it is claiming to

7.3.1.2. *Bilateral Initiatives*

The optimum illustrations of relevant bilateral initiatives are the so-called Shiprider Agreements which the US has concluded with a number of Caribbean States.[137] Generally, under these agreements, a host country officer aboard a US Coast Guard vessel which proceeds into the territorial sea of another State (the 'shiprider') represents the local government. However, law enforcement action cannot be taken against suspect vessels without express authorization from the flag or coastal State. Timely authorization is essential because it permits the Coast Guard to control the situation before the traffickers have time to jettison contraband, destroy the evidence, or evade apprehension. Flag State authorization may be *ad hoc* as each case occurs, or may be given on a comprehensive basis by means of bilateral agreements. These maritime counter-drug agreements recognize that international cooperation is critical to the successful suppression of drug smuggling at sea and aim to make territorial boundaries transparent to law enforcement—in the same way as they are to smugglers seeking refuge from interdiction.

The importance of these arrangements cannot be over-emphasized: apart from aiming to supplement the security forces of States which may not have sufficient resources to fight narcotics trafficking effectively, these agreements also aim to overcome any obstacles which may exist in the general international law regime. To this end, these arrangements may provide for hot pursuit to continue into the territorial sea of another State, for example. Furthermore, various bilateral treaties allow a warship of another State to continue surveillance activities even in the internal waters of a State, as long as there are representatives of the armed forces of that State on board the vessel.

The object of these agreements is to streamline the diplomatic process required to obtain flag State authority for law enforcement actions against foreign suspect vessels on the high seas. Usually, these bilateral agreements follow a 'six-part pattern' granting standing authority to take the following enforcement action:

---

have no documentation regarding its nationality on board; or there is no other information evidencing nationality. In such cases, should any documentation or evidence of nationality be found, paras 1–3 of Art. 16 will apply as appropriate; if no evidence of nationality is found, the vessel is to be dealt with as a stateless vessel in accordance with international law. See Art. 16(6) and (7).

137 Other examples of course exist, but will not be considered here. For example: Anglo-American Exchange of Notes concerning Cooperation in the Suppression of the Unlawful Importation of Narcotic Drugs (1981). See W.C. Gilmore, 'Narcotic Interdiction at Sea: UK–US Cooperation' (1989) 13 *Marine Policy* 218–230 and J. Siddle, 'Anglo-American Cooperation in the Suppression of Drug Smuggling' (1982) 31 *ICLQ* 726–747.

1. US authorities are entitled to board and search vessels flying the flag of a signatory nation.
2. A coastal State shiprider is empowered to authorize any patrols, boarding, searches, seizures, and arrests in sovereign waters; pursuit of suspect vessels into sovereign waters is permitted, as is the stopping, boarding and searching of vessels therein.
3. Entry into sovereign waters is provided for for the purpose of investigating suspect vessels and aircraft, also with permission to stop, board, and search.
4. Overflight by State aircraft in sovereign airspace and the authority to relay an order to land in the territory of a signatory nation are also features of the model agreement.
5. In the event that drugs are found on a vessel boarded and searched under these provisions, the Coast Guard takes no action except to detain the vessel, cargo and crew, thus preserving the flag or coastal State's option to exercise or waive prosecutorial jurisdiction.
6. The model agreement also contains provisions for the disposition of seized assets, including the transfer of forfeited assets or proceeds of their sale as a consequence of any interdictions.

Since these agreements deal with issues of national sovereignty on a cooperative basis, the US is not always able to reach agreement on all six parts of the model maritime agreements and, therefore, some agreements are more limited in scope.[138]

7.3.1.3. *The US–Bahamas 2004 Agreement: A Model Ship Rider Agreement*

While the US–Bahamas Agreement follows the general pattern of shiprider agreements, it has been selected for specific mention as it is especially interesting in that it provides a common attack against two major maritime threats: drug trafficking and migrant smuggling. Whereas the shiprider agreements generally focus only on illicit traffic in narcotic drugs, this agreement breaks new ground by showing that the same approach can also be effective in the fight against migrant smuggling.[139]

---

[138] See USCG, 'Statement of Rear Admiral E.R. Ruitta on Maritime Bilateral Counterdrug Agreements before the Sub-Committee on Criminal justice, Drug Policy, and Human Resources, Committee on Government Reform, US House of Representatives' (13 May 1999); USCG, 'Statement of Rear Admiral R. Dennis Sirois on Coast Guard Law Enforcement before the SubCommittee on Coast Guard and Maritime Transportation Committee on Transportation and Infrastructure', US House of Representatives (15 June 2005).

[139] The same approach is adopted in the Operational Procedures for Boarding and Inspecting Vessels Suspected of Illicit Traffic in Narcotic Drugs and Psychotropic Substances and of Smuggling Migrants by Sea, concluded between the Bureau of the Merchant Navy and Coastal Affairs of Ecuador and the United States Coast Guard (copy provided by the US Coast Guard). However, these operational procedures are nowhere near as detailed as the terms of the shiprider agreements.

The Agreement between the Government of the USA and the Government of the Commonwealth of the Bahamas concerning cooperation in maritime law enforcement (US–Bahamas Agreement) focuses on the suppression of illicit trafficking in narcotics and psychotropic substances and the unsafe transport and smuggling of migrants. As far as the latter is concerned, regard is had in the Preamble to the urgent need for international cooperation in the suppression of maritime migrant smuggling and, *inter alia*, Art. 17 of the Smuggling Protocol is referred to as calling on Parties to consider the conclusion of agreements additional to the Protocol further to prevent and combat the crime of migrant smuggling.

The general point of departure is set out in Art. 3 wherein it is stated that operations to suppress these crimes carried out in the territorial waters and airspace of a Party are the responsibility, and subject to the authority, of that particular Party. Furthermore, Art. 3 continues that, save for the application of Arts. 6 and 7,[140] nothing in the Agreement is to be interpreted as permitting law enforcement vessels or aircraft of one Party unilaterally to patrol the waters or airspace of the other Party. Once again, therefore, the aim is to leave intact the general principles of the law of the sea.

Art. 6 provides an exception to the above general principle by providing for operations in Bahamian territory, waters or airspace. The Agreement itself constitutes permission by the Bahamian Government for US enforcement officials to carry out operations without a Bahamian shiprider on board. Such operations may be conducted in Bahamian waters and airspace 'seaward of three nautical miles from the low-water line along the Bahamian coast, or in the case of islands having fringing reefs, seaward from the seaward low-water line of the reefs' (Art. 6(2)). Except as otherwise provided in the Agreement, US law enforcement vessels and aircraft are not to enter Bahamian waters and airspace landward of the area where patrol operations are authorized pursuant to Art. 6(2) above to pursue or investigate suspect vessels or aircraft without first seeking the express authorization of Bahamian law enforcement authorities, which authorization may be sought on a case-by-case basis (Art. 6(5)).

Art. 5 of the Agreement outlines the 'Shiprider Programme' according to which the Bahamas Shiprider Coordinator, in appropriate circumstances, designates shipriders[141] who, on behalf of the Bahamian Government and in accordance with Bahamian law, are empowered to grant the US law enforcement vessels and aircraft on which they are embarked authority to enter Bahamian territory, waters and airspace for the purpose of assisting Bahamian

[140] Art. 7 deals with overflight operations and procedures; Art. 6 is discussed hereunder.

[141] Defined in Art. 2(16) as a 'law enforcement official of one Party authorized to embark on a law enforcement vessel or aircraft of the other Party'.

law enforcement officials in boarding and searching suspect vessels, and, in the case of evidence of violations of Bahamian law for the purpose of assisting the shiprider in executing the disposition instructions of Bahamian law enforcement authorities in respect of the vessel, cargo and persons on board. Furthermore, the US law enforcement vessel (or aircraft) on which the shiprider is embarked is also granted authority to assist the shiprider to board and search suspect Bahamian-flagged vessels which are located seaward of any nation's territorial sea and within 200 nm of the baselines from which the territorial sea of The Bahamas is measured; should evidence of violations of Bahamian law be found, it is to assist the shiprider in carrying out the disposition instructions of Bahamian law enforcement authorities with regard to the vessel, cargo and persons on board. In cases arising in this scenario in which a suspect vessel claiming Bahamian nationality is not flying the flag of the Bahamas, not displaying any marks of its registration or nationality, and claiming to have no documentation on board the vessel, US law enforcement officials are given the right to proceed in accordance with Art. 9[142] unless and until the Bahamian Government confirms the suspect vessel's right to Bahamian nationality, in which case the Bahamian shiprider shall have the right to exercise primary jurisdiction over the boarding of the vessel.[143]

Art. 8 deals with the verification of nationality. Requests for the verification of nationality are to be dealt with quickly: a requested Party is to make its best efforts to respond to such requests[144] 'as expeditiously as possible, and in any case shall confirm or refute the claim of nationality within four (4) hours of the initial request' (Art. 8(3)).[145]

[142] That is, if no documentation or other physical evidence of nationality is available, the boarding Party, in this case the US, may assimilate the vessel to a vessel without nationality: see Art. 9(1). On the other hand, Art. 9 states that should any documentation or evidence be found, then the provisions of Art. 8 apply, which article regulates the verification of nationality.

[143] Art. 5(2) provides that US law enforcement officials may assist Bahamian shipriders conducting operations pursuant to Art. 5 only if expressly requested to do so by the shiprider, and only within the limits of the request and in the manner requested. The article continues by stating that such a request may be made, agreed to and acted upon only in accordance with the laws and policies of both Parties.

[144] If such requests are made orally, they are to be confirmed in writing as soon as possible. See Art. 8(2) which also lists the information which should be contained in the request.

[145] The boarding of vessels in other instances in accordance with international law is preserved by Art. 9(2). This is also provided in the following agreements concluded by the US with various States: Antigua and Barbuda, Art. 9; Belize, Art. 9; Barbados, Art. 17; Colombia, Art. 20; Costa Rica, Art. V(2); Dominica, Art. 9; Dominican Republic, Art. 9; Grenada, Art. 9; Haiti, Art. 15; Honduras, Art. VI(2); Jamaica, Art. 4; Nicaragua, Art. 9(3); Panama, Art. X(9); St. Kitts and Nevis, Art. 9; St. Lucia, Art. 9; St. Vincent and the Grenadines, Art. 9; Suriname, Art. 11; Trinidad and Tobago, Art. 10.

Art. 11 is central to the Agreement in that it provides for special procedures in cases involving unsafe transport of migrants by sea and the smuggling of migrants. Apart from the recognition of the obligation of *non-refoulement* in the Preamble, Art. 11(1) states that no person found on board a suspect vessel is to be involuntarily returned to a country where that person has a well-founded fear of persecution on grounds of race, religion, nationality, membership of a particular social group, or political opinion, except on grounds recognized as precluding protection as a refugee under the Refugee Convention and Protocol. The Agreement goes further than the Refugee Convention in that Art. 11(1)(b) refers to a country where it is likely that the person will be tortured, for any reason.

Provision is also made for the repatriation and return of migrants in that, in all cases, the Bahamian Government agrees, 'upon prior notification, to facilitate and accept without undue or unreasonable delay the return … of migrants having Bahamian nationality, citizenship, or permanent residence and, regardless of their nationality or country of origin, to give due consideration to any request by U.S. law enforcement authorities to accept the return of migrants found aboard vessels, wherever located, subject to the jurisdiction of The Bahamas or operated by Bahamian nationals' (Art. 11(2)). Each Party also agrees to prosecute migrant smugglers, to confiscate vessels involved in migrant smuggling, and to take appropriate action against Masters, officers, crew members and others on board suspect vessels which are engaged in the unsafe transport of migrants by sea (Art. 11(3)(4)). Lastly, the relevant Party is to report all unsafe or illegal practices associated with the smuggling or transport of migrants and the measures taken in this regard in accordance with the guidance of the IMO (Art. 11(5)).

In sum, the Agreement consolidates various existing agreements, codifies practices which occur in day-to-day operations and modernizes certain provisions, such as the 1992 Exchange of Notes granting the US permission to patrol Bahamian waters seaward of the three nautical mile limit and apprehend non-Bahamian vessels suspected of illicit drug trafficking.[146] Once again, the requirement of international cooperation is pivotal to this initiative. This cooperation also proceeds on the assumption that the flag State should in certain instances renege on its right and obligation of exclusive jurisdiction over vessels which fly their flag, and the coastal State should similarly permit action by foreign-flagged vessels in the maritime zones over which it exercises control.

[146] Statement by The Hon. F. Mitchell, Bahamian Minister of Foreign Affairs and the Public Service, 'Bahamas/US sign Comprehensive Maritime Agreement' (29 June 2004) Press Release, Bahamas Information Service.

Initiatives such as the US–Bahamas Agreement may indicate that the way forward in fighting current threats to maritime security is by implementing this obligation of cooperation.

7.3.1.4. *Analysis*

Two common patterns emerge from an analysis of the separate shiprider agreements.[147] These concern authorization to US vessels to enter the territorial sea of a State Party and the mechanism for authorization and deemed authorization in the case of requests for the verification of registry and boarding of vessels seawards of the territorial sea.

7.3.1.4.a. *Entry into the Territorial Sea*

The shiprider agreements provide a pattern of authorization of entry by US vessels into the territorial waters of the other State Party. A group of agreements provide for a shiprider on board a US vessel to enforce the laws of a State Party in the waters of that State Party.[148] Taking the Agreement between the US and Antigua and Barbuda as an example, Art. 5(d) provides that:

> … [t]he Government of Antigua and Barbuda may designate qualified law enforcement officials to act as law enforcement ship riders. Subject to Antigua and Barbuda law, these ship riders may, in appropriate circumstances:
>
> (d) enforce the laws of Antigua and Barbuda in waters of Antigua and Barbuda …[149]

Furthermore, this same Agreement provides for instances of entry into the territorial sea of Antigua and Barbuda in the absence of a shiprider on board a US vessel. Art. 8 begins with the general principle that '[t]he Government of the United States of America shall not conduct counter-drug operations in waters

[147] To date 24 have been concluded. Relevant provisions will be noted below.

[148] Recall the position under the Aruba Agreement: while Art. 11 requires that law enforcement operations in the waters of a State Party are subject to the authority of that Party, Art. 8(2) provides that in order to carry out the objectives of this Agreement each Party authorizes its designated law enforcement officials, or its competent national authority if notified to the Depositary, to permit the entry of law enforcement vessels under the Agreement into its waters. Art. 9 then goes on to permit each Party to authorize the designated law enforcement officials of another Party to embark on its law enforcement vessel and such official is given certain powers.

[149] The same provision is found in other agreements. See the agreements with Antigua and Barbuda, Art. 5(d); Belize, Art. 5(d); Dominica, Art. 5(d); Dominican Republic, Art. 5(d); Grenada, Art. 5(d); St. Kitts and Nevis, Art. 5(d); St. Lucia, Art. 5(d); St. Vincent and the Grenadines, Art. 5(d); Trinidad and Tobago, Art. 5(d); Costa Rica, Art. 2(d); Haiti, Art. 5(d); Suriname, Art. 4(3)(d); Honduras, Art. IV(2)(d); Guatemala, Art. 5(4)(b).

of Antigua and Barbuda without the permission of the Government of Antigua and Barbuda, granted by this Agreement or otherwise.' It however continues by providing that:

> [t]his Agreement constitutes permission by the Government of Antigua and Barbuda for United States counter-drug operations in any of the following circumstances:
>
> (b) a suspect vessel ... encountered seaward of the territorial sea of Antigua and Barbuda flees into waters of Antigua and Barbuda and is pursued therein by a U.S. vessel without a Antigua and Barbuda shiprider embarked, in which case any suspect vessel may be boarded and searched, and, if the evidence warrants, detained pending disposition instructions from Antigua and Barbuda; and
>
> (c) an Antigua and Barbuda shiprider is unavailable to embark on a U.S. vessel, in which case the U.S. vessel may enter waters of Antigua and Barbuda in order to ... board and search any suspect vessel, other than a Antigua and Barbuda flag vessel, and, if evidence so warrants, detain any such vessel pending disposition instructions from Antigua and Barbuda authorities.[150]

7.3.1.4.b. *Operations Seaward of the Territorial Sea*

Insofar as concerns the boarding of vessels seaward of the territorial sea and requests for verification of registry and boarding and search of vessels, persons and cargo on board, the shiprider agreements may be broadly divided into two groups. A class of agreements constitutes the actual authorization required to board and search the vessel:

> Whenever US Coast Guard officials encounter a vessel flagged to the other State Party which is located seaward of any nation's territorial sea and which is suspected of illicit traffic, the particular Agreement constitutes the authorization of the Government of that other State Party for the boarding and search of the suspect vessel and the persons found on board by such officials. If evidence of illicit traffic is found, Coast Guard officials are empowered to detain the vessel and persons on board pending expeditious disposition instructions from the Government of the other State Party.[151]

---

[150] The following agreements contain the same provision: Belize, Art. 8(b)(c); Dominica, Art. 8(b)(c); Dominican Republic, Art. 8(b)(c); Grenada, Art. 8(b)(c); St. Kitts and Nevis, Art 8(b)(c); St. Lucia, Art. 8(b)(c); St. Vincent and the Grenadines, Art. 8(b)(c); Trinidad and Tobago, Art. 8(b)(c); Costa Rica, Art. 6(b)(c); Haiti, Art. 9(b)(b); Suriname, Art. 6(2)(b)(c); Honduras, Art. V(1)(b)(c); Guatemala, Art. 6(2)(b)(c).

[151] Agreements with: Antigua and Barbuda, Art. 10; Belize, Art. 10; Dominica, Art. 10; Dominican Republic, Art. 10; Grenada, Art. 10; St. Kitts and Nevis, Art. 10; St. Lucia, Art. 10; St. Vincent and the Grenadines, Art. 10; Trinidad and Tobago, Art. 11. The same notion, using similar but not identical wording, is found in the agreements with: Costa Rica, Art. V(1); Haiti, Art. 14 and Suriname, Art. 10(1).

Another group of agreements provide for a mechanism in which authorization may be requested and received, or deemed to be received. An overview follows of the relevant provisions in these agreements in order to illustrate this best. The Agreement with Colombia states in Art. 8 that:

> The reply to the request for boarding and search shall be provided by the requested Party to the requesting Party at the earliest possible opportunity ... If the requested Party has not responded to the request for authorization to board and search within three (3) hours of receipt of the request, it shall be understood that the authorization has been granted.

Similarly, the Agreement with Jamaica states in Art. 3(2) that requests for verification of registry and authorization for boarding and search of the vessel, cargo and persons on board are to be answered 'expeditiously' and deemed authorization to board and search the vessel follows if there is no response from the flag State within three hours of its receipt in writing. The same holds for the Agreement with Barbados which stipulates in Art. 14(3) that 'a request for verification of registration shall be answered promptly but where no response is received from the requested Party within 3 hours of an oral request, the requested Party will not object to the requesting Party boarding the suspect vessel for the purpose of inspecting the vessel's documents, questioning persons on board and searching the vessel to determine whether it is engaged in illicit traffic.'

Deemed authorization of the flag State follows after a failure to respond to the request within two hours in Art. VI of the Agreement with Honduras, Art. 4 of the Agreement with Venezuela, Art. 9 of the Agreement with Nicaragua and Art. 7(3)(b) and (d) of the Agreement with Guatemala. Art. 7(3)(b) of the Agreement with Guatemala provides that '[t]he requested Party shall answer requests made for the verification of nationality within two (2) hours of the receipt of such requests ... [and] (d) [i]f there is no response from the requested Party within two (2) hours of its receipt of the request, the requesting Party will be deemed to have been authorized to board the suspect vessel for the purpose of inspecting the vessel's documents, questioning the persons on board, and searching the vessel to determine if it is engaged in illicit traffic.' This last Agreement additionally specifies the consequences of a failure to verify nationality within two hours. In this eventuality, the requested Party may either:

i. Nevertheless authorize the boarding and search by the Security Force Officials of the requesting Party; or
ii. Refute the claim of the suspect vessel to nationality.[152]

---

[152] Art. 7(3)(d). The same position is also noted in Art. X(4)–(6) of the Agreement with Panama.

7.3.2. *Acts of Maritime Terrorism*

Maritime terrorism and State reponses to it are of great interest, in that the location of the threat is usually the high seas which, as a rule, are beyond the jurisdiction of any State save for the flag State; cooperative arrangements are however effectively bypassing such rule and providing for non-flag State intervention by agreement.

The Proliferation Security Initiative (PSI), announced in Crakow, Poland, by President Bush on 31 May 2003, provides for the interdiction of vessels on the high seas.[153] The initiative is focused on the prevention of the proliferation of weapons of mass destruction (WMD) by land, sea and air and evidences US efforts at establishing cooperative partnerships to prevent the flow of WMD, their delivery systems and related materials, without however creating legally binding commitments.[154] To this end, on 4 September 2003 at a meeting in Paris, 11 States (Australia, France, Germany, Italy, Japan, the Netherlands, Poland, Portugal, Spain, the United States and the United Kingdom)[155] adopted a Statement of Interdiction Principles.[156]

The US has also entered into bilateral agreements with certain participating States, including Malta.[157] These arrangements are modelled on similar lines to the agreements in the drug smuggling sphere. According to the terms of these agreements, if either a US vessel or a vessel flying the flag of a partner State is

---

[153] The PSI has been described as an illustration of a unilateral initiative, followed by a 'coalition of the willing', as a means to bypass lengthy negotiations during which preferred goals are watered down. According to this pattern, arrangements are assembled initially through a series of bilateral contacts, rather than through a truly multilateral negotiation process, thereby marginalizing any opposition that may arise. See T. Findlay, 'Weapons of Mass Destruction' in E. Newman, R. Thakur and J. Tirman (eds), *Multilateralism Under Challenge? Power, International Order and Structural Change* (United Nations University Press, Tokyo, 2006), 216–217. For more information see R. Chesney, 'The Proliferation Security Initiative and WMD: Interdiction on the High Seas' (2003) 13 *National Security Review* 1; Benjamin Friedman Bipartisan Security Group, 'The Proliferation Security Initiative: The Legal Challenge' (Policy Brief) (Washington, D.C., September 2003); M. Byers, 'Policing the High Seas: the Proliferation Security Initiative' (2004) 98 *AJIL* 526–545; D. Freestone, R. Barnes and D. Ong, *The Law of the Sea: Progress and Prospects* (OUP, Oxford, 2006), 356–361 and the US Department of State website: www.state.gov/t/isn/c10390.htm. See also the Washington Declaration for PSI 5th Anniversary Senior-Level Meeting (28 May 2008) Media Note.

[154] T. McDorman, 'From the Desk of the Editor-in-Chief' (2005) 36 *ODIL* 382.

[155] While initially a cooperative arrangement between 11 States, it has widened its support base to include 91 participants as of 22 May 2008.

[156] http://usinfo.state.gov/products/pubs/proliferation/#statement.

[157] Agreement Between the Government Of the United States Of America And the Government Of Malta Concerning Cooperation to Suppress the Proliferation Of Weapons Of Mass Destruction, their Delivery Systems, and Related Materials by Sea 2007.

suspected of carrying WMD, their delivery systems or related materials, either Party can ask the other to confirm the nationality of the ship, and, if necessary, authorize boarding, search and possibly detention of the vessel and its cargo. Once again, a common pattern is noted: the ship boarding Agreement with Liberia (Art. 4(3)(b)-(d)) provides for a deemed authorization procedure in the same terms as those described for the Agreements with Guatemala and Panama, above. This is also the case in Art. 4(3)(b)-(d) of the Agreement with the Marshall Islands, except that in this case there is a four-hour time frame before authorization can be deemed to have been received. Art. 5(3)(b)(c) of the Agreement with Malta and Art. 4(3)(b)(c) of the Agreement with Cyprus are framed in the same terms as the Agreement with the Marshall Islands.[158]

Other agreements merely state a time limit within which the request should be responded to.[159] The ship boarding Agreement with Croatia can be contrasted with the above agreements because, while Art. 4(4)(b) states that the requested Party must respond to requests for verification of nationality and authorization to board within four hours of receipt, Art. 4(4)(d) specifically prohibits any other boardings without express consent:

> Except as otherwise permitted by international law, the requesting Party shall not board the vessel without the express written authorization of the Competent Authority of the requested Party.

7.3.3. *Suppression of Unlawful Acts against the Safety of Maritime Navigation*

The LOSC fails to provide for any measures to counter maritime terrorism, thus creating a loophole which, for years, caused an assimilation in classification between piracy and acts of maritime terrorism. For a long time, the international community overlooked the necessity of having a treaty approach to the problem of terrorism at sea. It was only after the *Achille Lauro* incident in October 1985—which fell outside the classification of the international crime of piracy—that the SUA Convention began to be negotiated. The Convention is modelled on the aviation security framework.[160] It seeks to ensure the prosecution and punishment of any person who unlawfully and intentionally commits one of the offences listed in Art. 3 of the Convention, all of which have one

[158] Note, however, that in these two agreements there is no equivalent to subpara. (d) specifying what is to occur if nationality is not verified in the stipulated period. Art. 4(3)(b)(c) of the Agreement with Mongolia is on the same lines; however here there is a two-hour time frame.

[159] See PSI Ship Boarding Agreements with Belize, Art. 4(3)(c) and the Bahamas, Art. 4(3)(b).

[160] The treaty rules governing the safety of aviation are the Tokyo Convention on Offences and Certain other Acts committed on board Aircraft (1963); the Hague Convention for the Suppression of the Unlawful Seizure of Aircraft (1970); the Montreal Convention for the Suppression of Unlawful Acts against the Safety of Civil Aviation (1971).

common element: all endanger or potentially endanger the safe navigation of ships.[161] After amendments in 2005 however, the list of offences has increased to such an extent that now the offences do not all necessarily relate to the inherent safety of the ship itself.[162]

One of the great strengths of the Convention is that its application is not limited to the high seas but that it applies to offences committed in all areas of the sea other than internal waters, as long as the vessel is engaged or is scheduled to engage on an international voyage or the offender is found in the territory of a State Party to the Convention. While breaking new grounds in the fight against maritime terrorism, a major shortcoming was that the Convention only provided for a mechanism by which to prosecute and punish offenders *ex post facto*; any form of policing jurisdiction which would allow the stopping, boarding, inspection and detention of the vessel was disregarded. As a result of Resolution 924(22) of January 2002, the SUA Convention was reviewed within the IMO's Legal Committee with a view to tailoring its provisions to current exigencies. This culminated in the Protocol of 2005 to the Convention for the Suppression of Unlawful Acts against the Safety of Maritime Navigation and the Protocol of 2005 to the Protocol for the Suppression of Unlawful Acts against the Safety of Fixed Platforms Located on the Continental Shelf.[163]

The most crucial amendment relates to the possibility of boarding by non-flag States, the Convention's regulation of which has been described as 'the most well-developed boarding procedures and safeguards in any instrument of its type.'[164] Art. 8 *bis* was introduced into the original Convention and is directed at permitting the boarding of ships in the event that they are suspected of being involved in a terrorist incident, either as perpetrators or as victims. This relates to ships located seaward of the territorial sea and is a striking example of a treaty exception to the principle of flag State exclusivity over the high seas. This new power is based on the boarding provisions found in the Vienna Drugs Convention 1988[165] and the Smuggling Protocol 2000.[166]

Art. 8*bis* relates to the permitted parameters of control which non-flag States may exercise with regard to a vessel. The boarding provisions under the new instrument consist of:

---

161 Note that the piracy regime and the regime established by the SUA Convention may have concurrent application. See J.L. Jesus, 'Protection of Foreign Ships against Piracy and Terrorism at Sea: Legal Aspects' (2002) 18 *IJMLC* 363–400.

162 See Arts. 3*bis*, 3*ter* and 3*quater*.

163 LEG/CONF.15/21 (1 November 2005) and LEG/CONF.15/22 (1 November 2001) respectively.

164 See LEG/CONF.15/15 (22 September 2005).

165 Art. 17.

166 Art. 8.

> A comprehensive set of procedures and protections designed to facilitate the boarding of a vessel suspected of being involved in a SUA offence, while ensuring that flag State jurisdiction is respected. The boarding procedures do not change existing international maritime law or infringe upon the traditional principle of freedom of navigation. Instead, the procedures eliminate the need to negotiate time consuming *ad hoc* boarding arrangements when facing the immediacy of ongoing criminal activity.[167]

The article commences by setting out the general duty of cooperation, noted in the other instruments reviewed, to the effect that States Parties are to cooperate to the fullest extent possible in the prevention and suppression of unlawful acts covered by the Convention in conformity with international law. All States are required to respond to requests made under this article 'as expeditiously as possible'.[168]

That the boarding of a ship is to be seen as an extreme measure is reflected in Art. 8(3).[169] In point of fact, in deliberations within the Legal Committee certain delegations were of the view that boarding should be permitted only for the more serious offences in Art. 3*bis*; however this view did not prevail.[170] Sub-Art. 4 specifies a general duty in that a State Party which has reasonable grounds to suspect that an offence under the Convention has been, is being or is about to be committed involving a ship flying its flag may request the assistance of other States Parties in preventing or suppressing this offence; the States Parties so requested are to use their 'best endeavours to render such assistance within the means available to them'.

A central principle upon which the boarding provision is based is that boarding is expressly authorized by the flag State, thus maintaining the authority of the flag State.[171] As far as the significance of retaining flag State exclusivity is concerned, there was general recognition of the fact that the inclusion of boarding provisions constituted a significant departure from the fundamental principles of the freedom of navigation on the high seas and exclusive flag State jurisdiction over its vessels. This right was therefore perceived as an exception to the general rule, where any exception must be 'precise, unambiguous and internationally accepted.'[172]

---

167 LEG.CONF.15/15 (22 September 2005), para. 22.

168 For a report of deliberations regarding whether to introduce a specific time limit or retain the terminology which was ultimately adopted see LEG 89/16 (4 November 2004), paras 46–49.

169 LEG 89/4/9 (24 September 2004), para. 4.

170 LEG 88/13 (18 May 2004), para. 67; LEG 89/4/9 (24 September 2004), paras 36, 68; LEG/SUA/WG.2/4 (9 February 2005), paras 70–72.

171 See LEG/CONF.15/15 (22 September 2005), para. 5.

172 LEG 88/13 (18 May 2004), para. 66.

Art. 8(5) sets out the procedure when law enforcement or other authorized officials of a State Party (the requesting State) encounter a ship flying the flag of another State Party (the first Party) and such ship is located seawards of the territorial sea of any State. Should the requesting Party have reasonable grounds to suspect that an offence under the Convention has been, is being or is about to be committed, flag State permission is required for the requesting State to board the vessel concerned. In such a case, a request for confirmation of nationality is first made.[173] Once nationality is confirmed, the requesting State must ask the flag State for its express authorization to board the vessel and to take appropriate measures with regard to that vessel. These appropriate measures may include stopping, boarding and searching the ship, its cargo and those on board, and questioning those on board in order to determine whether an offence has been, is being or is about to be committed. Sub-paragraph (c) permits the flag State either to decline such authorization, or to authorize stopping and boarding unconditionally, or subject to certain conditions, outlined in sub-paragraph (7), such as the obtaining of additional information from the requesting Party and conditions relating to responsibility for and the extent of the measures to be taken. In such a case, no additional measures may be taken without express authorization of the flag State unless they are necessary to avert imminent danger to life or if such further measures are permitted under a relevant bilateral or multilateral agreement. Alternatively, the flag State may opt to conduct the boarding and searching exercise with its own law enforcement officials, or together with the requesting Party. A tacit authorization procedure is provided for in Art. 8*bis*(5)(d) wherein, upon or after depositing its instrument of ratification, acceptance, approval or accession, a State may notify the Secretary-General that, as far as ships registered in that State are concerned, the requesting Party is granted such authorization if there is no response from the first Party within four hours of the acknowledgement of receipt of request to confirm nationality.[174] Furthermore, upon or after depositing its instrument of acceptance, a general authorization may be given

[173] Art. 8*bis*(2) stipulates the details of such requests: they should all contain, if possible, the name of the suspect ship, the IMO ship identification number, the port of registry, the ports of origin and destination, and any other relevant information.

[174] Note in this regard that the shipping community had reservations with regard to the tacit authorization procedure (allowing for boarding and searching of the ship in the event that no response is received from the first Party within 4 hours from the time a request for nationality of the vessel is made). Problems arising due to different time zones, different public holidays, and how to inform the Master of a ship that receipt of a request for nationality has been acknowledged were among the practical difficulties raised. See LEG 88/3/3 (19 March 2004), paras 4, 9; LEG 88/13 (18 May 2004), para. 73.

by the requested State with respect to ships flying its flag or displaying marks of its registry.[175] These notifications may be withdrawn at any time.[176]

7.4. *Common Elements*

In providing for a deemed authorization procedure, the agreements considered above have progressed beyond the terms of certain conventions requiring an 'expeditious' response to requests of this nature, as is noted in Art. 17(7) of the Vienna Drugs Convention and Art. 8(4) of the Smuggling Protocol. They are also an improvement on those conventions which merely impose a time limit within which requests for verification of registry and authorization to board vessels should ideally be responded to, but do not outline what action, if any, can be taken in default of a response, as is the case in the PSI Ship Boarding Agreements with Belize (Art. 4(3)(c)) and the Bahamas (Art. 4(3)(b)), for example.

In those cases where a time limit is imposed within which the requested State ought to respond to the request for verification of nationality and/or take authorized action *vis-à-vis* a vessel suspected of illicit activity, there is however a strong argument for the requesting Party to take action even in the case of a lack of response. In that event, it is submitted that the requesting State can, once it has again attempted to contact the Competent Authority of the requested State, legitimately take action *vis-à-vis* the suspect vessel where the Competent Authority is unavailable or cannot be reached, or cannot verify nationality or otherwise. In this scenario, where the requesting Party acts after the lapse of the stipulated time period or after a reasonable period has elapsed (in the cases where only 'expeditious' response is required), the burden of proof, as it were, shifts: the requesting State must explain why it had to act in the absence of a response; it must prove to the requested Party the necessity of immediacy of action. Any other interpretation would subvert the aims of these instruments.[177]

---

[175] Art. 8*bis*(5)(e). Presumably, only a request to confirm nationality must be made in such instance. Such notifications are to be encouraged as they cut down any time lag between the making of the request and the receipt of authorization, when immediacy is of the essence in most cases.

[176] In carrying out such exercises, the use of force is to be avoided except when necessary to ensure the safety of officials and persons on board, or if the officials conducting the boarding and search are obstructed in the execution of the exercise. Art. 8*bis*(9) states that '[a]ny use of force ... shall not exceed the minimum degree of force which is necessary and reasonable in the circumstance.' See LEG 89/16 (4 November 2004), paras 62–64; LEG/CONF.15/15 (22 September 2005), para. 26.

[177] Of course, this argument holds only for the case where no further provision is made for cases of lack of response. For example, it will be recalled that in the PSI Ship Boarding Agreement

Should action prove to have been unfounded, provisions of the kind stipulated in the 2005 Protocol to the SUA Convention would clearly be applicable: Art. 8*bis* (10)(b)(i)(ii) states that the State Party carrying out the boarding and search may be found liable under international law should the grounds for such measures being taken prove to be unfounded or where the measures taken are unlawful or exceed those reasonably required in the light of available information to implement the provisions of the article. States Parties are charged with providing effective recourse in respect of such damage, harm or loss.[178]

This interpretation holds more water if one considers the weight of the duty of cooperation. As mentioned at the outset, this duty must be interpreted as having some legal content and must indeed be taken seriously—not as a notion based on courtesy and goodwill. In relation to Art. 8(4) of the Smuggling Protocol it has been reported that although there is no obligation to grant authorization, Art. 7 contains a general duty to cooperate to the fullest extent in preventing and suppressing the smuggling of migrants and the granting or otherwise of this authorization is subject to this duty.[179] In this way, the duty of cooperation can be interpreted as imposing upon all States the duty to respond expeditiously to requests to verify nationality, to enter territorial waters and to board vessels on the high seas in the cause of suppressing certain threats to maritime security. Thus, States may not be permitted to refuse permission to a State which asks to board one of its vessels due to suspicion of migrant smuggling for example; and, furthermore, this consent must be given as soon as possible.

7.5. *Conclusion*

The agreements outlined in this chapter evidence a willingness on the part of States effectively to combat certain current threats to maritime security. While the arrangements detailed in section 7.2 of this chapter illustrate what has been done in the field of maritime migrant smuggling and rescue at sea, the agreements in section 7.3 offer us precedents for entry in the territorial waters of coastal States as well as mechanisms for the obtaining of flag State authorization to board vessels outside territorial waters.

In response to the question whether the existing legal framework can be used in the fight against maritime migrant smuggling, it can be stated that,

between the US and Croatia, Art. 4(4)(d) prohibits any unauthorized boardings other than in accordance with international law.

178 See also Art. 9(2) of the Migrant Smuggling Protocol.

179 McClean (n 27), 407.

while not necessarily easy (due to the humanitarian considerations discussed earlier in the book), it is possible to do so by adapting the models mainly evident in the drug trafficking initiatives, which have also been taken on in the fight against maritime terrorism. Within the drug smuggling scenario, the US has been highly successful in combating the maritime drug trade within the Caribbean region. It goes without saying, however, that drug trafficking does not come hampered with the same difficulties as migrant smuggling: drugs are commodities; human rights do not play as prominent a role in the fight against drug trafficking as they do in migrant smuggling. This, it may be argued, is a fundamental stumbling block in the effort to utilize the same principles to fight maritime migrant smuggling. To this it may however be countered that the US–Bahamas Agreement groups both crimes together—providing a highly useful reference paradigm and showing in no uncertain terms that the same principles may be employed in both these forms of organized crime.

Part III

State Practice

Chapter Eight

State Practice

This chapter does not purport to be an analysis of all relevant State practice, neither does it claim to cover the immigration regulations of the various cases selected. Rather, it attempts to illustrate salient points within the cases chosen which relate to the jurisdictional powers of States in the current international legal framework. These three examples were determined to be the best paradigms to illustrate the pitfalls and the prospects of State action in the fight against maritime migrant smuggling, and the potential future for international regulation in this area.

Insofar as State practice is concerned, some States have developed a specific policy with regard to interception, while others are still in the process of formulating one. Australia and the USA, for example, have both adopted interception policies under which official vessels patrol common transit routes and forcibly prevent maritime arrivals. Each country however acts in a different geographic zone: since September 1999, Australia has, through its Navy and the National Maritime Unit of its Customs Service, intercepted vessels carrying migrants within its territorial sea and contiguous zone.[1] The USA, in contrast, prevents entry into US territorial waters by patrolling the migrant transit routes on the high seas and intercepting vessels there. This practice began in 1981; however, as shall be discussed below, the current practice dates from 1992, under which US President G.H.W. Bush, by means of an Executive Order, rejected the extraterritorial application of US law on refugee protection.[2] Both Australia and the US have based their policies on the understanding that their obligations towards asylum-seekers are territorially bound, thus emphasizing the sovereignty argument mentioned earlier.[3]

---

1 Authorized by the Border Protection Legislation Amendment Act 1999.

2 US Office of the President, Executive Order 12807 of 24 May 1992, 'Interdiction of Illegal Aliens', 57 Fed Reg 23133 (1992). See also G. Goodwin-Gill and J. McAdam, *The Refugee in International Law* (3rd edn, OUP, Oxford, 2007), 141–145; J.C. Morris, 'The Spaces in Between: American and Australian Interdiction Policies and their Implications for the Refugee Protection Regime' (2003) 21 *Refuge* 4 for a summary of US interdiction policy history).

3 *Ibid.*, 51.

The EU is developing a policy on maritime migrant smuggling which falls within the wider policy on migration and asylum. The EU is faced with grave concerns on the part of some of its Member States such as Italy, Greece, Malta and Spain, which have been at the front-line of arrivals by sea. Partly in view of this, there has been a shift towards maritime patrols which are intended to serve both humanitarian and deterrent objectives.

Ultimately, whatever the policy adopted by States, the main issues remain the same: interception, disembarkation, how to deal with rescue operations and claims for asylum, and how to prevent irregular entry through smuggling operations via the maritime borders are all interconnected issues which face every State bordering the sea.

8.1. *Australia*

8.1.1. *Background*

Australia has in place a framework of measures designed to prevent unauthorized maritime arrivals. These measures were put in place during the 1990s in response to significant arrivals of migrants and asylum-seekers boarding vessels in Indonesia, and have served policy goals well, although their validity in terms of international instruments such as the Refugee Convention 1951 has been open to criticism.[4]

The core of Australia's policy has been termed the 'Pacific Strategy', established in the wake of the *Tampa* incident in September 1999 and comprising a framework of prevention and enforcement measures aimed at deterring boat arrivals.[5] 'Operation Relex' is an example of the aggressive interception policy employed by the Australian authorities. Alongside the interception policy, one finds the excision of certain offshore territories from Australia's migration zone, defined in Section 5 of the Migration Act 1958 as including Australia's territory and proclaimed ports.[6] By limiting the area in which a person can effectively

---

[4] For an overview of Australia's immigration and asylum system and regional initiatives such as the Regional Cooperation Agreement with Indonesia see J. van Selm and B. Cooper, 'The New Boat People: Ensuring Safety and Determining Status' (Migration Policy Institute, Report) (January 2006) 80–84. See also J. Vrachnas et al., *Migration and Refugee Law—Principles and Practices in Australia* (Cambridge University Press, Cambridge, 2005).

[5] See Parliament of Australia, Senate, 'Select Committee for an Inquiry into a Certain Maritime Incident' (23 October 2002) (A Certain Maritime Incident) Chapters 10 and 11.

[6] Australia's migration zone is the area consisting of the States, the Territories, Australian resource installations and Australian sea installations and, to avoid doubt, includes: (a) land which is part of a State or Territory at mean low water; and (b) sea within the limits of both

request asylum, Australia has purportedly shrunk the territory over which it has legal responsibility, while simultaneously expanding, through its interception policy, the area of its jurisdictional control. It is because of this that interception and excision of territory are sometimes referred to as complementary policies.[7]

This section will discuss Australia's approach in relation to irregular boat arrivals by first looking at major legislative interventions both prior to and after the arrival of the *Tampa* in August 2001. After this, Operation Relex will be referred to as an illustration of the interception policy practised by Australia.

8.1.2. *The Development of a Border Control Strategy*

In response to the undetected landing on the East coast of mainland Australia in 1999 of two vessels carrying unauthorized arrivals, the Australian government created the Coastal Surveillance Task Force charged with making recommendations on the strengthening of Australia's coastal surveillance regime. Amongst the 18 recommendations made was the need to create a coordinated approach to unauthorized arrivals.[8] This in turn led to the creation of a second task force in late 1999. The Unauthorized Arrivals in Australia Task Force's report resulted in the adoption of a 'comprehensive and integrated unauthorized arrivals strategy' involving three key elements: the prevention of irregular migration, the disruption of people smugglers and their clients *en route* and the development of appropriate reception arrangements.[9] However, there was no apparent effect on the number of unauthorized arrivals by sea.

8.1.3. *Key Legislation*

The offence of people smuggling was created by the Migration (Legislation Amendment) Act (No. 1) 1999, which amended the Migration Act 1958, making it an offence for a person to 'organize or facilitate the bringing or coming to Australia of a group of five or more persons where he knows they would become illegal immigrants'.[10] It also made it an offence to present false or forged documents, to make false or misleading statements or to pass documents

a State or a Territory and a port; and (c) piers, or similar structures, any part of which is connected to such land or to ground under such sea; but does not include sea within the limits of a State or Territory but not in a port.

7 Morris (n 2), 55, 58.

8 Prime Minister's Coastal Surveillance Task Force—Report (June 1999), para. 7.

9 Minister Philip Ruddock, Background Paper on Unauthorized Arrivals Strategy (2001).

10 Migration Act, s.232A.

to help a group gain illegal entry into Australia.[11] The Crimes at Sea Act 2000 extended the criminal jurisdiction of the Commonwealth and States to the limits recognized under the LOSC.[12] The Act establishes a cooperative scheme to apply the criminal law of Australian States extraterritorially in the areas adjacent to the coast of Australia.[13]

The main piece of legislation amending the Migration Act 1958 prior to 2001 was the Border Protection (Legislation Amendment) Act 1999, enacted with the aim of providing for enhanced protection of Australia's borders, which expanded Australia's capacity to board, search and detain ships and persons on board those ships at sea for immigration purposes.[14] The ultimate aim of this legislative exercise was the combating of the crime of people smuggling by creating new powers which would allow the competent Australian authorities to undertake enforcement action beyond Australian territorial waters, as is made evident in the relevant Parliamentary debates.[15]

8.1.4. *The Arrival of the* MV Tampa

It was the arrival of the *MV Tampa* in August 2001 which pushed Australian immigration policy into the limelight and marked the beginning of an aggressive border control strategy. An overview of the relevant facts follows.[16]

Prior to the arrival of the *Tampa*, 1,212 persons arrived in six boats in the first three weeks of August 2001. The boats arrived at the Australian offshore territories of Ashmore Reef and Christmas Island. In accordance with the established policy of the time (which was soon to change) as provided by the Migration Act, all of these boats were detained and those on board were taken to detention centres on mainland Australia for on-shore immigration processing.

11 Migration Act, s.233A.

12 This legislation, together with the Border Protection (Legislation Amendment) Act 1999, was a result of the realization that the then current maritime enforcement legislation did not fully implement the powers available under international law. See Prime Minister's Coastal Surveillance Task Force—Report (June 1999), para. 34.

13 Preamble. See also N. Hancock, 'Crimes at Sea Bill 1999' (Bills Digest No. 79 1999–2000) (10 November 1999) Department of the Parliamentary Library, Australia.

14 This Act also amended the Customs Act 1901.

15 'Border Protection Legislation Amendment Bill 1999' (Second Reading Speech, House of Representatives, Debates, 22 September 1999) 10147–10151.

16 See also *Victorian Council for Civil Liberties Inc v Minister for Immigration and Multicultural Affairs* (2001) 110 FCR 452, paras 14–43 (*VCCL v MIMA*); *Ruddock v Vadarlis* (2001) 110 FCR 491 (Fed. Ct.), paras 131–146; M. White, 'MV Tampa and Christmas Island Incident' [2002] *BIMCO Review* 116–123; N. Hancock, 'Border Protection (Validation and Enforcement Powers)' (Bills Digest No. 62 2001–2002) (20 September 2001) 5; N. Hancock, 'Refugee Law—Recent Legislative Developments' (Current Issues Brief No. 5 2001–2002) (18 September 2001) 9.

On 26 August 2001, 433 boat people (mostly Afghanis) were rescued from an Indonesian-flagged vessel, the *Palapa*, which was sinking in international waters between Indonesia and Christmas Island, technically in the Indonesian search and rescue area. This vessel was known by Australian authorities to be used by people smugglers to facilitate the arrival of asylum-seekers in Australia. The rescuing vessel was the *MV Tampa* (a Norwegian cargo ship *en route* from Fremantle in Australia to Singapore), which diverted its course to respond to a call from the Australian Coast Watch. The *Tampa's* Captain, Arne Rinnan, headed for Indonesia after failing to obtain assistance from the Australian authorities as to where to take the boat people, but then was pressured by the rescuees on board to change his course and head for the Australian territory of Christmas Island after five of those rescued threatened to commit suicide should he refuse to do so.[17] When the *Tampa* was close to Christmas Island, but outside Australian territorial waters, Captain Rinnan was asked by the Australian authorities to change course for Indonesia. However, due to mounting concerns regarding the health of the people on board, the *Tampa* entered Australian territorial waters off Christmas Island (stopping approximately four nm from the shore) on 29 August 2001 after having radioed an emergency signal for help and receiving none.[18] Within approximately two hours the *MV Tampa* was boarded by 45 Australian Special Air Services troops which effectively took control of the ship.[19]

That evening, the Australian government introduced legislation into Parliament which was intended to place beyond doubt the domestic legal basis for actions taken in relation to the *Tampa* and all foreign ships within the territorial sea of Australia, thus permitting the *Tampa* to be removed from territorial waters as a matter of Australian law.[20] Although the Bill was not specifically directed to the situation of the *Tampa*, it would have been retrospective, and

---

17 Australian search and rescue authorities seemed to indicate that the Captain was within his rights to change his course towards Christmas Island. However, DIMIA was opposed to the arrival of the ship, noting that carrier sanctions would apply. This was also the official government position. See P. Mares, *Borderline: Australia's Approach to Refugees and Asylum Seekers in the Wake of the Tampa* (University of New South Wales Press, Sydney, 2001), 122–123. Note that DIMIA (Department of Immigration and Multicultural Indigenous Affairs) has now been changed to DIAC (Department of Immigration and Citizenship).

18 As far as Australia's obligations towards asylum-seekers are concerned, it is arguable that Australia's obligations arose, at the latest, when the vessel entered Australian territorial waters. Furthermore, Australia also had the obligation to rescue the *Tampa* as a vessel in distress. See F. Feld, 'The *Tampa* Case: Seeking Refuge in Domestic Law' [2002] *Australian Journal of Human Rights* 11. See www.austlii.edu.au/au/journals/AJHR/2002/11.html.

19 The 5 Indonesian crew members rescued by the *Tampa* were landed on Christmas Island by the authorities and charged with people smuggling.

20 S.4(1).

thus applicable to the ship.[21] This power of removal was to be extended to any ship within the territorial waters, regardless of whether it was carrying persons seeking asylum or was otherwise engaged in any activity prejudicial to the peace, good order or security of Australia. Notably, section 4(1) provided for the discretion of an officer[22] to direct the Master or any person in charge of the vessel to remove a ship from Australian territorial waters and section 4(3) authorized the use of reasonable force to that end. Court proceedings concerning such actions were not to be permitted[23] and any applications for a protection visa under the Migration Act (effectively, an application for refugee status), by any person on board a vessel at the time when a direction is in force for the vessel to be removed from the territorial sea would be invalid.[24] The legislation was to have effect in spite of any other law.[25] The Bill, while passed in the House of Representatives, was however defeated in the Senate on 30 August 2001.[26]

On 30 August, the Norwegian ambassador to Australia was permitted to board the *Tampa*. He received a letter from the boat people pleading that they were refugees and effectively applying for asylum in Australia. The next day, two applications concerning the boat people were lodged in the Federal Court before Justice Anthony North. The applicants—Victorian Council for Civil Liberties and solicitor Eric Vadarlis—sought *habeas corpus* and an injunction against the removal of the ship. North J granted a temporary injunction and set the hearing for Monday, 3 September 2001. The respondents were restrained until the following day from taking any steps to remove the *MV Tampa* from Australian territorial waters—on the basis of preserving the authority of the court to consider the merits of the application the next day; had the *Tampa* been removed, the court's consideration of the issues would have been frustrated.[27] The first argument made by the applicants was that under section 245F(9) of the Migration Act there is no power to detain persons without bringing them to the migration zone; therefore, the detention was unlawful.[28]

---

21 Clause 2 of the Bill states that 'This Act is taken to have commenced on 29 August 2001 at 9.00am. legal time in the Australian Capital Territory.'

22 In proposed s.3 of the Border Protection Bill, an 'officer' included the following when authorized by the Prime Minister or Minister, either orally or in writing: (a) the Secretary or an employee of the Department; (b) an officer under the Customs Act 1901; (c) a member of the Australian Federal Police; (d) a member of the Australian Defence Force.

23 S.8.

24 S.9.

25 S.10.

26 The Bill was defeated in the Senate by the combined votes of the Labour, Democrats and Green parties.

27 *VCCL v MIMA*, (2001) 110 FCR 452, paras 29–30.

28 *Ibid.*, paras 138–161.

The law allows an officer to detain any persons found on board the ship and take them to the migration zone or to a place outside Australia. The latter part of section 245F(9), permitting removal to a place outside Australia, was not however included in the initial amendments of 1999 (in the Border Protection (Legislation Amendment) Act) but was introduced by the Border Protection Act of 2001. Therefore, in the *Tampa* court proceedings under section 245F(9), to which the Border Protection Act 2001 did not apply, the applicants argued that the rescuees were detained by members of the Australian Defence Force—'officers' for the purposes of the section. The duty of these officers was to take them or cause them to be taken to the migration zone; there was no power to detain persons without taking them into the migration zone. Therefore, detention of the vessel without such removal of persons to the migration zone was unlawful. The respondents maintained that the applicants had no standing to bring the claim, and at any rate, there was no detention of the ship itself (as the vessel could go anywhere except Australia) and section 245F(9) is predicated on detention of the vessel. Another argument put forward by the respondent was that the power to detain and take the persons on board into the migration zone is a police power conferred for law enforcement purposes and not for the purpose of conferring benefits on individuals.

These points did not fall to be determined however, since North J found that the applicants failed to establish that the Migration Act was applicable to the situation of the rescuees and the applicants did not have a sufficient interest in bringing the case.[29]

The applicants then argued an alternative basis for their claims: if the Migration Act did not apply to the situation of the rescuees, then they were detained without lawful authority. This principle is so well established that the respondents failed to challenge it. Their argument was that the rescuees were not held in detention—they were free to go anywhere they wished, except Australia.[30] The Government also stated that it had the executive power to repel people from its borders as a necessary facet of national sovereignty.[31]

---

[29] *Ibid.*, paras 149–150. Similarly, the applicants' argument based on s.189 of the Migration Act was also turned down owing to the fact that Mr Vadarlis lacked standing to pursue it for reasons given in paras 123–137. The applicants were held to lack standing on the basis of an earlier judgment: *Australian Conservation Foundation Incorporated v Commonwealth of Australia* [1979] HCA 1, (1980) 146 CLR 493.

[30] *VCCL v MIMA*, (2001) 110 FCR 452, para. 45. For the order for release argument see paras 50–109.

[31] *Ibid.*, para. 102.

Meanwhile, Australian authorities had been conducting discussions with various governments, and agreements with New Zealand and Nauru were announced on 1 September 2001.[32] These agreements lie at the heart of the so-called 'Pacific Strategy'.[33] New Zealand agreed to process 150 of the asylum-seekers, particularly women, children and family groups, and to settle those determined to be refugees. Nauru would take the rest (mostly men) and had agreed to act as a processing centre for the asylum-seekers, provided that Australia cover all costs and that any refugees be resettled in Australia or other countries. The agreement with Nauru was reached on 10 September, where a First Administrative Arrangement and a 13-point Statement of Principles was signed which stated *inter alia* that Nauru would 'provide a temporary processing site' for the migrants 'with the understanding that the refugees would be processed and out of the country by May 2002'. In return for this gesture, Australia was to compensate Nauru with a $30 million aid package.[34] Arrangements were made to transfer the boat people to the Australian troopship *Manoora* (on 3 September), which would take them to Papua New Guinea.[35] From there, they would be flown to New Zealand and Nauru. On 7 September, *en route* to Nauru, the Australian navy personnel intercepted and boarded an Indonesian vessel, the *Aceng*, in international waters. The Australian naval crew proceeded to transfer the 200 passengers (believed to be Iraqis) to the *Manoora*, and they continued on their way to Nauru.

The parties to the actions in the Federal Court agreed to the lifting of the court's injunction on condition that the government would return the asylum-seekers if the applicants' case was successful.[36] On 11 September 2001, North J found that the applicants did not have standing to bring any of the applications,

---

32 For an overview of the negotiations and agreements see 'A Certain Maritime Incident' (n 5), Chapter 10.

33 The other main prongs of the strategy involve Australia's increased aggressive efforts to intercept unauthorized vessels before they reach Australian territory, and the excision of many of its offshore territories from its migration zone. It has been criticized from various fronts. See, e.g., P. Mathew, 'Australian Refugee Protection in the Wake of the *Tampa*' (2002) 96 *AJIL* 661–676, at 676; Human Rights Watch, 'By Invitation Only: Australian Asylum Policy' (Report) (December 2002) Vol. 14 No. 10(C), Chapter 3; UNHCR, 'UNHCR criticises Australia for turning boat people away,' (11 November 2003) Press Release; A. Hewitt, 'The Pacific Solution is no Solution' (OXFAM Report).

34 OXFAM, 'Adrift in the Pacific: The Implications of Australia's Pacific Refugee Solution' (Report) (February 2002) 9.

35 On 10 October 2001, the Prime Minister made an announcement that the Government of Papua New Guinea had also agreed to establish a processing centre for unauthorized boat arrivals. See Arrangement with Papua New Guinea to Process Unauthorised Arrivals (10 October 2001) Media Release.

36 *VCCL v MIMA*, (2001) 110 FCR 452, para. 42.

except that for a writ of *habeas corpus*. On this issue he found that the rescuees had been unlawfully detained on the *Tampa*[37] and ordered that they be brought to the migration zone (i.e. effectively mainland Australia) to be dealt with according to law.

The Government successfully appealed North J's decision in *Ruddock v Vadarlis* (2001)[38] where the Commonwealth developed an argument based on the prerogative of the Crown (an argument which had not formed a noticeable part of the argument before North J). It argued that the inherent powers of any nation include a power to determine who enters the territory of that nation, and that this is a power exercisable by the Executive, regardless of any power existing under statute. French J (with whom Beaumont J agreed) held that although the extensive legislative powers in the Migration Act 1958 had not been invoked, the Government retained executive power (under Section 61 of the Constitution) to keep aliens from entering Australia and this executive power had not been abrogated by the Migration Act.[39] Rather simplistically, it was held that there was no breach of Art. 33 of the Refugee Convention either, as the rescuees had not been returned to the frontiers of persecution.[40] Further, as the aliens had no legal right to enter Australia, no detention had taken place and any restraint on liberty which might have been imposed was not subject to *habeas corpus*.[41]

Black CJ dissented, maintaining that, while the power to expel people entering Australia illegally is undoubted, this is a power which derives solely from statute; the existence of a prerogative or executive power to expel aliens was doubtful and the enactment of extensive legislative powers (through the Migration Act 1958) had excluded any relevant executive powers.[42] Moreover, the restriction of the asylum-seekers' liberty had been so significant as to amount to detention; since this was not justified by the powers conferred by Parliament under the Migration Act, it was not justified by law.[43] A subsequent application for special leave to appeal to the High Court on behalf of the asylum-seekers proved unsuccessful because the boat people were no longer detained within Australian jurisdiction, and the case was therefore moot.

37 Regarding detention see *ibid*., para. 81.
38 110 FCR 491 (Fed. Ct.).
39 *Ibid*., paras 193, 202.
40 *Ibid*., paras 126, 203.
41 *Ibid*., paras 212–215.
42 *Ibid*., paras 9–64.
43 *Ibid*., paras 65–89.

8.1.5. *The 2001 Legislative Package—Interception and Excision Perfected*

Following the incident, both Houses of Parliament passed six Bills on 27 September 2001.[44] Three of the laws making up this new legislative scheme, embodying the Pacific Strategy, are worthy of note.[45] These had the purpose of 'strengthening Australia's territorial integrity and to reduce incentives for people to make hazardous voyages to Australian territories.'[46]

8.1.5.1. *Interception and the Border Protection (Validation and Enforcement Powers) Act 2001*

Reference has already been made to the Border Protection (Validation and Enforcement Powers) Act 2001, amending both the Migration Act 1958 and the Customs Act 1901. It was enacted in order to validate the actions of the Commonwealth and others in relation to the *MV Tampa* and other vessels,[47] and to provide increased powers of interdiction.[48] This was introduced into Parliament on the day the Full Court's judgment was handed down, leading to the 'inescapable inference ... that the Government was going to seek to validate its actions regardless of what the decision of the Full Court might be.'[49]

The Act introduces mandatory minimum sentences (of five and eight years for first and repeat offenders, respectively), under the people smuggling provisions in the Migration Act.[50] Furthermore, it clarifies and expands border protection powers, including search and interdiction powers, under the Migration Act 1958 and the Customs Act 1901. Unlike the earlier Border Protection Bill 2001, Commonwealth officers are not authorized to tow vessels into international waters.[51]

---

44 Border Protection (Validation and Enforcement Powers) Act 2001; Migration Amendment (Excision from Migration Zone) Act 2001; Migration Amendment (Excision from Migration Zone) (Consequential Provisions) Act 2001; Migration Legislation Amendment Act (No. 1) 2001; Migration Legislation Amendment Act (No. 5) 2001; Migration Legislation Amendment Act (No. 6) 2001.

45 For information on the domestic legal initiatives taken by Australia see Mathew (n 33) 662–663; B. York, 'Australia and Refugees, 1901–2002: Annotated Chronology Based on Official Sources' (Chronology No. 2 2002–2003) (16 June 2003); J. Philips and A. Millbank, 'Protecting Australia's Borders' (Research Note 2003–2004 No. 22) (24 November 2003) Department of Parliamentary Library, Australia; R. Barnes, 'Refugee Law at Sea' (2004) 53 *ICLQ* 66–67.

46 DIAC Fact Sheet No. 65, 'New Humanitarian Visa System' (30 January 2007).

47 Part 2, ss.5–6.

48 Sched. 2, cl. 7, inserting s.245F(8) into the Migration Act.

49 Feld (n 18).

50 Migration Act, s.233C(2)(a)(b).

51 Possibly owing to the blatant interference with the freedom of navigation caused by towing the vessels back through international waters.

The Border Protection Act also settles the issue of the relationship between executive power and legislative power which proved central to the *Tampa* court litigation. Section 7A of the Migration Act[52] now provides that 'the existence of statutory powers under this Act does not prevent the exercise of any executive power of the Commonwealth to protect Australia's borders, including, where necessary, by ejecting persons who have crossed those borders.'[53]

The Border Protection (Validation and Enforcement Powers) Act finished the work commenced by the Border Protection (Legislation Amendment) Act in 1999. Through these pieces of legislation, the competent Australian authorities were given vast interdiction powers, as provided for in Division 12A of the Migration Act 1958. An overview of the relevant provisions follows.

A major innovation of the 2001 legislative package consisted in the power to stop, board and search vessels, whether situated in territorial waters, the contiguous zone or high seas, and detain and remove those on board. Division 12A of the Migration Act deals with the chasing, boarding, searching and control of movement of ships and aircraft.[54] Through this legislation, the authorities were given added powers, generally limited to boarding, searching, seizure and arrest without a warrant, in the overall task of protecting Australia's borders from irregular boat arrivals.

A general power for the Commander of a Commonwealth ship (or aircraft)[55] to request to board a vessel is set out under section 245B wherein the Commander may request the Master of a ship to permit him, a member of his crew or an officer to board the Master's ship. Once this request is made, sections 245F and 245G give the power to board the Master's vessel, even if the Master does not comply with the request. With respect to the making of the request, the Commander may use 'any reasonable means' to do so[56] and, in order to avoid any doubt, the request is held to have been made even if there is no Master on board the vessel or if the Master did not receive or understand the request.[57] A penalty of two years' imprisonment applies if the Master fails to comply with the request.[58]

---

52 Inserted by Sched. 2, cl. 2.

53 This power of removal would literally extend to the high seas. See P. Mathew, 'Legal Issues Concerning Interception', IARLJ Conference 2002, 87, 88.

54 Reference will be made only to ships, although the provisions apply equally to aircraft.

55 The terms 'Commander' and 'Commonwealth ship' are defined in ss.245B(12), introduced by the Border Protection (Validation and Enforcement Powers) Act 2001, and 245A, respectively.

56 S.245B(8).

57 S.245B(9).

58 S.245B(10); although note s.245B(11) where the Master need not comply with the request should a 'reasonable excuse' exist.

Section 245B also sets out the circumstances in which a request for boarding may be made and specifies the particular maritime zones in which such a request may validly be made:[59]

a. A request may be made to board a foreign ship in Australia's territorial sea. This request must be made 'for the purposes of th[e] Act'; in other words, those purposes stipulated in section 4 of the Migration Act, foremost amongst which is 'to regulate, in the national interest, the coming into, and presence in, Australia of non-citizens'. Such stipulation does not however seem to be necessary, since, according to jurisdictional principles, Australia would be empowered to exercise territorial jurisdiction over any vessel in its territorial sea. Possibly, this stipulation is made with the right of innocent passage in mind, in order to avoid any doubt; should the vessel be suspected of carrying illegal migrants (one of the negations of innocent passage), a request may be made to board the vessel precisely owing to such suspicion.
b. A request may also be made for the boarding of Australian ships[60] situated outside the territorial sea of any foreign country. Here, the request is not specifically tied to the 'purposes of the Act'.
c. Requests to board foreign vessels may be made where they are situated in Australia's contiguous zone or within 500 metres of an Australian resources installation or Australian sea installation. In such case the request to board must be made for a stipulated purpose: if the Commander wishes to establish the identity of the foreign vessel or should he reasonably suspect that the Master's ship 'is, will be or has been involved in a contravention, or an attempted contravention, in Australia of [the Migration] Act.'
d. Provision is also made with respect to foreign vessels outside any of the above-mentioned maritime zones, thus situated in the EEZ or high seas. Section 245B(5) allows a request to board to be made where the Commander 'reasonably suspects that the Master's ship is being used or was used in direct support of, or in preparation for, a contravention in Australia of [the Migration] Act, where the contravention involves another ship (whether a foreign ship or an Australian ship)' and 'the request is made as soon as practicable after the contravention happens.'[61] The reference here is to the so-called 'mother ships' which remain technically beyond the jurisdiction of coastal States while their boats commit offences within Australia.[62]
e. Furthermore, requests may be made to board foreign ships on the high seas where Australia has an agreement with the country whose flag the foreign vessel is entitled to fly which 'enables the exercise of Australian jurisdiction over ships of that country.'[63]

---

59 The instances outlined below reflect s.245B(2)–(7).

60 Defined in s.245A.

61 S.245B(5)(c) and (d).

62 See LOSC Art. 111(1) and (4).

63 A request under this subsection should not however be made if the circumstances outlined in the previous paragraph subsist. Note also s.245F(14) which provides that in such a situation

f. Lastly, requests to board stateless vessels on the high seas may also be made, in line with the general principle of the law of the sea, where the Commander wishes to establish the identity of the Master's ship.[64]

The power to chase the vessel, found in section 245C, is couched in the same language as that used in LOSC Art. 111. To facilitate the boarding of a foreign ship whose Master has not complied with the request to board made under section 245B, section 245C(1) enables a Commonwealth ship whose Commander made the initial request to board in any of the locations stipulated in section 245B[65] to chase the foreign ship to any place outside the territorial sea of another State. This chase may continue even when the Commonwealth ship involved in the chase loses sight of or trace of the foreign ship from radar or other sensing devices.[66] However, as under Art. 111 LOSC, under section 245C(5) the chase may not be resumed after being interrupted. A similar right also exists, under section 245D, with respect to the Commander of a Commonwealth vessel chasing an Australian ship to any place outside the territorial sea of a foreign country. The main difference is that an Australian ship can be chased without being requested to stop. Also, the chase of an Australian ship may be resumed if interrupted.

The means which may be used to facilitate the boarding of a foreign ship or Australian ship anywhere outside the territorial sea of a foreign State are laid out in section 245C(6) and 245D(3), respectively. The Commander may use 'any reasonable means' to enable him to board the chased ship.[67] These means include 'necessary and reasonable force' and 'where necessary, and after firing a gun as a signal, firing at or into the chased ship to disable it or compel it to be brought to for boarding.'[68]

What may be described as the core provision in this Division is section 245F which provides extensive powers to board, search and detail the vessel and persons on board. This section effectively applies to all ships hereunto mentioned, with section 245F(1) mentioning ships outside the territorial sea of any foreign country if a request to board has been made under section 245B

where an agreement does exist, the officer may then exercise any powers prescribed by such agreement in relation to the ship and persons found on board.

64 Note that a request under this subsection should not be made if the circumstances outlined in either of the two immediately preceding paragraphs subsist.

65 Or any other Commonwealth ship for that matter: see s.245C(2).

66 S.245C(4).

67 S.245C(6) dealing with the boarding of foreign ships includes the words 'consistent with international law', which are curiously omitted from the section on boarding Australian ships.

68 S.245C(6)(a)(b) and s.245D(3)(a)(b).

(irrespective of whether the request has been refused);[69] if the foreign ship is a mother ship pursued on the high seas under section 245C(3) and, lastly, if the ship is an Australian ship. The apparent overlap here is with Australian ships: these are mentioned both in section 245B(3) regarding requests to board and in section 245F(1)(c). Arguably therefore, this section applies to all Australian ships whether or not a request to board has been made.

Under section 245F(3) an officer[70] may board and search the ship and may search, examine and secure any goods contained on the vessel. He may require those on the ship to answer questions and produce documents in relation to: the ship, its voyage, cargo, crew and passengers, the identity and presence of those on board or a contravention or attempted contravention or involvement in an offence against the Migration Act, either in or outside Australia. The officer may copy or take extracts of the documents found or produced.[71] He may also arrest, without warrant, a person on the ship whether in or out of Australia. Where the vessel is in Australia, the arrest may be carried out if the officer reasonably suspects that the person has committed, is committing or is attempting to commit or is involved in, a migration offence either in or outside Australia. Insofar as concerns a vessel outside Australia, the arrest may be effected if the officer reasonably suspects that the person has committed, is committing or is attempting to commit, or is involved in the commission of a migration offence in Australia.[72]

Under section 245F(8), introduced by item 7 of the Border Protection (Validation and Enforcement Powers) Act, vessels may be detained and taken 'to a port, or to another place (including a place within the territorial sea or the contiguous zone in relation to Australia) that he or she considers appropriate'. The three enumerated cases where vessels may be so detained and brought to another place are if:

a. a vessel in Australia is reasonably suspected to be or to have been involved in a contravention of the Migration Act in- or outside Australia;
b. an Australian ship outside Australia is reasonably suspected to be, to have been, or that it will be involved in a contravention, either in- or outside Australia, of the Act; and

69 The section does not apply however where a request to board the ship has been made under s.245B(6) or (7) unless an officer is satisfied under s.245G(3) that the ship is indeed an Australian ship.

70 Defined in s.245F(18).

71 S.245F(3)(a)–(e).

72 S.245F(3)(f). Note s.245F(4) which states that 'any exercise of the power of arrest referred to in subsection (3) in the contiguous zone in relation to Australia is subject to the obligations of Australia under international law, including obligations under any treaty, convention or other agreement or arrangement between Australia and another country or countries.'

c. a foreign ship outside Australia is reasonably suspected to be, to have been, or that it will be involved in a contravention of the Act in Australia.

Prior to this amendment, where a ship was detained it could be taken only 'to a port, or other place.' The reference to 'port or other place' in the Migration Act (prior to amendment) was replaced with the following: 'to a port, or to another place (including a place within the territorial sea or the contiguous zone in relation to Australia)'.

Notwithstanding the opaque drafting, the effect of this amendment is that the areas to which an officer may move a detained ship have thereby been expressly extended to encompass the taking of boats within the territorial sea or contiguous zone. Since applications for protection visas can be made only in the migration zone, this amendment effectively prohibits illicit arrivals from making such application should they be taken to a place outside the Australian migration zone. The understanding is therefore that removal to a place outside the migration zone was not permitted prior to the amendment—or else, if permitted, then at least the power to do so was at best unclear. General rules of interpretation (such as the *eiusdem generis* rule) would lead one to understand that the 'other place' mentioned prior to the amendment being effected would require transfer of the vessel to a place of a similar nature to a port—possibly a bay, land territory or anchorage; in other words, transfer to the Australian migration zone. This is made even clearer by the analogous section 185(3) of the Customs Act 1901, referring to a 'port, airport or other place.' Ports and airports are understood as being points of entry. Therefore, the reference to 'other place' is to be understood, in the normal course of events, as being a similar place. Post-amendment however, this is not necessarily so. First, the inclusive reference to the territorial sea and contiguous zone clearly allows movement to those parts of the oceans. The specific term 'including' shows that this is not exhaustive—therefore, movement back out towards the high seas would also appear to be licit under this new article, despite the interference with the freedom of navigation which this would imply. Furthermore, a further indication that the high seas are also included in such other 'place' is seen in section 245F(8AA) which also permits movement on the high seas in order for such place to be reached. It should be recalled that when a vessel is directed to a place outside Australia, there is the possibility of a breach of the *non-refoulement* principle since the potential refugees are effectively being sent back 'into orbit.' Owing to this consideration, the provisions in section 245F(8) and (9) stand to be criticized as they permit, respectively, the removal of vessels to a place (including a place outside Australia) and the possibility that persons on board a detained ship may be sent to areas outside Australia.

Item 8 of the Border Protection (Validation and Enforcement Powers) Act introduced new provisions as far as persons on board the detained vessel are concerned.[73] Where a vessel is detained, section 245F(8A) provides that any restraint on the liberty of any persons on board resulting from the detention of the vessel is not unlawful and proceedings in this regard cannot be instituted. An officer has certain powers over persons on board detained ships, including to detain any persons found on board the ship and to take them or cause them to be taken to the migration zone or to a place outside Australia.[74] Section 245F(9A) complements the previous section, in that it provides an express power to place such persons on a ship, restrain them or remove them from a ship—in order to move them for the purpose of section 245F(9). Again, section 245F(9B) provides that no proceedings, whether civil or criminal, may be instituted in respect of any action taken under section 245F(9A) against the Commonwealth, the officer or any person assisting the officer in detaining the vessel where the person who took action acted in good faith and used no more force than is authorized by section 245F(10), which allows the use of such force as is 'necessary and reasonable.'[75]

As far as ships on the high seas are concerned, section 245G regulates the situation of a vessel on the high seas flying the flag of a State with which Australia has an agreement and of a stateless vessel on the high seas. This provision applies where a request was made under section 245B(6)[76] or (7)[77] and where the ship is outside the outer edge of the contiguous zone of Australia and outside the territory of any country, including Australia.[78] In either case, an officer[79] is granted the power to board the ship in order to establish its identity. In so doing he may ask those on board the ship questions regarding the identity and voyage of the ship and he may require the production of documents to that end. Furthermore, he may also request access to the ship's navigation instruments with respect to the ship's voyage. If the vessel is Australian, all the powers of boarding and searching as laid down in section 245F apply. Should the ship be registered in a country with which Australia has an agreement, then the officer is bound by the terms of that agreement; otherwise, should

[73] These are ss.245F(8A), (8B), (9), (9A) and (9B).

[74] S. 245F(9). They may also be returned to the vessel under s.245FB.

[75] S.245F(11)-(13) provides for limits on the use of force exercised in boarding and searching the vessel and examining goods on board, in arresting or detaining a person on board, and in arresting a person fleeing to escape arrest. These should arguably also be read together with s.245F(10) when determining the force 'authorized' by that subsection.

[76] Request to board a ship of a country with which Australia has an agreement.

[77] Request to board a ship without nationality.

[78] S.245G(1).

[79] Defined in s.245G(7).

no agreement exist with the State of registry, the officer is to leave the vessel 'as soon as is practicable.'[80] Where the vessel is stateless, the officer has the power to search her.

8.1.5.2. *Excision of the External Territories—the Migration Amendment (Excision from Migration Zone) Act 2001*[81] *(Excision Act)*

This Act effectively purports to alter Australia's migration zone, and thus represents another measure whereby Australia sought to 'discourage unauthorised arrivals, people smuggling and to promote the integrity of Australia's entry and visa processes.'[82] The 'migration zone' is the area in which valid applications for an Australian visa may be made. It is defined in section 5 of the Migration Act 1958 and refers to the physical territory and proclaimed ports. The definition therefore is different from that of 'Australia' in the Migration Act, since 'Australia' also includes the territorial sea. Through this Act, certain territories are excluded from the migration zone.

In terms of Australian law, under the Migration Act 1958 one criterion for a protection visa to be granted (which effectively recognizes the individual as a refugee)[83] is that the person is 'in Australia'. However, the Excision Act (which operates retrospectively so as to validate actions taken *vis-à-vis* the *Tampa*) removes particular territories (including Christmas Island and the Cocos, Ashmore and Cartier Islands, main landing points during the 1990s)[84] from the migration zone in order to ensure that 'offshore entry persons'[85] cannot make valid applications for protection visas in Australia.[86] These territories are known as 'offshore excised places', now redefined in section 5 of the Migration Act.

The Excision Act thus introduces the concept of the 'offshore entry person' which section 5 of the Migration Act defines as a person who entered an excised offshore place after the excision time for that place and became an unlawful non-citizen by reason of that entry. This new category of unauthorized arrival is thus barred from applying for a protection visa, by virtue of the new section

80 S.245F(5).

81 See DIAC Fact Sheet No. 81, 'Australia's Excised Offshore Places' (30 January 2007).

82 'Migration Amendment (Excision from Migration Zone) Bill 2001' (Explanatory Memorandum) (2001) 2.

83 A 'Protection Visa' is the method by which Australia satisfies its obligations under the Refugee Convention.

84 In July 2005 the Migration Amendment Regulations 2005 (No. 6) excised all Australian islands across Northern Australia from 210 South on the Queensland coast (vicinity of Makay) to 230 South on the Western Australian coast (Tropic of Capricorn south of Exmouth).

85 Defined in s.5 of the Migration Act.

86 Migration Act, s.46A, inserted by the Excision Act.

46A(1). However, the Minister for Immigration, by virtue of the same section, may exercise a non-compellable discretion to permit an offshore entry person to make a valid application.

Evaluation of what is permitted under international law is not an easy task when one takes into account that international law and the Refugee Convention did not foresee the phenomenon of boat people; neither did they foresee the refusal to grant the right to seek asylum to those in a State's territorial sea, and much less did they consider the exclusion of certain territories from the area in which asylum may be requested. The Migration Act 1958 permits applications for asylum within the migration zone. The definition of the migration zone effectively means that no person wishing to make an application for refugee status can do so from the territorial sea; rather they must land on Australian soil in order to do so. The act of excising certain territories from the migration zone further limited the right to claim asylum.

International law does not specify when the obligation to consider an asylum claim arises. However, there are various indications that such position constitutes a violation of the right to seek asylum. Key provisions in the 1969 Vienna Convention on the Law of Treaties (VCLT) dictate that a State is bound to carry out its international treaty obligations in good faith and to interpret a treaty in accordance with the ordinary meaning to be given to its terms in their context and in the light of its object and purpose.[87] Furthermore, Art. 28 VCLT provides that a treaty is binding in respect of the entire territory of a State. The fact that, according to Art. 27, States may not invoke internal laws as a justification for their failure to perform a treaty obligation clearly indicates that the domestic act of excising territory for the purposes of lodging a valid asylum claim (whether this 'territory' is the territorial sea or offshore territories) is contrary to international law.[88] The effect of excision effectively means that physical entry into the geographical limits of Australia does not necessarily qualify as entry sufficient to permit an individual to apply for asylum. This discord between the international law definition of territory and its domestic interpretation for certain purposes cannot be right.

[87] Art. 31.

[88] Australia continues to maintain that it is not breaching international law since a country has the right to determine which non-citizens may enter its territory, and on what conditions. The *non-refoulement* obligation does not guarantee a right of asylum or a right of residence, and therefore consideration of any claims in another State and resettlement of a refugee in a safe country discharge Australia's international obligations. See DIAC Fact Sheet No. 81, 'Australia's Excised Offshore Place' (30 January 2007). See also 'Guidelines for Commercial Shipping Rescuing Persons at Sea in or Adjacent to the Australian Search and Rescue Region' (June 2005).

8.1.5.3. *Migration Amendment (Excision from Migration Zone) (Consequential Provisions) Act 2001*[89]

This Act forms the final prong of the Pacific Strategy by enabling Australian officials either to detain offshore entry persons in Australia or to take them to a 'declared country', thus providing for mandatory detention or overseas processing.[90] The Bill was introduced into Parliament on the same day as the Excision Act and makes further provisions relevant to offshore entry persons and potential asylum-seekers. Its purpose is to amend the Migration Act 1958 to clarify the powers and obligations relative to the detention and movement of persons who arrive unlawfully at excised places, and also to amend the Migration Regulations 1994 so as to create a new temporary visa category for such offshore entry persons.[91]

As far as mandatory detention is concerned, 'offshore entry persons' are exempted from the mandatory detention provisions in section 189 of the Migration Act. However, if an officer knows or reasonably suspects that a person in an excised offshore place is an unlawful non-citizen[92] who is 'in Australia but outside the migration zone' and is seeking to enter an excised offshore place without a visa, then the officer *may* detain that person.[93] This power overlaps with the powers relating to the detention of ships and the detention of those aboard detained ships within the territorial sea.[94]

The taking of offshore entry persons to declared countries is provided for in section 198A of the Migration Act.[95] Offshore entry persons can no longer be taken into immigration detention in Australia, and they do not enjoy the limited rights of immigration detainees. Moreover, they are precluded from instituting or continuing any proceedings against Commonwealth action

---

89 See also DIAC Fact Sheet No. 70, 'Border Control' (30 January 2007).

90 Migration Act, ss.189(3)(4) and 198A(1), respectively.

91 Migration Regulations 1994, cl. 447 as amended by the Consequential Provisions Act 2001. See DIAC Fact Sheets: No. 60, 'Australia's Refugee and Humanitarian Programme' (5 March 2007); No. 61, 'Seeking Asylum within Australia' (30 January 2007); No. 64, 'Temporary Protection Visas' (27 June 2007); No. 65, 'New Humanitarian Visa System' (30 January 2007). For further information on Australia's visa policy see Vrachnas et al. (n 4), Chapter 13; R. Wazana, 'Fear and Loathing Down Under: Australian Refugee Policy and the National Imagination' (2004) 22 *Refuge* 83–95 at 90; Human Rights Watch, 'By Invitation Only: Australian Asylum Policy' (n 33) 81–90.

92 An 'unlawful non-citizen' is a person who is within the migration zone but does not possess a visa.

93 s.189(3)(4).

94 D. Spooner and N. Hancock, 'Migration Amendment (Excision from Migration Zone) (Consequential Provisions) Bill 2001' (Bills Digest No. 70 2001–2002) (26 September 2001) Department of the Parliamentary Library, Australia.

95 Inserted by the Migration Amendment (Excision from Migration Zone) (Consequential Provisions) Act 2001 (Consequential Provisions Act).

relating to their entry, status, detention and removal.[96] This power to remove such persons also includes the power to place, restrain, or remove them from a vessel, with such force as is necessary and reasonable, and this power can be exercised in- or outside Australia.[97]

A 'declared country' is any country which the Minister declares in writing under section 198A(3) of the Migration Act.[98] This declaration process is intended to ensure that the Minister is satisfied that appropriate arrangements are in place to prevent the *refoulement* of a person removed from Australia for processing in another country. However, there is no express requirement that the declared country be a Party to the Refugee Convention. Insofar as such non-party States may not be bound by the dictates of the Refugee Convention this could have serious ramifications with regard to the protection of asylum-seekers. For example, if a State negates the assertion that the *non-refoulement* obligation is a norm of customary international law, it will not hold itself bound by Art. 33 of the Convention and, therefore, the asylum-seekers may indeed be sent to the frontiers of a State where they would be liable to persecution.

Claims are assessed by Australian government officials in accordance with the Refugee Convention, but asylum-seekers have no recourse to Australian courts or tribunals.[99] The negation of such access,[100] together with the excision of certain territories, raises concerns about a second Guantanamo since individuals held at the US naval base have no legal rights:

> The 2001 Excision Acts place refugees in a Guantanamo Bay situation, outside the reach of the rule of law, with no legal protection of their rights and no guarantee of proper scrutiny and accountability.[101]

The aim of such amendments is to deter further movement from, or the bypassing of, other safe countries; it thus constitutes an attempt to stem 'forum-

---

[96] S.494AA.

[97] S.198A(2).

[98] The Minister may declare that a particular country: (i) provides access, for persons seeking asylum, to effective procedures for assessing their need for protection, and (ii) provides protection for persons seeking asylum, pending determination of their refugee status, and (iii) provides protection to persons who are given refugee status, pending their voluntary repatriation to their country of origin, or resettlement in another country, and (iv) meets relevant human rights standards in providing that protection.

[99] DIAC Fact Sheet No. 76 'Offshore Processing Arrangements' (6 June 2007).

[100] See Section 494AA, introduced by the Consequential Provisions Act.

[101] A. Bartlett, 'Migration Legislation Amendment (Migration Zone Excision Repeal) (Consequential Provisions) Bill 2006, Migration Legislation Amendment (Migration Zone Excision Repeal) Bill 2006' (Motion and Speech, Second Reading Speech, House of Representatives). See also International Commission of Jurists, Australian Section, 'Submission to the Senate Legal and Constitutional References Committee, Inquiry into the Migration Legislation (Further Border Protection Measures) Bill 2002 and related matters'.

shopping' on the part of reputed asylum-seekers. These measures are directed at creating further disincentives to unauthorized arrival in Australia by those who use people smugglers with the aim of achieving a resettlement place they may well not need—a place taken from refugees with no other options available to them.[102] The effect of this legislation however, may fall foul of Australia's international obligations: it may well permit *refoulement* to a place of persecution or torture; it discriminates against asylum-seekers; it permits detention of asylum-seekers in Australia and the agreements with declared countries contemplate detention as well.[103]

8.1.6. *Interception Illustrated: Operation Relex*

Operation Relex, which commenced on 28 August 2001, is a classic illustration of a State's attempt to intercept vessels in a bid to prevent unauthorized boat arrivals. Based upon the legislative measures taken in 2001, described above, it consisted mainly of preventing unauthorized vessels from crossing into Australia's contiguous zone and was thus fundamentally a 'forward defence strategy', marking a shift in border protection strategy and the nature of previous operations away from the more reactive position associated with 'Operation Cranberry' which sought to detect and intercept unauthorized boats *inside* Australian waters and escort them to Australian ports.[104] The operation was aimed at preventing 'in the first instance, the incursion of unauthorized vessels into Australian waters such that, ultimately, people smugglers and asylum-seekers would be deterred from attempting to use Australia as a destination.'[105]

---

[102] Minister Philip Ruddock, 'Migration Amendment (Excision from Migration Zone) (Consequential Provisions) Bill 2001' (Second Reading Speech, House of Representatives, Debates, 18 September 2001) 30381.

[103] Mandatory detention has been argued to be contrary to a number of international conventions such as the Refugee Convention (Art. 31), the ICCPR (Arts. 7 and 9(1)); the Torture Convention (Art. 16); and the Convention on the Rights of the Child (Art. 37). The key issue appears to be the prohibition on unnecessary or arbitrary detention. As stated in various communications by the Human Rights Committee, detention must not only be lawful but necessary and reasonable in all circumstances. See, e.g., *A v Australia (1997)* Communication No. 560/1993, UN Doc CCPR/C/59/D/560/1993 (1997), para. 9.4; *Alphen v The Netherlands (1990)* Communication No. 305/1988, UN Doc CCPR/C/39/D/305/1988, para. 5.8; *Chu Kheng Lim v The Minister for Immigration, Local Government and Ethnic Affairs* (1992) 176 CLR 1; United Nations Human Rights Committee, *Concluding Observations of the Human Rights Committee: Australia*, UN Doc CCPR/CO/69/AUS (28 July 2000); *Amuur v France* (1996) 22 ECtHR 533, para. 48.

[104] Evidence to Senate Select Committee on a Certain Maritime Incident, Parliament of Australia, Canberra (Evidence, CMI) 5 April 2002, at 488, 502 (Rear Admiral Ritchie).

[105] 'A Certain Maritime Incident' (n 5) 13. Attention was also given to ensuring the safety of all persons involved. See *ibid.*, at 14 *et seq*, paras 2.8–2.14.

Interception under Operation Relex generally followed a common pattern. Air and naval surveillance[106] of the areas of the country's northern approaches enabled vessels to be detected while still outside Australia's contiguous zone. These suspected illegal entry vessels (SIEVs) were warned to stay out of Australian waters by Australian naval vessels.[107] If the boat failed to turn back then, once it was within the contiguous zone, Australian authorities were empowered to use more forceful deterrence measures, such as firing warning shots into the ocean. In the face of continuing refusal, an armed party would be dispatched to board the vessel and assume control, whereupon attempts were made to return the boat to the high seas. Australian authorities made no attempt to ascertain whether any passengers might have been seeking to make a protection claim.[108]

The initial instructions were to intercept and board an SIEV which persisted in its attempt to enter Australian territorial waters and hold unauthorized arrivals for shipment in sea transport to a country to be designated. This policy was adjusted, where possible, to intercept, board and *return* the SIEVs to Indonesia (as these vessels were Indonesian vessels).[109] The evidence given to a Senate Select Committee on a 'Certain Maritime Incident' (23 October 2002) gives a detailed account of the workings of Operation Relex. An overview follows.

SIEVs would be intercepted on the high seas, generally in the vicinity of Christmas Island or the Ashmore Reef. Defence personnel had authority to board the vessels only once they entered Australia's contiguous zone. Interceptions could occur much further out than 24 nm; however, naval vessels would then have to shadow the SIEV until it entered the contiguous zone before any action could be taken. In the first instance, then, warning messages were delivered to the Masters of the boats, informing them that 'they were suspected of having illegal people on board and that they should not take the people to Australia because they were not welcome.'[110]

Naval frigates are not directly involved in the interception and boarding of SIEVs. Rather, the large frigates would be kept 'over the horizon' and out of sight, while fast rigid hull inflatable boats (RHIBs) would be sent forward to meet the SIEV in what is termed 'long range insertion'.[111] This approach was designed to minimize the risk of a safety-of-life-at-sea situation being

[106] Evidence, CMI 488, 502 (Rear Admiral Smith, 5 April 2002).
[107] Also customs vessels within the purview of the Customs Act 1901.
[108] Evidence, CMI 661 (Rear Admiral Smith, 5 April 2002).
[109] Evidence, CMI 508 (Rear Admiral Smith, 5 April 2002). With this new policy the requirement to issue a warning to vessels in international waters was cancelled.
[110] 'A Certain Maritime Incident' (n 5) 25, para. 2.62.
[111] See Discussion on Standard Operating Procedure in Evidence, CMI 502 (Rear Admiral Smith, 5 April 2002).

generated: the sight of a large vessel capable of rescuing all persons on board the SIEV would be the catalyst for attempts to sabotage the SIEV or jumping overboard, thereby necessitating a rescue situation.[112]

Upon interception of an SIEV, the personnel on board the RHIB would issue a warning to the Master of the vessel, if one was identified or, otherwise the crew.[113] The warning informed the Master/crew that he or it would be breaching Australian law if they proceeded into Australian territory and that they would be subject to severe penalties under that law.[114] The text of the warning was supplied in both English and Bahasa (Indonesian), given that the crews were invariably Indonesian nationals. It recommended that the crew turn the boat round and return to Indonesia. It appears that in every instance the warnings were ineffective in stopping the boats from continuing into Australian waters, thus calling for the next phase of the interception procedures once the vessels entered the contiguous zone, 24 nm off Christmas Island.[115]

The naval vessel would then shadow the SIEV as it proceeded towards the Australian contiguous zone. Warnings would continue to be given to the vessel prior to boarding. The boarding of the vessel could be either compliant or non-compliant. Where the boarding was compliant the SIEV was often broken down and in need of assistance, or else responded to a request to heave to, allowing the embarkation of the boarding party. In the case of a non-compliant boarding, requests to heave to were usually ignored, requiring more forceful measures to be used to embark the boarding party. In at least one instance, machine gun warning shots were fired into the water ahead of the SIEV and a searchlight was used to illuminate both the weapon firer and the area in the water ahead of the vessel where the rounds were to land.[116] Other tactics involved manoeuvring the naval vessel close to the SIEV to create a distraction, allowing 'an assault type non-compliant boarding, using the RHIB, to be effected whilst the vessel was still underway.'[117]

Once embarked, the boarding party commandeered the ship and prevented any further damage being occasioned to the vessel.[118] Initially, the boarding party comprised naval personnel only. As Operation Relex progressed, it was decided that an armed presence in the boarding party was required in order to

[112] *Ibid.*
[113] *Ibid.*
[114] *Ibid.*, at 503.
[115] *Ibid.*, at 504.
[116] The vessel in question was SIEV 4: Evidence, CMI 159 (Commander Norman Banks, 25 March 2002).
[117] *Ibid.*, at 159.
[118] Evidence, CMI 136 (Vice Admiral David Shackleton, 25 March 2002).

ensure control of the vessel.[119] This armed presence was known as the Transit Security Element and included members of the Australian Army.

The members of the boarding party, although armed, were told that the use of force should always be consistent with the situation they found themselves in and should be kept to a minimum.[120]

Once boarding had been effected, the established policy would be to:

> ... reinforce the warning and turn the vessel around and either steam it out of our contiguous zone ourselves under its own power or—as had happened on a number of occasions—if the engine had been sabotaged in our process of boarding, we would then tow the vessel outside our contiguous zone into international waters. At that point, our boarding party withdrew as we had no jurisdiction in international waters. Our initial policy was to do that up to three times and, after having done it the third time, to seek further advice from government with the view to those vessels being taken to Ashmore Island or to Christmas Island.[121]
>
> The boarding party would remain on the SIEV until it reached the outer limit of the Australian contiguous zone, at which point it would return to the naval vessel. The naval vessel would closely escort the SIEV, if it was not under tow, until the Indonesian 24 mile limit, at which point it would instruct the vessel to continue back towards Indonesia. The naval vessel would then withdraw over the horizon, outside the nominal visual range and would monitor the SIEV using an electro-optical tracking system. The SIEVs invariably just turned around and came back again.[122]

Initially, any SIEV which persisted in its attempts to enter Australia or which foundered while attempting to enter Australia, was contained by the Australian Defence Force (ADF) until a decision was made where the boat and/or passengers were to be taken. The aim was that no-one from any SIEV was to land on Australian territory. Many people were contained on vessels in Australian territorial waters but none was allowed to land. The Pacific Strategy saw the establishment of two processing camps on Nauru (one for the *Tampa* arrivals and one for subsequent arrivals) and one camp on Manus Island. The people on board the SIEVs were not returned to Indonesia, but taken to one of the camps for processing.

In early October 2001, a request was conveyed to the People Smuggling Taskforce (PSTF) to prepare a report on the feasibility of returning SIEVs to Indonesia once intercepted. The PSTF discussed the matter on 11 October 2001 and provided the draft report to the Secretaries Committee on National Security

[119] Evidence, CMI 453 (Rear Admiral Geoffrey Smith, 4 April 2002).
[120] Evidence, CMI 660 (Rear Admiral Geoffrey Smith, 11 April 2002).
[121] Evidence, CMI 504 (Rear Admiral Geoffrey Smith, 5 April 2002).
[122] Evidence, CMI 462 (Rear Admiral Geoffrey Smith, 4 April 2002).

on 12 October 2001, informing it that, subject to a number of limitations particularly relating to the seaworthiness of the vessel, it was possible to return the SIEVs to Indonesia.[123] The report acknowledged that not every vessel could be returned. The overriding considerations would be safety-of-life-at-sea issues and Australia's international law obligations to assist those in distress at sea.[124] Interestingly, the caveats failed to mention any consideration of people's potential asylum claims.

The 'tow-back' policy essentially constituted the interception of SIEVs and forcible return of the vessels under Navy escort to within close proximity of Indonesian territorial waters. Australian vessels involved in tow-backs did not at any stage enter Indonesian territorial waters—they escorted the SIEVs to the edge of the Indonesian contiguous zone, from which point the SIEVs continued under their own steam back into Indonesian territorial waters.[125] The Indonesian government was apparently notified of the return of each of the four SIEVS subject to the tow-back policy.[126] Australian involvement ceased once the Indonesian government was informed that the boats had been returned to Indonesian territorial waters, arguably amounting to a breach of Australia's international obligation to ensure that no asylum-seeker is subjected to *refoulement* owing to the fact that Indonesia is not a Party to the Refugee Convention and may argue that it is not bound by the *non-refoulement* obligation set out in Art. 33.

This 'tow-back' policy could be seen to be in violation of the current law of the sea regime, in that it could be perceived as being contrary to the freedom of navigation on the high seas. However, it has been reported that Australia has in its favour the apparent acquiescence of Indonesia in the practice and that, furthermore, the policy is in accord with the practice of other States such as Malaysia, Italy and the US and, as such, could even be argued to be part of customary international law.[127]

8.1.7. *Recent measures*

Australia's recent move has been the creation of an Australian Maritime Identification System (AMIS).[128] In its original formulation, as announced on

---

[123] Evidence, CMI 917 (Jane Halton, 16 April 2002).
[124] Evidence, CMI 662 (Rear Admiral Geoffrey Smith, 11 April 2002).
[125] Evidence, CMI 1452–3 (Dr Geoff Raby, 1 May 2002).
[126] Evidence, CMI 823 (Edward Killesteyn, 16 April 2002).
[127] Tate Lieutenant Commander NP, RAN, 'People Smuggling: Defending Australia's National Interest' (2003) Geddes Papers, 48.
[128] For use of new terminology see 'Strengthening Australia's Offshore Maritime Security' (Industry Briefing Paper, February 2005).

14 December 2004, the AMIS was described as a 'Maritime Identification Zone' and was designed to strengthen Australia's offshore maritime security by increasing awareness of the maritime domain. The provision of this information was intended to enhance the effectiveness of civil and military maritime surveillance, particularly in protecting offshore oil and gas facilities from terrorism.[129] However, following concerns voiced by Australia's neighbours over a perceived unilateral assertion of authority, Australian officials began referring to the 'zone' as the AMIS.[130]

The reformulation resulted in only a few modifications to the original proposal and in fact has had more effect in terms of organizing and streamlining Australian bureaucracy than anything else.[131] Australia will seek information from vessels which are 1,000 nm or 48 hours' steaming distance from the Australian mainland and intending to enter Australian ports. In the case of vessels proposing to transit the Australian EEZ or territorial waters, information is to be sought on a voluntary basis at 500 nm or 24 hours' steaming distance from the Australian mainland. Within Australia's 200 nm EEZ, all vessels are to be identified other than day recreational vessels. The information to be sought is to relate to the ship's identity, crew, cargo, location, course, speed and intended port of arrival.[132] The original proposal gave the ADF authority to enforce this measure by carrying out interdictions of vessels. This is no longer the case under the new regime. Through AMIS, Australia's Border Protection Command aims to 'develop and maintain a comprehensive picture of vessels operating within 1000 nms of the Australian coast ... track and assess vessels as they near the coast; maintain an ongoing overall and specific assessment to ensure that any threats posed by suspect vessels are met and contained; and if necessary organize a response before any threat reaches shore.'[133]

The requirement to give information prior to vessels entering port is not new: reference was made (in Chapter 4) to the US '96 hour advance notice of arrival rule' and the initiatives spearheaded by the IMO to increase awareness of the maritime domain such as the AIS and LRIT. In fact, the LRIT will assist Australia with its aims under AMIS; however, the information available through the LRIT is not as detailed as Australia's requirements. In asserting rights to information in areas of the high seas 'Australia is attempting to assert rights

[129] N. Klein, 'Legal Limitations on ensuring Australia's Maritime Security' (2006) 7 *MelbJIL* 306. See www.austlii.edu.au/au/journals/MelbJIL/2006/13.html.

[130] *Ibid.* See also N. Klein, 'Legal Implications of Australia's Maritime Identification System' (2006) 55 *ICLQ* 338–339.

[131] Information given via email by Dr Natalie Klein, University of Melbourne.

[132] See www.customs.gov.au/site/page.cfm?u=5783.

[133] See www.customs.gov.au/site/page.cfm?u=5779.

and exercise jurisdiction that are arguably not attributable to coastal States.'[134] This exercise therefore demonstrates both 'the need to improve maritime security and the limitations faced by States under the current international legal regime.'[135]

8.1.8. *Conclusion*

The introduction of an Australian border control policy coincided with the ending of boat arrivals and was hailed as a success by the Administration. However, questions about the validity in international law of such initiatives remain. Australia maintains that it honoured its obligations under international law through the Pacific Strategy arrangements, as was commented upon in the *Tampa* appeal judgment:

> Finally, it should be added that this is a municipal, and not an international, court. Even if it were, whilst customary international law imposes an obligation upon a coastal state to provide humanitarian assistance to vessels in distress, international law imposes no obligation upon the coastal state to resettle those rescued in the coastal state's territory. This accords with the principles of the Refugee Convention.[136]

It is interesting that the defeated Border Protection Bill of 2001 contained a provision, clause 4(1), which stated that 'an officer may, in his or her absolute discretion, direct the Master or other person in charge of a ship that is within the outer limits of the territorial sea of Australia to take the ship, and any person on board the ship, outside the territorial sea.' This provision does not find a replacement in the Border Protection (Validation and Enforcement Powers) Act 2001. While at first sight what was stated above may appear to lead to the same effect, there is a significant difference—the omission of the officer's 'absolute discretion' is replaced by a reasonable suspicion on the part of the officer that the ship 'is or has been involved in a contravention [of the Migration Act], either in or outside Australia' (section 245F(8)(a)). Should such suspicion exist, direction of the vessel out towards the high seas is possible and legal. As far as those on board are concerned, section 245F(9) directs that they be taken to the migration zone or to a place outside Australia. This addition, introduced by the Border Protection Act 2001, ensures the operation of the Pacific Strategy—places outside Australia are made available for any asylum claims to be heard.

---

134 Klein (n 130), 340 gives a detailed account of implications insofar as high seas freedoms and EEZ rights are concerned.

135 Klein (n 129), 308.

136 Beaumont J, para. 126. See also French J, at para. 203.

While Australia maintains that its refugee protection obligations are thereby met, this may not be the case since there is no guarantee that such countries will necessarily be parties to the Refugee Convention.

8.2. *United States*

Interception of unauthorized persons approaching US shores is part of a border enforcement strategy and is today presented as a national security measure, formalized by Proclamation 4865 of 1981,[137] marking the commencement of the current interception policy.[138] Interception takes place on the high seas, and is dictated by three key instruments which in turn, have given rise to a fair amount of court litigation.

On 29 September 1981 President Reagan issued Proclamation 4865 on 'High Seas Interdiction of Illegal Aliens', which stated *inter alia* that the 'continuing illegal migration by sea of large numbers of undocumented aliens into the southeastern United States' constituted 'a serious national problem detrimental to the interests of the United States.' In order to safeguard US sovereignty '[t]he entry of undocumented aliens from the high seas is hereby suspended and shall be prevented by the interdiction of certain vessels carrying such aliens.' The Presidential Proclamation was accompanied by Executive Order 12324 of 29 September 1981 on 'Interdiction of Illegal Aliens'[139] which outlined the 'continuing problem of migrants coming to the United States, by sea, without necessary entry documents' and ordered 'the suspension and interdiction of such entry.' Apart from stating the aim of concluding cooperative arrangements with foreign governments, the core provision authorized the Coast Guard to 'enforce the suspension of the entry of undocumented aliens and the interdiction of any defined vessel carrying such aliens.' Members of the Coast Guard were authorized to interdict ships on the high seas ('outside the territorial waters of the United States'), to 'stop and board' suspect vessels and to make inquiries of those on board, examine documents and take such action as necessary to establish the registry, condition and destination of the vessel and the status of those on board. Such vessels and passengers were to be returned to the country from which they came.[140] However, pursuant to Section 2(c)(3), no person determined to be a refugee was to be returned without his consent.

---

[137] 46 Fed Reg 48109 (1981), 3 CFR, 1981 Comp, 180.

[138] See L.D. Rosenberg, 'The Courts and Interception: The United States Interdiction Experience and its Impact on Refugees and Asylum Seekers', IARLJ Conference 2002, 233–259 for an overview of US interception policy and related litigation in the US courts.

[139] 46 Fed Reg 48109, 3 CFR (1981 Comp) 180.

[140] Section 2(c).

These directions and powers applied only to certain specified vessels, outlined in Section 2(b) as being:

a. vessels flying the US flag;
b. vessels owned 'in whole or in part by the United States, a citizen of the United States or a corporation incorporated under the laws of the United States.' Vessels which have been granted nationality by a foreign nation in accordance with Art. 5 HSC were expressly exempted;
c. vessels without nationality;
d. vessels assimilated to vessels without nationality because of an attempt to fly more than one flag, in accordance with Art. 6(2) HSC;
e. vessels flying the flag of a State with which the US had an arrangement authorising such action, such as the US–Haiti Agreement.

Six days prior to the Proclamation and Executive Order, a Bilateral Executive Agreement had been signed with the Haitian government on 23 September 1981. The Agreement was a cooperative programme of interdiction and selective return of certain Haitian migrants to Haiti. The Exchange of Notes provided for the boarding of Haitian vessels by members of the US Coast Guard[141] who were given the authority to 'address inquiries, examine documents and take such measures as are necessary to establish the registry, condition and destination of the vessel and the status of those on board the vessel.' Under the terms of the Agreement, the US agreed to 'the presence of a representative of the Navy of Haiti as liaison aboard any United States vessel engaged in the implementation of th[e] cooperative programme'. In the event that such measures suggested a violation of US or Haitian immigration laws, the Republic of Haiti consented to the US Coast Guard detaining the vessel and those on board on the high seas. In such case, the authorities of the US were promptly to inform the Haitian authorities of the action taken and keep them abreast of any developments. Upon prior notification being given, the Haitian government agreed to the return of Haitian vessels (and outgoing US vessels) and persons on board to a Haitian port; alternatively, if circumstances permitted, the Haitian ship could also be released, on the high seas, to representatives of the Haitian government. While both States agreed to prosecute illegal traffickers and confiscate the vessels used, Haiti gave assurances that 'Haitians returned to their country and who are not traffickers will not be subject to prosecution for illegal departure.' At the same time, it was provided that the US 'does not intend to return to Haiti any Haitian migrants whom the United States authorities determine to qualify for refugee status.'

In point of fact, the Proclamation and Executive Order were intended to stop illegal migration from Haiti, although in subsequent years the same law

[141] Permission was also requested for US authorities to board any private Haitian-flagged vessels suspected of carrying illegal immigrants to US shores.

was used for immigrants from Cuba.[142] In the decade to follow, approximately 25,000 Haitians were interdicted. Haitians interdicted on the high seas were interviewed at sea to determine whether they were political refugees with a credible fear of persecution. If this was so, the individual would be screened in, and permitted to enter, the US to apply for political asylum. The others were screened out and repatriated to Haiti.[143]

While the installation of a popularly-elected President in Haiti caused boat departures and interceptions to decrease significantly during 1989 and 1990, a military coup in late 1991 caused departures to soar in 1992. Following the coup, the Coast Guard suspended repatriations. However, when on 18 November 1991 the Coast Guard announced the recommencement of the programme of interdiction and forced repatriation, the Haitian Refugee Center, representing a class of interdicted Haitians, filed a complaint in the US District Court for the Southern District of Florida alleging that the Government had failed to provide adequate procedures to protect Haitians who qualified for asylum. The District Court granted temporary relief which precluded any repatriations until 4 February 1992, when a reversal on appeal in the Court of Appeals for the Eleventh Circuit and a denial of *certiorari* by that court effectively terminated that litigation.[144] The Department of Defense consequently established temporary facilities at the US Naval Base in Guantanamo, Cuba, to accommodate them during the screening process.

In the meantime, the Haitian exodus expanded dramatically. During the six months after October 1991, the Coast Guard interdicted over 34,000 Haitians. With these swiftly escalating numbers of interdicted vessels carrying undocumented Haitians the Navy determined that it could no longer safely accommodate Haitians at Guantanamo. As a result of the overwhelming refugee flows, overcrowding in Guantanamo Bay and sinking of unseaworthy vessels, screening and protecting the nation's borders were no longer feasible.[145]

President G.H.W. Bush issued Executive Order 12807 on 24 May 1992 (also known as the 'Kennebunkport Order')[146] calling for 'instruction to the Coast Guard in order to enforce the suspension of the entry of undocumented aliens at sea and the interdiction of any defined vessel carrying such aliens.' This resulted in the interdiction on the high seas and direct return to Port-au-

[142] For information on various US interdiction operations see van Selm et al. (n 4), 72–75.

[143] Even under this original system in which those found to have a credible fear were screened in, it appeared that few *bona fide* claims to refugee status were presented. See *Haitian Refugee Center v Gracey*, 809 F 2d 794, 797 (DC Cir 1987).

[144] Reported in *Sale v Haitian Centers Council*, 113 S. Ct. 2549, 509 US 155 at 163 (1993) (*Sale v HCC*).

[145] 509 US 155 at 163 (1993).

[146] 'Interdiction of Illegal Aliens', 57 Fed Reg 23133 (1992).

Prince of individuals fleeing Haiti, with no prior screening for asylum-seekers. Executive Order 12807 terminated the screening process provided in Order 12324 and allowed the Coast Guard to interdict Haitians on the high seas and immediately repatriate them to Haiti without making any determination of refugee status. Thus, Executive Order 12807, superseding Executive Order 12324, instituted a new interdiction programme of 'summary return without screening' and led to the forcible return of *bona fide* refugees without any process or questioning to Haiti. The 1981 Agreement with Haiti, together with Executive Order 12324 were thereby abrogated.[147]

The instructions under the new Executive Order included:

1. Stopping and boarding vessels intercepted beyond the US territorial sea;
2. Questioning those on board, examining their documents and taking action as necessary;
3. Returning the vessel and its passengers to the country from which they came, though with the stipulation that the Attorney General may at his discretion decide that a refugee will not be returned without his consent.

The US policy under the Kennebunkport Order gave rise to litigation on behalf of Haitian refugees who were repatriated without screening. Class actions were initiated in the Federal Courts, by the Haitian Refugee Center and the Haitian Centers Council, two non-profit organizations assisting Haitian emigrants. Whether the interception of Haitian refugees on the high seas contravened domestic and international law was litigated in both *Haitian Refugee Center v Baker*[148] and *Haitian Centers Council v McNary*.[149] The US Court of Appeals for the 11th Circuit in *Baker* and the 2nd Circuit in *McNary* reached contrary conclusions.

A core issue in the *McNary* litigation concerned whether §243(h)(1) of the Immigration and Nationality Act (INA), prohibiting the return of aliens to a State where they face a credible fear of persecution, applies beyond the geographic borders of the US. The US Court of Appeals for the Second Circuit, on 29 July 1992, issued an order enjoining the programme. It thus reversed the district court's decision and held that §243(h)(1), as amended, was applicable to aliens intercepted in international waters, thereby extending the protection of the Act to such aliens. The Kennebunkport Order was therefore illegal since it permitted the Coast Guard to return Haitians to their persecutors without a prior determination of refugee status.[150]

---

[147] This policy was also adopted by President Clinton who chose not to modify the Order on his election. This policy remained until May 1994 when full refugee status determination interviews on board ships were announced (16 *Refugee Reports*, 28 February 1995, 11).

[148] 953 F.2d 1498 (11th Cir. 1992), *cert. denied* 112 S.Ct. 1245 (1992).

[149] 969 F.2d 1350 (1992), *cert. granted* 113 S.Ct. 52 (1992) (No. 92–344).

[150] 969 F.2d 1366–1367.

In reaching its decision the Court of Appeals applied the plain meaning doctrine to its construction of § 243(h)(1) INA. Prior to 1980, this section had created a distinction between those aliens who were 'within the United States' and others not within the country's borders. In removing the words 'within the United States' the court observed that 'Congress does not intend, *sub silentio*, to enact statutory language that it has earlier discarded.'[151] The court also rejected the Government's argument that Art. 33 of the Refugee Convention and the Protocol did not apply extraterritorially on the high seas.[152] The Court of Appeals in *Baker I* indicated that the Haitians had not yet reached the territory of the United States, thus implying that the court did not believe that Art. 33 had extraterritorial application.[153]

Three days later, the Supreme Court stayed the Second Circuit's decision in *McNary* in a two paragraph order without explanation.[154] On 29 July 1992, the Government filed an application for a stay of the Second Circuit's decision with the Supreme Court, which the Court granted on 1 August 1992. The petition for a writ was granted and *Haitian Centers Council v McNary* was restyled as *Sale v Haitian Centers Council.*

The litigation in the Supreme Court turned upon the respondents' contention[155] that Executive Order 12807 violated § 243 (h)(1) of the INA, the text of which reads:

> [T]he Attorney General shall not deport or return any alien … to a country if the Attorney General determines that such alien's life or freedom would be threatened in such country because of race, religion, nationality, membership in a particular social group or political opinion. (8 USC § 1253(h)(1) (1988 ed., Supp. IV).

In the words of the Supreme Court, '[t]he question presented in this case is whether such forced repatriation, "authorized to be undertaken only beyond the territorial sea of the United States" violates § 243(h)(1) of the Immigration and Nationality Act of 1952.'[156] The Supreme Court held that neither § 243(h)(1) nor Art. 33 of the Refugee Convention limited the Presidential power to order repatriation of undocumented aliens intercepted on the high

[151] 969 F.2d 1359.

[152] However, the issue whether Art. 33 was self-executing was not addressed by the Court of Appeals because it found that § 243(h)(1) did indeed prohibit the US from returning aliens to their prosecutors no matter where in the world these actions are taken. See 969 F.2d 1367.

[153] *Haitian Refugee Center v. Baker (Baker I)* 949 F. 2d 1109 (11th Cir. 1991).

[154] *McNary v Haitian Centers Council* 61 USLW 3082 (US 1 August 1992) petition for cert. filed (US 24 August 1992) (No. 92–344). Justices Blackmun and Stevens dissented.

[155] The respondents were organizations representing interdicted Haitians and a number of Haitians who were being detained at Guantanamo naval base.

[156] 509 US 158.

seas. It began by analysing the text and structure of the INA. § 243(h)(1) clearly restricted the actions of the Attorney General in proceedings regarding the determination of whether deportable or excludable aliens could remain in the US; it therefore limited the actions of the Attorney General in the performance of her normal responsibilities such as conducting deportation and exclusion proceedings—proceedings which are to be performed within the United States. Nowhere in Part V (in which § 243 is found) is it indicated that similar proceedings can be conducted outside the country or that this Part could have an extraterritorial application. The court noted that even if the relevant portion of the statute was not limited to strictly domestic procedures, 'the presumption that Acts of Congress do not ordinarily apply outside our borders would support an interpretation of § 243(h) as applying only within United States territory.'[157] Therefore, while the provision bound the Attorney General, the same could not be said for the President's powers in this respect.[158]

This provision was part of the Refugee Act of 1980 which amended the INA in relevant part by removing the words 'within the United States' from § 243(h) and adding the word 'return'. Respondents contended that the 1980 amendment deleting the words 'within the United States' from the prior text of § 243(h) obviously gave the statute extraterritorial effect. However, the Supreme Court referred to *Leng May Ma* v *Barber*[159] in order to explain the distinction between 'deportation' or 'expulsion,' on the one hand, and 'exclusion,' on the other.[160] The 1980 amendment was seen to have erased the long-maintained distinction between deportable and excludable aliens, thus extending the statute's protection to both types of aliens.[161]

The Supreme Court stated that the addition of the phrase 'or return' and the deletion of the phrase 'within the United States' were the only relevant changes made by the 1980 amendment to § 243(h)(1), and were fully explained by the intent to apply § 243(h) to exclusion as well as to deportation proceedings.

---

[157] 509 US 173, citing *EEOC v Arabian Am Oil Co* 499 US 244, 248 (1991); *Foley Bros v Filardo* 336 US 281, 285 (1945); and *Argentine Republic v Amerada Hess Shipping Corp*, 488 US 428, 440 (1989).

[158] Although § 243(h)(1) refers only to the Attorney General, the Court of Appeals had found it 'difficult to believe that the proscription of § 243(h)(1)—returning an alien to his persecutors—was forbidden if done by the attorney general but permitted if done by some other arm of the executive branch': 969 F. 2d 1360.

[159] 357 US 185 (1958).

[160] 509 US 174–175.

[161] A 'deportable' alien was an alien who had been admitted into the US but who had to be expelled (8 USC § 1251 (1994)). An 'excludable' alien was an alien who was ineligible for admission into the US; such an alien could be paroled into the US pending the initiation of exclusion proceedings, but, although physically present within the US, the alien was deemed excludable (8 USC § 1182(a) (1994), 8 USC § 1182(d)(5)).

That intent is plainly identified in the legislative history of the amendment.[162] There was no change in the 1980 amendment. However, that could be explained by an assumption that Congress also intended to provide for the statute's extraterritorial application.[163]

The court however did go on to make an interesting argument, noting that owing to the fact that the 1980 Act was intended to bring US law into line with Art. 33 of the Refugee Convention, it could be argued that the extraterritorial obligations imposed by Art. 33 were so clear that Congress, in acceding to the Protocol and then amending the statute to harmonize the two, meant to give the latter a correspondingly extraterritorial effect.[164] This possibility led the Supreme Court to analyse the text and negotiating history of the Convention itself. Both the text of the Convention and the negotiating history of Art. 33 are completely silent regarding the geographical reach of the provision. Two points however led the Supreme Court to hold that Art. 33 was not intended to be given any extraterritorial effect.

The court referred to the fact that because Art. 33(2) had an explicitly territorial application—stating that an alien may not claim the protection of the first paragraph of Art. 33 if he poses a danger to the country in which he is located—it follows that Art. 33(1) must obviously have a similarly territorial reach. The reason for this line of argument was that, if Art. 33(1) applied extraterritorially, then dangerous aliens on the high seas would fall outside the application of the Art. 33(2) exception, and because they could then invoke Art. 33(1) they would be in a more privileged position than those aliens residing in the country which sought to expel them.[165]

Furthermore, the court adopted somewhat contorted reasoning when looking at the parallel use of the words 'expel or return (*refouler*)' in the Convention and 'deport or return' in § 243(h)(1). After noting that 'expel' has the same meaning as 'deport', it went on to conclude that 'return' has a legal meaning which is narrower than its common meaning. It reinforced this otherwise unfounded argument by looking at English translations of '*refouler*' which do not include the word 'return' and concluding that within the context of the Refugee Convention 'return' denoted 'a defensive act of resistance or exclusion at a border rather than an act of transporting someone to a particular destination.'[166] Reference was made to Edwards J's understanding in *Haitian Refugee Center v Gracey*, that ' "expulsion" would refer to a "refugee already admitted

[162] See H.R. Rep. No. 96–608, p. 30 (1979); S. Rep. No. 96–256, p. 17 (1979).
[163] 509 US 176.
[164] 509 US 178.
[165] 509 US 179–180.
[166] 509 US 180–182.

into a country" and that "return" would refer to a "refugee already within the territory but not yet resident there."' Authorities were also cited which purportedly supported the view that the provision was not intended to apply to conduct outside national borders.[167]

Furthermore, after going through the records of the negotiating conference, the Supreme Court concluded:

> The negotiating history, which suggests that the Convention's limited reach resulted from a deliberate bargain, is not dispositive, but it solidly supports our reluctance to interpret Art. 33 to impose obligations on the contracting parties that are broader than the text commands. We do not read that text to apply to aliens interdicted on the high seas.[168]

The decision was seen as being 'seriously flawed,' causing 'monumental injury to the human rights norm of *non-refoulement*.'[169] Blackmun CJ's dissent most clearly illustrates these flaws. His dissenting opinion begins with a look at the Refugee Convention owing to the fact that the 1980 Refugee Act was enacted precisely to bring US Law into line with Art. 33 of the Convention. The most basic argument made is that Art. 33(1) is without geographical limitation, a stance which the Government had consistently taken until litigation ensued.[170]

Further criticism was directed at the way the majority found that 'return' did not mean return, but instead had a distinctive legal meaning. The US Supreme Court gave an interpretation of the word 'return' in an international Convention based on a domestic distinction between 'deportation' and 'exclusion'. Without explanation, the majority asserted that in the light of this distinction the word 'return' as used in the Convention referred to the exclusion of aliens 'who are on the threshold of initial entry.' Rather than taking this contorted route, the Supreme Court ought to have construed the treaty according to its ordinary meaning as directed by the 1969 VCLT in Art. 31(1). The ordinary meaning of the Convention text did not ban the 'exclusion' of aliens who had reached some indeterminate 'threshold'; it banned their 'return.' The ordinary dictionary meaning of 'return' is 'to bring, send, or put (a person or thing) back to or in a former position.' Thus, the term described precisely what the petitioners were doing to the Haitians.[171] The majority's reliance on translations of '*refouler*' also comes under attack as using a nonsensical line of argument.[172]

167 For example, N. Robinson, *Convention Relating to the Status of Refugees: Its History, Contents and Interpretation* (Institute of Jewish Affairs, NY, 1953),162–163 and A. Grahl Madsen, *The Status of Refugees in International Law* (A.W. Sijthoff, Leiden,1972) vol. 2, 94.

168 509 US 187.

169 T.D. Jones, 'Sale v Haitian Council' (1994) 88 *AJIL* 126; Rosenberg (n 138), 243.

170 509 US 190.

171 509 US 191.

172 509 US 192.

Perhaps the harshest criticism may be levelled at the way the majority seized upon the fact that, because Art. 33(2) contains a geographical limitation, the entire article must apply territorially. In other words, a territory-based meaning was given to Art. 33(1) solely because of the need for consistency with Art. 33(2). What the provisions actually refer to is the fact that, since a refugee can be ejected from a State only on national security grounds under Art. 33(2), it is difficult to conceive of a situation in which a refugee not yet at or in a State's territory could be subject to such exclusion. Read in this light, it is perfectly logical that this limited prerogative to avoid the duty of *non refoulement* would be limited to situations in which a clear and critical risk could in fact arise.[173]

The majority's reliance on the *travaux préparatoires* is also criticized as being unnecessary and only to be resorted to as a last resort when the terms of the document are obscure or lead to manifestly absurd or unreasonable results (according to Art. 32 VCLT). Be that as it may, the majority's reliance on a remark by the Netherlands' delegate at the negotiating conference in order to support the contention that Art. 33 does not apply extraterritorially was misplaced for two reasons. There is no evidence that the delegate's statement was actually agreed to; and even if it had been accepted as reflecting the dominant view of the negotiating conference, the comment dealt with the right of a nation to close its borders—a point clearly not at issue here. Furthermore, none of the secondary sources the majority referred to in order to substantiate its claims suggest that States Parties can seize refugees outside their territory and return them to places of persecution; what they do acknowledge is that nations need not admit refugees or grant them asylum.[174]

When commenting on the text and history of the statutory provision at issue, Blackmun views the deletion of the phrase 'within the United States' as making it clear that a refugee cannot be returned to his persecutors, whether he is in the United States or not.[175] The reference to a single case (*Leng May Ma v Barber*, 1958) which had been decided 22 years before the enactment of the amendment was thus considered seriously misguided. Furthermore, the presumption against extraterritoriality which runs throughout the majority's reasoning is also stated to have no role here: if any rule of interpretation were to be applied in this case, it should be the rule that 'an act of congress ought never to be construed to violate the law of nations if any other possible construction remains.'[176]

[173] J.C. Hathaway, *The Rights of Refugees under International Law* (Cambridge University Press, Cambridge, 2005), 336.
[174] 509 US 194–197.
[175] 509 US 202.
[176] 509 US 207, referring to *Murray* v *The Charming Betsy*, 6 US (2 Cranch) 64, 117–118 (1804).

The Supreme Court's interpretation of 'return' not only removes the ordinary meaning of the term, but neutralizes the core duty of the Convention, which is to prevent the sending of refugees back to places of persecution. It is also an interpretation which conflicts with the basic notion of the Convention, set out in the Preamble, which is to afford refugees the widest exercise of fundamental rights and freedoms. With this decision the Supreme Court seems to have contorted any proper application of the Convention since:

> Under [the US Government's] reading, the availability of the most fundamental protection afforded to refugees turns not on the refugee's need for protection, but on his or her own ability to enter clandestinely the territory of another country.[177]

The decision also negates the general understanding that obligations do indeed arise not only in a territorial context, but also in any case where a State Party exercises some form of effective extraterritorial jurisdiction, of which the case of US interception by military vessels on the high seas provides an example.[178]

It is safe to say that the decision is not in line with current international law, and its line of reasoning has not been adopted in further litigation where it has been stated to be 'impermissible to return refugees from the high seas to their country of origin.'[179] Notwithstanding this, US policy in this sphere does not appear to have shifted. The characterization of boat arrivals as a threat to national security due to the diversion of Coast Guard resources indicates a complete shift in the treatment of boat arrivals: from a policy of rescue and prevention to a policy of pure deterrence.[180]

Generally, the account of US practice outlined above flies in the face of current international law, disregarding the extraterritorial effect of humanitarian principles of law. On the other hand, the last chapter documented that the US has been at the forefront of seeking cooperation with its neighbours in the fight against common threats—notably, drug smuggling and, to a lesser degree, maritime migrant smuggling. Some thoughts on this approach will be discussed in the conclusion to this chapter.

---

177 UNHCR, Brief as Amicus Curiae filed Dec 21, 1992 in McNary v Haitian Centers Council Case No. 92–344 (US SC) at 18, reprinted in (1994) 6(1) IJRL 85.

178 Other examples listed by Hathaway include whenever a State's consular or other agents take control of persons abroad; where the State exercises some significant public power in foreign territory which it has occupied, or in which it is present by consent, invitation or acquiescence: Hathaway (n 173), 339.

179 *R (European Roma Rights Centre and Others) v Immigration Officer at Prague Airport* [2003] EWCA Civ 666 (Eng. CA, 20 May 2003), para. 35.

180 Van Selm et al. (n 4), 76.

8.3. *European Union*

8.3.1. *EU Law and Policy on Asylum and Immigration*

One of the main aims of the EU is the establishment of an area of freedom, security and justice without internal borders. The objective is to guarantee the freedom of movement of persons with concomitant security by combating crime—applicable to citizens of the Union and non-citizens alike. Precisely because this freedom is also guaranteed to non-citizens of the Union, '[t]his in turn requires the Union to develop common policies on asylum and immigration, while taking into account the need for a consistent control of external borders to stop illegal immigration and to combat those who organize it and commit related international crimes.'[181]

The fight against illegal immigration in the EU sphere is thus firmly rooted in the development of a common and comprehensive asylum and immigration policy.[182] The general aim of EU policy in this field is legal and safe access to protection within Europe to those in need of such protection, while at the same time deterring people smugglers and traffickers.[183] There is a general recognition of the fact that people smuggling is a threat to the asylum system as it misuses and abuses the system of international protection.[184] At the same time, this system of protection cannot be made available to all immigrants. The challenge thus lies in sifting the hybrid migratory flows which involve genuine asylum-seekers as well as economic migrants. EU policy in this field is not specifically directed at maritime landings of irregular migrants, although

[181] Tampere European Council, 15–16 October 1999, Presidency Conclusions, point 3. For a description of the legal basis for Community action in this field see P.S.R.F. Mathijsen, *A Guide to European Union Law* (8th edn, Sweet and Maxwell, London, 2004), 189; K. Lenaerts and P. Van Nuffel, *Constitutional Law of the European Union* (2nd edn, Sweet and Maxwell, London, 2005), 215.

[182] 'A Common Policy on Illegal Immigration' (Communication), COM(2001)672 final, 15 November 2001. Note that this approach, of merging asylum and immigration, has come under attack due to the fact that '[i]mmigration law is about controlling entry, refugee law is about providing international protection': G. Gilbert, 'Is Europe living up to its Obligations to Refugees?' (2004) 15 *EJIL* 968; A. Sianni, 'Interception Practices in Europe and Their Implications' (2003) 21 *Refuge* 4, 25–34.

[183] 'Towards a Common Asylum Procedure and a Uniform Status, valid throughout the Union, for Persons granted Asylum' (Communication), COM(2000)755 final, 22 November 2000.

[184] See, e.g., 'Towards more accessible, equitable and managed asylum systems' (Communication), COM(2003)315, 3 June 2003, 4, where reference is made to the UNHCR's Agenda for Protection and Convention Plus system wherein there is acknowledgement of the fact that 'the asylum and international protection system can come under serious threat if it is used for other purposes or repeatedly misused, notably by networks of smugglers in human beings.'

some documents focus on this fact. Because of this, a short overview of the general policy will be given in order to understand the stance taken with regard to all irregular migrants, including those arriving at Europe's maritime borders.

The plan to create a common system for immigration and asylum commenced with the Tampere Summit (October 1999 to May 2004) which established a two-stage strategy for the attainment of the common system for immigration and asylum.[185] The Tampere Presidency Conclusions emphasized the need for a comprehensive approach to migration incorporating respect for human rights and freedoms, and, in regard to asylum measures, the full application of the Refugee Convention, especially the *non-refoulement* principle. As far as management of migration flows is concerned, cooperation with countries of origin and transit was considered to be an essential tool, together with tackling illegal migration at its source and combating human trafficking and economic exploitation of migrants, the creation of a visa policy and the creation of border control services providing exchange programmes and technology transfer.

The continuation of the Tampere initiative was determined at the meeting of the European Council in November 2004. The Hague Programme, endorsed by the European Council in November 2004, took into account the final evaluation of the Tampere programme and established a set of priorities in order to lead to the establishment of an area of freedom, security and justice in the EU within five years; legal and illegal immigration policies were, of course, included in this initiative. The Commission presented an Action Plan in May 2005 with a set of measures and a timeline to implement the programme adopted in the Hague—in other words, the overall priorities set out in the Hague Programme were turned into concrete actions, including a timetable for their adoption and implementation. The Council approved this Action Plan on 2 June 2005 and this was the reference point for the Commission and Council over the coming five years.[186]

---

185 The results were published in 2004: 'Area of Freedom, Security and Justice: Assessment of the Tampere Programme and Future Orientations' (Communication), COM(2004)4002 final, 2 June 2004.

186 'The Hague Programme: Ten Priorities for the next five years—The Partnership for European Renewal in the field of Freedom, Security and Justice' (Communication), COM(2005)184 final, 10 May 2005. This Communication launched the five year action plan on Freedom, Justice and Security. Relevant areas identified are: the definition of a balanced approach to migration, the setting up of a common asylum procedure and the development of an integrated management system of the Union's external borders.

8.3.2. *Focus on Illegal Immigration*

It is evident that EU initiatives are based on the understanding that combating human smuggling is a complementary element in a policy which seeks to fight illegal immigration since, in many cases, illegal entry into a Member State would not be possible without the services of smugglers.[187] As in other international and regional initiatives, notwithstanding the 'substantial links' between these crimes,[188] a distinction is sought to be drawn between 'smuggling' and 'trafficking'. The definitions provided in various Community documents make it clear that smuggling is connected with the support of an illegal border crossing and illegal entry. Smuggling, therefore, always has a transnational element. It will be recalled that this is not necessarily the case with trafficking, where the key element is the exploitative purpose. Trafficking involves the intent to exploit a person, independently of the question how the victim arrives at the location where the exploitation takes place.[189]

The key points necessary in the fight against illegal immigration were outlined in the Commission's Communication on a Common Policy on Illegal Immigration in 2001.[190] However, the two documents of significance for immediate purposes, directly addressing the prevention of human smuggling are Council Directive 2002/90/EC, providing a common definition of this infringement,[191] and Council Framework Decision 2002/946/JHA, establishing the minimum rules for penalties, liability of legal persons and jurisdiction.[192]

---

[187] 'On the Development of a Common Policy on Illegal Immigration, Smuggling and Trafficking of Human Beings, External Borders and the Return of Illegal Residents' (Communication), COM(2003)323 final, 3 June 2003, 10.

[188] *Ibid*; 'Combating Trafficking in Human Beings and on Combating the Sexual Exploitation of Children and Child Pornography' (Communication), COM(2000)854 final/2, 22 January 2001, 4 and 10.

[189] 'Common Policy on Illegal Immigration' (Communication), COM(2001)672 final, 15 November 2001, 21.

[190] *Ibid*. The six possible actions outlined are: visa policy; an infrastructure for information exchange, cooperation and coordination; border management, containing the first steps towards the creation of a European border guard (mentioned again in the Communication 'Towards Integrated Management of the External Borders of the Member States of the European Union', COM(2002)233 final, 7 May 2002); police cooperation; aliens and criminal law; return and readmission policy.

[191] Council Directive of 28 November 2002 defining the facilitation of unauthorised entry, transit and residence. 2002/90/EC [2002] OJ L328/17.

[192] Council Framework Decision of 28 November 2002 on the strengthening of the penal framework to prevent the facilitation of unauthorised entry, transit and residence. 2002/946/JHA [2002] OJ L328/1.

These sister measures were adopted in pursuance of a French proposal presented to the Council on 28 July 2000.[193]

The general infringement defined in the Directive is assisting unauthorized border crossing, and the instigation, complicity or attempt thereof.[194] Each Member State is directed to implement the Directive by 5 December 2004[195] by imposing appropriate sanctions on:

a. any person who intentionally assists a person who is not a national of a Member State to enter or transit across the territory of a Member State in breach of the laws of the State concerned on the entry or transit of aliens;
b. any person who, for financial gain, intentionally assists a person who is not a national of a Member State to reside within the territory of a Member State in breach of the laws of the State concerned on the residence of aliens.[196]

An exemption is created by Art. 1(2) wherein it is stated that 'any Member State may decide not to impose sanctions with regard to the behaviour defined in paragraph 1(a) by applying its national law and practice for cases where the aim of the behaviour is to provide humanitarian assistance to the person concerned.'[197]

The Framework Decision is aimed at harmonizing the penal framework to establish penalties which are 'effective, proportionate and dissuasive … which may entail extradition.'[198] Member States are to establish jurisdiction over infringements committed in whole or in part within their own territory, by one of their nationals or for the benefit of a legal person established in their territory.[199] The Decision applies without prejudice to the international law framework on refugees and other instruments relating to human rights, especially Arts. 31 and 33 of the Refugee Convention as amended by its Protocol.[200]

8.3.3. *Border Control*

The external borders of the Union play an essential role in managing the influx of persons and providing a common area of identity and security. In order

193 [2000] OJ C253/1.
194 Arts. 1 and 2.
195 Directive, Art. 4; Decision, Art. 9.
196 Art. 1.
197 This exemption was not found in the initial proposal.
198 Art. 1. These may include confiscation of the means of transport, prohibition on practising directly or through an intermediary the occupational activity in the exercise of which the offence was committed, or deportation. Increased prison sentences are established where the offence is committed by a person belonging to a criminal organization or where the lives of the aliens are endangered.
199 See Arts. 2 and 3 regarding the liability of legal persons.
200 Art. 6. This was inserted on the suggestion of the UNHCR.

to offset security *lacunae* created by the abolition of internal border controls, improved police cooperation became vital. One of the main catalysts in this area is the Commission's Communication on Integrated Management of the External Borders of the Member States of the European Union.[201] This Communication provides, *inter alia*, for the creation of an External Borders Practitioners' Common Unit which was to be tasked with managing operational cooperation at the external borders of the Member States. This was the predecessor of today's Agency for the Management and Control of Operational Cooperation at the External Borders of the Member States of the EU.[202]

This agency, known as Frontex, was set up by a Regulation in October 2004, wherein it was recognized that 'responsibility for the control and surveillance of external borders lies with the Member States.'[203] Frontex commenced work on 1 May 2005 with its base in Warsaw and the aim of 'facilitating and rendering more effective the application of existing and future Community measures related to the management of the external borders.'[204] It thus coordinates cooperation between the Member States and assists them in the implementation of Community law on the control and surveillance of the external borders—land, maritime borders and airports—on a harmonized basis.[205] It has no law enforcement powers, nor does it have legislative or policy-making powers, but it supports the national authorities by providing technical and training aid and risk assessment to Member States.[206]

Through this agency it is hoped that Community measures in this area will be more easily applied in a harmonized manner throughout the Union, thereby ensuring a high level of control and surveillance of external borders. As mentioned in various Community instruments, the EU 'already possesses

[201] COM(2002)233 final, 7 May 2002.

[202] See 'On the development of a common policy on illegal immigration, smuggling and trafficking of human beings, external borders and the return of illegal residents' (Communication), COM(2003)323 final, 3 June 2003, where the Commission stated that due to the limitations the Common Unit had shown with regard to the coordination of operational cooperation, certain operational tasks could be entrusted to a new permanent Community structure able to exercise day-to-day management and coordination tasks and to respond in time to emergency situations.

[203] Council Regulation (EC) 2007/2004 [2004] OJ L349/1.

[204] 'Report on the Evaluation and Future Development of the Frontex Agency' (Communication), COM(2008)67 final, 13 February 2008.

[205] Note also the Council Conclusions on the improvement of cooperation between Member States, the Commission and Frontex in the field of return, 2807th Justice and Home Affairs Council Meeting, Luxembourg, 12 and 13 June 2007.

[206] For further information see Refugees Council and ECRE, 'Joint response to Select Committee on the European Sub-Committee F (Home Affairs): Frontex Inquiry' (24 September 2007) PP3/09/2007/extPC; ECRE, 'Defending Refugees' Access to Protection in Europe' (Report) (December 2007), 10–18; and the Frontex Homepage at http://Frontex.europa.eu.

an exact *acquis communautaire* in the area of external frontiers, but the principal current difficulty is the ability to organize between the Member States all the operational synergies which would permit action to be better co-ordinated and therefore a more homogenous level of security at all the external frontiers.'[207]

8.3.4. *Focus on Maritime Borders*

The recognition that increasing numbers of illegal immigrants arrived by sea indicated the importance of an effective mechanism for control and surveillance of the external maritime borders of the EU, together with the need for the adoption of appropriate legislative and operational initiatives at the European level aimed at improving sea border controls. To this end the Commission was invited to conduct a Feasibility Study to see how these controls could be improved.[208] This Feasibility Study had two principal aims: to identify the gaps and weaknesses existing at these borders and to provide a list of the appropriate measures in order to have an equivalent level of effective protection at the external borders.[209] It identified a number of deficiencies in the system including surveillance methods, the underestimation of the actual levels of illegal immigration by sea and the general problem of how to deal with illegal immigrants who are picked up at sea, who cannot be sent back across a border and who are often bogus asylum-seekers.

The Feasibility Study[210] begins by highlighting the fact that the characteristics of maritime borders pose specific problems with regard to their surveillance which, although extremely expensive for the States concerned,[211] is essential if the phenomenon of illegal immigration is to be reduced to a minimum. Maritime borders are approached from areas of the seas where the general principle of freedom of the sea dominates, and this does not make it easy to condition the entry of a ship to a declaration or prior authorization, unlike in air travel where every aircraft must submit a flight plan. Furthermore, due to the large number of potential points of entry on the coastline (there are precisely 387 maritime

[207] 'Towards Integrated Management of the External Borders of the Member States of the European Union' (Communication), COM(2002)233 final, 7 May 2002.

[208] Council of the European Union (EC), 'Proposal for a Comprehensive Plan to Combat Illegal Immigration and Trafficking of Human Beings in the European Union', 6621/1/02 JAI 30 FRONT 19 MIGR 10 VISA 29 REV 1, 27 February 2002, 20–21.

[209] 'On the development of a common policy on illegal immigration, smuggling and trafficking of human beings, external borders and the return of illegal residents' (Communication), COM(2003)323 final, 3 June 2003, 8 and 19.

[210] Final Report, 19 September 2003, 11490/1/03 FRONT 102 COMIX 458 REV 1.

[211] Management of maritime borders is not a shared responsibility between Member States.

authorized crossing points, not counting other accessible ports and beaches), surveillance cannot cover one entry point but must adopt a 'variable-depth surface.'[212]

The Study proposes a European initiative for improving the security of maritime borders,[213] stressing the urgent need for a European policy for the management of maritime borders. The objective is the improvement of control of immigration by sea by vigorously targeting both focal routes and random routes where they exist,[214] while at the same time ensuring that mechanisms are in place to monitor entry flows at ports in the Schengen area. Insofar as proposals of a legal nature are concerned, these include the launching of a process based on the arrangement established in the Aruba Agreement tailored for the Mediterranean; the establishing of a joint European mandate to amend the principal instruments of international maritime law starting with the LOSC and SOLAS, through the Smuggling Protocol;[215] and creating a Community-level legal status for ships flying the flag of a European country.

The main focus of the Study is on economic migration. There is a recognition of the mixed influx of groups reaching the shores of the EU Member States; however, 'the minority of genuine refugees conceals the mass of economic migrants. Whereas the former declare their nationality, the latter are often undocumented and claim a nationality that is known to give easy entitlement to refugee status. They often also apply to the authorities of the Member States for political asylum to benefit from the longest possible period for examination of their situation.'[216]

When analyzing the international legal regime, it was noted *inter alia* that the SOLAS and SAR Conventions, as well as the Refugee Convention, the CATOC and Smuggling Protocol are applicable to all European Member States.[217] The Study notes that the international legal resources and applicable domestic laws are not used to their full potential.[218]

Finally, when discussing maritime surveillance arrangements a number of potential problems are voiced:

> The main obstacles to policing by joint forces are of a legal nature. Can a vessel belonging to a Member State intervene in the territorial waters of another Member State? What asylum and immigration rights apply, those of the ship's flag

---

[212] Feasibility Study (n 210) 8.
[213] *Ibid.*,71–88.
[214] See *ibid.*, 9–10 for definitions.
[215] Referred to in the Study as the 'Palermo Protocol.'
[216] Feasibility Study (n 210), 16.
[217] *Ibid.*, 20, 24.
[218] *Ibid.*, 20, 21.

> or the country of destination? Is it possible simply to treat illegals on the high seas as shipwrecked persons on the basis that they are not actually illegals until they land in a European area port? What if they claim asylum on board ship?[219]

In pursuance of the ultimate aim of controlling illegal immigration by sea, the Study posited certain recommendations of an operational, organizational and funding nature,[220] and, more significantly for immediate purposes, a number of legal initiatives to combat illegal immigration by sea.

In the section relating to the enforcement of existing provisions in the law of the sea regime, the Study seems unduly naïve in its assessment of areas of improvement. The enforcement of the law of the sea regime is predicated upon forcing flag States to fulfil their obligations,[221] especially within their territorial waters, and ensure effective control of ships flying their flag. However, the Study then goes on to maintain that the States of departure must be made to take responsibility for law enforcement in the case of vessels sailing from their coast. From this one may arguably infer that it is the primary responsibility of the coastal State in enforcing standards for which the flag State is ultimately liable.[222] Perhaps a better reading of this section would indicate that both flag States and coastal States share responsibility in this area. Having established this responsibility, the Study notes that no inter-State cases have ever been brought against a flag State or port State concerning compliance with their obligations. The reason cited for this is the desire to maintain friendly diplomatic and trade relations. The recommendation is therefore that an explicit procedure for bringing flag States to justice needs to be established. The efficacy of this approach is however open to debate: such a procedure already exists under the LOSC and there is little reason why a European-wide arrangement would prove preferable to this system.

Another recommendation concerns the application of the SOLAS Convention, which imposes the duty to render assistance at sea on the Master of a ship who must change course to respond to a distress call. IMO Resolution A.867(20) on combating unsafe practices associated with the trafficking or transport of migrants by sea (27 November 1997) calls on governments to 'cooperate in the interests of safety of life at sea by increasing their efforts to suppress and prevent unsafe practices associated with the trafficking or transport of migrants by sea and by ensuring that effective and prompt action is

[219] *Ibid.*, 43.

[220] *Ibid.*, 44–54, 74–78.

[221] This is also reiterated in UNGA 'Report of the Office of the United Nations High Commissioner for Refugees: The Treatment of Persons Rescued at Sea: Conclusions and Recommendations from Recent Meetings and Expert Round Tables convened by the Office of the United Nations High Commissioner for Refugees' (11 April 2008) UN Doc A/AC.259/17, 2.

[222] Feasibility Study (n 210) 55–56.

taken against such unsafe practices.' However, it is stated that the measures to implement this Resolution—set out in MSC/Circ.896 (16 December 1998)—exist only on paper; they are not mandatory measures. The Study thus recommends Member State patrols to intercept vessels or carry out rescue operations at sea. The purpose of these patrols is preventive, to protect human life at sea by taking passengers off overloaded boats and taking them back where they came from.[223] This however seems to be an oversimplification of the issue as it ignores the fact that 'where they came from' is more often than not impossible to determine immediately. Furthermore, it disregards the claims for asylum which are nearly always made on interception.[224]

Certain amendments to the law of the sea regime are also proposed. The Study sees it as necessary explicitly to spell out the responsibility of the flag State. In order to enforce the existing law, the Study urges cases to be brought and damages to be sought by States which are victims of illegal immigration against those States whose civilian vessels use their territorial sea for non-peaceful purposes. The legal basis for this seems to be Art. 21(4) LOSC, which states that 'foreign ships exercising the right of innocent passage through the territorial sea shall comply with all … generally accepted international regulations relating to the prevention of collisions at sea.' The Study maintains that, as in the case of pollution, there is a need for international procedures to challenge flag States which neglect their duty to control the seaworthiness of vessels sailing under their flag. Apart from financial sanctions—which are rarely effective against States—there is need for collective sanctions, which could include a partial or total boycott of a State's flag in the ports of other countries:[225]

> The law of the sea should therefore formally spell out the responsibility of the State that agrees to register sub-standard ships or allows them to sail from its coast and does not carry out any checks. What is needed are additional collective sanctions that are sufficiently deterrent when a direct causal link has been established between the vessel's sub-standard condition and the lack of effective control by the flag State.[226]

What is interesting about this suggestion is that it seems to mention not only flag State responsibility, but also the responsibility of those States which permit vessels to sail from their coasts without carrying out the necessary checks and controls. Since most vessels used in migrant smuggling are unseaworthy, this

[223] *Ibid.*, 57.
[224] The oversight is repeated later in the context of supplementing European law: section B4.3.1 (Feasibility Study), 61.
[225] Feasibility Study (n 210), 58.
[226] *Ibid.*

proposal seems to advocate that flag States and States from which such vessels sail are to be held responsible not so much for the fact of migrant smuggling from their shores but for their failure to ensure the seaworthiness of those vessels. This should have an effect on migrant smuggling from their shores: it may not prove lucrative for the organizers of migrant smuggling to maintain seaworthy vessels and this could have the result of diminishing the frequency of such operations. However, this proposal does not take into account that many vessels used in migrant smuggling are stateless.

Unmanned vehicles operated at sea and extending the principle of freedom of navigation to them is also seen to be necessary in the fight against illegal migration. The purpose of this is to deploy semi-permanent surveillance stations at sea or in the airspace above coasts at risk, in order to improve maritime surveillance by developing an early warning system. However, these remote-controlled vessels are in a 'legal vacuum': they are not provided for in the LOSC; furthermore, SOLAS Chapter V, Regulation 14 requires States to 'undertake, each for its national ships, to maintain, or, if it is necessary, to adopt, measures for the purpose of ensuring that, from the point of view of safety of life at sea, all ships shall be sufficiently and efficiently manned.' This Regulation is not among the list of authorized exemptions in Regulation 4(b) of Chapter 1 of the SOLAS Convention. Therefore, either the LOSC needs to provide expressly for such vessels or there needs to be an *ad hoc* extension of the exemptions provided for in SOLAS, as they are not currently regulated under international law.[227]

A link is sought to be forged between drug smuggling and migrant smuggling, as the Study proposes the harmonization of the conditions for intervention under the Smuggling Protocol with those of the Vienna Drugs Convention.[228] The Smuggling Protocol contains three articles on the illegal smuggling of migrants by sea[229]—the aim being to widen the scope of the mutual aid and cooperation measures which already exist under Art. 17 of the Drugs Convention. However, Art. 8 of the Protocol is not a cooperation instrument and does not provide for coercive powers to be granted to the signatory States. It must therefore be supplemented by the provisions of Art. 9 of the Drugs Convention dealing with other forms of cooperation and training and obliging States to 'co-operate closely with one another, consistent with their respective domestic legal and administrative systems, with a view to enhancing the effectiveness of law enforcement action to suppress the commission of offences established in [the Convention].'

[227] *Ibid.*, 58–60.
[228] *Ibid.*, 60.
[229] The actual text of the Study uses the term 'trafficking' throughout.

The Study also recommends that Art. 108 LOSC (which deals with the suppression of illicit traffic in drugs and psychotropic substances) be amended so as to link the fight against drug trafficking to the fight against illegal immigration. This is proposed because the Smuggling Protocol states that the offences it defines should be the subject of preventive and repressive measures in accordance with the law of the sea; the provisions of the LOSC currently do not provide for migrant smuggling. By inserting a reference to maritime migrant smuggling in the provision dealing with illicit traffic in drugs and psychotropic substances not only would the provisions of the Protocol be more coherent, but this could lead to an assimilation of the treatment of illicit traffic in drugs and migrant smuggling.

When analysing improvements in European law, the Study calls for the harmonization of criminal procedures with regard to illegal trafficking so as to prevent the phenomenon of forum shopping: trafficking in illegal immigrants should not be less severely punished than other types of trafficking using the same means, and if trafficking is inadequately punished in one Member State this will act as a magnet for traffickers.[230]

The Study however seems to proceed on the assumption that 'formal recognition must be given to the legal principle that the deck of a ship flying the flag of a Member State is not national territory and, consequently, the law applicable is not that of the territory of the flag State.' It maintains that, as it is, the different interpretations do not allow the pooling of naval resources to carry out joint operations. Through this recognition, by means of a directive which would 'lay down the conditions for including the principle of the extraterritoriality of ships in the national law of the Member States that do not apply it', the Study seems to attempt to place vessels in a legal vacuum, thus making it possible 'for the ships of one Member State to operate on behalf of another Member State in that State's territorial waters, and at the same time allows shipwrecked immigrants to be returned directly to the country of departure or sent to a host country without crossing a European maritime frontier.'[231] However, it is submitted that removing flag State jurisdiction is not an ideal solution. It would be preferable were EU Member States to enter into agreements similar to the US Shiprider Agreements and the Aruba Agreement and authorize entry into their territorial seas under such terms. Furthermore, an apparent contradiction follows, in that the Study also sees it necessary to provide that in the case of a ship in the internal waters of an EU Member State, whatever flag it is flying, the law applicable will not be that of the territory of the port State. The reason for this is that stowaways could then be kept on board the ship that brought them into

[230] Feasibility Study (n 210), 62.
[231] *Ibid.*, 61.

the European port and the same ship can return them to their country of origin under the responsibility of its Master. Again, however, it does not seem useful to suspend the operation of certain basic norms of international law. It seems more feasible to work within the confines of general precepts and allow non-flag State or non-coastal State intervention on the basis of the consent of States evidenced through treaties. In point of fact, the most effective proposal is to create a Mediterranean law by adapting the principles of the Aruba Agreement to the migration problem in the Mediterranean.[232]

While the Study raises a number of relevant points and attempts to provide solutions, it sometimes proceeds on an over-simplification of the facts. Apart from the questionable benefit of amending certain fundamental principles of the law of the sea, the report is inconsistent, at times advocating the removal of flag State jurisdiction and then calling for its application in other instances such as within ports. It is true that the doctrine of the internal economy of the vessel applies to ships in ports; however, the presence of stowaways on board a vessel may very persuasively be argued to be an instance where the port State may legitimately exercise jurisdiction. Furthermore, laying responsibility on the Master of the vessel in the case of stowaways on board a ship in port surely cannot be the solution to the problem. Also, no consideration is given to the potential presence of asylum-seekers on board the vessel, imposing certain obligations upon States, as discussed earlier. It is true that the Report covers only the situation of economic migrants; however, it seems naïve to tackle one class of irregular migrants to the exclusion of the other, seeing that a major part of the problem concerns sifting through these categories of individuals.

Subsequently, the Council, on 27 November 2003, adopted a Programme to improve action taken to combat illegal immigration across the maritime borders of the Member States of the European Union, with the intention of achieving the coordinated and effective management of the maritime borders within a minimum time.[233] The programme contains proposals for measures, to be organized operationally on unified lines, for increasing port-to-port controls among Member States and in the traffic with third countries, for patrols in territorial waters and on the high seas, for the treatment of immigrants found

---

232 *Ibid.*, 63.

233 Programme of measures to combat illegal immigration across the maritime borders of the Member States of the European Union 15236/03 FRONT 170 COMIX 717, 28 November 2003. This was adopted by the Brussels European Council (12–13 December 2003), 5381/04 POLGEN 2, 5 February 2004, 6. For a fuller overview of EU actions in this area see Programme of Measures at 3–5 and the Draft Council conclusions evaluating the progress made with regard to the implementation of the Programme of measures to combat illegal immigration across the maritime borders of the Member States of the European Union, 15087/04 FRONT 201 COMIX 709, 22 November 2004, 3–4.

on board vessels, for agreements with third countries of origin or transit and for a single management structure for maritime coordination centres. It also identifies sources of EU funding. It deals with operational port-control and coastline-control measures, together with issues such as the necessity of readmission agreements with countries of origin or transit and the possibility of technical and organizational assistance in accordance with the relevant EU and national legislation.

The principal means of ensuring the success of any measures taken is enhanced international relations with the third countries from which illegal migration flows originate or through which they pass.[234] The Programme adopts the concept of the virtual maritime border in order to reinforce the legal borders of Member States by means of joint operations and specific measures in the places where illegal migratory flows originate or transit.[235]

The core point to be noted is the recognition that:

> If cooperation between Member States is to be uniform and more effective, there is an especial need to reaffirm the principle of solidarity in intercepting vessels carrying illegal immigrants, by means of meticulous application of the law of the sea for the immediate rescue of ships whose seaworthiness is in doubt.[236]

8.3.5. *Sea Border Patrols*

At the informal meeting of the EU Heads of State and Government at Hampton Court (27 October 2005) there was a general call for a comprehensive approach to tackle migration issues. In the follow-up document reference was made to the Hague Programme, which identified the humanitarian tragedies that occur in the Mediterranean, and to illegal migration as the most pressing issue, as well as the general call on States to intensify their cooperation. In response to that

---

[234] See, e.g., Council of the European Union, Justice and Home Affairs, Press Release 8849/05 (Presse 114) 2664th Council Meeting, Luxembourg, 2–3 June 2005, Cooperation with Libya on Migration Issues: Council Conclusions, 15; Presidency Conclusions, Brussels European Council (15–16 December 2005) 15914/05, Global Approach to Migration: Priority Actions focusing on Africa and the Mediterranean, annex 1, 9.

[235] Council of the European Union, Justice and Home Affairs, Press Release 14995/03 (Presse 334) 2548th Council Meeting, Brussels, 27–28 November 2003, Illegal Immigration Across the Maritime Borders of the EU, 15.

[236] *Ibid.*, 10. The Brussels European Council of 17 and 18 June 2004 (Presidency Conclusions, 10679/2/04 REV 2, CONCL 2, 19 July 2004, para. 11) called for the Council to review the implementation of this Programme by the end of 2004. In November 2004, the Council noted the progress made but maintained that further progress was needed with regard to both operational and legislative measures. See 'Draft Council conclusions evaluating the progress made with regard to the implementation of the Programme of measures to combat illegal immigration across the maritime borders of the Member States of the European Union' 15087/04 FRONT 201 COMIX 709, 22 November 2004.

call for action, certain short-term actions were devised, amongst which were Frontex's task of launching a Study in 2006 on the possibilities of reinforcing the monitoring and surveillance of the Mediterranean, and considering the feasibility of a Mediterranean Coastal Patrol Network which would ensure permanent contact and coordination between Member States' sea border surveillance authorities and search and rescue services and would also connect similar services of North African countries that could be involved in the development of this project.[237]

2006 was witness to a renewed impetus in the fight against illegal immigration by sea, caused in large part by pressure from receiving States such as Italy, Malta and Spain.[238] The June European Council[239] referred to the Global Approach to Migration agreed upon in December 2005,[240] and called for enhanced efforts on maritime operational cooperation with a view to developing adequate surveillance capacities at the sea borders as well as on the establishment of Rapid Border Intervention Teams.[241]

---

[237] 'Priority actions for responding to the challenges of migration: First follow-up to Hampton Court' (Communication), COM(2005)621 final, 30 November 2005, 4–5. Another task was entrusted to the Commission, which was to present an analysis of the existing international law instruments on the law of the sea and their efficiency in tackling illegal migration. Much attention was also given to the necessity of dialogue and cooperation with non-Member States such as Africa, especially sub-Saharan countries of origin.

[238] See Joint Letter, dated 25 September 2006, addressed to the European Union Presidency, from the Heads of States of Cyprus, France, Greece, Italy, Malta, Portugal, Slovenia and Spain. It is also envisaged that the initiatives being taken in the field of asylum will assist these States in the wider aspect of the granting of asylum. See, e.g., Council of the European Union, Justice and Home Affairs, Luxembourg, 18 April 2008, 2863rd Council Meeting, Press Release 8297/08 (Presse 96) Practical Cooperation in the Field of Asylum: Council Conclusions.

[239] Presidency Conclusions, Brussels European Council, 15–16 June 2006, 10633/06 CONCL 2 (17 July 2006) 4.

[240] Council of the European Union, 13 December 2005, 15744/05, ASIM 66, RELEX 761, Global Approach to Migration: Priority Actions focusing on Africa and the Mediterranean. The Global Approach aims to formulate comprehensive and coherent policies which address a broad range of migration-related issues, bringing together various policy areas. See also Council of the European Union, Justice and Home Affairs, Luxembourg, 17–18 June 2007, 2807th Council Meeting, Press Release 10267/7 (Presse 125), Extending and Enhancing the Global Approach to Migration: Council Conclusions.

[241] The Rapid Border Intervention Teams are to be sent to Member States to provide rapid operational assistance, for a limited period of time, to a requesting Member State facing a situation of urgent and exceptional pressure, especially at the arrival at points of the external borders of large numbers of third country nationals trying to enter the territory of a Member State illegally. See Council of the European Union, 2794th Council Meeting, Justice and Home Affairs, Luxembourg, 19–20 April 2007. See also Council and Parliament Regulation (EC) 863/2007 establishing a mechanism for the creation of Rapid Border Intervention Teams and amending Council Resolution (EC) No. 2007/2004 as regards that mechanism and regulating the tasks and powers of guest officers [2007] OJ L199/30.

Frontex has taken a front seat in the introduction of sea border patrols. The first EU-coordinated operation to be launched was *Hera II* (aimed at stemming illegal immigration to the Canary Islands), which began on 11 August 2006, with an EU budget of 3.2 million Euros to be spent during the nine weeks of the operation. This was the first time that border patrols at sea were undertaken as a direct result of an EU initiative and coordinated by an EU body, thus representing the first example of a coordinated response to the problem.

A similar operation—*Nautilus* (5–15 October 2006)—with a coordinating base at Lampedusa (the EU territory closest to Libya) and an EU budget of 1.2 million Euros, consisted in a surveillance patrol mission in the strait between North Africa and Malta, a main route being operated by human traffickers in the Mediterranean, where boats laden with immigrants leave Libya and pass through the Maltese SAR area *en route* to the coast of southern Sicily. Five Member States—Malta, Italy, Greece, France and Germany—participated in this operation by aerial and maritime means.[242] No vessels were intercepted in this short time. A second mission took place in July and September 2007. The objective of this joint operation was to strengthen the control of the Central Mediterranean maritime border using the technical means of several Member States, and also to support the Maltese authorities in interviews with the migrants. Some 3,000 boat people were intercepted during this operation.

In 2008, *Nautilus III* again covered the same strait between Sicily, Malta and Libya but was intended to run for 23 weeks, with 10 participating Member States and with an increased budget of over 8 million Euros.[243] The commencement of *Nautilus III* was delayed due to disagreement between Malta, Italy, France and Germany over which State should be responsible for immigrants rescued in Libya's search and rescue zone.[244] Agreement was eventually reached that the rules regarding disembarkation of persons rescued at sea were to remain the same as in the previous year's operation: migrants rescued in the Libyan SAR area would be taken to Libya and, when this was not possible, to the closest safe haven. According to the previous year's agreement, when Libya refused to take illegal immigrants, both Germany and France had agreed to assume responsibility for the illegal immigrants saved by their assets. Migrants rescued in the Maltese SAR area were taken to the closest land area—either Malta or Lampedusa.[245]

---

[242] A previously-planned operation called *Jason 1* proved to be a non-starter due to Libya's refusal to cooperate.

[243] I. Camilleri, 'EU Border Patrols "imminent"', *The Sunday Times* (Malta, 13 April 2008).

[244] I. Camilleri, 'EU Patrols on hold as States grapple over destination of rescued illegal immigrants', *The Times* (Malta, 27 April 2008).

[245] I. Camilleri, 'Nautilus III starts today', *The Times* (Malta, 17 May 2008).

While a large number of vessels are in need of rescue due to their overcrowding, unseaworthiness and perhaps deliberate sabotaging of the vessel, there are other vessels which will not be in need of rescue and will therefore be intercepted nonetheless in order to deter their progress to European shores. It is not disclosed what actually happens when boats are intercepted by Frontex vessels, save for the fact that force cannot be used, and that the migrants are told what they are doing is illegal. The reason cited for this dearth of information is 'security reasons.' It seems that intercepted boats are redirected to the territorial waters. However, Frontex cannot actually stop a vessel carrying irregular migrants when on the high seas; it can only follow the vessel and apprehend it when it enters the territory of an EU Member State.[246] It seems that no particular attention is paid to the fact that asylum-seekers may be on board such vessel. The general assumption seems to be that, according to statistics, only 10 out of every 1,000 illegal immigrants reaching Malta and Italy put forward justified claims.

The EU Commission had asked Libyan authorities to sanction EU patrols in its territorial waters, to cooperate in the patrols, and also to allow repatriation (on the lines of the bilateral agreement of the type which exists with Italy, or in the shape of an EU–Libya Agreement). The intention was to stop boats leaving Libyan waters immediately and send them back to their point of departure. Libya's cooperation was therefore considered necessary for these illegal immigrants to be sent back and for Libya to take action against the traffickers. However, Libyan support has not been forthcoming.[247]

What makes *Nautilus* different from operations such as the one off the coast of the Canary Islands, for example, is the lack of cooperation from Libya. In the situation off the Canary Islands, in which Senegal and Mauritania are cooperating, intercepted boats are landed in the Canary Islands and asylum applications are processed there. If any are found to be irregular, the individuals are returned to their country of departure. Furthermore, on board each Member State's patrolling vessel there is a Senegalese and a Mauritanian officer who have the right to order the vessel carrying illegal immigrants to turn back.[248]

In point of fact, Frontex officials have admitted that the joint patrols are not Malta's solution to illegal immigration, as cooperation from countries of departure is crucial to the success of the mission.[249] Furthermore, Illka Laitinen,

---

[246] I. Camilleri, 'Frontex no solution as Libya fails to Cooperate', *The Times* (Malta, 11 July 2008).

[247] It should however be noted at this point that even with Libya's cooperation, in the case of any genuine asylum-seekers, the option of sending the vessels back to Libyan shores could well fall foul of the *non refoulement* obligation, especially as Libya is not a Party to the Refugee Convention.

[248] I. Camilleri, 'Frontex no solution as Libya fails to Cooperate' *The Times* (Malta, 11 July 2008).

[249] *Ibid.*

Frontex's executive director, admitted the failure of the Frontex mission in the Mediterranean.[250] Reasons submitted, apart from Libya's lack of cooperation, were the fact that traffickers were forcing immigrants to sink their boats so that they would be rescued by Frontex vessels. Furthermore, it was also stated that the success of the operation in the Canary Islands could well be causing traffickers to target Malta and Italy as an alternative.[251] Nevertheless, while it is acknowledged that border control is not a panacea for the problem of illegal immigration, it can, however, when combined with other elements, help to create a significant improvement in this area, as indicated in the situation around the Canary Islands. The aim must be, therefore, for maritime border patrols to be incorporated into a fully-fledged, integrated border control policy with the cooperation of third States.[252]

A general comment on Frontex patrols is that, rather than the issue relating to the number of vessels actually intercepted and turned back, a more complex concern perhaps lies in the general understanding within the EU that many immigrants are not seeking humanitarian protection but are simply economic migrants, a group which is not protected under the Refugee Convention. Possibly, this is the reason why the solution of sending the vessels back to the point of departure is so readily aired. The EU is quick to state that the operations are part of a comprehensive EU approach to addressing migration and not intended to build and reinforce a 'Fortress Europe', but are of a humanitarian character, aiming at saving lives at sea, apart from reducing illegal immigration and combating human trafficking. This may well be true: however, the assumption that anyone making an asylum claim will be assisted, and if necessary taken on board the patrolling vessels, seems over-simplistic and rather naïve. What safeguards have been adopted to ensure that unfounded claims made at sea will be identified and filtered out? Arguably, no such safeguards exist. At any rate, the UNHCR has advised against the processing of asylum claims whilst at sea. Once again, therefore, the problem of disembarkation of individuals to determine their status raises its head.

The humanitarian aspect of migrant smuggling cannot be ignored. The UNHCR High Commissioner for Refugees, Antonio Guterres, when addressing the EU and African Ministers at the Morocco Conference on Migration and Development (10–11 July 2006) brings this point into clear relief:

---

[250] Arrivals on Lampedusa increased by 190 % in the first six months of 2008 compared with the same period in 2007, and Malta had registered an increase thus far of 32 % on the whole of 2007.

[251] I. Camilleri, 'Frontex chief admits failure' *The Times* (Malta, 21 September 2008).

[252] See I. Laitinen, 'EU Member States' assistance is a must if Frontex operations are to succeed', *The Times* (Malta, 6 October 2008); T. Borg, 'Frontex—deterring human trafficking', *The Times* (Malta, 25 September 2008).

> While recognising the difficulties that such movements can pose for states in terms of national and local security, we must ensure that the measures taken to curb irregular migration do not prevent refugees from gaining the international protection they need and to which they are entitled.

To this end, the 10 Point Action Plan unveiled by the UNHCR at the Conference[253] set out key areas in which action is required to tackle migratory movements in countries of origin, transit and destination. While recognizing that border controls are essential for combating international crime, including smuggling and trafficking, and in order to avert security threats, the plan stresses the need for practical protection safeguards to ensure that such measures are not applied in an indiscriminate or disproportionate manner and do not lead to refugees being returned to countries where their lives or liberty would be at risk. It called for the training of border guards and immigration officials so that they know how to respond to asylum applications and how to meet the needs of separated children, victims of trafficking and other groups with special needs.

8.3.6. *Recent Initiatives*

In its Communication on Reinforcing the Management of the European Union's Southern Maritime Borders,[254] the Commission noted that the reinforcement of the management of the EU's southern maritime borders was essential for the further development of a European model for integrated border management, and that the management of the EU's external borders was based on principles of solidarity, mutual trust and co-responsibility among Member States, founded on full respect for human rights.[255] It referred to the unprecedented levels of irregular arrivals in the Member States situated in the Mediterranean and Atlantic regions in the previous two years and pointed to the need to cooperate with African and Middle Eastern transit countries.[256] It was also of the opinion that asylum considerations were an important part of the response and an effective option for persons requiring international protection.[257]

As regards control of the maritime borders, the Commission found that a two-pronged approach was necessary:

---

253 Addressing Mixed Migratory Movements: A 10 Point Plan of Action, UNHCR, June 2006. This has since been revised and re-named 'Refugee Protection and Mixed Migration: A 10-Point Plan of Action' (January 2007) Rev. 1.

254 COM(2006)733 final, 30 November 2006.

255 Para. 4.

256 Paras 5 and 7.

257 Para. 10.

> Operational measures to fight illegal immigration, protect refugees and reinforce control and surveillance of the external maritime border which can be implemented immediately, and
>
> Building on the existing relations and practical cooperation already established with third countries, pursuing and strengthening our dialogue and cooperation with third countries on these operational measures in the context of the Association Agreements and ENP Action Plans as well as in the context of the Cotonou Agreement.[258]

This Communication forms part of the first prong. The Commission calls for the maximizing of the capacity of Frontex and for new tools for what it terms 'the next generation of integrated border management.' Here, reference is made to a Coastal Patrol Network for the southern maritime external borders to be established and managed by Frontex together with Member States of the region. This Coastal Patrol Network was seen as necessary in the Feasibility Study presented by Frontex on 14 July 2006 for the implementation of the Global Approach to Migration.[259] The Commission is of the opinion that 'this patrol network would have a real added value, making it possible for Member States to coordinate their patrol schedules, pool their civilian and military assets and exchange strategic and tactical information in real time.'[260] To this end, it also calls for serious consideration to be given to the possibility of establishing regional command centres at the southern maritime external borders, staffed and equipped by Member States and coordinated by Frontex. Another aspect of the next generation of integrated border management is the creation of a common European Surveillance System for Borders (EUROSUR) at the southern maritime external borders. Another very important aspect was stated to be the improvement of the capacity to deal with mixed flows. The prompt initial assessment of individual cases at points of arrival was seen as a challenge for the effective management of large mixed migratory flows. It was stated that Member States which face particular pressure on their capacities to perform this initial assessment should be able to make use of the expertise and manpower which exist in other Member States.[261]

The Commission here suggests 'the provision of rapid and well targeted operational assistance to the Member States concerned through the establishment and management of a pool of experts from Member States' administrations who

---

[258] Para. 8.

[259] The Commission has endorsed the proposal in 'A Future Maritime Policy' (Green Paper), COM(2006)257 final, 7 June 2006.

[260] Para. 22.

[261] Para. 26. The Communication at this point refers to 'Strengthened Practical Cooperation. New structures, new approaches: Improving the quality of decision making in the Common European Asylum System', COM(2006)67 final, 17 February 2006.

can be made available for deployment at short notice ... The asylum expert teams that would be established from this pool would be called to assist on a temporary basis the requesting Member State in performing this initial profiling through the provision, in particular, of interpretation services, case working and country of origin expertise.'[262] In its report, the European Council on Refugees and Exiles (ECRE) states that these teams would be deployed in emergency situations in order to facilitate a prompt initial assessment of individual cases at points of arrivals with respect to protection obligations of Member States. It notes that these emergency situations would however concern mass arrivals at the borders of Member States, and that therefore the problem would remain for those who never succeeded in reaching these borders because they were diverted in international waters.[263]

The Commission calls for the operational implementation of the international law of the sea and demonstrates its awareness of and consideration for certain fundamental issues:

> Determining more accurately the correct *modus operandi* for the purpose of intercepting vessels carrying, or suspected of carrying, illegal immigrants bound for the European Union would improve the much needed efficiency of joint operations to prevent and divert illegal immigration by sea involving the forces of different Member States which do not always have a common understanding of how and when to carry out interceptions ...
>
> An issue that should benefit from further elaboration and clarification is the determination of the most appropriate port for disembarkation following rescue at sea or interception, and the closely related issue of allocation of protection responsibilities between States taking part in interception and search and rescue operations for intercepted or rescued people seeking international protection. Indeed, the determination of the appropriate place for disembarkation often engages, in practice, the responsibility of the state concerned for the examination of the protection needs of the asylum seekers amongst the persons rescued or intercepted.
>
> Another issue which merits particular attention is the extent of the States' protection obligations flowing from the respect of the principle of non-refoulement, in the many different situations where State vessels implement interception or search and rescue measures.[264]

---

262 See also 'Future Common European Asylum System' (Green Paper), COM(2007)301 final, 6 June 2007.

263 ECRE Report (n 206).

264 Paras 33–34. The EU Council referred to the further reinforcing of the EU's Southern Maritime Borders in its Conclusions in the 2818th Justice and Home Affairs Council Meeting on 18 September 2007. See Press Release 12604/07 (Presse 194). See also Council of the European Union, Justice and Home Affairs, Luxembourg, 5–6 October 2006, 2752nd Council Meeting, Press Release 13068/06 (Presse 258) Reinforcing the Southern External Maritime

States particularly affected by the arrival of irregular migrants do not view EU intervention in this field as sufficient. Spain, for example, submitted a statement to the Transport, Telecommunications and Energy Council in November 2007 stating that incidents of maritime rescue have shown a lack of efficient Community legislation in this field. This could threaten the fulfilment of the fundamental principles of solidarity and assistance among the Member States of the EU. To this end, it proposed a series of measures including a legislative regulation harmonizing rescue procedures in all Member States, from the moment of rescue to the disembarkation of rescuees in a safe place. Specifically, it proposed the following:

- The establishment of the obligation for all vessels flying an EU flag, to rescue those persons who are in danger at sea, irrespective of whether or not they are in waters belonging to the jurisdiction of the European Union States or in their SAR areas . . .
- Encourage the said obligation via the creation of compensation mechanisms for vessels which have been economically affected as a consequence of the rescue of castaways at sea, so that the fact of having carried out the said operation does not cause them any detriment.
- Establish sanctions against vessels which ignore, do not inform or do not attend, in an unjustified manner, to distress calls from crafts.
- Create surveillance and alert systems, of a permanent nature, on the coasts of the European Union States, either incorporated within the national surveillance and rescue services or within the Frontex Agency itself, in order to adopt the necessary measures to proceed with the immediate rescue of persons in danger at sea.
- Draw up the possible most specific definition of 'port or place of refuge,' which, in any case, should contain as a minimum the following elements:
  - That the life and safety of the survivors is no longer threatened.
  - That their basic human needs, such as food, shelter and medical assistance can be satisfied.
  - That agreements may be reached for transporting the survivors to their next or final destination.
- Ensure the obligation of European States to have adequate rescue means at one's disposal which guarantee a certain level of effectiveness in the waters of their jurisdiction or in their SAR area of responsibility . . .
- Guarantee the cooperation, coordination and collaboration among the different Authorities of the Member States and between the latter and those of third countries at the origin of the immigration or as stopping points of the same, via the establishment of systems of alert and rapid intervention for rescue situations.[265]

Borders: Council Conclusions.

265 EU Council, 'Rescue at Sea—Information from the Spanish and Italian Delegations' (Information Note) (23 November 2007) 14758/07, MAR 109.

Apart from the level of EU intervention in this field, there is also a concern regarding the attention given to possible asylum situations. As was indicated above, management of asylum claims does not seem to form part of Frontex's duties.[266] Indeed, it has been reported that there is no evidence that Frontex takes potential protection issues into account when planning and coordinating joint operations.[267]

Furthermore, on 13 February 2008, the Commission set out its Border Management Package regarding which Vice-President Frattini (the Commissioner responsible for Justice, Freedom and Security at the time) commented:

> This package puts forward new ideas on the table for the control of our borders, at check points as well as along the length of the border, using the most advanced technology to reach the highest level of security, whilst at the same time facilitating the procedures for bona fide third country nationals wishing to enter the Schengen area. These ideas will promote legitimate free movement of people, whilst also dealing with unexpected migratory pressure, especially at the southern maritime border of the Union, and reducing the trafficking of human beings into the EU.[268]

Again, in relation to the above, ECRE notes that 'the EU's approach fails to properly address the fact that while all EU countries have a right to control their borders, they also have an obligation to provide international protection to persons fleeing persecution.'[269] Therefore, it seems that while the EU exhorts respect for fundamental principles such as *non-refoulement* as noted in the Communication on Reinforcing the Management of the European Union's Southern Maritime Borders[270] and in the Commission's Study on the international law instruments in relation to illegal immigration by sea,[271] the application of such principles has not yet reached an optimum level.

8.3.7. *EU Practice as compared with Australian and US Action*

With respect to the stemming of boat arrivals in particular, joint patrols may be part of the answer to stemming boat arrivals, definitely preferable to unilateral measures aimed at deterring the arrival of boat people. Despite Libya's

---

266 ECRE, 'EU Border Management Package ignores right to seek asylum?' (News Release), PR1/02/3008/Ext/Pc, 13 February 2008.

267 ECRE Report (n 206), 12, 13. See further in this regard I. Camilleri, 'Frontex urged to be more aware of fundamental rights', *The Times* (Malta, 4 September 2008).

268 'A Comprehensive Vision for an Integrated European Border Management System for the 21st Century' (13 February 2008), Press Release IP/08/215.

269 ECRE News Release (n 266).

270 COM(2006)733 final, 20 November 2006.

271 SEC(2007)691, 15 May 2007.

reluctance to take part in the Mediterranean exercise, there is evidence of a certain willingness of States to cooperate to this end. Further evidence of such cooperation exists in the Prum Convention 2005 (becoming known as the Schengen III Agreement), concluded by Belgium, Germany, Spain, France, Luxembourg, the Netherlands and Austria with the aim of stepping up cross-border cooperation, particularly in combating terrorism, cross-border crime and illegal migration.[272]

The above overview of State action in the face of irregular maritime arrivals shows what divergent solutions have been adopted to a common problem. The Australian response focussed on excision and took a purely 'law of the sea' approach by creating specific zones where coastal State powers were modified. The US approach is more aggressive in that it leaves the current regime intact, but purposefully disregards any extraterritorial application of humanitarian principles. Both, it has been seen, suffer from critiques that they may fall foul of the current international legal framework. In this light, although still in a developmental phase, the EU approach should be contrasted as one which, basing itself on cooperation as opposed to unilateral action, should be regarded as preferable. It has been seen that this approach too suffers from drawbacks, primarily in the lack of information which exists surrounding the Frontex patrols and lack of cooperation from major players such as Libya. However, these could optimistically be described as teething problems, awaiting further fine-tuning through experience and through increased goodwill on the part of the States concerned.

8.4. *General Appraisal of State Practice*

A review of State practice is therefore useful in demonstrating primarily two opposing features. It shows that in some circumstances States have gone beyond what the law allows and what is actually necessary in stemming boat arrivals and fighting maritime smuggling. It also, however, demonstrates possible developments to enhance the ability to deal with the problem. This can be in two main areas. There is always the possibility of the creation of new customary international law, in the way that the law on hot pursuit and constructive

[272] Italy has since become a Party to the Convention (Date of signature: 4 July 2006). This Convention has been supplemented by the Administration and Technical Implementing Agreement to the Prum Convention and its Annex, Council of the European Union, Brussels, 22 January 2007, 5473/07, CRIMORG 13, ENFOPOL 9, MIGR 3. The Prum Treaty was transposed into the legal framework of the EU by Council Decision 2008/615/JHA [2008] OJ L210/12.

presence has developed. More immediately, it indicates the importance of cooperation agreements and signals them as the way forward in the fight against maritime migrant smuggling.

A basic distinction which has emerged throughout this chapter from the State practice chosen for review is the lack of cooperation demonstrated by both Australia and the USA as opposed to that purported to be used within the EU. On the face of it, the EU has put in place a more effective and systematic regime dedicated to fight migrant smuggling. Australia and the US, on the other hand, have failed to put any such system into practice, have acted alone, and in so doing have strayed beyond the limits of what was strictly necessary and legal. The reason for this may be stated to be the political climate existing in these regions: there can be no comparison between the integration existing at a European level as opposed to that in the Caribbean or Asia-Pacific region.

However, this may on further consideration not appear to be a wholly correct assumption. EU cooperation is necessary in a way that is not necessary in the US: the Caribbean situation is dominated by individuals from many States converging onto one State, the USA. In the European scenario, specifically the Mediterranean region, individuals hailing from a few States (North African States leaving Libyan shores) travel towards many States, which make up the EU. The cooperation existing at EU level is *intra*-EU, and is necessary because a threat to the borders of one State is a threat to all the members of the Union. However, the cooperation existing at EU level can be described as being no different from the cooperation existing between the federal units of the USA.

The USA actually takes things further, as shown in the last chapter: as opposed to EU practice, the US has been active in forming agreements with neighbouring States to fight threats common to them all. The Shiprider Agreements, the Aruba Agreement, the 2004 Agreement with the Bahamas, and more generally, its efforts in the PSI and Ship Boarding Agreements with various States all demonstrate the readiness of the USA to act in concert with other States; its readiness to cooperate with other States. Even Australia stands out, in contrast to the EU, in its regional agreements making up the Pacific Strategy—no matter how much these arrangements are open to question. The EU has been unable to conclude any such agreement with its North African neighbours; it has hitherto been unsuccessful in concluding certain fundamental agreements within its own Member States.

From this viewpoint, ironically, it is the USA that stands out as the primary player in this field, as the most advanced party in the effort to create cooperative mechanisms to combat migrant smuggling and other common threats to maritime security.

Therefore, when one tries to devise a pattern of conduct in the three States reviewed one notes a stark division between cooperation and the vigorous assertion of unilateral rights. Australian practice is devoid of cooperation with source countries. Here, cooperation is limited to dubious agreements under the Pacific Strategy, while the EU practice is characterized by an amount of internal cooperation (and no cooperation with source countries). The US practice falls into both groups (as Chapters 7 and 8 demonstrated)—cooperation with source countries and extensive unilateral action. It is this cooperation with source countries which, it is submitted, signals a future way forward in the fight against maritime migrant smuggling.

Chapter Nine

Conclusion

9.1. *A Workable Regime*

The study set out to determine whether the existing jurisdictional regime provides an adequate system to combat effectively the crime of maritime migrant smuggling. Specific regulation of the crime is both recent and limited, in the form of the Migrant Smuggling Protocol. Surrounding this however, there lies the general regime of the law of the sea, including provisions on the rescue of those in distress at sea, humanitarian principles of protection and human rights law. It could be argued that the lack of specific mention of maritime migrant smuggling in the LOSC is a drawback which militates against the proper and effective regulation of the crime insofar as it could be expected that a Constitution of the Oceans should be both comprehensive and up-to-date in the matters it strives to regulate. However, it is submitted that the answer to an effective regulatory framework would not necessarily be reached should the LOSC be revised in order to extend the exceptions to flag State exclusivity on the high seas to maritime migrant smuggling. On a practical level, this solution does not seem feasible due to the procedure necessary for amending the LOSC.[1] Apart from this, reference to the drug smuggling, slavery or piracy provisions in the LOSC, for example, soon shows that regulation in the LOSC does not necessarily provide a workable or effective regime. Furthermore, there is ample evidence, reviewed in Chapter 7, of States' willingness to cooperate in other fields such as drug trafficking, thus rendering the international regime more effective while at the same time leaving core principles, such as flag State exclusivity, intact.

The instruments studied in Chapter 7 were portrayed as implementations of the duty of cooperation which, it was noted, is an obligation having a certain legal content, which dictates coordinated action and which is not satisfied by mere acts of good neighbourliness and courtesy. Both the Ship Rider Agreements and the Ship Boarding Agreements in the context of the

[1] See Art. 155 LOSC.

PSI, together with the recently amended SUA Convention, work within the parameters of the existing framework of flag State exclusivity over the high seas and coastal State sovereignty in the territorial waters in order to create an efficient model of cooperation to fight contemporary maritime threats. Thus, they offer a useful paradigm in two areas: admission into the territorial waters of a coastal State Party to the particular Agreement and expeditious response to requests for verification of nationality and authorization to board vessels in operations seawards of the territorial waters of the States Parties.

As far as drug smuggling in the Caribbean is concerned, it is submitted that, due to their inclusion in a fair number of bilateral treaties, the obligations of giving timely response to requests to enter territorial waters, to verify nationality and to board vessels on the high seas can arguably constitute regional customary international law for the Caribbean area. In this way, a State may not be permitted to refuse its cooperation in authorizing the boarding of one of its vessels, and this cooperation dictates that consent must be given as soon as possible. It is submitted that these obligations are facets of the general duty of cooperation, which obligation is a common feature in the fight against all current security threats.

Extending these principles to the migrant smuggling sphere is possible, as long as adequate consideration is given to the particular nature of migrant smuggling and the close connection to human rights and humanitarian principles, as demonstrated by the US–Bahamas Agreement 2004. In this way, the drug trafficking models studied could signal a development in international law in two ways: firstly, through the creation of treaties embodying such principles in the migrant smuggling sphere. From the treaty law perspective, therefore, the process which commenced with the Migrant Smuggling Protocol, discussed in Chapter 7, should therefore be continued, and States should become Parties to this instrument if they have not yet done so. In the European context, Member States may wish to consider the creation of a regional framework along the lines laid out in the multilateral document to expedite the implementation of these obligations between them.[2] Secondly, these models could be the seeds for the generation of customary international law in the fight against migrant smuggling, should the practice be sufficiently widespread, uniform and consistent, accompanied by the requisite *opinio juris*. There is a strong chance of the creation of regional customary law to this effect, in each particular crime collectively combated.

Cooperation thus lies at the core of this study. It should also be because of the force of this obligation that a State is not entitled to leave it to other

2 The EU aspect was considered in Chapter 8.

States to rescue those in distress at sea. This point is strengthened by reference to the recent amendments made to the SAR Convention where, *inter alia*, paragraph 3.1.9 imposes a duty of coordination and cooperation upon all States to ensure the disembarkation of rescuees at a place of safety. If this hypothesis is correct, the introduction of the duty of cooperation and coordination by the recent IMO amendments when dealing with the rescue of those in distress at sea has more force than initially noted. It can be seen to be an illustration of a new direction being taken in the suppression of threats to maritime security: the inclusion of the duty of cooperation, with its various component obligations, as the essential weapon in the arsenal needed to fight maritime security threats in the 21st century.

9.2. *The Way Forward*

As far as the maritime border patrols coordinated by Frontex are concerned, their effectiveness would benefit greatly from a specific *modus operandi* agreed to by the States concerned. Potential bilateral or regional agreements or, at least, guidelines could lay the foundation for a common understanding between participating States of how and when to carry out interceptions, and the procedure to be followed during these operations.[3] As far as the principle of *non-refoulement* is concerned, specific delineation of what actions trigger the obligation should be included in the agreements and/or guidelines outlined above.

There is a pressing need to define the circumstances in which a State is obliged to assume responsibility for processing the asylum claims of those rescued at sea, especially when they are rescued outside the SAR area of an EU Member State or on the high seas. Guidelines would be helpful in this regard. They could also pinpoint factors signalling the most appropriate State in which to disembark in order to assist States in their obligation to coordinate and cooperate in ensuring the disembarkation of rescuees to a place of safety. Similarly, the sharing of responsibilities between the States participating in interception or SAR operations with regard to obligations such as the repatriation of migrants, access to asylum procedures and the international protection to be given to migrants is an essential consideration.

Of course, as far as the patrols in the Mediterranean region are concerned, the lack of support from Libya greatly militates against the success of such

[3] Commission Staff Working Document, Study on the international law instruments in relation to illegal immigration by sea, Brussels, 15.5.2007, SEC(2007)691. This document proceeded to pose a number of suggestions for future progress, most of which are dealt with here.

joint exercise. Cooperation by Libya by controlling the departures of vessels laden with irregular immigrants and by permitting the surveillance of other States' vessels in its territorial waters would greatly aid the cause of preventing migrant smuggling. However, at this point it should be stressed that merely turning intercepted vessels back to Libyan shores is not the answer to the overall situation. This method of preventing irregular arrivals in Europe would violate the *non-refoulement* principle, as Libya is not a Party to the Refugee Convention and there is no guarantee that Libya will not send these migrants back to their countries of origin, where they may indeed be subject to persecution.

In line with this, it is submitted that, especially within the EU context, no cooperative regime purporting to tackle maritime migrant smuggling can be said to be complete without having regard to the bigger picture. This entails the addressing of the migration issue at its source, and also tackling the second limb of humanitarianism mentioned in Chapter 6: that is, the act of processing and hearing claims for asylum and the granting of refugee status in the case of a successful claim. The necessity of considering this added aspect of humanitarianism mirrors precisely the dual nature of maritime migrant smuggling: a crime against national security, a violation of State sovereignty and an infraction of immigration regulations on the one hand, and a breach of human rights on the other. State action, based on cooperative frameworks, must perforce consider both these aspects in order effectively to combat the crime of maritime migrant smuggling. At all times it should be recalled that responsibilities lie with all States concerned; the answer to the problem of migrant smuggling is not to be found at the expense of any one State's resources and security. In this respect, a system of burden-sharing within the EU context[4] should be given due weight as one facet of a solution giving further voice to the duty of cooperation among States.

[4] Referred to in Chapter 7.

Bibliography[1]

Adamoli, Sabrina, Di Nicola Andrea, Ernest Savona and Paola Zoffi, *Organised Crime Around the World* (European Institute for Crime Prevention and Control (HEUNI), Helsinki, 1998)

Aiken, Sharryn J., 'Manufacturing "Terrorists": Refugees, National Security and Canadian Law' (2000) 19 *Refuge* 3, 54–73

——, 'Manufacturing "Terrorists": Refugees, National Security and Canadian Law' (2001) 19 *Refuge* 4, 116–133

Aleinikoff, Alexander T. and Vincent Chetail (eds), *Migration and International Legal Norms* (TMC Asser Press, The Hague, 2003)

Allain, Jean, 'The *Jus Cogens* Nature of Non-refoulement' (2001) 13 *IJRL*, 533–558

Ataner, Attila, 'Refugee Interdiction and the Outer Limits of Sovereignty' (2004) 3 *JLE* 1, 7–29

Bagaric, Mirko, Kim Boyd, Penny Dimopoulos, Sue Tongue and John Vrachnas, *Migration and Refugee Law in Australia: Cases and Commentary* (Cambridge University Press, Cambridge, 2007)

Bailet, François N., Frew W. Crickard and Glen J. Herbert, *Integrated Maritime Enforcement: A Handbook* (Centre for Foreign Policy Studies, Dalhousie University, 1999)

Bantekas, Illias and Susan Nash, *International Criminal Law* (2nd edn, Cavendish Publishing, London, 2003)

Barnes, Richard, 'Refugee Law at Sea' (2004) 53 *ICLQ* 47–77

Barsky, Robert F., 'An Essay on the Free Movement of Peoples' (2001) 19 *Refuge* 4, 8489

Berkenkopf, Karen, 'Italy allows aid ship carrying Sudanese refugees to enter Sicilian port', *Lloyd's List* (13 July 2004)

——, 'Aid ship officers in refugee storm arrested', *Lloyd's List* (14 July 2004)

——, 'Italy releases Cap Anamur crew', *Lloyd's List* (20 July 2004)

——, 'Greens in Cap Anamur arrests protest', *Lloyd's List* (22 July 2004)

Bonello, Jesmond, 'Malta and Libya discuss fight against immigration', *The Times of Malta* (25 October 2003)

Borg, Tonio, 'Frontex—deterring human trafficking', *The Times of Malta* (25 September 2008)

Bossin, Michael, 'Bill C-31: Limited Access to Refugee Determination and Protection' (2001) 19 *Refuge* 4, 55–61

Bostock, Chantal Marie-Jeanne, 'The International Legal Obligations owed to the Asylum Seekers on the *MV Tampa*' (2002) 14 *IJRL* 2 and 3, 279–301

Brolan, Claire, 'An Analysis of the Human Smuggling Trade and the *Protocol Against the Smuggling of Migrants by Land, Air and Sea (2000)* from a Refugee Protection Perspective' (2002) 14 *IJRL* 561–596

[1] All website references correct as at 31st August 2009.

Brouwer, Andrew and Judith Kumin, 'Interception and Asylum: When Migration Control and Human Rights Collide' (2003) 21 *Refuge* 4, 6–24
Busuttil, Cynthia, 'European approach needed to immigration', *The Times of Malta* (24 October 2006)
——, 'Minister upbeat about Frontex despite chief's admission of failure', *The Times of Malta* (22 September 2008)
Busuttil, Simon, 'A dangerous road to tread', *The Times of Malta* (1 October 2008)
Byers, Michael, 'Terrorism, the Use of Force and International Law after 11 September' (2002) 51 *ICLQ* 401–414
——, 'Policing the High Seas: the Proliferation Security Initiative' (2004) 98 *AJIL* 526–545
Byrne, Rosemary, Gregor Noll and Jens Vedsted-Hansen, 'Understanding Refugee Law in an Enlarged European Union' (2004) 15 *EJIL* 355–379
Camilleri, Ivan, 'EU to step up fight against illegal migration', *The Times of Malta* (12 May 2005)
——, 'Malta urges EU to tackle African States', *The Times of Malta* (3 September 2005)
——, 'Amnesty urges EU to ease pressure on Malta', *The Times of Malta* (12 October 2005)
——, 'EU proposes coastal patrol for Mediterranean', *The Times of Malta* (1 December 2005)
——, 'MEPs for fact-finding mission', *The Times of Malta* (22 February 2006)
——, 'Frattini defends Malta over illegal immigration', *The Times of Malta* (3 March 2006)
——, 'European Parliament adopts Malta resolution', *The Times of Malta* (7 April 2006)
——, 'Amendment to Dublin Convention "highly unlikely"', *The Times of Malta* (8 April 2006)
——, 'EU to offer Malta air and sea patrols', *The Times of Malta* (24 May 2006)
——, 'EU agency to discuss air, sea patrols with Malta', *The Times of Malta* (1 June 2006)
——, 'Six EU members in Operation Malta', *The Times of Malta* (22 June 2006)
——, 'Five EU patrols for "Operation Malta"', *The Times of Malta* (26 June 2006)
——, 'EU seeking Libyan cooperation on patrols', *The Times of Malta* (1 July 2006)
——, 'Illegal migration patrols to start in four weeks' time', *The Times of Malta* (6 August 2006)
——, 'EU launches first patrols', *The Times of Malta* (12 August 2006)
——, 'Italy, Libya to run joint patrols', *The Times of Malta* (14 September 2006)
——, 'Amnesty International calls for monitoring of patrols', *The Times of Malta* (19 September 2006)
——, 'EU grants Malta 1.3 m Euro in aid on immigration', *The Times of Malta* (20 September 2006)
——, 'Frattini pledges 3 m Euro in aid to Libya', *The Times of Malta* (23 September 2006)
——, 'Operation Nautilus starts today', *The Times of Malta* (4 October 2006)
——, 'Call for new methods to tackle illegal migration', *The Times of Malta* (21 October 2006)
——, 'EU allocates 8 m Euro for sea patrols', *The Times of Malta* (21 April 2007)

——, 'EPP Malta conference to discuss illegal immigration', *The Times of Malta* (22 April 2007)
——, 'Malta participates in EU intelligence sharing network', *The Times of Malta* (25 May 2007)
——, 'Malta proposal sent to Frattini', *The Times of Malta* (8 June 2007)
——, 'Malta pushes EU for concrete action', *The Times of Malta* (12 June 2007)
——, 'Lukewarm response to Malta's bid', *The Times of Malta* (13 June 2007)
——, 'Frontex patrols resume on September 10', *The Times of Malta* (25 August 2007)
——, 'Frattini stands up for Malta', *The Times of Malta* (4 September 2007)
——, 'Patrols resume today', *The Times of Malta* (10 September 2007)
——, 'EU ministers to discuss Malta's burden-sharing proposal', *The Times of Malta* (18 September 2007)
——, 'EU Border Patrols "imminent"', *The Sunday Times of Malta* (13 April 2008)
——, 'Still no headway on burden sharing', *The Times of Malta* (24 April 2008)
——, 'EU Patrols on hold as States grapple over destination of rescued illegal immigrants', *The Times of Malta* (27 April 2008)
——, 'Sea Patrols to start next week', *The Times of Malta* (9 May 2008)
——, 'Nautilus III starts today', *The Times of Malta* (17 May 2008)
——, 'Frontex no solution as Libya fails to Cooperate', *The Times of Malta* (11 July 2008)
——, 'Frontex urged to be more aware of fundamental rights', *The Times of Malta* (4 September 2008)
——, 'Busuttil proposes solidarity mechanism for 2009 EU budget', *The Times of Malta* (16 September 2008)
——, 'No burden sharing, no deal, Malta says', *The Times of Malta* (19 September 2008)
——, 'Frontex chief admits failure', *The Times of Malta* (21 September 2008)
——, 'Malta facing uphill battle', *The Times of Malta* (24 September 2008)
——, 'Malta close to deal on burden sharing', *The Times of Malta* (25 September 2008)
——, 'Malta gets its way', *The Times of Malta* (26 September 2008)
Cassese, Antonio, 'Terrorism is also Disrupting Some Crucial Legal Categories of International Law' (2001) 12 *EJIL* 993–1001
——, *International Criminal Law* (2nd edn, Oxford University Press, Oxford, 2008)
Cassola, Arnold, 'Refugees in Malta—a Maltese and European concern', *The Sunday Times of Malta* (9 November 2003)
Chatham House, 'Ship-Boarding: An Effective Measure against Terrorism and WMD Proliferation?' (Summary of Discussion of International Law Discussion Group) (24 November 2005) available at www.chathamhouse.org.uk/publications/papers/download/-/id/318/file/3288_ilp241105.doc
Chen, Jeffrey, 'Time to evaluate the likelihood of terrorism at sea', *Lloyd's List* (19 July 2005)
Chesney, Robert, 'The Proliferation Security Initiative and WMD: Interdiction on the High Seas' (2003) 13 *National Security Review* 1
Churchill, Robin R. and Alan V. Lowe, *The Law of the Sea* (3rd edn, Manchester University Press, Manchester, 1999)
Churchill, Robin, 'The MOX Plant Litigation: The First Half-Life' (2004) 53 *ICLQ* 643–676

Claude-Valentin, Marie, *Preventing Illegal Immigration: Juggling Economic Imperatives, Political Risks and Individual Rights* (Council of Europe, Strasbourg, 2003)

Colombos, John C., *International Law of the Sea* (6th edn, Longman Group Limited, London, 1967)

Coombs, Mary, 'State v Stepansky. 761 So. 2d 1027 (Fla.), cert, Denied, 121 S. Ct. 385 (2000)' (2001) 95 *AJIL* 438–445

Crook, John R. (ed.), 'US Concludes Additional Proliferation Security Initiative Ship Boarding Agreements' (2005) 99 *AJIL* 919–920

Cummins, Sally J. and David P. Steward (eds), *Digest of United States Practice in International Law 2001* (Office of the Legal Advisor, United States Department of State, International Law Institute, Washington, DC, 2001)

——, *Digest of United States Practice in International Law 2002* (Office of the Legal Advisor, United States Department of State, International Law Institute, Washington, DC, 2002)

——, *Digest of United States Practice in International Law 2003* (Office of the Legal Advisor, United States Department of State, International Law Institute, Washington, DC, 2003)

Cummins, Sally J. (ed.), *Digest of United States Practice in International Law 2004* (Oxford University Press, Oxford, 2004)

——, *Digest of United States Practice in International Law 2005* (Oxford University Press, Oxford, 2005)

Davies, Martin, 'Obligations and Implications for Ships Encountering Persons in Need of Assistance at Sea' (2003) 12 *Pac Rim L & Pol'y J* 109–141

Davis-Mattis, Laleta, 'International Drug Trafficking and the Law of the Sea: Outstanding Issues and Bilateral Responses with Emphasis on US–Caribbean Agreements' (2000) 14 *Ocean Yearbook* 360–385

De La Fayette, Louise, 'Access to Ports in International Law' (1996) 11 *IJMLC* 1–22

De Londras Fiona, '*Saadi v Italy*: European Court of Human Rights Reasserts the Absolute Prohibition on Refoulement in Terrorism Extradition Cases' (2008) 12 ASIL Insight 9 http://www.asil.org/insights080513.cfm

Della Torre, Emilia, 'A Discussion of the Recent Excision of Christmas Island from Australia's Migration Zone in the Light of Australia's International Refugee Obligation of Non-refoulement' [2003] *AJHR* 20, available at www.austlii.edu.au/au/journals/AJHR/2003/20.html

Dench, Janet, 'Controlling the Borders: C-31 and Interdiction' (2001) 19 *Refuge* 4, 34–40

Dench, Janet and François Crepeau, 'Interdiction at the Expense of Human Rights: A Long-term Containment Strategy' (2003) 21 *Refuge* 4, 2–5

Dennis, William C., 'The Sinking of the *I'm Alone*' (1929) 23 *AJIL* 351–362

Department of the Navy, Office of the Chief of Naval Operations and Headquarters, U.S. Marine Corps, Department of Homeland Security and U.S. Coast Guard, 'The Commander's Handbook on the Law of Naval Operations' (July 2007) NWP 1-14M/MCWP 5-12.1/COMDTPUB P5800.7A http://www.nwc.navy.mil/cnws/ild/documents/1-14m_(jul_2007)_(nwp).pdf

Duff, John A., 'A Note on the United States and the Law of the Sea: Looking Back and Moving Forward' (2004) 35 *ODIL*, 195–219

Dupuy, Rene-Jean and Daniel Vignes, *A Handbook on the New Law of the Sea* (Martinus Nijhoff Publishers, Dordrecht, 1991) vols. 1 and 2

Eason, Craig, 'Freedom and security: the dilemma of vessel tracking', *Lloyd's List* (21 April 2006)

——, 'IMO seeks backing on Somalia piracy', *Lloyd's List* (11 July 2007)

Edwards, Alice, 'Tampering with Refugee Protection: The Case of Australia' (2003) 15 *IJRL* 192–211

Erdogan, Bulent, 'Italy releases rescue ship Cap Anamur' *Lloyd's List*, (25 February 2005)

Evans, Alona E., 'Aircraft Hijacking: Its Cause and Cure' (1969) 63 *AJIL* 695–710

Evans, Malcolm D (ed.), *International Law* (Oxford University Press, Oxford, 2003)

Fairplay Daily News, 'Are Security Alert Systems any use?', *Fairplay Daily News* (28 March 2008)

——, 'EU "24 hour" rule running late', *Fairplay Daily News* (4 April 2008)

Farrugia, Massimo, 'Ability to respond to genuine refugees "being overwhelmed"', *The Times of Malta* (24 September 2005)

——, 'EU "lacks means" to ease irregular migration burdens', *The Times of Malta* (11 May 2006)

Feld, Francine, 'The *Tampa* Case: Seeking Refuge in Domestic Law' [2002] *AJHR* 11, available at www.austlii.edu.au/au/journals/AJHR/2002/11.html

Feller, Erika, 'Asylum, Migration and Refugee Protection: Realities, Myths and the Promise of Things to Come' (2006) 18 *IJRL* 509–536

Feller, Erika, Volker Turk and Frances Nicholson (eds), *Refugee Protection in International Law: UNHCR's Global Consultations on International Protection* (Cambridge University Press, Cambridge, 2003)

Fenech, Natalino, 'Frendo lashes out at EU', *The Times of Malta* (1 July 2006)

——, 'US admiral describes experiences with immigrants', *The Times of Malta* (2 November 2006)

Fenwick, Charles G., '"Piracy" in the Caribbean' (1961) 55 *AJIL* 426–428

Fitzmaurice, Gerald, 'Some Results of the Geneva Convention on the Law of the Sea' (1959) 8 *ICLQ* 73

Fitzpatrick, Joan, 'Temporary Protection of Refuges: Elements of a Formalized Regime' (2000) 94 *AJIL* 279–306

Franck, Thomas M., 'Terrorism and the Right of Self-Defense' (2001) 95 *AJIL* 839–843

Frank, Jerry, 'UN's refugee agency raises Somalia alarm', *Lloyd's List* (9 July 2007)

——, 'Two-track approach to security at sea', *Lloyd's List* (4 October 2007)

Freestone, David, Richard Barnes and David Ong (eds), *The Law of the Sea: Progress and Prospects* (Oxford University Press, Oxford, 2006)

Frelick, Bill, 'Haitian Boat Interdiction and Return: First Asylum and First Principles of Refugee Protection' (1993) 26 *Cornell Intl LJ* 675–694

——, 'In-Country Refugee Processing of Haitians: The Case Against' (2003) 21 *Refuge* 4, 66–72

Gallagher, Anna, 'Human Rights and the New UN Protocols on Trafficking and Migrant Smuggling: A Preliminary Analysis' (2001) 23 *Human Rights Quarterly* 975–1004

Gavouneli, Maria, *Functional Jurisdiction in the Law of the Sea* (Martinus Nijhoff Publishers, Dordrecht, 2007)

Gilbert, Geoff, 'Is Europe living up to its Obligations to Refugees?' (2004) 15 *EJIL* 963–987
Gilmore, William C., 'Hot Pursuit and Constructive Presence in Canadian Law Enforcement: A Case Note' (1988) 12 *Marine Policy*, 105–111
——, 'Narcotic Interdiction at Sea: UK–US Cooperation' (1989) 13 *Marine Policy*, 218–230
——, 'Hot Pursuit: The Case of R v Mills and others' (1995) 44 *ICLQ* 949–958
——, 'Narcotics Interdiction at Sea: the 1985 Council of Europe Agreement' (1996) 20 *Marine Policy*, 3–14
——, 'Drug Trafficking at Sea: The Case of *R v Charrington and Others*' (2000) 49 *ICLQ* 477–489
——, *Agreement Concerning Co-operation in Suppressing Illicit Maritime and Air Trafficking in Narcotic Drugs and Psychotropic Substances in the Caribbean Area, 2003* (TSO, London, 2005)
Goodwin-Gill, Guy, 'Non-refoulement and the New Asylum-seekers' (1986) 26 *Va. J. Int'l Law* 897–918
Goodwin-Gill, Guy and Jane McAdam, *The Refugee in International Law* (3rd edn, Oxford University Press, Oxford, 2007)
Grahl-Madsen, Atle, *The Status of Refugees in International Law*, (AW Sijthoff, Leiden, 1972) vol. 2
——, *Commentary on the Refugee Convention 1951, arts. 2–11, 13–37* (reprinted by UNHCR, Geneva, 1997)
Gray, Christine, *International Law and the Use of Force* (2nd edn, Oxford University Press, Oxford, 2004)
Grech, Herman, 'Call for national strategy on migrants', *The Times of Malta* (29 October 2004)
——, 'Malta proposes resettlement in EU countries', *The Times of Malta* (11 July 2005)
——, 'Libya unable to protect itself let alone Europe', *The Times of Malta* (5 August 2005)
——, 'Migrants perish after refusing help from Malta', *The Times of Malta* (19 November 2005)
——, 'S. European leaders rally on migration', *The Times of Malta* (26 September 2006)
——, 'Coastal states urged to help people in distress at sea', *The Times of Malta* (2 June 2007)
——, 'Barroso to call on EU to help Malta', *The Times of Malta* (16 June 2007)
——, 'Libya invites army for talks on search and rescue zone', *The Times of Malta* (17 July 2007)
——, 'Malta, Libya meet today on search and rescue', *The Times of Malta* (22 August 2007)
Grey, Michael, 'Measures to stop terrorism must be seen as practical in order to work', *Lloyd's List* (30 September 2004)
——, 'IMO to host diplomatic debate to step up anti-terrorist action', *Lloyd's List* (5 November 2004)
——, 'IMO calls in UN security council over Somalia', *Lloyd's List* (29 June 2007)
Grotius, Hugo, *The Free Sea* (ed. D. Armitage, Liberty Fund, Ind., 2004)

Guild, Elspeth, 'The Europeanisation of Europe's Asylum Policy' (2006) 18 *IJRL* 630–651

Gunaratna, Rohan, 'Terrorist threat to shipping is "imminent and growing"', *Lloyd's List* (29 September 2004)

Halberstam, Malvina, 'Terrorism on the High Seas: The Achille Lauro, Piracy and the IMO Convention on Maritime Safety' (1988) 82 *AJIL*269–310

Hand, Marcus, 'IMO backs joint anti-terror patrols in Malacca Strait', *Lloyd's List* (4 March 2005)

——, 'Hijacking off Indonesia spoils talk of piracy decline', *Lloyd's List* (5 October 2005)

——, 'Terrorists "could see ports as soft targets"', *Lloyd's List* (21 October 2005)

——, 'Three nations co-ordinate strait patrols', *Lloyd's List* (25 April 2006)

——, 'IMB calls for Somalia piracy action', *Lloyd's List* (12 June 2007)

——, 'Abduction raises fears of new era of pirate attacks', *Lloyds List* (16 August 2007)

Harris, Jonathan, 'Haitian Centers Council, Inc. v McNary' (1993) 87 *AJIL* 112–117

Harvard Research in International Law, 'Article 7. Protection—Security of the State' (1935) 29 *AJIL* Supplement, 543–561

Harvey, Colin J., 'Refugees, Rights and Human Security' (2001) 19 *Refuge* 4, 94–99

Hathaway, James C., 'Refugee Law is not Immigration Law' in *World Refugee Survey 2002* (United States Committee for Refugees, 2002)

——, *The Rights of Refugees under International Law* (Cambridge University Press, Cambridge, 2005)

Hathaway, James and Colin J. Harvey, 'Framing Refugee Protection in the New World Disorder' (2001) 34 *Cornell Intl LJ* 257–320

Hesse, Hartmut G., 'Maritime Security in a Multilateral Context: IMO Activities to Enhance Maritime Security' (2003) 18 *IJMLC* 327–339

Hinrichs, Ximena, 'Measures against Smuggling of Migrants at Sea: A Law of the Sea Related Perspective' (2003) 36 *Revue belge de droit international* 413–451

Hirst, Michael, *Jurisdiction and the Ambit of the Criminal Law* (Oxford, Oxford University Press, 2003)

Howard, Jessica, 'To Deter and Deny: Australia and the Interdiction of Asylum Seekers' (2003) 21 *Refuge* 4, 35–50

IMO / UNHCR, 'Guide to Principles and Practice as Applied to Migrants and Refugees' (Leaflet) (2006) Available online: www.imo.org/includes/blastDataOnly.asp/data_id =15282/UNHCRIMOleafletpersonsrescuedatsea.pdf

International Organisation for Migration, *International Migration Law: Glossary on Migration* (IOM, Geneva, 2004) http://www.ir.metu.edu.tr/iom/pdf/iom2.pdf

Jennings, Robert and Arthur Watts (eds), *Oppenheim's International Law* (9th edn, Longman, London, 1996) vol. I *Peace*

Jessup, Philip C., *The Law of the Territorial Waters and Maritime Jurisdiction* (G.A. Jennings Co Inc, New York, 1927)

Jesus, Jose Luis, 'Protection of Foreign Ships against Piracy and Terrorism at Sea: Legal Aspects' (2003) 18 *IJMLC* 363–400

Jones, Thomas David, 'Sale v Haitian Council, Inc' (1994) 88 *AJIL* 114–126

Jones, Thomas David and Judith Hippler Bello, 'Cuban Bar Association, Inc v Christopher. 43 F.3d 1412. Haitian Refugee Center, Inc. v Christopher. 43 F.3d 1431' (1996) 90 *AJIL* 477–483

Joshi, Rajesh, 'Maritime security strategy continues to confound', *Lloyd's List* (10 November 2005)

Kanter, James, 'EU vows to step up efforts on migrants', *International Herald Tribune* (16 June 2006)

Kasoulides, George C., *Port State Control and Jurisdiction—Evolution of the Port State Control Regime* (Martinus Nijhoff, Dordrecht, 1993)

Katselli, Elena and Sangeeta Shah, 'September 11 and the UK Response' (2003) 52 *ICLQ* 245–255

Keith, Kenneth J., Marc Joyau, Tony Angelo (eds.) *Stemming the Tide or Keeping the Balance—The Role of the Judiciary* (Conference Proceedings) (NZ Association for Comparative Law and the *Revue Juridique Polynesienne* in association with the New Zealand centre for Public Law of the Victorian University of Wellington, Wellington, 2003)

Kelley, Ninette and Jean-François Duriex, 'UNHCR and Current Challenges in International Refugee Protection' (2004) 22 *Refuge* 1, 6–17

Kenney, Frederick J. and Vasilios Tasikas, 'The Tampa Incident: IMO Perspectives and Responses on the Treatment of Persons Rescued at Sea' (2003) 12 *Pac Rim L & Pol'y J* 143–178

Klein, Natalie, 'Legal Limitations on Ensuring Australia's Maritime Security' (2006) 7 *MelbJIL* 306, available at www.austlii.edu.au/au/journals/MelbJIL/2006/13.html

——, 'Legal Implications of Australia's Maritime Identification System' (2006) 55 *ICLQ* 337–368

Knight, Stephen M., 'Defining Due Process Down: Expedited Removal in the United States' (2001) 19 *Refuge* 4, 41–47

Kourula, Pirkko, *Broadening the Edges: Refugee Definition and International Protection Revisited* (Martinus Nijhoff, The Hague, 1997)

Kreijen, Gerard, Marcel Brus, Jorris Duursma, Elizabeth De Vos, John Dugard (eds), *State, Sovereignty and International Governance* (Oxford University Press, Oxford, 2002)

van Krieken, Peter J. (ed.), *The Consolidated Asylum and Migration Acquis—The EU Directives in an Expanded Europe* (TMC Asser Press, The Hague, 2004)

Kwiatkowska, Barbara, 'Creeping Jurisdiction beyond 200 Miles in the Light of the 1982 LOSC and State Practice' (1991) 22 *ODIL* 2, 153–187

Laitinen, Illika, 'EU member States' assistance is a must if Frontex operations are to succeed', *The Times of Malta* (6 October 2008)

Lambert, Helene, 'Article 3 of the European Convention on Human Rights and the Protection of Refugees and Rejected Asylum Seekers against Refoulement from Europe' (1999) 48 *ICLQ* 515–544

Landon, Felicity, 'Genuine link call may end owners' right to choose', *Lloyd's List* (1 September 2004)

——, 'EU to push for coastal rights overhaul', *Lloyd's List* (26 May 2006)

Lee, Roy and Moritaka Hayashi (eds), *New Directions in the Law of the Sea: Global Developments* (Oceania Publications, Dobs Ferry, NY, 1996)

Legomsky, Stephen H., 'The USA and the Caribbean Interdiction Program' (2006) 18 *IJRL* 677–695

Lenaerts, Koen and Piet Van Nuffel, *Constitutional Law of the European Union* (2nd edn, Sweet and Maxwell, London, 2005)

Lloyd's List DCN, 'Australia drops plans for a 1000-mile sea security zone', *Lloyd's List* (12 July 2005)

Lonbay, Julian, 'Current Developments: European Community Law. II. Free Movement of Persons' (2001) 50 *ICLQ* 168–174

——, 'Current Development: European Community Law. II. The Free Movement of Persons' (2004) 53 *ICLQ* 479–487

Lowe, Alan Vaughan, 'The Right of Entry into Maritime Ports in International Law' (1977) 14 *San Diego Law Review*, 597–622

Lowe, Vaughan, '"Clear and Present Danger": Responses to Terrorism' (2005) 54 *ICLQ* 185–196

Magner, Tara, 'A Less than "Pacific" Solution for Asylum Seekers in Australia' (2004) 16 *IJRL* 53–90

Mansted, Rachel, 'The Pacific Solution—Assessing Australia's Compliance with International Law' (2007) 3 *Bond University Student Law Review* 1–11

Mares, Peter, '*Borderline: Australia's Approach to Refugees and Asylum Seekers in the Wake of the Tampa*' (University of New South Wales Press, Sydney, 2001)

Martin, David A. (ed), *The New Asylum Seekers: Refugee Law in the 1980s. The 9th Sokol Colloquium on International Law* (Martinus Nijhoff, Dordrecht, 1988)

Massa, Ariadne, 'Saving lives at sea "is an unqualified obligation"', *The Times of Malta* (6 July 2007)

Masterson, William E., *Jurisdiction in Marginal Seas* (The Macmillan Co, New York, 1929)

Mathew, Penelope, 'Australian Refugee Protection in the Wake of the Tampa' (2002) 96 *AJIL* 661–676

——, 'Legal Issues concerning Interception' (2003) 17 *Georgetown Immigration Law Journal*, 221–249

Mathijsen, Petrus SRF, *A Guide to European Union Law* (8th edn, Sweet and Maxwell, London, 2004)

McClean, David, *International Co-operation in Civil and Criminal Matters* (2nd edn, Oxford University Press, Oxford, 2002)

——, *Transnational Organized Crime: A Commentary on the UN Convention and its Protocols* (Oxford University Press, Oxford, 2007)

McDorman, Ted L., 'From the Desk of the Editor-in-Chief' (2005) 36 *ODIL*, 381–386

McDougal Myres S., William T. Burke and Ivan A. Vlasic, 'The Maintenance of Public Order at Sea and the Nationality of Ships' (1960) 54 *AJIL* 25–116

McLaughlin, John, 'Container Ports to be a Global Shield in Anti-Terror Initiative', *Lloyds List* (24 December 2003)

——, 'E-seal Technology Studies with View to Setting New Standards', *Lloyds List* (14 January 2004)

——, 'US urges ships to report in', *Lloyd's List* (14 July 2004)

——, 'US may go it alone on merchant ship tracking', *Lloyd's List* (16 August 2004)

——, 'Security shortfalls let terror thrive', *Lloyd's List* (20 August 2004)
——, 'US Coast Guard plumbs new depths in port security', *Lloyd's List* (7 February 2005)
——, '"More must be done" on port security', *Lloyd's List* (20 May 2005)
——, 'Ports still vulnerable to terror, NY/NJ man says', *Lloyd's List* (23 June 2005)
McLaughlin, Rob, 'United Nations Mandated Naval Interdiction Operations in the Territorial Sea?' (2002) 51 *ICLQ* 249–278
Melander, Ingrid, 'EU Commission wants rapid-reaction migration units', *The Times of Malta* (17 February 2006)
——, 'EU states at sea over how to tackle illegal immigrants', *The Times of Malta* (20 September 2006)
Menefee, Samuel Pyeatt, 'Foreign Naval Intervention in Cases of Piracy' (1999) 14 *IJMLC* 353–370
Moles Stephanie (Commander, RAN), 'The Law of the Sea Convention 1982 and the Refugee Convention 1951 Provisions: How They Might Impact on Extant Australian Government Policy concerning Illegal Immigration' [2003] *Geddes Papers*, available at www.defence.gov.au/adc/docs/Publications/Geddes%20Papers%202003/08%20The%20Law%20of%20the%20Sea_Com%20Moles.pdf
Morris, Jessica C., 'The Spaces in Between: American and Australian Interdiction Policies and their Implications for the Refugee Protection Regime' (2003) 21 *Refuge* 4, 51–62
Morrison John, 'The Trafficking and Smuggling of Refugees: The end game in European Asylum policy?' (UNHCR Evaluation and Policy Unit, Geneva, 2000) (Prepublication edition) http://www.arnehansen.net/Morrisonrapport.pdf
Muller, Benjamin, 'Globalization, Security, Paradox: Towards a Refugee Biopolitics' (2004) 22 *Refuge* 1, 49–57
Murphy, Sean D (ed.), 'Reviews, Release, and Trials of Detainees at Guantanamo Bay' (2002) 98 *AJIL* 353–355
——, 'Extraterritorial Application of US Laws to Crimes on Foreign Vessels' (2003) 97 *AJIL* 183–185
——, 'US Reaction to Belgian Universal Jurisdiction Law' (2003) 97 *AJIL* 984–987
——, '"Proliferation Security Initiative" for Searching Potential WMD Vessels' (2004) 98 *AJIL* 355–357
Nafziger, James AR, 'The General Admission of Aliens under International Law' (1983) 77 *AJIL* 804–847
Nash, Leich Marian, 'Illegal Haitian Migrants' (1982) 76 *AJIL* 374–377
Nash, Leich Marian (ed.), 'US–UK Agreement on Vessels Trafficking Drugs' (1982) 76 *AJIL* 377–379
Newman, Edward and Joanne van Selm (eds), *Refugees and Forced Displacement: International Security, Human Vulnerability and the State* (United Nations University Press, Tokyo, 2003)
Newman, Edward, Ramesh Thakur and John Tirman (eds), *Multilateralism Under Challenge? Power, International Order and Structural Change* (United Nations University Press, Tokyo, 2006)
Nicholson, Frances and Patrick Twomey, *Refugee Rights and Realities: Evolving Concepts and Regimes* (Cambridge University Press, Cambridge, 1999)

Nordquist, Myron H. (Editor-in-chief), *United Nations Convention on the Law of the Sea 1982: A Commentary* (Martinus Nijhoff Publishers, Dordrecht, 1985) vols. I–VI

O'Connell, Daniel Patrick, *The International Law of the Sea* (ed. I.A. Shearer, Clarendon Press, Oxford, 1982) vol. I

O'Connell, Daniel Patrick (Shearer Ivan Anthony ed), *The International Law of the Sea* (Clarendon Press, Oxford, 1984) vol. II

O'Grey, William, 'Are seafarers terrorists, or our best security system?', *Lloyd's List* (30 September 2004)

O'Mahoney, Hugh, 'IMO to tackle Singapore and Malacca Strait terror threats', *Lloyd's List* (24 November 2004)

——, 'Security top concern for IMO-USCG talks', *Lloyd's List* (18 February 2005)

——, 'US gears up to stop speedboat terrorists', *Lloyd's List* (15 December 2006)

Obokata, Tom, '"Trafficking" and "Smuggling" of Human Beings in Europe: Protection of Individual Rights or States' Interests?' (2001) 5 *Web Journal of Current Legal Issues*, available at http://webjcli.ncl.ac.uk/2001/issue5/obok5.html

——, 'Trafficking of Human Beings as a Crime Against Humanity: Some Implications for the International Legal System' (2005) 54 *ICLQ* 445–458

——, 'Smuggling of Human Beings from a Human Rights Perspective: Obligations of Non-State and State Actors under International Human Rights Law' (2005) 17 *IJRL* 394–415

Ochoa-Ruiz, Natalia and Esther Salacanca-Aguado, 'Exploring the Limits of International Law relating to the Use of Force in Self-Defence' (2005) 16 *EJIL* 499–524

Osler, David, 'Bimco smoothes C-TPAT signing' *Lloyd's List*, (6 April 2004)

——, 'US demands 2000-mile track and trace zone', *Lloyd's List* (12 August 2004)

——, 'New container security device developed by GE', *Lloyd's List* (20 September 2004)

——, 'Australia proposes an ambitious 1000-mile nautical security zone', *Lloyd's List* (16 December 2004)

——, 'US admits aim to make all nations sign 24-hour rule', *Lloyd's List* (24 January 2005)

——, 'Compulsory security audits threaten port throughput efficiency', *Lloyd's List* (6 June 2005)

——, 'UN Security Council urged to act on Somalia piracy', *Lloyd's List* (25 November 2005)

——, 'UN approves IMO Somali plan', *Lloyd's List* (20 March 2006)

——, 'Indonesian waters still world's worst among piracy hotspots', *Lloyd's List* (4 May 2006)

Ovey, Clare and Robin C.A. White, *Jacobs and White: European Convention on Human Rights* (4th edn, Oxford, Oxford University Press, 2006)

Oxman, Bernard H. and Vincent Bantz, 'The M/V "Saiga" (No. 2) (Saint Vincent and the Grenadines v Guinea), Judgment (ITLOS Case No. 2)' (2000) 94 *AJIL* 140–150

Oxman-Martinez, Jacqueline, Andrea Martinez and Jill Hanley, 'Human Trafficking: Canadian Govt Policy and Practice' (2001) 19 *Refuge* 4, 14–23

Ozcayir, Oya Z., 'The International Convention on Maritime Search and Rescue (SAR)' (2006) 12 *J. Int Marit Law* 282–288

Pallis, Mark, 'Obligations of States towards Asylum Seekers at Sea: Interactions and Conflicts Between Legal Regimes' (2002) 14 *IJRL* 329–364

Peers, Steve, 'EU Responses to Terrorism' (2003) 52 *ICLQ* 227–244

Phuong, Catherine, 'Enlarging "Fortress Europe": EU Accession, Asylum, and Immigration in Candidate Countries' (2003) 52 *ICLQ* 641–663

Pickering, Margaret, Sally Cummins, David Stewart (eds), *Digest of United States Practice in International Law 1989–1990* (Office of the Legal Advisor, United States Department of State International Law Institute, Washington, DC, 1989–1990)

Piotrowicz, Ryszard and Sam Blay, 'The Case of the MV Tampa: State and Refugee Rights Collide at Sea' (2002) 76 *Aust LJ* 12–18

Pugh, Michael (ed.), *Maritime Security and Peacekeeping: A Framework for United Nations Operations* (Manchester University Press, Manchester, 1994)

Pugh, Michael, 'Europe's Boat People: Maritime Cooperation in the Mediterranean' [2000] *Chaillot Paper* 41, Institute for Security Studies Western European Union, available at http://aei.pitt.edu/501/01/chai41e.html

Ramcharan, Bertrand G., *Human Rights and Human Security* (Kluwer Law International, The Netherlands, 2002)

Ratner, Steven R., 'Belgium's War Crimes Statute: A Postmortem' (2003) 97 *AJIL* 888–897

Reydams, Luc, *Universal Jurisdiction: International and Municipal Legal Perspectives* (Oxford University Press, Oxford, 2003)

Robinson, Nehemiah, *Convention Relating to the Status of Refugees: Its History, Contents and Interpretation* (Institute of Jewish Affairs, NY, 1953)

Rosenberg, Lory Diana, 'The Courts and Interception: The United States Interdiction Experience and its Impact on Refugees and Asylum Seekers' (2003) 17 *Georgetown Immigration L J* 199–219

Roth, Brad R., 'Sosa v Alvarez-Machain; United States v Alvarez-Machain. 124 S.Ct. 2739' (2004) 98 *AJIL* 798–804

Rothwell, Donald R., 'The Law of the Sea and the MA Tampa Incident: Reconciling Maritime Principles with Coastal State Sovereignty' (2002) 13 *Pub LR* 118–127

Rubenstein, Kim, 'Citizenship, Sovereignty and Migration: Australia's Exclusive Approach to Membership of the Community' (2002) 13 *Pub LR* 102–109

Rubin, Alfred P., 'Is Piracy Illegal?' (1976) 70 *AJIL* 92–95

Ruth, Alexandra and Mirja Trilsch, 'Bankovic v Belgium (Admissibility) App. No. 52207/99' (2003) 97 *AJIL* 168–172

Salt, John, *Current Trends in International Migration in Europe* (Council of Europe Publishing, Strasbourg, 2005)

Sarrar, Salah, 'Gaddafi: Africa migration to Europe inevitable', *The Times of Malta* (24 November 2006)

Schloenhardt, Andreas, *Migrant Smuggling: Human Trafficking and Organised Crime in Australia and the Asia Pacific Region* (Martinus Nijhoff, Leiden, 2003)

——, 'To Deter, Detain and Deny: Protection of Onshore Asylum Seekers in Australia' (2002) 14 *IJRL* 302–328

van Selm, Joanne and Cooper Betsy, *The New Boat People: Ensuring Safety and Determining Status* (Migration Policy Institute, Report) (2006) http://www.migrationpolicy.org/pubs/Boat_People_Report.pdf

Shachar, Ayelet, 'The Shifting Border of Immigration Regulation' (2007) 3 *Stanford Journal of Civil Rights and Civil Liberties* 165

Shearer, Ivan Anthony, 'Problems of Jurisdiction and Law Enforcement Against Delinquent Vessels' (1986) 35 *ICLQ* 320–343

Shepherd, Harold, 'Towards a Common European Asylum System: Asylum, Human Rights and European Values' (2004) 22 *Refuge* 1, 96–107

Shigeru, Oda, 'The Concept of the Contiguous Zone' (1962) 11 *ICLQ* 131–153

Sianni, Areti, 'Interception Practices in Europe and their Implications' (2003) 21 *Refuge* 4, 25–34

Siddle, John, 'Anglo-American Cooperation in the Suppression of Drug Smuggling' (1982) 31 *ICLQ* 726–747

Sinclair, Ian, *The Vienna Convention on the Law of Treaties* (2nd edn, Manchester University Press, Manchester, 1984)

Sohn, John E. and Louis B. Noyes, *Cases and Materials on the Law of the Sea* (Transnational Publishers, New York, 2004)

Speares, Sandra, 'Australia to set new reporting rules for ships', *Lloyd's List* (14 July 2004)

——, 'Trials of defining whether a cargo is safe or a danger', *Lloyd's List* (10 August 2005)

——, 'IMO member nations bury differences to pass updated anti-terror treaties', *Lloyd's List* (17 October 2005)

——, 'Piracy focus "has subtly switched to war on terror"', *Lloyd's List* (1 February 2006)

Spiteri, Lino, 'Preparing for immigration change', *The Times of Malta* (28 September 2008)

Stares, Justin, 'Worldwide accord on 24-hour box rule', *Lloyd's List* (6 August 2004)

——, 'EU lines up container security expansion', *Lloyd's List* (16 November 2004)

——, 'Brussels takes stride towards launch of Euro-coastguard', *Lloyd's List* (17 February 2005)

——, 'Europe one step closer to US-style 24 hour rule', *Lloyd's List* (25 February 2005)

——, 'EU maritime task force to tackle Law of the Sea', *Lloyd's List* (5 April 2005)

——, 'Brussels urged not to seek wider influence in maritime matters', *Lloyd's List* (15 July 2005)

——, 'EU pushes through 24-hour cargo rule despite protests', *Lloyd's List* (31 October 2006)

——, 'EU has "no intention" to send customs officials abroad', *Lloyd's List* (8 February 2007)

Strati, Anastasia, Maria Gavouneli, Nikolaos Skourtos (eds), *Unresolved Issues and New Challenges to the Law of the Sea: Time Before and Time After* (Martinus Nijhoff, Leiden, 2006)

Sztucki, Jerzy, 'The Conclusions on the International Protection of Refugees adopted by the Executive Committee' (1989) 1 *IJRL* 285–318

Tate, N.P., Lieutenant Commander, RAN, 'People Smuggling: Defending Australia's National Interest' [2003] *Geddes Papers*, available at www.defence.gov.au/ADC/docs/Publications/Geddes%20Papers%202003/07%20People%20Smuggling_Lie%20Com%20Tate.pdf

Testa, Michael, 'Steady flow of illegal migrants', *The Times of Malta* (24 May 2007)

Texeire Fiona, 'At the Gate of Fortress Europe: Irregular Immigration and Malta' (Malta, 2006) http://www.alternattiva.org.mt/filebank/documents/Fiona%20TEXEIRE-%20At%20the%20Gate%20of%20Fortress%20Europe.pdf

Triggs, Gillian, 'International Law and Asylum Seekers: A Legal Twilight Zone' (2001) 4 *The Asia–Australia Papers*, 17–30

Trimble, Phillip R., 'The Supreme Court and International Law: the Demise of Restatement Section 403' (1995) 89 *AJIL* 53–57

Tsamenyi, Martin Palma, 'Legal Considerations in the Implementation of Long-range Identification and Tracking Systems for Vessels' (2007) 13 *J. Int Marit Law* 42–55

Turner, Thomas, 'Security in Malacca Strait show signs of improvement', *Lloyd's List* (4 April 2006)

UK Ministry of Defence (ed.), *The Manual of the Law of Armed Conflict* (Oxford University Press, Oxford, 2005)

United Nations, *Commentary on the UN Convention against Illicit Traffic in Narcotic Drugs and Psychotropic Substances 1998*, E/CN.7/590 (United Nations, New York, 1998)

——, *Trends in Total Migrant Stock: The 2005 Revision* (UN Publications, New York, 2007)

——, *Yearbook of the International Law Commission 1950* (United Nations Publications, New York, 1957) vol. II

——, *Yearbook of the International Law Commission 1951* (United Nations Publications, New York, 1957) vol. II

——, *Yearbook of the International Law Commission 1956* (United Nations Publications, New York, 1956) vol. I

——, *Yearbook of the International Law Commission 1956* (United Nations Publications, New York, 1957) vol. II

——, *Yearbook of the International Law Commission 1973* (United Nations Publications, New York, 1975) vol. II

United Nations Division for Ocean Affairs and the Law of the Sea, Office for Legal Affairs, *The Law of the Sea, Exclusive Economic Zone: Legislative History of Articles 56, 58 and 59 of the United Nations Convention on the Law of the Sea* (United Nations, New York, 1992)

——, *The Law of the Sea: Obligations of States Parties under the United Nations Convention on the Law of the Sea and Complementary Instruments* (United Nations, New York, 2004)

United Nations High Commissioner for Refugees, *The State of the World's Refugees* (Oxford University Press, Oxford, 2006)

United Nations Office for Ocean Affairs and the Law of the Sea, *The Law of the Sea, Navigation on the High Seas: Legislative History of Part VII, Section I (Articles 87, 89, 90–94, 96–98) of the United Nations Convention on the Law of the Sea* (United Nations, New York, 1989)

United Nations Office on Drugs and Crime, *Practical Guide for Competent National Authorities under Article 17 of the United Nations Convention Against Illicit Traffic in Narcotic Drugs and Psychotropic Substances of 1988* (UN Publications, New York, 2003)

——, *Legislative Guide for the Implementation of the UN Convention against Transnational Organised Crime and the Protocols thereto* (United Nations, New York, 2004) www.unodc.org/pdf/crime/legislative_guides/01%20Introduction%20and%20List%20of%20Experts.pdf

——, *Travaux Préparatoires of the Negotiations for the Elaboration of the United Nations Convention against Transnational Organised Crime and the Protocols thereto* (United Nations, New York, 2006) www.unodc.org/pdf/ctoccop_2006/04-60074_ebook-e.pdf

United States Coast Guard, Department of Homeland Security, 'Model Maritime Operations Guide' (2003) http://www.uscg.mil/international/docs/mmog.pdf

UNCHR, 'Problems related to the Rescue of Asylum-Seekers in Distress at Sea' (26 August 1981) EC/SCP/18

——, 'Report on the Meeting of the Working Group of Government Representatives on the Question of Rescue of Asylum-Seekers at Sea' Geneva (5–7 July 1982) EC/SCP/21

——, 'International Protection, Preliminary Report on Suggestions Retained by the Working Group of Government Representatives on the Question of Rescue of Asylum-Seekers at Sea' (1 October 1982) EC/SCP/24

——, 'International Protection, Problems related to the rescue of Asylum-Seekers in Distress at Sea' (1 September 1983) EC/SCP/30

——, 'International Protection, Problems related to the rescue of Asylum-Seekers in Distress at Sea' (28 August 1984) EC/SCP/35

——, 'International Protection, Problems related to the rescue of Asylum-Seekers in Distress at Sea' (8 July 1985) EC/SCP/42

——, 'International Protection, Note on Stowaway Asylum-Seekers' (22 July 1988) EC/SCP/51

——, *Handbook on Procedures and Criteria for Determining Refugee Status under the 1951 Convention and 1967 Protocol relating to the Status of Refugees* HCR/IP/4/Eng/REV.1 (UNHCR 1979; re-edited, Geneva, January 1992)

——, Brief of the Office of the United Nations High Commissioner for Refugee as *Amicus Curiae* in Support of Respondents in *McNary v Haitian Centres Council*, 509 US 155, (1993), (Case No. 92–344) 18 reprinted in (1994) 6(1) IJRL 85

——, 'Interception of Asylum-Seekers and Refugees: The International Framework and Recommendations for a Comprehensive Approach' (9 June 2000) EC/50/SC/CRP.17

——, *Refugee Law: A Guide to International Refugee Law* (Inter-Parliamentary Union and UNHCR, Geneva, 2001) www.unhcr.org/publ/PUBL/3d4aba564.pdf

——, 'Protection of Refugees in Mass Influx Situations: Overall Protection Framework' (19 February 2001) EC/GC/01/4

——, 'Mechanisms of International Cooperation to Share Responsibilities and Burdens in Mass Influx Situations' (19 February 2001) EC/GC/01/7

——, 'Regional Workshops in Ottawa, Ontario (Canada) and in Macau—Incorporating Refugee Protection Safeguards into Interception Measures' Ottawa, Ontario, Canada. (14–15 May 2001) EC/GC/01/13

——, 'Refugee Protection and Migration Control: Perspectives from UNHCR and IOM' Global Consultations on International Protection (31 May 2001) EC/GC/01/11

——, 'Reception of Asylum Seekers, Including Standards of Treatment, in the context of Individuals Asylum Systems' (4 September 2001) EC/GC/01/17

——, 'Background Note Concerning the Competence of the United Nations High Commissioner for Refugees (UNHCR) in Relation to Rescue at Sea Matters' as distributed to the participants in COMSAR 6, Working Group 1, during the Committee session held in London, 18 to 20 February 2002

——, 'Background Note on the Protection of Asylum Seekers and Refugees Rescued at Sea' (18 March 2002) http://www.refugeelawreader.org/512/Background_Note_on_the_Protection_of_Asylum_Seekers_and_Refugees_Rescued_at_Sea.pdf

——, 'Rescue-at-Sea: Specific Aspects Relating to the Protection of Asylum-Seekers and Refugees. Expert Roundtable, Lisbon 25–26 March 2002, Summary of Discussions' (11 April 2002) http://www.unhcr.org/refworld/docid/3cd14e3b4.html

——, 'Ensuring International Protection and Enhancing International Cooperation in Mass Influx Situations—Advance Summary Findings of the Study Commissioned by UNHCR' (7 June 2004) EC/54/GC/CRP.11

——, *Selected Reference Materials: Rescue at Sea, Maritime Interception and Stowaways* (UNHCR, Geneva, 2006) http://www.unhcr.org/refworld/docid/45b8d8b44.html

——, 'Refugee Protection and Mixed Migration: A 10-Point Plan of Action' (January 2007) Rev. 1. http://www.unhcr.org/refworld/docid/45b0c09b2.html

——, *A Thematic Compilation of Executive Committee Conclusions, Office of the United Nations High Commissioner for Refugees* (3rd edn, Department of International Protection, Geneva, 2008) www.unhcr.org/publ/PUBL/3d4ab3ff2.pdf

Van Dyke, Jon M., 'The Disappearing Right to Navigational Freedom in the Exclusive Economic Zone' (2005) 29 Marine Policy 2, 107–121

Van Zwanenberg, Anna, 'Interference with Ships on the High Seas' (1961) 10 *ICLQ* 785–817

Vorbach, Jospeh E., 'The Vital Role of Non-State Actors in the Pursuit of Safer Shipping' (2001) 32 *ODIL* 1, 27–42

Vrachnas, John, Kim Boyd, Mirko Bagaric, Penny Dimopoulos, *Migration and Refugee Law—Principles and Practices in Australia* (Cambridge University Press, Cambridge, 2005)

Warbrick, Colin and Dominic McGoldrick (eds), 'Current Developments: Drug Trafficking at Sea: The Case of R v Charrington and Others' (2000) 49 *ICLQ* 447–489

Warton, Andrew, 'The Changing Tide of People Smuggling' (2002) 75 *Platypus Magazine* 14–19, available at www.afp.gov.au/__data/assets/pdf_file/3963/changingTide.pdf

Wazana, Richard, 'Fear and Loathing Down Under: Australian Refugee Policy and the National Imagination' (2004) 22 *Refuge* 1, 83–95

Wedgwood, Ruth, 'United States v Verdugo-Urquidez' (1990) 84 *AJIL* 747–755

White, Michael, 'MV Tampa and Christmas Island Incident' [2002] *BIMCO Review* 116–123

——, 'Tampa Incident: Shipping, International and Maritime Legal Issues' (2004) 78 *Australian Legal Journal* 101–113

Wilhelm, Ernst, '*MV Tampa*: The Australian Response' (2003) 15 *IJRL* 159–191

Wise, Jennings C., 'The Rights of Visit and Search, Capture, Angary and Requisition' (1922) 16 *AJIL* 391–399

Xuereb, Matthew, '129 illegal migrants arrive: Debate on burden-sharing pact festers', *The Times of Malta* (29 September 2008)

——, 'Government rejects MLP's call to veto the EU migration pact', *The Times of Malta* (29 September 2008)

Young, Wendy, 'Resettlement and Processing of Haitian Refugees' (2002) 21 *Refuge* 4, 63–66

Zammit, Roseanne, 'MEPs to seek changes to migration rules', *The Times of Malta* (5 April 2006)

Index

www.ingramcontent.com/pod-product-compliance
Lightning Source LLC
LaVergne TN
LVHW080847300926
849162LV00003B/354